THE SWORD OF DAMOCLES

ANNA KATHARINE GREENE

[ZHINGOORA BOOKS]

This edition is published by
Zhingoora Books.

Apart from any fair dealing for the purposes
of research or private study, or criti-cism or
review, this publication may only be
reproduced, stored or transmitted, in any
form or by any means, with the prior
permission in writing of the publishers. All
disputes are subject to exclusive jurisdiction
of Mandsaur Courts only. For any
suggestions and feedback or book on new
concept/domain, please contact us at the email
given below.

contact@Zhingoora.com

CONTENTS.

BOOK I. TWO MEN.

I.—A Wanderer

II.—A Discussion

III.—A Mysterious Summons

IV.—Searchings

V.—The Rubicon

VI.—A Hand Clasp

VII.—Mrs. Sylvester

VIII.—Shadows of the Past

IX.—Paula

X.—The Barred Door

XI.—Miss Stuyvesant

XII.—Miss Belinda Makes Conditions

XIII.—The End of My Lady's Picture

BOOK II. LIFE AND DEATH.

XIV.—Miss Belinda has a Question to Decide

XV.—An Adventure—or Something More

XVI.—The Sword of Damocles

XVII.—Grave and Gay

XVIII.—In the Night Watches

XIX.—A Day at the Bank

XX.—The Dregs in the Cup

XXI.—Departure

XXII.—Hopgood

BOOK III. THE JAPHA MYSTERY.

XXIII.—The Poem

XXIV.—The Japha Mansion

XXV.—Jacqueline

XXVI.—A Man's Justice and a Woman's Mercy

XXVII.—The Lone Watcher

XXVIII.—Sunshine on the Hills

XXIX.—Mist in the Valley

BOOK IV. FROM A. TO Z.

XXX.—Miss Belinda Presents Mr. Sylvester with a Christmas Gift

XXXI.—A Question

XXXII.—Full Tide

XXXIII.—Two Letters

XXXIV.—Paula Makes her Choice

XXXV.—The Falling of the Sword

XXXVI.—Morning

XXXVII.—The Opinion of a Certain Noted Detective

XXXVIII.—Bluebeard's Chamber

XXXIX.—From A. to Z

XL.—Half-past Seven

BOOK V. WOMAN'S LOVE.

XLI.—The Work of an Hour

XLII.—Paula Relates a Story She has Heard

XLIII.—Determination

XLIV.—In Mr. Stuyvesant's Parlors

XLV.—"The Hour of Six is Sacred!"

XLVI—The Man Cummins

BOOK I.

TWO MEN.

I.

A WANDERER.

"There's no such word."—BULWER.

A wind was blowing through the city. Not a gentle and balmy zephyr, stirring the locks on gentle ladies' foreheads and rustling the curtains in elegant boudoirs, but a chill and bitter gale that rushed with a swoop through narrow alleys and forsaken courtyards, biting the cheeks of the few solitary wanderers that still lingered abroad in the darkened streets.

In front of a cathedral that reared its lofty steeple in the midst of the squalid houses and worse than squalid saloons of one of the dreariest portions of the East Side, stood the form of a woman. She had paused in her rush down the narrow street to listen to the music, perhaps, or to catch a glimpse of the light that now and then burst from the widely swinging doors as they opened and shut upon some tardy worshipper.

She was tall and fearful looking; her face, when the light struck it, was seared and desperate; gloom and desolation were written on all the lines of her rigid but wasted form, and when she shuddered under the gale, it was with that force and abandon to which passion lends its aid, and in which the soul proclaims its doom.

Suddenly the doors before her swung wide and the preacher's voice was heard: "Love God and you will love your fellow-men. Love your fellow-men and you best show your love to God."

She heard, started, and the charm was broken. "Love!" she echoed with a horrible laugh; "there is no love in heaven or on earth!"

And she swept by, and the winds followed and the darkness swallowed her up like a gulf.

II.

A DISCUSSION.

"Young men think old men fools, and old men know young men to be so."—Ray's Proverbs.

"And you are actually in earnest?"

"I am."

The first speaker, a fine-looking gentleman of some forty years of age, drummed with his fingers on the table before him and eyed the face of the young man who had repeated this assent so emphatically, with a certain close scrutiny indicative of surprise.

"It is an unlooked-for move for you to make," he remarked at length. "Your success as a pianist has been so decided, I confess I do not understand why you should desire to abandon a profession that in five years' time has procured you both competence and a very enviable reputation—for the doubtful prospects of Wall Street, too!" he added with a deep and thoughtful frown that gave still further impressiveness to his strongly marked features.

The young man with a sweep of his eye over the luxurious apartment in which they sat, shrugged his shoulders with that fine and nonchalant grace which was one of his chief characteristics.

"With such a pilot as yourself, I ought to be able to steer clear of the shoals," said he, a frank smile illumining a face that was rather interesting than handsome.

The elder gentleman did not return the smile. Instead of that he remained gazing at the ample coal-fire that burned in the grate before him with a look that to the young musician was simply inexplicable. "You see the ship in haven," he murmured at last; "but do not consider what storms it has weathered or what perils escaped. It is a voyage I would encourage no son of mine to undertake."

"Yet you are not the man to shrink from danger or to hesitate in a course you had marked out for yourself, because of the struggle it involved or the difficulties it presented!" the young man exclaimed almost involuntarily as his glance lingered with a certain sort of fascination on the powerful brow and steady if somewhat melancholy eye of his companion.

"No; but danger and difficulty should not be sought, only subdued when encountered. If you were driven into this path, I should say, 'God pity you!' and hold you out my hand to steady you along its precipices and above its sudden quicksands. But you are not driven to it. Your profession offers you the means of an ample livelihood while your good heart and fair talents insure you ultimate and honorable success, both in the social and artistic world. For a man of twenty-five such prospects are not common and he must be difficult to please not to be satisfied with them."

"Yes," said the other rising with a fitful movement but instantly sitting again; "I have nothing to complain of as the world goes, only—Sir," he exclaimed with a sudden determination that lent a force to his features they had hitherto lacked, "you speak of being driven into a certain course; what do you mean by that?"

"I mean," returned the other; "forced by circumstances to enter a line of business to which many others, if not all others are preferable."

"You speak strongly, speculation evidently has none of your sympathy, notwithstanding the favorable results which have accrued to you from it. But excuse me, by circumstances you mean poverty, I suppose, and the lack of every other opening to wealth and position. You would not consider the desire to make a large fortune in a short space of time a circumstance of a sufficiently determining nature to reconcile you to my entering Wall Street speculation?"

The elder gentleman rose, not as the other had done with a restless impulse quickly subsiding at the first excuse, but forcibly and with a feverish impatience that to appearance was somewhat out of proportion to the occasion. "A large fortune in a short space of time!" he reiterated, pausing where he had risen with an eagle glance at his companion and a ringing tone in his voice that bespoke a deep but hitherto suppressed agitation. "It is the alluring inscription above the pitfall into which many a noble youth has fallen; the battle-cry to a struggle that has led many a strong man the way of ruin; the guide-post to a life whose feverish days and sleepless nights offer but poor compensation for the sudden splendors and as sudden reverses attached to it. I had rather you had accounted for this sudden freak of yours by the strongest aspiration after power than by this cry of the merely mercenary man who in his desire to enjoy wealth, prefers to win it by a stroke of luck rather than conquer it by a life of endeavor." He stopped. "I am aware that this tirade against the ladder by which I myself have risen so rapidly, must strike you as in ill-taste. But Bertram, I am interested in your welfare and am willing to incur some slight charge of inconsistency in order to insure it," and here he turned upon his companion with that expression of extreme gentleness which lent such a peculiar charm to his countenance and explained perhaps the almost unlimited power he held over the hearts and minds of those who came within the circle of his influence.

"You are very good, sir," murmured his young friend, who to explain matters at once was in reality the nephew of this Wall Street magnate, though from the fact of his having taken another name on entering the musical profession, was not generally known as such. "No one, not even my father himself, could have been more considerate and kind; but I do not think you understand me, or rather I should say I do not think I have made myself perfectly intelligible to you. It is not for the sake of wealth itself or the eclat attending its possession that I desire an immediate fortune, but that by means of it I may attain another object dearer than wealth, and more precious than my career."

The elder gentleman turned quickly, evidently much surprised, and cast a sudden inquiring glance at his nephew, who blushed with a modest ingenuousness pleasing to see in one so well accustomed to the critical gaze of his fellow-men.

"Yes," said he, as if in answer to that look, "I am in love."

A deep silence for a moment pervaded the apartment, a sombre silence almost startling to young Mandeville, who had expected some audible expression to follow this announcement if only the good-natured "Pooh! pooh!" of the matured man of the world in the presence of ardent youthful enthusiasm. What could it mean? Looking up he encountered his uncle's eye fixed upon him with the last expression he could have anticipated seeing there, namely that of actual and unmistakable alarm.

"You are displeased," Mandeville exclaimed. "You have thought me proof against such a passion, or perhaps you do not believe in the passion itself!" Then with a sudden remembrance of the notable if somewhat indolent loveliness of his uncle's wife, blushed again at his unusual want of tact, while his eye with an involuntary impulse sought the large panel at their right where, in the full bloom of her first youth, the lady of the house smiled upon all beholders.

"I do not believe in that passion influencing a man's career," his uncle replied with no apparent attention to the other's embarrassment. "A woman needs be possessed of uncommon excellences to justify a man in leaving a path where success is certain, for one where it is not only doubtful but if attained must bring many a regret and heart-ache in its train. Beauty is not sufficient," he went on with sterner and sterner significance, "though it were of an angelic order. There must be worth." And here his mind's eye if not that of his bodily sense, certainly followed the glance of his companion.

"I believe there is worth," the young man replied; "certainly, it is not her beauty that charms me. I do not even know if she *is* beautiful," he continued.

"And you believe you love!" the elder exclaimed after another short pause.

There was so much of bitterness in the tone in which this was uttered, that Mandeville forgot its incredulity. "I think I must," returned he with a certain masculine naïveté not out of keeping with his general style of face and manner, "else I should not be here. Three weeks ago I was satisfied with my profession, if not enthusiastic over it; to-day I ask nothing but to be allowed to enter upon some business that in three years' time at least will place me where I can be the fit mate of any woman in this land, that is not worth her millions."

"The woman for whom you have conceived this violent attachment is, then, above you in social position?"

"Yes, sir, or so considered, which amounts to the same thing, as far as I am concerned."

"Bertram, I have lived longer than you and have seen much of both social and domestic life, and I tell you no woman is worth such a sacrifice on the part of a man as you propose. No woman of to-day, I should say; our mothers were different. The very fact that this young lady of whom you speak, obliges you to change your whole course of life in order to obtain her, ought to be sufficient to prove to you—" He stopped suddenly, arrested by the young man's lifted hand. "She does not oblige you, then?"

"Not on her own account, sir. This lily," lifting a vase of blossoms at his elbow, "could not be more innocent of the necessities that govern the social circle it adorns, than the pure, single-minded girl to whom I have dedicated what is best and noblest in my manhood. It is her father—"

"Ah, her father!"

"Yes, sir," the young man pursued, more and more astonished at the other's tone. "He is a man who has a right to expect both wealth and position in a son-in-law. But I see I shall have to tell you my story, sir. It is an uncommon one and I never meant that it should pass my lips, but if by its relation I can win your sympathy for a pure and noble passion, I shall consider the sacred seal of secrecy broken in a good cause. But," said he, seeing his uncle cast a short and uneasy glance at the door, "perhaps I am interrupting you. You expect some one!"

"No," said his uncle, "my wife is at church; I am ready to listen."

The young man gave a hurried sigh, cast one look at his companion's immovable face, as if to assure himself that the narrative was necessary, then leaned back and in a steady business-like tone that softened, however, as he proceeded, began to relate as follows:

III.

A MYSTERIOUS SUMMONS.

"Without unspotted, innocent within,She feared no danger, for she knew no sin."—
Dryden.

It was after a matinée performance at ——— Hall some two weeks ago that I stopped
to light a cigar in the small corridor leading to the back entrance. I was in a
dissatisfied frame of mind. Something in the music I had been playing or the manner
in which it had been received had touched unwonted chords in my own nature. I felt
alone. I remember asking myself as I stood there, what it all amounted to? Who of all
the applauding crowd would watch at my bedside through a long and harassing
sickness, or lend their sympathy as they now yielded their praise, if instead of
carrying off the honors of the day I had failed to do justice to my reputation. I was
just smiling over the only exception I could make to this sweeping assertion, that of
the pale-eyed youth you have sometimes observed dogging my steps, when Briggs
came up to me.

"There is a woman here, sir, who insists on seeing you; she has been waiting through
half the last piece. Shall I tell her you are coming out?"

"A woman!" exclaimed I, somewhat surprised, for my visitors are not apt to be of the
gentler sex.

"Yes sir, an old one. She seems very anxious to speak to you. I could not get rid of
her no how."

I hurried forward to the muffled figure which he pointed out cowering against the
wall by the door. "Well, my good woman, what do you want?" I asked, bending
towards her in the hopes of catching a glimpse of the face she held partly concealed
from me.

"Are you Mr. Mandeville?" she inquired in a tone shaken as much by agitation as
age.

I bowed.

"The one who plays upon the piano?"

"The very same," I declared.

"You are not deceiving me," she went on, looking up with a marked anxiety plainly visible through her veil. "I haven't seen you play and couldn't contradict you, but—"

"Here!" said I calling to Briggs with a kindly look at the old woman, "help me on with my coat, will you?"

The "Certainly, Mr. Mandeville," with which he complied seemed to reassure her, and as soon as the coat was on and he was gone, she grasped me by the arm and drew my ear down to her mouth.

"If you are Mr. Mandeville, I have a message for you. This letter," slipping one into my hand, "is from a young lady, sir. She bade me give it to you myself. She is young and pretty," she pursued as she saw me make a movement of distaste, "and a lady. We depend upon your honor, sir."

I acknowledge that my first impulse was to fling her back the note and leave the building; I was in no mood for trifling, my next to burst into a laugh and politely hand her to the door, my last and best, to open the poor little note and see for myself whether the writer was a lady or not. Proceeding to the door, for it was already twilight in the dim passage way, I tore open the envelope which was dainty enough and took out a sheet of closely written paper. A certain qualm of conscience assailed me as I saw the delicate chirography it disclosed and I was tempted to thrust it back and return it unread to the old woman now trembling in the corner. But curiosity overcame my scruples, and hastily unfolding the sheet I read these lines:

"I do not know if what I do is right; I am sure aunty would not say it was; but aunty never thinks anything is right but going to church and reading the papers to papa. I am just a little girl who has heard you play, and who would think the world was too beautiful, if she could hear you say to her just once, some of the kind things you must speak every day to the persons who know you. I do not expect very much—you must have a great many friends, and you would not care for me—but the least little look, if it were all my own, would make me so happy and so proud I should not envy anybody in the world, unless it was some of those dear friends who see you always.

"I do not come and hear you play often, for aunty thinks music frivolous, but I am always hearing you no matter where I am, and it makes me feel as if I were far away from everybody, in a beautiful land all sunshine and flowers. But nurse says I must not write so much or you will not read it, so I will stop here. But if you *would* come it would make some one happier than even your beautiful music could do."

That was all; there was neither name nor date. A child's epistle, written with a woman's circumspection. With mingled sensations of doubt and curiosity I turned back to the old woman who stood awaiting me with eager anxiety.

"Was this written by a child or woman?" I asked, meeting her eye with as much sternness as I could assume.

"Don't ask me—don't ask me anything. I have promised to bring you if I could, but I cannot answer any questions."

I stepped back with an incredulous laugh. Here was evidently an adventure. "You will at least tell me where the young miss lives," said I, "before I undertake to fulfil her request."

She shook her head. "I have a carriage at the door, sir," said she. "All you have got to do is to get into it with me and we shall soon be at the house."

I looked from her face to the letter in my hand, and knew not what to think. The spirit of simplicity and ingenuousness that marked the latter was scarcely in keeping with this air of mystery. The woman observing my hesitation moved towards the door.

"Will you come, sir?" she inquired. "You will not regret it. Just a moment's talk with a pretty young girl—surely—"

"Hush," said I, hearing a hasty step behind me. And sure enough just then my intimate friend Selby came along and grasping me by the arm began dragging me towards the door. "You are my property," said he. "I've promised, on my word of honor as a gentleman and a musician, to bring you to the Handel Club this afternoon. I was afraid you had escaped me, but—" Here he caught sight of the small black figure halting in the door-way, and paused.

"Who's this?" said he.

I hesitated. For one instant the scale of my whole future destiny hung trembling in the balance, then the demon of curiosity got the better of my judgment, and with the rather unworthy consideration that I might as well enjoy my youth while I could, I released myself from my friend's detaining hand and replied, "Some one with whom I have very particular business. I cannot go to the Handel Club to-day," and darting out without further delay, I rejoined the old woman on the sidewalk.

Without a word she drew me towards a carriage I now observed standing by the curbstone a few feet to the left. As I got in I remember pausing a moment to glance at the man on the box, but it was too dark for me to perceive anything but the fact that he was dressed in livery. More and more astonished I leaned back in my seat and endeavored to open conversation with my mysterious companion. But it did not work. Without being actually rude, she parried my questions in such a way that by the end of five minutes I found myself as far from any knowledge of the real situation of the case as when I started. I therefore desisted from any further attempts and turned to look out, when I made a discovery that for the first time awoke some vague feelings of alarm within my breast. This was, that the window was not covered by a curtain as I supposed, but by closed blinds which when I tried to raise them resisted all my efforts to do so.

"It is very close here," I muttered, in some sort of excuse for this display of uneasiness. "Cannot you give us a little air?" But my companion remained silent, and I felt ashamed to press the matter though I took advantage of the darkness to remove to a safer place a roll of money which I had about me.

Yet I was far from being really anxious, and did not once meditate backing out of an adventure that was at once so piquant and romantic. For by this time I became conscious from the sounds about me that we had left the side street for one of the avenues and were then proceeding rapidly up town. Listening, I heard the roll of omnibuses and the jingle of car-bells, which informed me that we were in Broadway, no other avenue in the city being traversed by both these methods of conveyance. But after awhile the jingle ceased and presently the livelier sounds of constant commotion inseparable from a business thoroughfare, and we entered what I took to be Madison Avenue at Twenty-third Street.

Instantly I made up mind to notice every turn of the carriage, that I might fix to some degree the locality towards which we were tending. But it turned but once and that after a distance of steady travelling that quite overthrew any calculation I was able to make at that time of the probable number of streets we had passed since entering the avenue. Having turned, it went but about half a block to the left when it stopped. "I shall see where I am when I get out," thought I; but in this I was mistaken.

First we had stopped in the middle of a block of houses built, as far as I could judge, all after one model. Next the fact of the front door being open, though I saw no one in the hall, somewhat disconcerted me, and I hurried across the sidewalk and up the stoop in a species of maze hardly to be expected from one of my naturally careless disposition. The next moment the door closed behind me and I found myself in a well-lighted hall whose quiet richness betokened it as belonging to a private dwelling of no mean pretensions to elegance.

This was the first surprise I received.

"Follow me," said the old woman, hurrying me down the hall and into a small room at the end. "The young lady will be here in a moment," and without lifting her veil or affording me the least glimpse of her features, she retired, leaving me to face the situation before me as best I might.

It was anything but a pleasant one as it appeared to me at that moment, and for an instant I seriously thought of retracing my steps and leaving a domicile into which I had been introduced in such a mysterious manner. Then the quiet aspect of the room, which though sparsely furnished with a piano and chairs was still of an order rarely seen out of gentlemen's houses, struck my imagination and reawakened my curiosity, and nerving myself to meet whatever interview might be accorded me, I waited. It was only five minutes by the small clock ticking on the mantel-piece, but it seemed an hour before I heard a timid step at the door, and saw it swing slowly open, disclosing—well, I did not stop to inquire whether it was a child or a woman. I merely saw the shrinking modest form, the eager blushing face, and bowed almost to the ground in a sudden reverence for the sublime innocence revealed to me. Yes, it did not take a second look to read that tender countenance to its last guileless page. Had she been a woman of twenty-five I could not have mistaken her expression of pure delight and timid interest, but she was only sixteen, as I afterwards learned, and younger in experience than in age.

Closing the door behind her, she stood for a moment without speaking, then with a deepening of the blush which was only a child's embarrassment in the presence of a stranger, looked up and murmured my name with a word or so of grateful acknowledgment that would have called forth a smile on my lips if I had not been startled by the sudden change that passed over her features when she met my eyes. Was it that I showed my surprise too plainly, or did my admiration manifest itself in my gaze? an admiration great as it was humble, and which was already of a nature such as I had never before given to girl or woman. Whatever it was, she no sooner met my look than she paused, trembled, and started back with a confused murmur, through which I plainly heard her whisper in a low distressed tone, "Oh, what have I done!"

"Called a good friend to your side," said I in the frank, brotherly way I thought most likely to reassure her. "Do not be alarmed, I am only too happy to meet one who evidently enjoys music so well."

But the hidden chord of womanhood had been struck in the child's soul, and she could not recover herself. For an instant I thought she would turn and flee, and struck as I was with remorse at my reckless invasion of this uncontaminated temple, I could not but admire the spirited picture she presented as, with form half turned and face bent back, she stood hesitating on the point of flight.

I did not try to stop her. "She shall follow her own impulse," said I to myself, but I felt a vague relief that was deeper than I imagined, when she suddenly relinquished her strained attitude, and advancing a step or so began to murmur:

"I did not know—I did not realize I was doing what was so very wrong. Young ladies do not ask gentlemen to come and see them, no matter how much they desire to make their acquaintance. I see it now; I did not before. Will you—can you forgive me?"

I smiled; I could not help it. I could have taken her to my heart and soothed her as I would a child, but the pallor of womanhood, which had replaced the blush of the child, awed me and made my own words come hesitatingly.

"Forgive you? You must forgive me! It was as wrong for me," I went on with a wild idea of not mincing matters with this pure soul, "to obey your innocent request, as it was for you to make it. I am a man of the world and know its *convenances*; you are very young."

"I am sixteen," she murmured.

The abrupt little confession, implying as it did her determination not to accept any palliation of her conduct which it did not deserve, touched me strangely. "But very young for that," I exclaimed.

"So aunty says, but no one can ever say it any more," she answered. Then with a sudden gush, "We shall never see each other again, and you must forget the motherless girl who has met you in a way for which she must blush through life. It is no excuse," she pursued hurriedly, "that nurse thought it was all right. She always approves of everything I do or want to do, especially if it is anything aunt would be likely to forbid. I have been spoiled by nurse."

"Was nurse the woman who came for me?" I asked.

She nodded her head with a quick little motion inexpressibly charming. "Yes, that was nurse. She said she would do it all, I need only write the note. She meant to give me a pleasure, but she did wrong."

"Yes," thought I, "how wrong you little know or realize." But I only said, "You must be guided by some one with more knowledge of the world after this. Not," I made haste to add, struck by the misery in her child eyes, "that any harm has been done. You could not have appealed to the friendship of any one who would hold you in greater respect than I. Whether we meet again or not, my memory of you shall be sweet and sacred, I promise you that."

But she threw out her hand with a quick gesture. "No, do not remember me. My only happiness will lie in the thought you have forgotten." And the last remnants of the child soul vanished in that hurried utterance. "You must go now," she continued more calmly. "The carriage that brought you is at the door; I must ask you to take it back to your home."

"But," I exclaimed with a wild and unbearable sense of sudden loss as she laid her hand on the knob of the door, "are we to part like this? Will you not at least trust me with your name before I go?"

Her hand dropped from the knob as if it had been hot steel, and she turned towards me with a slow yearning motion that whatever it betokened set my heart beating violently. "You do not know it, then?" she inquired.

"I know nothing but what this little note contains," I replied, drawing her letter from my pocket.

"Oh, that letter! I must have it," she murmured; then, as I stepped towards her, drew back and pointing to the table said, "Lay it there, please."

I did so, whereupon something like a smile crossed her lips and I thought she was going to reward me with her name, but she only said, "I thank you; now you know nothing;" and almost before I realized it she had opened the door and stepped into the hall.

As I made haste to follow her, the sound of a low, "He is a gentleman, he will ask no questions," struck my ear, and looking up, I saw her just leaving the side of the old nurse who stood evidently awaiting me half down the hall. Bowing with formal ceremony, I passed her by and proceeded to the front door. As I did so I caught one glimpse of her face. It had escaped from all restraint and the expression of the eyes was overpowering. I subdued a wild impulse to leap back to her side, and stepped at once over the threshold. The nurse joined me, and together we went down the stoop to the street.

"May I inquire where you wish to be taken?" she asked.

I told her, and she gave the order to the coachman, together with a few words I did not hear; then stepping back she waited for me to get in. There was no help for it. I gave one quick look behind me, saw the front door close, realized how impossible it would ever be for me to recognize the house again, and placed my foot on the carriage step. Suddenly a bright idea struck me, and hastily dropping my cane I stepped back to pick it up. As I did so I pulled out a bit of crayon I chanced to have in my pocket, and as I stooped, chalked a small cross on the curbstone directly in front of the house, after which I recovered my cane, uttered some murmured word of apology, jumped into the carriage and was about to shut the door, when the old nurse stepped in after me and quietly closed it herself. By the pang that shot through my breast as the carriage wheels left the house, I knew that for the first time in my life, I *loved.*

IV.

SEARCHINGS.

"Patience, and shuffle the cards."—Cervantes.

If I had expected anything from the presence in the carriage of the woman who had arranged this interview, I was doomed to disappointment. Reticent before, she was absolutely silent now, sitting at my side like a grim statue or a frozen image of watchfulness, ready to awake and stop me if I offered to open the door or make any other move indicative of a determination to know where I was, or in what direction I was going. That her young mistress in the momentary conversation they had held before our departure had succeeded in giving her some idea of the shame with which she had felt herself overwhelmed and her present natural desire for secrecy, I do not doubt, but I think now, as I thought then, that the unusual precautions taken both at that time and before, to keep me in ignorance of the young lady's identity, were due to the elderly woman's own consciousness of the peril she had invoked in yielding to the wishes of her young and thoughtless mistress; a theory which, if true, argues more for the mind than the conscience of this mysterious woman. However, it is with facts we have to deal, and you will be more interested in learning what I did, than what I thought during that short ride in perfect darkness.

The mark which I had left on the curbstone behind me sufficiently showed the nature of my resolve, and when we made the first turn at the end of the block I leaned back in my seat and laying my finger on my wrist, began to count the pulsations of my blood. It was the only device that suggested itself, by which I might afterward gather some approximate notion of the distance we travelled in a straight course down town. I had just arrived at the number seven hundred and sixty-two, and was inwardly congratulating myself upon this new method of reckoning distance, when the wheels gave a lurch and we passed over a car track. Instantly all my fine calculations fell to the ground. We were not in Madison Avenue, as I supposed; could not be, since no track crosses that avenue below Fifty-ninth Street, and we were proceeding on as we could not have done had we gained the terminus of the avenue at Twenty-third Street. Could it be that the carriage had not been turned around while I was in the house, and that we had come back by way of Fifth Avenue? I could not remember—in fact, the more I tried to think which way the horses' heads were directed when we went into the house, the more I was confused. But presently I considered that wherever we were, we certainly had not passed over the narrow strip of smooth pavement in front of the Worth monument, and therefore could not have reached Twenty-third Street by way of Fifth Avenue. We must be up town, and that track we crossed must have been at Fifty-ninth Street. And soon, as if to assure me of this, we took a turn, quickly followed at a block's length by another, after which I had no difficulty in recognizing the smooth pavement of the entrance to the Park or the roll down Fifth Avenue afterwards. "They have thought to confuse me by an extra mile or so of travel," thought I, with some complacency, "but the streets of New York are too simply laid out to lend themselves to any such easy mode of mystification." Yet I have thought since then how, with a smarter man on the box, the affair might have been conducted so as to have baffled the oldest citizen in any attempt at calculation.

When we stopped in front of the Albemarle I quietly thanked the woman who had conducted me, and stepped to the ground. Instantly the door shut behind me, the carriage drove off, and I was left standing there like a man suddenly awakened from a dream.

Entering my hotel, I ordered supper, thinking that the very practical occupation of eating would serve to divert my mind into its ordinary channels. But the dream, if dream it was, had made too vivid an impression to be shaken off so easily. It followed me to the hall in the evening and mingled with every chord I struck.

I could scarcely sleep that night for thinking of the sweet child's face that had blossomed into a woman's before my eyes, and what a woman! With the first hint of daylight I rose, and as soon as it was in any degree suitable to be out, hired a cab and proceeded to the corner of Fifty-ninth Street and Madison Avenue, where, according to my calculations of the evening before, we had crossed the car track which had first interrupted me in that very original method of computing distance of which I have already spoken, a method by the way, which you must acknowledge is an improvement on the boy's plan of finding his way back from the woods by means of the bread-crumbs he had scattered behind him, forgetting that the birds would eat up his crumbs and leave him without a clew. Bidding the driver proceed at the ordinary jog trot down the avenue, I laid my finger on my wrist, and counted each throb of my pulse till I had reached the magical number seven hundred and sixty-two. Then putting my head out of the window, I bade him stop. We were in the middle of a block, but that did not disconcert me. I had not expected to gain more than an approximate idea of the spot where we had first turned into the avenue, it being impossible to regulate the horses' pace so as to tally with that taken by the span of the night before, even if the pulsations in my wrist were to be absolutely relied upon. Noting the streets between which we had paused, I bade the driver to turn down one and come back by the other, occupying myself in the meanwhile, in searching the curbstone for the small mark I had left in front of her door the night before. But though we drove slowly and I searched carefully, not a trace did I perceive of that tell-tale sign, and forsaking those two streets, I ordered my obedient Jehu to try the two outlying ones below and above. He did so, and I again consulted the curbstone, but with no better success. No mark or remnants of a mark was to be found anywhere. Nor, though we travelled through three or four other streets in the same way, did we come upon any clew liable to assist me in my search. Clean discouraged and somewhat out of temper with myself for my pusillanimity of the evening before in not having braved the anger of my companion by opening the carriage door at the first corner and leaping out, I commanded to be taken back to the hotel, where for a whole miserable day I racked my brain with devices for acquiring the knowledge I so much desired. The result was futile, as you may imagine; nor will I stop to recount the various expedients to which I afterwards resorted in my vain attempt to solve the mystery of this young girl's identity.

Enough that they all failed, even the very promising one of searching the various photographic establishments of the city, for the valuable clew which her picture would give me. And so a week passed.

"It is time this mad infatuation was at an end," said I to myself one morning as I sat down to write a letter. "There is no hope of my ever seeing her again, and I am but frittering away the best emotions of my life in thus indulging in a dream that is not the prelude to a reality." But in spite of the wise determination thus made, I soon found my thoughts recurring to their old channel, and seized with sudden impatience at my evident weakness, took up the letter I had been writing and was about to read it, when to my great amazement I perceived that instead of inditing the usual words of a business communication, I had been engaged in scribbling a certain number up and down the page and even across the bottom where my signature should have been.

"Am I a fool?" I exclaimed, and was about to tear the sheet in two, when glancing again at the number, which was a simple thirty-six, I asked myself where I had got those especial figures. Instantly there arose before my mind's eye the vision of a brown-stone front with its vestibule and door. It was, then, the number of a house; but what house? a *chateau en Espagne* or a *bona fide* New York dwelling, which for some reason had unconsciously impressed itself upon my memory? I could not answer. There on the page was the number thirty-six, and equally plain in my mind was the look of the brown-stone front to which that number belonged—and that was all.

But it was enough to awaken within me the spirit of inquiry. The few houses thus numbered in that quarter of the city where I had lately been, were not so hard to find but that a morning given to the business ought to satisfy me whether the vision in my mind had its basis in reality. Taking a cab, I rode up town and into that region of streets I had traversed so carefully a week before. For I was assured that if the impression had been made by an actual dwelling it had been done at that time.

Following the same course I then took, I consulted the appearance of the various houses to which that number was assigned. The first was built of brick; that was not it. The next one had pillars to the vestibule; and that was not it. The third, to use an Irish bull, was no house at all, but a stable, while the fourth was an elegant structure of much more pretension than the plain and simple front I had in my mind or memory. I was about to utter a curse upon my folly and go home, when I remembered there was yet a street or two taken in my zig-zag course of the week before, which I had not yet tested. "Might as well be thorough," I muttered, and bade my driver proceed down —— Street.

What was there in its aspect that dimly excited me at the first glance? A dim remembrance, a certain ghostly assurance that we had reached the right spot? As we neared the number I sought, I could not suppress an exclamation of surprise. For there before me to its last detail, stood the house which involuntarily presented itself to my mind, when my eye first fell upon that mysterious number scribbled at the foot of the page I was writing.

It was, then, no chimera of an overwrought brain, this vision of a house-front which had been haunting me, but a distinct remembrance of an actual dwelling seen by me in my former journey through this street. But why this house-front above all others; what was there in it to make such an impression? Looking at it I could not determine, but after we had passed, something, I cannot tell what, brought back another remembrance, trivial in itself, but yet a link in the chain that was destined sooner or later to lead me out of the maze into which I had stumbled. It was merely this; that as I rode along the streets on that memorable morning, searching for that mark on the curbstone from which I hoped so much, I had come upon a spot where the pavement had been freshly washed. With that unconscious action of the brain with which we are familiar, I looked at the sidewalk a moment, running even then with the water that had been cast upon it, and then gave a quick glance at the house. That glance, account for it as you will, took in the picture before it as the camera catches the impression of a likeness, and though in another instant I had forgotten the whole occurrence, it needed but a certain train of thought or perhaps a certain state of emotion to revive it again.

A noble cause for such an act of unconscious cerebration you will say, a freshly washed pavement: *Le jeu ne faut pas la chandelle.* And so I thought too, or would have thought if I had not been so interested in the pursuit in which I was engaged, and if the idea had not suggested itself that water and a broom might obliterate chalk-marks from curbstones, and that the imps that preside over our mental forces would not indulge in such a trick at my expense unless the play *was* worth the candle. At all events, from the moment I made this discovery, I fixed my faith on that house as the one which held the object of my search, and though I contented myself with merely noting the number of the street as we left it, I none the less determined to pursue my investigations, till I had learned beyond the possibility of a doubt whether my conjectures were not true.

A perseverance worthy of a better cause you will say, but you are no longer twenty-five and under the influence of your first passion. I own I was astonished at myself and frequently paused in the pursuit I had undertaken, to ask if I were the same person who but a fortnight before laughed at the story of a man who had gone mad over the body of an unknown woman he had saved from a wreck only to find her dead in his arms.

The first thing I did was to ascertain the name of the gentleman occupying the house I have specified. It was that of one of our wealthiest and most respectable bankers, a name as well known in the city—as your own for instance. This was somewhat disconcerting, but with a dogged resolution somewhat foreign to my natural disposition, I persevered in my investigations, and learning in the next breath that the gentleman alluded to was a widower with an only child, a young daughter of about sixteen or so, recovered my assurance, though not my equanimity. Seeking out my friend Farrar, who as you know is a walking gazette of New York society, I broached the subject of Mr.—excuse me if I do not mention his name; allow me to say, Preston's domestic affairs, and learned that Miss Preston, "A naive little piece for so great an heiress," I remember Farrar called her, had left town within a day or two for a visit to some friends in Baltimore. "I happen to know," said he with that careless sweep of his hand at which you have so often laughed, "because my friend Miss Forsyth met her at the depot. She was intending to be gone—two weeks, I think she said. Do you know her?"

That last question sprung upon me unawares, and I am afraid I blushed. "No," I returned, "I have not that honor but an acquaintance of mine has—well—has met her and—"

"I see, I see," broke in Farrar with his most disagreeable smile. Then with a short laugh, meant to act as a warning, I suppose, added as he walked off, "I hope your friend is in fair circumstances and not connected with the fine arts. Music is Mr. Preston's detestation, while Miss Preston though too young to be much sought after yet, will in two years' time have the pick of the city at her command."

"So!" thought I to myself; "my little innocent charmer is an embryo aristocrat, eh? Well then, I was a greater fool than I imagined." And I walked out of the hotel where

I had met Farrar, with the very sensible conclusion to drop a subject that promised nothing but disappointment.

But the fates were against me, or the good angels perhaps, and at the next corner I met an old acquaintance, the very opposite of Farrar in character, who with a long love story of his own fired, my imagination to such an extent that in spite of myself I turned down —— Street, and was proceeding to pass her house, when suddenly the thought struck me, "How do I know that this unapproachable daughter of one of our most prominent citizens is one and the same person with my dainty little charmer? Widowers with young daughters are not so rare in this great city that I need consider the question as decided, because by a half superstitious freak of my own I have settled upon this house as the one I was in the other night. My inamorata may be the offspring of a musician for all I know." And inflamed at the thought of this possibility—I remembered the piano, you see—I gave to the winds all my fine resolutions and only asked how I could determine for once and all, whether I had ever crossed the threshold of the house before me. Some men would have run up the stoop, rung the bell and asked to see Mr. Preston on some pretended business he could easily conjure up to suit the occasion, but my face is too well known for me to risk any such attempt, besides I was too anxious to win the confidence of the young girl to shock her awakened sense of propriety by seeming to seek her where she did not wish to be found. And yet I must enter that house and see for myself if it was the one that held her on that memorable evening.

Pondering the question, I looked back at the door so obstinately closed against my curiosity, when to my satisfaction and delight it suddenly opened and a man stepped out, whom I instantly recognized as a business agent for one of the largest piano-forte manufactories in the city. "The heavens smile upon my enterprise," thought I, and waited for the man to come up with me. He was not only a friend of mine but largely indebted to me in various ways, so that I knew I had only to urge a request for it to be immediately granted, and that, too, without any questions or gossip.

You will not be interested in anything but the result, which was somewhat out of the usual course, and may therefore shock you. But you must remember that I am telling you of matters which young men usually keep to themselves, and that whatever I did, was accomplished in a spirit of respect only a shade less constraining in its power than the love that was at once my impelling force, and my constant embarrassment.

To come, then, to the point, a piano was to be set up in that house on that very day, Mr. Preston having yielded to the solicitations of his daughter for a new instrument. My friend was to be engaged in the transfer, and at my solicitation for leave to assist in the operation, gave his consent in perfect confidence as to my possessing good and sufficient reasons for such a remarkable request, and appointed the hour at which I was to meet him at the ware-rooms.

Behold me, then, at half-past two that afternoon, assisting with my own hands in carrying a piano up the stoop of that house which, four hours before, I had regarded as unapproachable. Dressed in a workman's blouse and with my hair well roughened under a rude cap that effectually disguised me, I advanced with but little fear of detection. And yet no sooner had I entered the house and seen at a glance that the aspect of the hall coincided with my rather vague remembrance of that through which I had been ushered a week before, than I was struck by a sudden sense of my situation, and experiencing that uncomfortable consciousness of self-betrayal, which a blush always gives a man, stumbled forward under my heavy burden, feeling as if a thousand eyes were fixed upon me and my cherished secret, instead of the two sharp but totally unsuspicious orbs of the elderly matron that surveyed us from the top of the banisters. "Be careful there, you'll knock a hole through that glass door!" though a natural cry under the circumstances, struck on my ears with the force and mysterious power of a secret warning, and when after a moment of blind advance I suddenly lifted my eyes and found myself in the little room, which like a silhouette on a white ground, stood out in my memory in distinct detail as the spot where I had first heard my own heart beat, I own that I felt my hands slipping from my burden, and in another moment had disgraced my character of a workman if I had not caught the sudden ring of a well known voice in the hall, as nurse answered from above some question propounded by the elderly lady with the piercing eyes. As it was, I recovered myself and went through my duties as promptly and deftly as if my heart did not throb with memories that each passing hour and event only served to hallow to my imagination.

At length the piano was duly set up and we turned to leave. Will you think I am too trivial in my details if I tell you that I lingered behind the rest and for an instant let my hand with all its possibilities for calling out a soul from that dead instrument, lie a moment on the keys over which her dainty fingers were so soon to traverse?

V.

THE RUBICON.

"I'll stake my life upon her faith."—Othello.

Once convinced of the identity of my sweet young friend with the Miss Preston at whose feet a two year hence, the wealth and aristocracy of New York would be kneeling, I drew back from further effort as having received a damper to my presumptuous hopes that would soon effectually stifle them. Everything I heard about the family—and it seemed as if suddenly each chance acquaintance that I met had something to say about Mr. Preston either as a banker or a man, only served to confirm me in this view. "He is a money worshipper," said one. "The bluest of blue Presbyterians," declared another. "The enemy of presumption and anything that looks like an overweening confidence in one's own worth or capabilities," remarked a third. "A man who would beggar himself to save the honor of a corporation with which he was concerned," observed a fourth "but who would not invite to his table the most influential man connected with it if that man was unable to trace his family back to the old Dutch settlers to which Mr. Preston's own ancestors belonged."

This latter statement I have no doubt was exaggerated for I myself have seen him at dinners where half the gentlemen who lifted the wine glass were self-made in every sense of the term. But it showed the bent of his mind and it was a bent that left me entirely out of the sweep of his acquaintanceship much less that of his exquisite daughter, the pride of his soul if not the jewel of his heart.

But when will a man who has seen or who flatters himself that he has seen in the eyes of the woman he admires, the least spark of that fire which is consuming his own soul, pause at an obstacle which after all has its basis simply in circumstances of position or will. By the time the two weeks of her expected absence had expired, I had settled it in my own mind that I would see her again and if I found the passing caprice of a child was likely to blossom into the steady regard of a woman, risk all in the attempt to win by honorable endeavor and persistence this bud of loveliness for my future wife.

How I finally succeeded by means of my friend Farrar in being one evening invited to the same house as Miss Preston it is not necessary to state. You will believe me it was done with the utmost regard for her feelings and in a way that deceived Farrar himself, who if he is the most prying is certainly the most volatile of men. In a crowded parlor, then, in the midst of the flash of diamonds and the flutter of fans Miss Preston and I again met. When I first saw her she was engaged in conversation with some young companion, and I had the pleasure of watching for a few minutes, unobserved, the play of her ingenuous countenance, as she talked with her friend, or sat silently watching the brilliant array before her. I found her like and yet unlike the vision of my dreams. More blithesome in her appearance, as was not strange considering her party attire and the lustre of the chandelier under which she sat, there was still that indescribable something in her expression which more than the flash of her eye or the curve of her lip, though both were lovely to me, made her face the one woman's face in the world for me; a charm which circumstances might alter, or suffering impair, but of which nothing save death could ever completely divest her and not death either, for it was the seal of her individuality, and that she would take with her into the skies.

"If I might but advance and sit down by her side without a word of explanation or the interference of conventionalities how happy I should be," thought I. But I knew that would not do, so I contented myself with my secret watch over her movements, longing for and yet dreading the advance of my hostess, with its inevitable introduction. Suddenly the piano was touched in a distant room and not till I saw the quick change in her face, a change hard to explain, did I recognize the selection as one I was in the habit of playing. *She* had not forgotten at least, and thrilled by the thought and the remembrance of that surge of color which had swept like a flood over her cheek, I turned away, feeling as if I were looking on what it was for no man's eyes to see, least of all mine.

My hostess' voice arrested me and next moment I was bowing to the ground before Miss Preston.

I am not a boy; nor have I been without my experiences: life with its vicissitudes has taught me many a lesson, subjected me to many a trial, yet in all my career have I never known a harder moment than when I raised my eyes to meet hers after that lowly obeisance. That she would be indignant I knew, that she might even misinterpret my motives and probably withdraw without giving me an opportunity to speak, I felt to be only too probable, but that she would betray an agitation so painful I had not anticipated, and for an instant I felt that I had hazarded my life's happiness on a cast that was going against me. But the necessity of saving her from remark speedily restored me to myself, and following the line of conduct I had previously laid out, I addressed her with the reserve of a stranger, and neither by word, look or manner conveyed to her a suggestion that we had ever met or spoken to each other before. She seemed to appreciate my consideration and though she was as yet too much unused to the ways of the world to completely hide her perturbation, she gradually regained a semblance of self-possession, and ere long was enabled to return short answers to my remarks, though her eyes remained studiously turned aside and never so much as ventured to raise themselves to the passing throng much less to my face, half turned away also.

Presently however a change passed over her. Pressing her two little hands together, she drew back a step or two, speaking my name with a certain tone of command. Struck with apprehension, I knew not why, I followed her. Instantly like one repeating a lesson she spoke.

"It is very good in you to talk to me as though we were the strangers that people believe us. I appreciate it and thank you very much. But it is not being just true; that is I feel as if I were not being just true, and as we can never be friends, would it not be better for us not to meet in this way any more?"

"And why," I gently asked, with a sense of struggling for my life, "can we never be friends?"

Her answer was a deep blush; not that timid conscious appeal of the blood that is beating too warmly for reply, but the quick flush of indignant generosity forced to do despite to its own instincts.

"That is a question I would rather not answer," she murmured at length. "Only it is so; or I should not speak in this way."

"But," I ventured, resolved to know on just what foundations my happiness was tottering, "you will at least tell me if this harsh decree is owing to any offence I myself may have inadvertently given. The honor of your acquaintance," I went on, determined she should know just what a hope she was slaying, "is much too earnestly desired, for me to wilfully hazard its loss by saying or doing aught that could be in any way displeasing to you."

"You have done nothing but what was generous," said she with increasing womanliness of manner, "unless it was taking advantage of my being here, to learn my name and gain an introduction to me after I had desired you to forget my very existence."

I recoiled at that, the chord of my self-respect was touched. "It was not here I learned your name, Miss Preston. It has been known to me for two weeks. At the risk of losing by your displeasure what is already hazarded by your prudence, I am bound to acknowledge that from the hour I left your father's house that night, I have spared no effort compatible with my deep respect for your feelings, to ascertain who the young lady was that had done me such an honor, and won from me such a deep regard. I had not intended to tell you this," I added, "but your truth has awakened mine, and whatever the result may be, you must see me as I am."

"You are very kind," she replied governing with growing skill the trembling of her voice. "The acquaintance of a girl of sixteen is not worth so much trouble on the part of a man like yourself." And blushing with the vague apprehension of her sex in the presence of a devotion she rather feels than understands, she waved her trembling little hand and paused irresolute, seemingly anxious to terminate the interview but as yet too inexperienced to know how to manage a dismissal requiring so much tact and judgment.

I saw, comprehended her position and hesitated. She was so young, uncle, her prospects in life were so bright; if I left her then, in a couple of weeks she would forget me. What was I that I should throw the shadow of manhood's deepest emotion across the paradise of her young untrammelled being. But the old Adam of selfishness has his say in my soul as well as in that of my fellow-men, and forgetting myself enough to glance at her half averted face, I could not remember myself sufficiently afterwards to forego without a struggle, all hope of some day beholding that soft cheek turn in confidence at my approach.

"Miss Preston," said I, "the promise of the bud atones for its folded leaves." Then with a fervor I did not seek to disguise, "You say we cannot be friends; would your decision be the same if this were our first meeting?"

Again that flush of outraged feeling. "I don't know—yes I think—I fear it would."

I strove to help her. "There is too great a difference between Bertram Mandeville the pianist, and the daughter of Thaddeus Preston."

She turned and looked me gently in the eye, she did not need to speak. Regret, shame, longing flashed in her steady glance.

"Do not answer," said I, "I understand; I am glad it is circumstances that stand in the way, and not any misconception on your part as to my motives and deep consideration for yourself. Circumstances can be changed." And satisfied with having thus dropped into the fruitful soil of that tender breast, the seed of a future hope, I bowed with all the deference at my command and softly withdrew.

But not to rest. With all the earnestness with which a man sets himself to decide upon the momentous question of life or death, I gave myself up to a night of reflection, and seated in my solitary bachelor apartment, debated with myself as to the resolution at which I had dimly hinted in my parting words to Miss Preston.

That I am a musician by nature, my success with the the public seems to indicate. That by following out the line upon which I had entered I would attain a certain eminence in my art, I do not doubt. But uncle, there are two kinds of artists in this world; those that work because the spirit is in them and they cannot be silent if they would, and those that speak from a conscientious desire to make apparent to others the beauty that has awakened their own admiration. The first could not give up his art for any cause, without the sacrifice of his soul's life; the latter—well the latter could and still be a man with his whole inner being intact. Or to speak plainer, the first has no choice, while the latter has, if he has a will to exert it. Now you will say, and the world at large, that I belong to the former class. I have risen in ten years from a choir boy in Trinity Church to a position in the world of music that insures me a full audience wherever and whenever I have a mind to exert my skill as a pianist. Not a man of my years has a more promising outlook in my profession, if you will pardon the seeming egotism of the remark, and yet by the ease with which I felt I could give it up at the first touch of a master passion, I know that I am not a prophet in my art but merely an interpreter, one who can speak well but who has never felt the descent of the burning tongue and hence not a sinner against my own soul if I turn aside from the way I am walking. The question was, then, should I make a choice? Love, as you say, seems at first blush too insecure a joy, if not often too trivial a one, to unsettle a man in his career and change the bent of his whole after life; especially a love born of surprise and fed by the romance of distance and mystery. Had I met her in ordinary intercourse, surrounded by her friends and without the charm cast over her by unwonted circumstances, and then had felt as I did now that of all women I had seen, she alone would ever move the deep springs of my being, it would be different. But with this atmosphere of romance surrounding and hallowing her girl's form till it seemed almost as ethereal and unearthly as that of an angel's, was I safe in risking fame or fortune in an attempt to acquire what in the possession might prove as bare and common-place as a sweep of mountain heather stripped of its sunshine. Curbing every erratic beat of my heart, I summoned up her image as it bloomed in my fancy, and surveying it with cruel eyes, asked what was real and what the fruit of my own imagination. The gentle eye, the trembling lip, the girlish form eloquent with the promise of coming womanhood,—were these so rare, that beside them no other woman should seem to glance or smile or move? And her words! what had she said, that any simple-minded, modest yet loving girl might not have uttered under the circumstances. Surely my belief in her being the one, the best and the dearest was a delusion, and to no delusion was I willing to sacrifice my art. But straight upon that conclusion came sweeping down a flood of counter-reasons. If not the wonder she seemed, she was at least a wonder to me. If I had seen her under romantic circumstances, and unconsciously been influenced by them, the influence had remained and nothing would ever rob her form of the halo thus acquired. Whether I ever won her to my fireside or not, she must always remain the fairy figure of my dreams, and being so, the gentle eye and tender lip acquired a value that made them what they seemed, the exponent of love and happiness. And lastly if love well or illy founded was an uncertain joy, and the passion for a woman a poor substitute for the natural incentive of talent or ambition, *this* love had within it the beginning of something deeper than joy, and in the passion thus cheaply characterized, dwelt a force and living fire that notwithstanding all I have hitherto achieved, has ever been lacking from my dreams of endeavor.

As you will see, the most natural question of all did not disturb me in these cogitations: And that was, whether in making the sacrifice I proposed, I should meet with the reward I had promised myself. The fancies of a young girl of sixteen are not usually of a stable enough character to warrant a man in building upon them his whole future happiness, especially a young girl situated like Miss Preston in the midst of friends who would soon be admirers, and adulators who would soon be her humble slaves. But the doubt which a serious contemplation of this risk must have presented, was of so unnerving a character, I dared not admit it. *If* I made the sacrifice, I must meet with my reward. I would listen to no other conclusion. Besides, something in the young girl herself, I cannot tell what, assured me then as it assures me now, that whatever virtues or graces she might lack, that of fidelity to a noble idea was not among them; that once convinced of the purity and value of the flame that had been lit in her innocent breast, nothing short of the unworthiness of the object that had awakened it, would ever serve to eliminate or extinguish it. That I was not worthy but would make it the business of my life to become so, was certain; that she would mark my endeavors and bestow upon me the sympathy they deserved, I was equally sure. No one would ever make such a sacrifice to her love as I was willing to do, and consequently in no one would I find a rival.

The morning light surprised me in the midst of the struggle, nor did I decide the question that day. Mr. Preston might not be as determined in his prejudices against musicians as my friends or even his daughter had imagined. I resolved to see him. Taking advantage of his connection with the ———— Club, I procured an introducer in the shape of a highly respected person of his own class, and went one evening to the Club-rooms with the full intention of making his acquaintance if possible. He was already there and in conversation with some business associates. Procuring a seat as near him as possible, I anxiously surveyed his countenance. It was not a reassuring one, and studied in this way, had the effect of dampening any hopes I may have cherished in the outset. He soften to the sounds of sweet strains or the voice of youthful passion! As soon as the granite rock to the surge of the useless billow. His very necktie spoke volumes. It was an old fashioned stock, full of the traditions of other days, while his coat, shabbier than any I would presume to wear, betrayed in every well-worn seam the pride of the aristocrat and millionaire who in his native city and before the eyes of his fellow magnates does not need to carry the evidences of his respectability upon his back.

"It would be worse than folly for me to approach him on such a subject," I mentally ejaculated. "If he did not stare the musician out of countenance he would the newly risen man." And I came very near giving up the whole thing.

But the genius that watches over the affairs of true love was with me notwithstanding the unpropitious state of my surroundings. In a few minutes I received my expected introduction to Mr. Preston, and I found that underneath the repelling austerity of his expression, was a kindly spark for youth, and a decided sympathy for all instances of manly endeavor if only it was in a direction he approved; further that my own personality was agreeable to him and that he was disposed to regard me with favor until by some chance and very natural allusion to my profession by the friend standing between us, he learned that I was a musician, when a decided change came over his countenance and he exclaimed in that blunt, decisive way of his that admits of no reply:

"A jingler on the piano, eh? Pretty poor use for a man to put his brains to, I say, or even his fingers. Sorry to hear we cannot be friends." And without waiting for a reply, took my introducer by the arm and drew him a step or so to one side. "Why didn't you say at once he was Mandeville the musician," I overheard him ask in somewhat querulous tones. "Don't you know I consider the whole race of them an abomination. I would have more respect for my bank clerk than I would for the greatest man of them all, were it Rubenstein himself." Then in a lower tone but distinctly and almost as if he meant me to hear, "My daughter has a leaning towards this same fol-de-rol and has lately requested my permission to make the acquaintance of some musical characters, but I soon convinced her that manhood under the disguise of a harlequin's jacket could have no interest for her; that when a human being, man or woman has sunk to be a mere rattler of sweet sounds, he has reached a stage of infantile development that has little in common with the nervous energy and business force of her Dutch ancestry. And my daughter stoops to make no acquaintances she cannot bid sit at her father's table."

"Your daughter is a child yet, I thought," was ventured by his companion.

"Miss Preston is sixteen, just the age at which my mother gave her hand to my respected father sixty-seven years ago." And with this drop of burning lead let fall into my already agitated bosom they passed on.

He would have more respect for his bank clerk! Would his bank clerk or what was better, a young man with means at his command, working in a business capacity more in consonance with the tastes he had evinced, have a chance of winning his daughter? I began to think he might. "The way grows clearer!" I exclaimed.

But it was not till after another interview with him ten minutes later in the lobby that I finally made up my mind. He was standing quite alone in an obscure corner, fumbling in an awkward way with his muffler that had caught on the button of his coat. Seeing it, I hastened forward to his assistance and was rewarded by a kind enough nod to embolden me to say,

"I have been introduced to you as a musician; would my acquaintance be more acceptable to you if I told you that the pursuit of art bids fair in my case to yield to the exigencies of business? That I purpose leaving the concert-room for the banker's office and that henceforth my only ambition promises to be that of Wall Street?"

"It most certainly would," exclaimed he, holding out his hand with an unmistakable gesture of satisfaction. "You have too good a countenance to waste before a piano-top strumming to the smirks of women and the plaudits of weak-headed men. Let us see you at the desk, my lad. We are in want of trustworthy young men to take the place of us older ones." Then politely, "Do you expect to make the change soon?"

"I do," said I.

And the Rubicon was passed.

VI.

A HAND CLASP.

"*Fer.*—Here's my hand.

Mir.—And mine with my heart in it."—Tempest.

Once arrived at a settled conclusion, I put every thought of wavering out of my mind. Deciding that with such a friend in business circles as yourself, I needed no other introducer to my new life, I set apart this evening for a confab with you on the subject. Meanwhile it is pretty generally known that I make no more engagements to appear through the country.

I have but one more incident to relate. Last Sunday in walking down Fifth Avenue I met her. I did not do this inadvertently. I knew her custom of attending Bible class and for once put myself in her way. I did not give her time to remonstrate.

"Do not express your displeasure," said I, "this shall never be repeated. I merely wish to say that I have concluded to leave a profession so little appreciated by those whose esteem I most desire to possess; that I am about entering a banker's office where it shall be my ambition to rise if possible, to wealth and consequence. If I succeed— you shall then know what my incentive has been. But till I succeed or at least give such tokens of success as shall insure respect, silence must be my portion and patience my sole support. Only of one thing rest assured, that until I inform you with my own lips that the hope which now illumines me is gone, it will continue to burn on in my breast, shedding light upon a way that can never seem dark while that glow rests upon it." And bowing with the ceremonious politeness our positions demanded, I held out my hand. "One clasp to encourage me," I entreated.

It seemed as if she did not comprehend. "You are going to give up music, and for— for—"

"You?" said I. "Yes, don't forbid me," I implored; "it is too late."

Like a lovely image of blushing girlhood turned by a lightning flash into marble, she paused, pallid and breathless where she was, gazing upon me with eyes that burned deeper and deeper as the full comprehension of all that this implied gradually forced itself upon her mind.

"You make a chaos of my little world," she murmured at length.

"No," said I, "*your* world is untouched. If it should never be my good fortune to enter it, you are not to grieve. You are free, Miss Preston, free as this sunshiny air we breathe; I alone am bound, and that because I must be whether I will or no."

Then I saw the woman I had worshipped in this young fair girl shine fully and fairly upon me. Drawing herself up, she looked me in the face and calmly laid her hand in mine. "I am young," said she, "and do not know what may be right to say to one so generous and so kind. But this much I can promise, that whether or not I am ever able to duly reward you for what you undertake, I will at least make it the study of my life never to prove unworthy of so much trust and devotion."

And with the last lingering look natural to a parting for years, we separated then and there, and the crowd came between us, and the Sunday bells rang on, and what was so vividly real to us at the moment, became in remembrance more like the mist and shadow of a dream.

VII.

MRS. SYLVESTER.

Love is more pleasant than marriage, for the same reason that romances are more amusing than history.—Chamfort.

"He draweth out the thread of his verbosity, finer than the staple of his argument."—Loves Labor Lost.

Young Mandeville having finished his story, looked at his uncle. He found him sitting in an attitude of extreme absorption, his right arm stretched before him on the table, his face bent thoughtfully downwards and clouded with that deep melancholy that seemed its most natural expression, "He has not heard me," was the young man's first mortifying reflection. But catching his uncle's eye which at that moment raised itself, he perceived he was mistaken and that he had rather been listened to only too well.

"You must forgive me if I have seemed to rhapsodize," the young man stammered. "You were so quiet I half forgot I had a listener and went on much as I would if I had been thinking aloud."

His uncle smiled and throwing off the weight of his reflections whatever they might be, arose and began pacing the floor. "I see you are past surgery," quoth he, "any wisdom of mine would be only thrown away."

Young Mandeville was hurt. He had expected some token of approval on his uncle's part, or at least some betrayal of sympathy. His looks expressed his disappointment.

"You expected to convert me by this story," continued the elder, pausing with a certain regret before his nephew; "nothing could convert me but—"

"What?" inquired Mandeville after waiting in vain for the other to finish.

"Something which we will never find in the whirl of New York fashionable life. A woman with faith to reward and soul to understand such unqualified trust as yours."

"But I believe Miss Preston is such a girl and will be such a woman. Her looks, her last words prove it."

"Nothing proves it but time and as for your belief, I have believed too." Then as if fearing he had said too much, assumed his most business-like tone and observed,

"But we will drop all that; you have resolved to quit music and enter Wall Street, your object money and the social consideration which money secures. Now, why Wall Street?"

"Because I can think of no other means for attaining what I desire, in the space of time I would consent to keep a young lady of Miss Preston's position waiting."

"Humph! and you have money, I suppose, which you propose to risk on the hazard?"

"Some! enough to start with; a small amount to you, but sufficient if I am fortunate."

"And if you are not?"

The young man opened his arms with an expressive gesture, "I am done for, that is all."

"Bertram," his uncle exclaimed with a change of tone, "has it ever struck you that Mr. Preston might have as strong a prejudice against speculation as against the musical profession?"

"No, that is, pardon me but I have sometimes thought that even in the event of success I should have to struggle against his inherited instincts of caste and his natural dislike of all things new, even wealth, but I never thought of the possibility of my arousing his distrust by speculating in stocks and engaging in enterprises so nearly in accord with his own business operations."

"Yet if I guess aright you would run greater risk of losing the support of his countenance by following the hazardous course you propose, than if you continued in the line of art that now engages you."

"Do you know—"

"I know nothing, but I fear the chances, Bertram."

"Then I am already defeated and must give up my hopes of happiness."

A smile thin and indefinable crossed the other's face. "No," said he, "not necessarily." And sitting down by his nephew's side, he asked if he had any objections to enter a bank. "In a good capacity," he exclaimed.

"No indeed; it would be an opportunity surpassing my hopes. Do you know of an opening?"

"Well," said he, "under the circumstances I will let you into the secret of my own affairs. I have always had one ambition, and that was to be at the head of a bank. I have not said much about it, but for the last five years I have been working to this end, and to-day you see me the possessor of at least three-fourths of the stock of the Madison Bank. It has been deteriorating for some time, consequently I was enabled to buy it low, but now that I have got it I intend to build up the concern. I am able to throw business of an important nature in its way, and I dare prophesy that before the year is out you will see it re-established upon a solid and influential footing."

"I have no doubt of it, sir; you have the knack of success, any thing that you touch is sure to go straight."

"Unhappily yes, as far as business operations go. But no matter about that;—" as if the other had introduced some topic incongruous to the one they were considering— "the point is this. In two weeks time I shall be elected President of the Bank; if you will accept the position of assistant cashier,—the best I can offer in consideration of your total ignorance of all details of the business,—it is open to you—"

"Uncle! how generous! I—"

"Hush! your duties will be nominal, the present cashier is fully competent; but the leisure thus afforded will offer you abundant opportunity to make yourself acquainted with all matters connected with the banking system as well as with such capitalists as it would be well for you to know. So that when the occasion comes, I can raise you to the cashier's place or make such other disposal of your talents as will best insure your rapid advance."

The young man's eyes sparkled; with a sudden impetuous movement he jumped to his feet and grasped his uncle's hand. "I can never thank you enough; you have made me your debtor for life. Now let any one ask me who is my father, and I will say—"

"He was Edward Sylvester's brother. But come, come, this extreme gratitude is unnecessary. You have always been a favorite with me, Bertram, and now that I have no child, you seem doubly near; it is my pleasure to do what I can for you. But—" and here he surveyed him with a wistful look, "I wish you were entering into this new line from love of the business rather than love of a woman. I fear for you my boy. It is an awful thing to stake one's future upon a single chance and that chance a woman's faith. If she should fail you after you had compassed your fortune, should die—well you could bear that perhaps; but if she turned false, and married some one else, or even married you and then—"

"What?" came in silvery accents from the door, and a woman richly clad, her trailing velvets filling the air at once with an oppressive perfume, entered the room and paused before them in an attitude meant to be arch, but which from the massiveness of her figure and the scornful carriage of her head, succeeded in being simply imperious.

Mr. Sylvester rose abruptly as if unpleasantly surprised. "Ona!" he exclaimed, hastening, however, to cover his embarassment by a courteous acknowledgement of her presence and a careless remark concerning the shortness of the services that had allowed her to return from church so early. "I did not hear you come in," he observed.

"No, I judge not," she returned with a side glance at Mandeville. "But the services were not short, on the contrary I thought I should never hear the last amen. Mr. Turner's voice is very agreeable," she went on, in a rambling manner all her own, "it never interferes with your thoughts; not that I am considered as having any," she interjected with another glance at their silent guest, "a woman in society with a reputation for taste in all matters connected with fashionable living, has no thoughts of course; business men with only one idea in their heads, that of making money, have more no doubt. Do you know, Edward," she went on with sudden inconsequence, which was another trait of this amiable lady's conversation, "that I have quite come to a conclusion in regard to the girl Philip Longtree is going to marry; she may be pretty, but she does not know how to dress. I wish you could have seen her to-night; she had on mauve with old gold trimmings. Now with one of her complexion—But I forget you haven't seen her. Bertram, I think I shall give a German next month, will you come? Oh, Edward!" as if the thought had suddenly struck her, "Princess Louise *is* the sixth child of Queen Victoria; I asked Mr. Turner to-night. By the way, I wonder if it will be pleasant enough to take the horses out to-morrow? Bird has been obliging enough to get sick just in the height of the season, Mr. Mandeville. There are a thousand things I have got to do and I hate hired horses." And with a petulant sigh she laid her prayer-book on the table and with a glance in the mirror near by, began pulling off her gloves in the slow and graceful fashion eminently in keeping with her every movement.

It was as if an atmosphere of worldliness had settled down upon this room sanctified a moment before by the utterances of a pure and noble love. Mr. Sylvester looked uneasy, while Bertram searched in vain for something to say.

"I seem to have brought a blight," she suddenly murmured in an easy tone somewhat at variance with the glance of half veiled suspicion which she darted from under her heavy lids, at first one and then the other of the two gentlemen before her. "No, I will not sit," she added as her husband offered her a chair. "I am tired almost to death and would retire immediately, but I interrupted you I believe in the utterance of some wise saying about matrimony. It is an interesting subject and I have a notion to hear what one so well qualified to speak in regard to it—" and here she made a slow, half lazy courtesy to her husband with a look that might mean anything from coquetry to defiance—"has to say to a young man like Mr. Mandeville."

Edward Sylvester who was regarded as an autocrat among men, and who certainly was an acknowledged leader in any company he chose to enter, bowed his head before this anomalous glance with a gesture of something like submission.

"One is not called upon to repeat every inadvertent phrase he may utter," said he. "Bertram was consulting me upon certain topics and—"

"You answered him in your own brilliant style," she concluded. "What did you say?" she asked in another moment in a low unmoved tone which the final act of smoothing out her gloves on the table with hands delicate as white rose leaves but firm as marble, did not either hasten or retard.

"Oh if you insist," he returned lightly, "and are willing to bear the reflection my unfortunate remark seems to cast upon the sex, I was merely observing to my nephew, that the man who centered all his hopes upon a woman's faith, was liable to disappointment. Even if he succeeded in marrying her there were still possibilities of his repenting any great sacrifice made in her behalf."

"Indeed!" and for once the delicate cheek flushed deeper than its rouge. "And why do you say this?" she inquired, dropping her coquettish manner and flashing upon them both, the haughty and implacable woman Bertram had always believed her to be, notwithstanding her vagaries and fashion.

"Because I have seen much of life outside my own house," her husband replied with undiminished courtesy; "and feel bound to warn any young man of his probable fate, who thinks to find nothing but roses and felicity beyond the gates of fashionable marriage."

"Ah then, it was on general principles you were speaking," she remarked with a soft laugh that undulated through an atmosphere suddenly grown too heavy for easy breathing. "I did not know; wives are so little apt to be appreciated in this world, Mr. Mandeville, I was afraid he might be giving you some homely advice founded upon personal experience." And she moved towards their guest with that strange smile of hers which some called dangerous but which he had always regarded as oppressive.

She saw him drop his eyes, and smiled again, but in a different way. This woman, whom no one accused of anything worse than levity, hailed every tribute to her power, as a miser greets the glint of gold. With a turn of her large but elegant figure that in its slow swaying reminded you of some heavy tropical flower, hanging inert, intoxicated with its own fragrance, she dismissed at once the topic that had engaged them, and launched into one of her choicest streams of inconsequent talk. But Mandeville was in no mood to listen to trivialities, and being of a somewhat impatient nature, presently rose and excusing himself, took a hurried leave. Not so hurried however that he did not have time to murmur to his uncle as they walked towards the door:

"You would make comparison between the girl I worship and other women in fashionable life. Do not I pray; she is no more like them than a star that shines is like a rose that blooms. My fate will not be like that of most men that we know, but better and higher."

And his uncle standing there in the grand hall-way, with the fresh splendors of unlimited wealth gleaming upon him from every side, looked after the young man with a sigh and repeated, "Better and higher? God in his merciful goodness grant it."

VIII.

SHADOWS OF THE PAST.

"Memory, the warder of the brain."—Macbeth.

It was long past midnight. The fire in the grate burned dimly, shedding its lingering glow on the face of the master of the house as with bowed head and folded hands he sat alone and brooding before its dying embers.

It was a lonesome sight. The very magnificence of the spacious apartment with its lofty walls and glittering works of art, seemed to give an air of remoteness to that solitary form, bending beneath the weight of its reflections. From the exquisitely decorated ceiling to the turkish rugs scattered over the polished floor, all was elegant and luxurious, and what had splendors like these to do with thoughts that bent the brows and overshadowed the lips of man? The very lights burned deprecatingly, illuminating beauties upon which no eye gazed and for which no heart beat. The master himself seemed to feel this, for he presently rose and put them out, after which he seated himself as before, only if possible with more abandon, as if with the extinguishing of the light some eye had been shut whose gaze he had hitherto feared. And in truth my lady's image shone fainter from its heavy panel, and the smile which had met with unrelenting sweetness the glare of the surrounding splendor, softened in the mellow glimmer of the fire-light to an etherial halo that left you at rest.

One, two, THREE, the small clock sounded from the mantel and yet no stir took place in the sombre figure keeping watch beneath. What were the thoughts which could thus detain from his comfortable bed a man already tired with manifold cares? It would be hard to tell. The waters that gush at the touch of the diviner's rod are tumultuous in their flow and rush hither and thither with little heed to the restraining force of rule and reason. But of the pictures that rose before his eyes in those dying embers, there were two which stood out in startling distinctness. Let us see if we can convey the impression of them to other eyes and hearts.

First, the form of his mother. Ah grey-bearded men weighted with the cares of life and absorbed in the monotonous round of duties that to you are the be all and end all of existence, to whom morning means a jostling ride to the bank, the store or the office, and with whom night is but the name for a worse unrest because of its unfulfilled promises of slumber, what soul amongst you all is so callous to the holy memories of childhood, as not to thrill with something of the old time feeling of love and longing as the memory of that tender face with its watchful eye and ready smiles, comes back to you from the midst of weary years! Your mother!

But Edward Sylvester with that black line across his life cutting past from present, what makes him think of his mother to-night; and the cottage door upon the hillside where she used to stand with eager eyes looking up and down the road as he came trudging home from school, swinging his satchel and shouting at every squirrel that started across the road or peeped from the branches of the grand old maples overhead! And the garret-chamber under the roof, the scene of many a romp with Elsie and Sonsie and Jack, neighbors' children to whom the man of to-day would be an awe and a mystery! And the little room where he slept with Tom his own blue-eyed brother so soon to die of a wasting disease, but full of warm blood then and all alive with boyish pranks. He could almost hear the wild clear laugh with which the mischievous fellow started upon its travels, the rooster whose legs he had tied a short space apart with one of Sonsie's faded ribbons, a laugh that became unrestrained when the poor creature in attempting to run down hill, rolled over and over, cutting such a figure before his late admirers, the hens, that even Elsie smiled in the midst of her gentle entreaties. And Jocko the crow, whom taming had made one of the boys! poor Jocko! is it nearly thirty years since you used to stalk in majesty through the village streets, with your neat raven coat closely buttoned across your breast and your genteel caw, caw, and condescending nod for old acquaintances? The day seems but as yesterday when you marred the stolen picnic up in the woods by flying off with a flock of your fellow black-coats, nor is it easy to realize that the circle of tow-headed fellows who hailed with shouts your ignominious return after a day or so's experience of the vaunted pleasures of freedom, are now sharp featured men without a smile for youth or a thought beyond the hard cold dollar buried deep in their pockets.

And the church up over the hills! and the long Sunday walk at mother's side with the sunshine glowing on the dusty road and beating on the river flowing far beyond! The same road, the same river of Monday and Tuesday but how different it looked to the boy; almost like another scene, as if Sunday clothes were on the world as well as upon his restless little limbs. How he longed for it to be Monday though he did not say so; and what a different day Saturday would have been if only there was no long, sleepy Sunday to follow it.

But the mother! She did not dread that day. Her eyes used to brighten when the bell began to ring from the old church steeple. Her eyes! how they mingled with every picture! They seemed to fill the night. What a sparkle they had, yet how they used to soften at his few hurried caresses. He was always too busy for kisses; there were the snares in the north woods to be looked after; the nest in the apple-tree to be inquired into; the skates to be ground before the river froze over; the nuts to be gathered and stored in that same old garret chamber under the eaves. But now how vividly her least look comes back to the tired man, from the glance of wistful sympathy with which she met his childish disappointments to the flash of joy that hailed his equally childish delights.

And another scene there is in the embers to-night; a remembrance of later days when the mother with her love and yearning was laid low in the grave, and manhood had learned its first lessons of passion and ambition from the glance of younger eyes and the smile of riper lips. Not the picture of a woman, however; that was already present beside him, shining from its panel with an insistence that not even the putting out of the lights could quite quench or subdue, but of a child young, pure and beautiful, sitting by the river in the glow of a June sunshine, gazing at the hills of his boyhood's home with a look on her face such as he had never before seen on that of child or woman. A simple picture with a simple villager's daughter for its centre, but as he mused upon it to-night, the success and triumph of the last ten years faded from his sight like the ashes that fell at his feet, and he found himself questioning in vain as to what better thing he had met in all the walks of his busy life than that young child's innocence and faith as they shone upon him that day from her soft uplifted eyes.

He had been sitting the whole warm noontide at the side of her whose half gracious, half scornful, wholly indolent acceptance of his homage, he called love, and enervated by an atmosphere he was as yet too inexperienced to recognize as of the world, worldly, had strolled forth to cool his fevered brow in the fresh autumn breeze that blew up from the river. He was a gay-hearted youth in those days, heedless of everything but the passing moment; nature meant little to him; and when in the course of his ramble he came upon the form of a child sitting on the edge of the river, he remembers wondering what she saw in a sweep of empty water to interest her so deeply. Indeed he was about to inquire when she turned and he caught a glimpse of her eyes and knew at once without asking. Yet in those days he was anything but quick to recognize the presence of feeling. A face was beautiful or plain to him, not eloquent or expressive. But this child's countenance was exceptional. It made you forget the cotton frock she wore, it made you forget yourself. As he gazed on it, he felt the stir of something in his breast he had never known before, and half dreaded to hear her speak lest the charm should fail or the influence be lost. Yet how could he pass on and not speak. Laying his hand on her head, he asked her what she was thinking of as she sat there all alone looking off on the river; and the wee thing drew in her breath and surveyed him with all her soul in her great black eyes before she replied, "I do not know, I never know." Then looking back she dreamily added, "It makes me want to go away, miles away,"—and she held out her tiny arms towards the river with a longing gesture; "and it makes me want to cry."

And he understood or thought he did and for the first time in his life looked upon the river that had met his gaze from childhood, with eyes that saw its exceeding beauty.

Ah it was an exquisite scene, a rare scene, mountain melting into mountain and meadow vanishing into meadow, till the flow of silver waters was lost in a horizon of azure mist. No wonder that a child without snares to set or nuts to gather, should pause a moment to gaze upon it, as even he in the days gone by would sometimes stop on Sabbath eves to snatch a kiss from his mother's lips.

"It is like a fairy land, is it not?" quoth the child looking up into his face with a wistful glance. "Do you know what it is that makes me feel so?"

He smiled and sat down by her side. Somehow he felt as if a talk with this innocent one would restore him more than a walk on the hills. "It is the spirit of beauty, my child, you are moved by the loveliness of the scene; is it a new one to you?"

"No, oh no, but I always feel the same. As if something here was hungry, don't you know?" and she laid her little hand on her breast.

He did not know, but he smiled upon her notwithstanding, and made her talk and talk till the gush of the sweet child spirit with its hidden longings and but half understood aspirations, bathed his whole being in a reviving shower, and he felt as if he had wandered into a new world where the languors of the tropics were unknown, and passion, if there was such, had the wings of an eagle instead of the siren's voice and fascination.

Her name was Paula, she said, and before leaving he found that she was a relative of the woman he loved. This was a slight shock to him. The lily and the cactus abloom on one stalk! How could that be? and for a moment he felt as if the splendors of the glorious woman paled before the lustre of the innocent child. But the feeling, if it was strong enough to be called such, soon passed. As the days swept by bringing evenings with light and music and whispered words beneath the vine-leaves, the remembrance of the pure, sweet hour beside the river, gradually faded till only a vague memory of that gentle uplifted face sweet with its childish dimples, remained to hallow now and then a passing reverie or a fevered dream.

But to-night its every lineament filled his soul, vying with the memories of his mother in its vividness and power. O why had he not learned the lesson it taught. Why had he turned his back upon the high things of life to yield himself to a current that swept him on and on until the power of resistance left him and—O dwell not here wild thoughts! Pause not on the threshold of the one dark memory that blasts the soul and sears the heart in the secret hours of night. Let the dead past bury its dead and if one must think, let it be of the hope, which the remembrance of that short glimpse into a pure if infantile soul has given to his long darkened spirit.

One, two, three, FOUR; and the fire is dead and the night has grown chill, but he heeds it not. He has asked himself if his life's book is quite closed to the higher joys of existence? whether money getting and money holding is to absorb him body and soul forever; and with the question a great yearning seizes him to look upon that sweet child again, if haply in the gleam of her pure spirit, something of the noble and the pure that lay beneath the crust of life might be again revealed to his longing sight.

"She must be a great girl now," murmured he to himself, "as old as if not older than she whom Bertram adores so passionately, but she will always be a child to me, a sweet pure child whose innocence is my teacher and whose ignorance is my better wisdom. If anything will save me—"

But here the shadow settled again; when it lifted, the morning ray lay cool and ghostly over the hearthstone.

IX.

PAULA.

"The stars of midnight shall be dearTo her; and she shall lean her earIn many a secret placeWhere rivulets dance their wayward round,And beauty born of murmuring soundShall pass into her face."—Wordsworth.

A wintry scene. Snow-piled hills stretching beyond a frozen river. On the bank a solitary figure tall, dark and commanding, standing with eyes bent sadly on a long narrow mound at his feet. It is Edward Sylvester and the mound is the grave of his mother.

It is ten years since he stood upon that spot. In all that time no memories of his childhood's home, no recollection of that lonely grave among the pines, had been sufficient to allure him from the city and its busy round of daily cares. Indeed he had always shrunk at the very name of the place and never of his own will alluded to it, but the reveries of a night had awakened a longing that was not to be appeased, and in the face of his wife's cold look of astonishment and a secret dread in his own heart, had left his comfortable fireside, for the scenes of his early life and marriage, and was now standing, in the bleak December air, gazing down upon the stone that marked his mother's grave.

But tender as were the chords that reverberated at this sight, it was not to revisit this tomb he had returned to Grotewell. No, that other vision, the vision of young sweet appreciative life has drawn him more strongly than the memory of the dead. It was to search out and gaze again upon the innocent girl, whose eloquent eyes and lofty spirit had so deeply moved him in the past, that he had braved the chill of the Connecticut hills and incurred the displeasure of his wife.

Yet when he turned away from that simple headstone and set his face towards the village streets it was with a sinking of the heart that first revealed to him the severity of the ordeal to which he had thus wantonly subjected himself. Not that the wintry trees and snow covered roofs appealed to him as strongly as the same trees and homes would have done in their summer aspect. The land was bright with verdure when that shadow fell whose gloom resting upon all the landscape, made a walk down this quiet road even at this remote day, a matter of such pain to him. But scenes that have caught the reflection of a life's joy or a heart's sorrow, lose not their power of appeal, with the leaves they shake from their trees, and nothing that had met the eyes of this man from the hour he left this spot, no, not the glance of his wife as his child fell back dead in his arms, had shot such a pang to his soul as the sight of that long street with its array of quiet homes, stretching out before him into the dim grey distance.

But for all that he was determined to traverse it, ay to the very end, though his steps must pass the house whose ghostly portals were fraught with memories dismal as death to him. On then he proceeded, walking with his usual steady pace that only faltered or broke, as he met the shy eyes of some hurrying village maiden, speeding upon some errand down the snowy street, or encountered some old friend of his youth who despite his altered mien and commanding carriage, recognized in him the slim young bank cashier who had left them now ten long years ago to make a name and fortune in the great city.

It was noon by the time he gained the heart of the village, and school was out and the children came rushing by with just the same shout and scamper with which he used to hail that hour of joyous release. How it carried him back to the days when those four red walls towered upon him with awful significance, as with books on his back and a half eaten apple in his pocket he crept up the walk, conscious that the bell had rung its last shrill note a good half hour before. He felt half tempted to stop and make his way through the crowd of shouting boys and dancing girls to that same old door again, and see for himself if the huge LATE which in a fit of childish revenge he had cut on its awkward panels, was still there to meet the eyes of tardy boys and loitering girls. But the wondering looks of the children unused to behold a figure so stately in their simple streets deterred him and he passed thoughtfully on. So engrossed was he by the reminiscences of Tom and Elsie which the school house had awakened, that he passed the ominous mansion which had been his dread, and the bank where he had worked, and the arbor by the side of the road where he had sat out the first hours of his fatal courtship, almost without realizing their presence, and was at the end of the street and in full view of the humble cottage which the little Paula had pointed out as her home on that day of their first acquaintance.

"Good heaven! and I do not even know if she is alive," he suddenly ejaculated, stopping where he was and eying the lowly walls before him with a quick realization of the possibilities of a great disappointment. "Ten years have strown many a grave on the hillside and Ona would not mention it if she lost every relative she had in this town. What a fool I have been," thought he.

But with the stern resolution which had carried him through many a difficulty, he prepared to advance, when he was again arrested by seeing the door of the house he was contemplating, suddenly open and a girlish figure issue forth. Could it be Paula? With eager, almost feverish interest he watched her approach. She was a slight young thing and came towards him with a rapid movement almost jaunty in its freedom. If it were Paula, he would know her by her eyes, but for some reason he hoped it was not she, not the child of his dreams.

At a yard or two in front of him she paused astonished. This grave, tall figure with the melancholy brow, deep eyes and firmly compressed lips was an unaccustomed sight in this primitive town. Scarcely realizing what she did she gave a little courtesy and was proceeding on when he stopped her with a hurried gesture.

"Is Mrs. Fairchild still living?" he asked, indicating the house she had just left.

"Mrs. Fairchild? O no," she returned, surveying him out of the corner of a very roguish pair of brown eyes, with a certain sly wonder at the suspense in his voice. "She has been dead as long as I can remember. Old Miss Abby and her sister live there now."

"And who are they?" he hurriedly asked; he could not bring himself to mention Paula's name.

"Why, Miss Abby and Miss Belinda," she returned with a puzzled air. "Miss Abby sews and Miss Belinda teaches the school. I don't know anything more about them, sir."

The courteous gentleman bowed. "And they live there quite alone?"

"O no sir, Paula lives with them."

"Ah, she does;" and the young girl looking at him could not detect the slightest change in his haughty countenance. "Paula is Mrs. Fairchild's daughter."

"Yes, sir."

"Thank you," said he, and allowed the pretty brown-eyed miss to pass on, which she did with lingering footsteps and many a backward glance of the eye.

Halting at the door of that small cottage, Edward Sylvester reasoned with himself.

"She may be just such another fresh-looking, round-faced, mischievous-eyed school-girl. Spiritual children do not always make earnest-souled women. Let me beware what hopes I build on a foundation so unsubstantial." Yet when in a moment later the door opened and a weazen-faced dapper, little woman appeared, all smiles and welcome, he owned to a sensation of dismay that sufficiently convinced him what a hold this hope of meeting with something exceptionally sweet and high, had taken upon his hitherto careless and worldly spirit.

"Mr. Sylvester I am sure! I thought Ona would remember us after a while. Come in sir, do, my sister will be home in a few moments." And with a deprecatory flutter comical enough in a woman at least seventy odd years old, she led her distinguished guest into a large unused room where in spite of his remonstrances she at once proceeded to build a fire.

"It is a pleasure sir," she said to every utterance of regret on his part at the trouble he was causing. And though her vocabulary was thus made to appear somewhat small, her sincerity was undoubted. "We have counted the days, Belinda and I, since we sent the last letter. It may seem foolish to you, sir; but Paula is growing so fast and Belinda says is so uncommon smart for her age that we did think that it was time Ona knew just what a straight we were in. Do you want to see Paula?"

"Very much," he returned, shocked and embarrassed at the position in which he found himself put by the reticence of his wife on the subject of her relations. "They think I have come in reply to a letter," he mused, "and I did not even know my wife had received one."

"You will be surprised," she exclaimed with a complacent nod as the fire blazed up brightly; "every one is surprised who sees her for the first time. Is my niece well?" And thus it was he learned the relation between his wife of ten years and these simple inhabitants of the little cottage in Grotewell.

He replied as in duty bound, and presently by the use of a few dexterous questions succeeded in eliciting from this simple-minded old lady, the few facts necessary to a proper understanding of the situation. Miss Abby and Miss Belinda were two maiden ladies, sisters of Mrs. Fairchild and Ona's mother, who on the death of the former took up their abode in the little cottage for the purpose of bringing up the orphan Paula. They had succeeded in this by dint of the utmost industry, but Paula was not a common child, and Belinda, who was evidently the autocrat of the house, had decided that she ought to have other advantages. She had therefore written to Mrs. Sylvester concerning the child, in the hopes that that lady would take enough interest in her pretty little cousin to send her to boarding-school; but they had received no reply till now, all of which was perfectly right of course, Mrs. Sylvester being undoubtedly occupied and Mr. Sylvester himself being better than any letter.

"And does Paula herself know what efforts you have been making in her behalf," asked Mr. Sylvester upon the receipt of this information.

The little lady shook her head with vivacity. "Belinda advised me to say nothing," she remarked. "The child is contented with her home and we did not like to raise her expectations. You will never regret anything you may do for her," she went on in a hurried way with a peep now and then towards the door as if while enjoying a momentary freedom of speech, she feared an intrusion that would cut that pleasure short. "Paula is a grateful child and never has given us a moment of concern from the time she began to put pieces of patchwork together. But there is Belinda," she suddenly exclaimed, rising with the little dip and jerk of her left shoulder that was habitual to her whenever she was amused or excited. "Belinda," she cried, going to the door and speaking with great impressiveness, "Mr. Sylvester is in the parlor." And almost instantly a tall middle aged lady entered, whose plain but powerful countenance and dignified demeanor, stamped her at once as belonging to a very different type of woman from her sister.

"I am very glad to see you sir," she exclaimed in a slow determined voice as dissimilar as possible from the piping tones of Miss Abby. "Is not Mrs. Sylvester with you?"

"No," returned he, "I have come alone; my wife is not fond of travelling in winter."

The slightest gleam shot from her bright keen eye. "Is she not well?"

"Yes quite well, but not over strong," he rejoined quietly.

She gave him another quick look, settled some matter with herself and taking off her bonnet, sat down by the fire. At once her sister ceased in her hovering about the room and sitting also, became to all appearance her silent shadow.

"Paula has gone up stairs to take off her bonnet," the younger woman said in a straightforward manner just short of being brusque. "She is a very remarkable girl, Mr. Sylvester, a genius I suppose some would call her, a child of nature I prefer to say. Whatever there is to be learned in this town she has learned. And in a place where nature speaks and good books abound that is not inconsiderable. I have taken pride in her talents I acknowledge, and have endeavored to do what I could to cultivate them to the best advantage. There is no girl in my school who can write so original a composition, nor is there one with a truer heart or more tractable disposition."

"You have then been her teacher as well as her friend, she owes you a double debt of gratitude."

A look hard to understand flashed over her homely face. "I have never thought of debt or gratitude in connection with Paula. The only effort which I have ever made in her behalf which cost me anything, is this one which threatens me with her loss." Then as if fearing she had said too much, set her firm lips still firmer and ignoring the subject of the child, astonished him by certain questions on the leading issues of the day that at once betrayed a truly virile mind.

"She is a study," thought he to himself, but meeting her on the ground she had taken, replied at once and to her evident satisfaction in the direct and simple manner that appeals the most forcibly to a strong if somewhat unpolished understanding, while the meek little Miss Abby glanced from one to the other with a humble awe more indicative of her appreciation for their superiority than of her comprehension of the subject.

But what with Miss Belinda's secret anxiety and Mr. Sylvester's unconscious listening for a step upon the stair, the conversation, brisk as it had opened, gradually languished, and ere long with a sort of clairvoyant understanding of her sister's wishes, Miss Abby arose and with her customary jerk left the room for Paula.

"The child is not timid but has an unaccountable aversion to entering the presence of strangers alone," Miss Belinda explained; but Mr. Sylvester did not hear her, for at that moment the door re-opened and Miss Abby stepped in with the young girl thus heralded.

Edward Sylvester never forgot that moment, and indeed few men could have beheld the picture of extraordinary loveliness thus revealed, without a shock of surprise equal to the delight it inspired. She was not pretty; the very word was a misnomer, she was simply one of nature's most exquisite and undeniable beauties. From the crown of her ebon locks to the sole of her dainty foot, she was perfect as the most delicate coloring and the utmost harmony of contour could make her. And not in the conventional type either. There was an individuality in her style that was as fresh as it was uncommon. She was at once unique and faultless, something that can be said of few women however beautiful or alluring.

Mr. Sylvester had not expected this, as indeed how could he, and for a moment he could only gaze with a certain swelling of the heart at the blooming loveliness that in one instant had transformed the odd little parlor into a bower fit for the habitation of princes. But soon his natural self-possession returned, and rising with his most courteous bow, he greeted the blushing girl with words of simple welcome.

Instantly her eyes which had been hitherto kept bent upon the floor flashed upward to his face and a smile full of the wonder of an unlooked for, almost unhoped for delight, swept radiantly over her lips, and he saw with deep and sudden satisfaction that the hour which had made such an impression upon him, had not been forgotten by her; that his voice had recalled what his face failed to do, and that he was recognized.

"It is Mr. Sylvester, your cousin Ona's husband," Miss Belinda interposed in a matter-of-fact way, evidently attributing the emotion of the child to her astonishment at the imposing appearance of their guest.

"And it was *you* who married Ona!" she involuntarily murmured, blushing the next moment at this simple utterance of her thoughts.

"Yes, dear child," Mr. Sylvester hastened to say. "And so you remember me?" he presently added, smiling down upon her with a sense of new life that for the moment made every care and anxiety shrink into the background.

"Yes," she simply returned, taking the chair beside him with the unconscious grace of perfect self-forgetfulness. "It was the first time I had found any one to listen to my childish enthusiasms; it is natural such kindness should make its impression."

"Little Paula and I met long ago," quoth Mr. Sylvester turning to the somewhat astonished Miss Belinda. "It was before my marriage and she was then—"

"Just ten years old," finished Paula, seeing him cast her an inquiring glance.

"Very young for such a thoughtful little miss," he exclaimed. "And have those childish enthusiasms quite departed?" he continued, smiling upon her with gentle encouragement. "Do you no longer find a fairy-land in the view up the river?"

She flushed, casting a timid glance at her aunt, but meeting his eyes again seemed to forget everything and everybody in the inspiration which his presence afforded.

"I fear I must acknowledge that it is more a fairy-land to me than ever," she softly replied. "Knowledge does not always bring disillusion, and though I have learned one by one the names of the towns scattered along those misty banks, and though I know they are no less prosaic in their character than our own humdrum village, yet I cannot rid myself of the notion that those verdant slopes with their archway of clouds, hide the portals of Paradise, and that I have only to follow the birds in their flight up the river to find myself on the verge of a mystery, the banks at my feet can never disclose."

"May the gates of God's Paradise never recede as those would do, my child, if like the birds you attempted to pierce them."

"Paula is a dreamer," quoth Miss Belinda in a matter-of-fact tone, "but she is a good girl notwithstanding and can solve a geometrical problem with the best."

"And sew on the machine and make a very good pie," timidly put in Miss Abby.

"That is well," laughed Mr. Sylvester, observing that the poor child's head had fallen forward in maidenly shame at her aunts' elogiums as well as at the length of the speech into which she had been betrayed. "It shows that her eyes can see what is at hand as well as what is beyond our reach." Then with a touch of his usual formal manner intended to restore her to herself, "Do you like study, Paula?"

In an instant her eyes flashed. "I more than like it; it feeds me. Knowledge has its vistas too," she added with an arch look, the first he had seen on her hitherto serious countenance. "I can never outgrow my recognition of the portals it discloses or the fairy-land it opens up to every inquiring eye."

"Even geometry," he ventured, more anxious to probe this fresh young mind than he had ever been to sound the opinions of the most notable men of the day.

"Even geometry," she smiled. "To be sure its portals are somewhat methodical in shape, allowing no scope to the fancy, but from its triangles and circles have been born the grandeurs of architecture, and upright on the threshold of its exact laws and undeviating calculations, I see an angel with a golden rod in his hand, measuring the heavens."

"Even a stone speaks to a poet," said Mr. Sylvester with a glance at Miss Belinda.

"But Paula is no poet," returned that lady with strict and impartial honesty. "She has never put a line on paper to my knowledge. Have you child?"

"No aunt, I would as soon imprison a falling sunbeam or try to catch the breeze that lifts my hair or kisses my cheek."

"You see," continued Mr. Sylvester still looking at Miss Belinda.

She answered with a doubtful shake of the head and an earnest glance at the girl as if she perceived something in that bright young soul, that even she had never observed before.

"Have you ever been away from home?" he now asked.

"Never, I know as little of the great world as a callow nestling. No, I should not say that, for the young bird has no Aunt Belinda to tell of the great cathedrals and the wonderful music she has heard and the glorious pictures she has seen in her visits to the city. It is almost as good as travelling one's self to hear Aunt Belinda talk."

It was now the turn of the mature plain woman to blush, which she did under Mr. Sylvester's searching eye.

"You have then been in the habit of visiting New York?"

"I have been there twice," she returned evasively.

"Since my marriage?"

"Yes sir;" with a firm closing of her lips.

"I did not know you were there or I should have insisted upon your remaining at my house."

"Thank you," said she with a quick triumphant glance at her demure little shadow, who looked back in amaze and was about to speak when Miss Belinda proceeded. "My visits usually have been on business; I should not think of troubling Mrs. Sylvester." And then he knew that his wife had been aware of those visits if he had not.

But he refrained from testifying to his discovery. "You speak of music," said he, turning gently back to Paula. "Have you a taste for it? Would it make you happy to hear such music as your aunt tells about?"

"O yes, I can conceive nothing grander than to sit in a church whose every line is beauty and listen while the great organ utters its song of triumph or echoes in the wonderful way it does, the emotions you have tried to express and could not. I would give a whole week of my life on the hills, dear as it is, for one such hour, I think."

Mr. Sylvester smiled. "It is a rare kind of coin to offer for such a simple pleasure, but it may meet with its acceptance, nevertheless;" and in his look and in his voice there was an appearance of affectionate interest that completed the subjugation of the watchful Miss Belinda, who now became doubly assured that whatever neglect had been shown her by her niece was not due to that niece's husband.

Mr. Sylvester recognized the effect he had produced and hastened to complete it, feeling that the good opinion of Miss Belinda would be valuable to any man. "I have been a boy on these hills," said he, "and know what it is to long for what is beyond while enjoying what is present. You shall hear the organ my child." And stopped, wondering to himself over the new sweet interest he seemed to take in the prospect of pleasures which he had supposed himself to have long ago exhausted.

"Hear the organ, I? why that means—O what does it mean?" she inquired, turning with a look of beaming hope towards her aunt.

"You must ask Mr. Sylvester," that uncompromising lady replied, with a straightforward look at the fire.

And he with a smile told the blushing girl that according to his reading, mortals went blindfold into fairy-land; and she understood what he meant and was silent, whereupon he turned the conversation upon more common-place subjects.

For how could he tell her then of the intention that had awakened in his breast at the first glimpse of her grand young beauty. To make her his child, to bequeath to her the place of the babe that had perished in his arms three long years before—That meant to give Ona a care if not a rival in his affections, and Ona shrank from care, and was not a subject for rivalry. And the *if*which this implied weighed heavily on his heart as moment after moment flew by, and he felt again the reviving power of an unsullied mind and an aspiring nature.

X.

THE BARRED DOOR.

"A school boy's tale; the wonder of an hour."—Byron.

"Did you know that your niece was gifted with rare beauty as well as talents?" asked Mr. Sylvester of Miss Belinda as a couple of hours or so later, they sat alone by the parlor fire, preparatory to his departure.

"No, that is," she hastily corrected herself, "I knew she was very pretty of course, prettier by far than any of her mates, but I did not suppose she was what you call a beauty, or at least would be so considered by a person accustomed to New York society."

"I do not know of a woman in New York who can boast of any such claims to transcendent loveliness. Such faces are rare outside of art, Miss Belinda; was Mrs. Fairchild a handsome woman?"

"She was my sister and if I may say so, my favorite sister, but she was no more agreeable to the eye than some others of her family," grimly returned the heavy browed spinster with a compression of her lips. "What beauty Paula has inherited came from her father. Her chief charm in my eyes, however, springs from her pure nature and the unselfish impulses of her heart."

"And in mine," rejoined he quietly. Then with a sudden change of tone as he realized the necessity of saying something definite to this woman in regard to his intentions toward the child, he remarked, "Her great and unusual talents and manifest disposition to learn, demand as you say, superior advantages to any she can have in a small country town like this, fruitful as it has already been to her under your wise and fostering care and such shall she have; but just when and how I cannot say till I have seen my wife and learned what her wishes are likely to be in regard to the subject."

"You are very kind, sir," returned Miss Belinda. "I have no doubt as to the good-will of your intentions, and the child shall be prepared at once for a change."

"And will *the child*," he exclaimed with a smile as Paula re-entered the room, "be so kind as to give me her company in the walk I must now take to the cars?"

"Of course," replied her aunt before the young girl could speak, "we owe you that much attention I am sure."

And so it was that when he came to retrace his way through the village with its heavy memories, he had a guardian spirit at his side that robbed them of their power to sadden and oppress.

"What shall I say for you to the grim, city streets when I get back?" inquired he as they hastened on over the snow covered road.

"Say to them from me? O you may give them my greeting," she responded half shyly, half confidingly. Evidently for her he was one of those rare persons whose presence is perfect freedom and with whom she could not only think her best but speak it also. "I should like to make their acquaintance, but indeed they would have to do well to vie in attraction with these white roads girded by their silver-limbed trees. The very rush of life must seem oppressive. So many hopes, so many fears, so many interests jostling you at every step! Yet the thought is exhilarating too; don't you find it so?"

It was the first question she had asked him and he knew not how to reply. Her eyes were so confiding, he could not bear to shake her faith in his imagined superiority. Yet what thoughts had he ever cherished in walking the busy streets, save those connected with his own selfish hopes and fears, plans and operations? "I have no doubt," said he after a moment's pause, "that I have felt this exhilaration of which you speak. Certainly the hurrying masses in Broadway awaken a far different sensation in a man, than this solitary stretch of country road."

"Yet the road has its companionships," she murmured. "In the city one thinks most of men, but in the country, of God. Its very solitude compels you."

"Compels you," he involuntarily answered. And shuddered as he said it, remembering days when he trod these very roads with anything but reverence in his heart for the Creator of the landscape before him. "Not every one has the inner vision, my child, to see the love and wisdom back of the works, or rather most men have a vision so short it does not reach so far. Yet I think I can understand what you mean and might even experience your emotions if my eyes had leisure to explore this space and my thoughts to rise out of their usual depressing atmosphere of care and anxiety. You did not think I was a busy man, he continued," observing her gaze of wonder. "You thought riches brought ease; if you ever come to think, 'most of men' you will learn that the wealthy man is the greatest worker, for his rest comes not night or day."

She shook her head with a sudden doubt. "It is a problem," she said, "which my knowledge of geometry does not help me to solve."

"No," assented he; "and one in which even your fanciful soul would fail to find any poetry. But stop, Paula; isn't this the place where I found you that day, and you showed me the view up the river?"

"Yes, and it was on that stone I sat; it has a milk-white cushion now; and there is where you stood, looking so tall and grand to my childish eyes! The gates are of pearl now," she said, pointing to the snow-covered slopes in the west. "I wish the sky had been clear to-night and you could have seen the effect of a rosy sunset falling over those domes of ice and snow."

"It would leave me less to expect when I come again," he responded almost gayly. "The next time we will have the sunset, Paula."

She smiled and they hastened on, presently finding themselves in the village streets. Suddenly she paused. "Small towns have their mysteries as well as great cities," said she; "we are not without ours, look."

He turned, followed with a glance the direction of her pointing finger and started in his sudden surprise. She had indicated to him the house whose ghostly and frowning front bore written across its grim gray boards, such an inscription of painful remembrance. "It is a solitary looking place, isn't it?" she went on, innocent of the pain she was inflicting. "No one lives there or ever will, I imagine. Do you see that board nailed across the front door?"

He forced himself to look. He did more, he fixed his eyes upon the desolate structure before him until the aspect of its huge unpainted walls with their long rows of sealed-up windows and high smokeless chimneys was impressed indelibly upon his mind. The large front door with its weird and solemn barrier was the last thing upon which his eye rested.

"Yes," said he, and involuntarily asked what it meant.

"We do not know exactly," she responded. "It was nailed across there by the men who followed Colonel Japha to the grave. Colonel Japha was the owner of the house," she proceeded, too interested to observe the shadow which the utterance of that name had invoked upon his brow. "He was a peculiar man I judge, and had suffered great wrongs they say; at all events his life was very solitary and sad, and on his deathbed he made his neighbors promise him that they would carry out his body through that door and then seal it up against any further ingress or egress forever. His wishes were respected, and from that day to this no one has ever entered that door."

"But the house!" stammered Mr. Sylvester in anything but his usual tone, "surely it has not been deserted all these years!"

"Ah," said she, "now we come to the greatest mystery of all." And laying her hand timidly on his arm, she drew his attention to the form of a decrepit old lady just then advancing towards them down the street "Do you see that aged figure?" she asked. "Every evening at this hour, winter and summer, stormy weather or clear, she is seen to leave her home up the street and come down to this forsaken dwelling, open the worm-eaten gate before you, cross the otherwise untrodden garden and enter the house by a side door which she opens with a huge key she carries in her pocket. For just one hour by the clock she remains there, and then she is seen to issue in the falling dusk, with a countenance whose heavy dejection is in striking contrast to the expression of hope with which she invariably enters. Why she makes this pilgrimage and for what purpose she secludes herself for a stated time each day in this otherwise deserted mansion, no man knows nor is it possible to determine, for though she is a worthy woman and approachable enough on all other topics, on this she is absolutely mute."

Mr. Sylvester started and surveyed the woman as she passed with an anxious gaze. "I know her," he muttered; "she was a connection of—of the family, who inhabited this house." He could not speak the name.

"Yes, so they say, and the owner of this house, though she does not live here. Did you notice how she looked at me? She often does that, just as if she wanted to speak. But she always goes by and opens the gate as you see her now and takes out the big key and—"

"Come away," cried Mr. Sylvester with sudden impulse, seizing Paula by the hand and hurrying her down the street. "She is a walking goblin; you must have nothing to do with such uncanny folk." And endeavoring to turn off this irresistible display of feeling by a show of pleasantry he laughed aloud, but in a strained and unnatural way that made her eyes lift in unconscious amazement.

"You are infected by the atmosphere of unreality that pervades the spot," said she, "I do not wonder." And with the gentle perversity that sometimes affects the most thoughtful amongst us, she went on talking upon the unwelcome subject. "I know of some folks who invariably cross to the other side of the street at night, rather than go through the shadows of the two gaunt poplars which guard that house. Yet there has been no murder committed there or any great crime that I know of, unless the disobedience of a daughter who ran away with a man her father detested, could be denominated by so fearful a word."

The set gaze with which Mr. Sylvester surveyed the landscape before him quavered a trifle and then grew hard and cold. "And so," said he in a tone meant more for himself than her, "even your innocent ears have been assailed by the gossip about Miss Japha."

"Gossip! I have never thought of it as gossip," returned she, struck for the first time by the change in his appearance. "It all happened so long ago it seems more like some quaint and ancient tale than a story of one of our neighbors. Besides, the fact that a wilful girl ran away from the house of her father, with the man of her choice, is not such a dreadful one is it, though she never returned to its walls with her husband, and her father was so overwhelmed by the shock, he was never seen to smile again."

"No," said he, giving her a hurried glance of relief, "I only wondered at the tenacity of old stories to engage the popular ear. I had supposed even the remembrance of Jacqueline Japha would have been lost in the long silence that has followed that one disobedient act."

"And so it might, were it not for that closely shut house with the sinister bar across its chief entrance, inviting curiosity while it effectually precludes all investigation. With that token ever before our eyes of a dead man's implacable animosity, who can wonder that we sometimes ponder over the fate of her who was its object."

"And no intimations of that fate have been ever received in Grotewell. For all that is known to the contrary, Jacqueline Japha may have preceded her father to the tomb."

Paula bowed her head, amazed at the gloomy tone in which this emphatic assertion was made by one whose supposed ignorance she had been endeavoring to enlighten. "You knew her history before, then," observed she, "I beg your pardon."

"And it is granted," said he with a sudden throwing off of the shadow that had enveloped him. "You must not mind my sudden lapses into gloom. I was never a cheerful man, that is, not since I—since my early youth I should say. And the shadows which are short at your time of life grow long and chilly at mine. One thing can illumine them though, and that is a child's happy smile. You are a child to me; do not deny me a smile, then, before I go."

"Not one nor a dozen," cried she, giving him her hands in good-bye for they had arrived at the depot by this time and the sound of the approaching train was heard in the distance.

"God bless you!" said he, clasping those hands with a father's heartfelt tenderness. "God bless my little Paula and make her pillow soft till we meet again!" Then as the train came sweeping up the track, put on his brightest look and added, "If the fairy-godmother chances to visit you during my departure, don't hesitate to obey her commands, if you want to hear the famous organ peal."

"No, no," she cried. And with a final look and smile he stepped upon the train and in another moment was whirled away from that place of many memories and a solitary hope.

XI.

MISS STUYVESANT.

"She smiled; but he could see ariseHer soul from far adown her eyes."—Mrs. Browning.

"She is a beauty; it is only right I should forewarn you of that."

"Dark or light?"

"Dark; that is her hair and eyes are almost oriental in their blackness, but her skin is fair, almost as dazzling as yours, Ona."

Mrs. Sylvester threw a careless glance in the long mirror before which she was slowly completing her toilet, and languidly smiled. But whether at this covert compliment to her greatest charm or at some passing fancy of her own, it would be difficult to decide. "The dark hair and eyes come from her father," remarked she in an abstracted way while she tried the effect of a bunch of snow-white roses at her waist with a backward toss of her proud blonde head. "His mother was a Greek. 'Tell it not in Gath, publish it not in the streets of Askelon,'" she exclaimed in a voice as nearly gay as her indolent nature would allow. For this lady of fashion was in one of her happiest moods. Her dress, a new one, fitted her to perfection and the vision mirrored in the glass before her was not lacking, so far as she could see in one charm that could captivate. "Do you think she could fasten a ribbon, or arrange a bow?" she further inquired. "I should like to have some one about me with a knack for helping a body in an emergency, if possible. Sarah is absolutely the destruction of any bit of ribbon she undertakes to handle. Look at that knot of black velvet over there for instance, wouldn't you think a raw Irish girl just from the other side would have known better than to tie it with half the wrong side showing?"

With the habit long ago acquired of glancing wherever her ivory finger chanced to point, the grave man of the world slowly turned his head full of the weightiest cares and oppressed by the burden of innumerable responsibilities, and surveyed the cluster of velvet bows thus indicated, with a mechanical knitting of the brows.

"I pay Sarah twenty-five dollars a month and that is the result," his wife proceeded. "Now if Paula—"

"Paula is not to come here as a waiting maid," her husband quickly interposed, a suspicion of color just showing itself for a moment on his cheek.

"If Paula," his wife went on, unheeding the interruption save by casting him a hurried glance over the shoulder of her own reflection in the glass, "had the taste in such matters of some other members of our family and could manage to lend me a helping hand now and then, why I could almost imagine I had my younger sister back with me again, who with her skill in making one look fit for the eyes of the world, was such a blessing to us in our old home."

"I have no doubt Paula could be taught to be equally efficient," her husband responded, carefully restraining any further show of impatience. "She is bright, I am certain, and ribbon-tying is not such a very difficult art, is it?"

"I don't know about that; by the way Sarah succeeds I should say it was about on a par with the science of algebra or—what is that horrid study they used to threaten to inflict me with at the academy whenever I complained of a headache? Oh I remember—conic sections."

"Well, well," laughed her husband, "she ought soon to to be an expert in it then; Paula is a famous little mathematician."

A silence followed this response; Mrs. Sylvester was fitting in her ear-rings. "I suppose," said she when the operation was completed, "that the snow will prevent half the people from coming to-night." It was a reception evening at the Sylvester mansion. "But so long as Mrs. Fitzgerald does not disappoint me, I do not care. What do you think of the setting of these diamonds?" she inquired, leaning forward to look at herself more closely, and slowly shaking her head till the rich gems sparkled like fire.

"It is good," came in short, quick tones from the lips of her husband.

"Well, I don't know, there might be a shade more of enamel on the edge of that ring. I shall speak to the jeweller about it to-morrow. But what were we talking about?" she dreamily asked, still turning her head from side to side before the mirror.

"We were talking about adopting your cousin in the place of our child who is dead," replied her husband with some severity, pausing in the middle of the floor which he was pacing, to honor her with a steady glance.

"O yes! Dear me! what an awkward clasp that man has given to these rings after all. You will have to fasten them for me." Then as he stepped forward with studied courtesy, yawned just a trifle and remarked, "No one could ever take the place of one's own child of course. If Geraldine had lived she would have been a blonde, her eyes were blue as sapphires."

He looked in his wife's face and his hands dropped. He thought of the day when those eyes, blue as sapphires indeed, flashed burning with death's own fever, from the little crib in the nursery, while with this same cool and self-satisfied countenance, the wife and mother before him had swept down the broad stairs to her carriage, murmuring apologetically as she gathered up her train, "O you needn't trouble yourself to look after her, she will do very well with Sarah."

She may have thought of it too, for the least little bit of real crimson found its way through the rouge on her cheek as she encountered the stern look of his eye, but she only turned a trifle more towards the glass, saying, "I forgot you do not admire the rôle of waiting maid. I will try and manage them myself, seeing that you have banished Sarah."

He exerted his self-control and again for the thousandth time buried that ghastly memory out of sight, actually forcing himself to smile as he gently took her hand from her ear and began deftly to fasten the rebellious ornaments.

"You mistake," said he, "love can ask any favor without hesitation. I do not object to waiting upon my own wife."

She gave him a little look which he obligingly took as a guerdon for this speech, and languidly held out her bracelets. As he stood clasping them on her arms, she quietly eyed him over from head to foot. "I don't know of a man who has your figure," said she with a certain tone of pride in her voice; "it is well you married a wife who does not look altogether inferior beside you." Then as he bowed with mock appreciation of the intended compliment, added with her usual inconsequence, "I dare say it would give me something to interest myself in. I don't suppose she has a decent thing to wear, and the fact of her being a dark beauty would lend quite a new impulse to my inventive faculty. Mrs. Walker has a daughter with black eyes, but dear me, what a guy she does make of her!"

With a sigh Mr. Sylvester turned to the window where he stood looking out at the heavy flakes of snow falling with slow and fluctuating movement between him and the row of brown stone houses in front. Paula considered as a milliner's block upon which to try the effect of clothes!

"Even Mrs. Fitzgerald with all her taste don't know how to dress her child," proceeded his wife, with a hurried, "Be still, Cherry!" to the importunate bird in the cage. "Now I should take as much pride in dressing any one under my charge as I would myself, provided the subject was likely to do credit to my efforts." And finding the bird incorrigible in his shrill singing, she moved over to the cage, where she stood balancing her white finger for the bird to peck at, with a pretty caressing motion of her lip, the little Geraldine of the wistful blue eyes, had never seen.

"You are welcome to do what you please in such matters," was her husband's reply. He was thinking again of that same little Geraldine; a fall of snow like the present always made him think of her and her innocent query as to whether God threw down such big flakes to amuse little children. "I give you *carte blanche*," said he with sudden emphasis.

Mrs. Sylvester paused in her attentions to the bird to give him a sharp little look which might have aroused his surprise if he had been fortunate enough to see it. But his back was towards her, and there was nothing in the languidly careless tone with which she responded, to cause him to turn his head. "I see that you would really like to have me entertain the child; but—"

She paused, pursing up her lips to meet the chattering bird's caress, while her husband in his impatience drummed with his fingers on the pane.

—"I must see her before I decide upon the length of her visit," continued she, as weary with the sport she drew back to give herself a final look in the glass. "Will you please to hand me that shawl, Edward."

He turned with alacrity. In his relief he could have kissed the snowy neck held so erectly before him, as he drew around it the shawl he had hastily lifted from the chair at his side. But that would not have suited this calm and languid beauty who disliked any too overt tribute to her charms and saved her caresses for her bird. Besides it would look like gratitude, and gratitude would be misplaced towards a wife who had just indicated her acceptance of his offer to receive a relative of her own into his house.

"She might as well come at once," was her final remark, as satisfied at last with the lay of every ribbon she swept in finished elegance from the room. "Mrs. Kittredge's reception comes off a week from Thursday, and I should like to see how a dark beauty with a fair skin would look in that new shade of heliotrope."

And so the battle was over and the victory won; for Mrs. Sylvester for all her seeming indifference was never known to change a decision she had once made. As he realized the fact, as he meditated that ere long this very room which had been the scene of so much frivolity and the witness to so many secret heart-burnings, would reëcho to the tread of the pure and innocent child, whose mind had flights unknown to the slaves of fashion, and in whose heart lay impulses of goodness that would satisfy the long smothered cravings of his awakened nature, he experienced a feeling of relenting towards the wife who had not chosen to thwart him in this the strongest wish of his childless manhood, and crossing to her dressing table, he dropped among its treasures a costly ring which he had been induced to purchase that day from an old friend who had fallen into want. "She will wear it," murmured he to himself, "for its hue will make her hand look still whiter, and when I see it sparkle I will remember this hour and be patient." Had he known that she had yielded to this wish out of a certain vague feeling of compunction for the disappointments she had frequently occasioned him and would occasion him again, he might have added a tender thought to the rich and costly gift with which he had just endowed her.

"I expect a young cousin of mine to spend the winter with me and pursue her studies," were the first words that greeted his ears as an hour or so later he entered the parlor where his wife was entertaining what few guests had been anxious enough for a sight of Mrs. Sylvester's newly furnished drawing-room, to brave the now rapidly falling snow. "I hope that you and she will be friends."

Curious to see what sort of a companion his wife was thus somewhat prematurely providing for Paula, he hastily advanced towards the little group from which her voice had proceeded, and found himself face to face with a brown-haired girl whose appealing glance and somewhat infantile mouth were in striking contrast to the dignity with which she carried her small head and managed her whole somewhat petite person.

"Miss Stuyvesant! my husband!" came in musical tones from his wife, and somewhat surprised to hear a name that but a moment before had been the uppermost in his mind, he bowed with courtesy and then asked if he was so happy as to speak to a daughter of Thaddeus Stuyvesant.

"If it will give you especial pleasure I will say yes," responded the little miss with a smile that irradiated her whole face. "Do you know my father?"

"There are but few bankers in the city who have not that pleasure," replied he with an answering look of regard. "I am especially happy to meet his daughter in my house to-night."

There was something in his manner of saying this and in the short inquiring glance which at every opportunity he cast upon her bright young face with its nameless charm of mingled appeal and reserve, that astonished his wife.

"Miss Stuyvesant was in the carriage with Mrs. Fitzgerald," said that lady with a certain dignity she knew well how to assume. "I am afraid if it had not been for that circumstance we should not have enjoyed the pleasure of her presence." And with the rare tact of which she was certainly a mistress, as far as all social matters were concerned, she left the aspiring magnate of Wall Street to converse with the daughter of the man whom all New York bankers were expected to know, and hastened to join a group of ladies discussing ceramics before a huge placque of rarest *cloissone*.

Mr. Sylvester followed her with his eyes; he had never seen her look more vivacious; had the hope of seeing a young face at their board touched some secret chord in her nature as well as his? Was she more of a woman than he imagined, and would she be, though in the most superficial of ways, a mother to Paula? Flushed with the thought, he turned back to the little lady at his side. She was gazing in an intent and thoughtful way at an engraving of Dubufe's "Prodigal Son" that adorned the wall above her head. There was something in her face that made him ask:

"Is that a favorite picture of yours?"

She smiled and nodded her small and delicate head.

"Yes sir, it is indeed, but I was not looking at the picture so much as at the face of that dark-haired girl that sits in the centre, with that far-away expression in her eyes. Do you see what I mean? She is like none of the rest. Her form is before us, but her heart and her interest are in some distant clime or forsaken home to which the music murmured at her side recalls her. She has a soul above her surroundings, that girl; and her face is indescribably pathetic to me. In the recesses of her being she carries a memory or a regret that separates her from the world and makes certain moments of her life almost holy."

"You look deep," said Mr. Sylvester, gazing down upon the little lady's face with strongly awakened interest. "You see more perhaps than the painter intended."

"No, no; possibly more than the engraving expresses, but not more than the artist intended. I saw the original once, when as you remember it was on exhibition here. I was a wee thing, but I never forgot that girl's face. It spoke more than all the rest to me; perhaps because I so much honor reserve in one who holds in his breast a great pain or a great hope."

The eye that was resting upon her, softened indescribably. "You believe in great hopes," said he.

The little figure seemed to grow tall; and her face looked almost beautiful. "What would life be without them?" she answered.

"True," returned Mr. Sylvester; and entering into the conversation with unusual spirit, was astonished to find how young she was and yet how thoroughly bright and self-possessed.

"Lovely girls are cropping up around me in all directions," thought he; "I shall have to correct my judgment concerning our young ladies of fashion if I encounter many more as sensible and earnest-hearted as this." And for some reason his brow grew so light and his tone so cheerful that the ladies were attracted from all parts of the room to hear what the demure Miss Stuyvesant could have to say to the grave master of the house, to call forth such smiles of enjoyment upon his usually melancholy countenance.

Take it all together, the occasion though small was one of the pleasantest of the season, and so Mrs. Sylvester announced when the last carriage had driven away, and she and her husband stood in the brilliantly lighted library, surveying a new cabinet of rare and antique workmanship which had been that day installed in the place of honor beneath my lady's picture.

"I thought you seemed to enjoy it, Ona," her husband remarked.

"O, it was an occasion of triumph to me," she murmured. "It is the first time a Stuyvesant has crossed our threshold, *mon cher*."

"Ha," he exclaimed, turning upon her a brisk displeased look. He was proud and considered no man his superior in a social sense. "Do you acknowledge yourself a parvenue that you rejoice at the entrance of any one special person into your doors?"

"I thought," she replied somewhat mortified, "that you betrayed unusual pleasure yourself at her introduction."

"That may be; I was glad to see her here, for her father is one of the most influential directors in the bank of which I shortly expect to be made president."

The nature of this disclosure was calculated to be especially gratifying to her, and effectually blotted out any remembrance of the break by which it had been introduced. After a few hasty inquiries, followed by a scene of quite honest mutual congratulation, the gratified wife left her husband to put out the lights himself or call Samuel as he might choose, and glided up stairs to delight the curious Sarah with the broken soliloquies and inconsequent self-communings which formed another of her peculiar habits.

As for her husband, he stood a few minutes where she left him, abstractedly eying the gorgeous vista that spread out before him down to the further mirror of the elaborate drawing-room, thinking perhaps with a certain degree of pride, of the swiftness with which he had risen to opulence and the certainty with which he had conquered position in the business as well as in the social world when he could speak of such a connection with Thaddeus Stuyvesant as a project already matured. Then with a hasty movement and a quick sigh which nothing in his prospects actual or apparent would seem to warrant, he proceeded to put out the lights, my lady's picture shining with less and less importunity as the flickering jets disappeared, till all was dark save for the faint glimmer that came in from the hall, a glimmer just sufficient to show the outlines of the various articles of furniture scattered about—and could it be the tall figure of the master himself standing in the centre of the room with his palms pressed against his forehead in an attitude of sorrow or despair? Yes, or whose that wild murmur, "Is it never given to man to forget!" Yet no, or who is this that calm and dignified, steps at this moment from the threshold? It must have been a dream, a phantasy. *This* is the master of the house who with sedate and regular step goes up flight after flight of the spiral staircase, and neither pauses or looks back till he reaches the top of the house where he takes out a key from his pocket, and opening a certain door, goes in and locks it behind him. It is his secret study or retreat, a room which no one is allowed to enter, the mystery of the house to the servants and something more than that to its inquisitive mistress. What he does there no man knows, but to-night if any one had been curious enough to listen, they would have heard nothing more ominous than the monotonous scratch of a pen. He was writing to Miss Belinda and the burden of his letter was that on a certain day he named, he was coming to take away Paula.

XII.

MISS BELINDA MAKES CONDITIONS.

"For of the soul the body form doth take,For soul is form, and doth the body make."—Spenser.

Miss Belinda was somewhat taken aback at the proposal of Mr. Sylvester to receive Paula into his own house. She had not anticipated any such result to her efforts; the utmost she had expected was a couple of years or so of instruction in some state Academy. Nor did she know whether she was altogether pleased at the turn affairs were taking. From all she had heard, her niece Ona was, to say the least, a frivolous woman, and Paula had a mind too noble to be subjected to the deteriorating influence of a shallow and puerile companionship. Then the child had great beauty; Mr. Sylvester who ought to be a judge in such matters had declared it so, and what might not the adulation of the thoughtless and the envy of the jealous, do towards belittling a nature as yet uncontaminated.

"We ought to think twice," she said to Miss Abby with some bitterness, who on the contrary never having thought once was full of the most childish hopes concerning a result which she considered with a certain secret complacency she would not have acknowledged for the world, had been very much furthered by her own wise recommendations to Mr. Sylvester in the beginning of his visit. Yet notwithstanding her doubts Miss Belinda allowed such preparations to be made as she considered necessary, and even lent her hand which was deft enough in its way, to the task of enlarging the child's small wardrobe. As for Paula, the thought of visiting the great city with the dear friend whose image had stood in her mind from early childhood as the impersonation of all that was noble, generous and protecting, was more than joyful; it was an inspiration. Not that she did not cling to the affectionate if somewhat quaint couple who had befriended her childhood and sacrificed their comfort to her culture and happiness. But the chord that lies deeper than gratitude had been struck, and fond as were her memories of the dear old home, the charm of that deep "My child," with its hint of fatherly affection, was more than her heart could stand; and no spot, no not the realms of fairy-land itself, looked so attractive to her fancy as that far fireside in an unknown home where she might sit with cousin Ona and alternately with her exert her wit to beguile the smile to his melancholy lips.

When therefore upon the stated day, Mr. Sylvester made his second appearance at the little cottage in Grotewell, it was to find Paula radiant, Miss Abby tearfully exultant and Miss Belinda—O anomaly of human nature—silent and severe. Attributing this however to her very natural regret at parting with Paula, he entered into all the arrangements for their departure on the following morning without a suspicion of the real state of her mind, nor was he undeceived until the day was nearly over and they sat down to have a few minutes of social conversation before the early tea.

They had been speaking on some local topic involving a question of right and wrong, and Mr. Sylvester's ears were yet thrilling to the deep ringing tones with which Paula uttered the words, "I do not see how any man can hesitate an instant when the voice of his conscience says no. I should think the very sunlight would daunt him at the first step of his foot across the forbidden line," when Miss Belinda suddenly spoke up and sending Paula out of the room on some trivial pretext, addressed Mr. Sylvester without reserve.

"I have something to say to you, sir, before you take from my home the child of my care and affection."

Could he have guessed what that something was that he should turn with such a flush of sudden anxiety to meet her determined gaze.

"The rules of our life here have been simple," continued she in a tone of voice which those who knew her well recognized as belonging to her uncompromising moods. "To do our duty, love God and serve our neighbor. Paula has been brought up to reverence those rules in simplicity and honor; what will your gay city life with its hollow devices for pleasure and its loose hold on the firm principles of life, do for this innocent soul, Mr. Sylvester?"

"The city," he said firmly but with a troubled undertone in his voice that was not unnoted by the watchful woman, "is a vast caldron of mingled good and evil. She will hear of more wrong doing, and be within the reach of more self-denying virtue, than if she had remained in this village alone with the nature that she so much loves. The tree of knowledge bears two kinds of fruit, Miss Belinda; would you therefore hinder the child from approaching its branches?"

"No, sir; I am not so weak as to keep a child in swaddling-clothes after the period of infancy is past, neither am I so reckless as to set her adrift on an unknown sea without a pilot to guide her. Your wife—" she paused and fixed an intent look upon the flames leaping before her. "Ona is my niece," she resumed in a lower tone of voice, "and I feel entitled to speak with freedom concerning her. Is she such a guide as I would choose for a young girl just entering a new sphere in life? From all I have heard, I should judge she was somewhat over-devoted to this world and its fashions."

Mr. Sylvester flushed painfully, but seeing that any softening of the truth would be wholly ineffectual with this woman, replied in a candid tone, "Ona is the same now as she was in the days of her girlhood. If she loves the world too well she is not without her excuse; from her birth it has strewn nothing but roses in her path."

"Humph!" came from the lips of the energetic spinster. Then with a second stern glance at the fire, continued, "Another question, Mr. Sylvester. Does your wife consent to receive my niece into her house, for the indefinite length of time which you mention, from interest in the girl herself or indeed from any motive I should judge worthy of Paula? It is a leading question I know, but this is no time for niceties of speech."

"Miss Belinda," replied he, and his voice was firm though his fingers slightly trembled where they rested upon the arms of his chair, "I will try and forget for a moment that Ona is my wife, and frankly confide to you that any such motive on her part, as would meet with your entire approval, must not be expected from a woman who has never fully recognized the solemn responsibilities of life. That she will be kind to Paula I have no doubt, that she may even learn to take an interest in her for her own sake, is also very possible, but that she will ever take your place towards her as guide or instructor, I neither anticipate nor would feel myself justified in leading you to."

The look which Miss Belinda cast him was anything but reassuring. "And yet," said she, "you will take away my darling and give her up to an influence that can not be for good, or your glance would not be so troubled or your lip so uncertain. You would set her young feet in a path where the very flowers are so thick they conceal its tendency and obscure its dangers. Mr. Sylvester you are a man who has seen life with naked eyes, and must recognize its responsibilities; dare you take this Paula, whom you have seen, out of the atmosphere of truth and purity in which she has been raised, and give her over to the enervating influences of folly and fashion? Will you assume the risk and brave the consequences?"

As though an electric shock had touched the nerve of his nature, Mr. Sylvester hastily rose and moved in a restless manner to the window. It was his favorite refuge in any time of sudden perplexity or doubt, and this was surely an occasion for both.

"Miss Belinda," he began and then paused, looking out on the hills of his boyhood, every one of which spoke to him at that moment with a force that almost sickened his heart and benumbed the faculties of his mind; "I recognize the love which leads you to speak in this way, and I bow before it, but—" here his tongue faltered again, that ready tongue whose quick and persuasive eloquence on public occasions had won for him the name of Silver-speech among his friends and admirers—"but there are others who love your Paula also, love her with a yearning that only the childless can feel or the disappointed appreciate. I had hoped—" here he left the window and approached her side, "to do more for Paula than to give her the temporal benefit of a luxurious home and such instruction as her extraordinary talents demand. If Ona upon seeing and knowing the child had found she could love her, I had intended to ask you to yield her to us unreservedly and forever, in short to make her my child in place of the daughter I have lost. But now—" with a quick gesture he began pacing the floor and left the sentence unfinished.

Miss Belinda's eyes which were of a light grey, wholly without beauty but with strange flashes of expression in them, left the fire and fell upon his face, and a tear of real feeling gathered beneath her lids.

"I had no idea," said he, "that you cherished any such intention as that. If I had I might have worded my apprehensions differently. The yearning feeling of which you speak, I can easily understand, also the strength of the determination it must take on the part of a man like yourself, to give up a hope of this nature. Yet—" Seeing him pause in his hurried pacing and open his lips as if to speak, she deferentially stopped.

"Miss Belinda," said he, in the firm and steadfast way more in keeping with his features than his agitated manner of a moment before, "I cannot give it up. The injury it would do me is greater than the harm, which one of Paula's lofty nature would be apt to acquire in any atmosphere into which she might chance to be introduced. She is not a child, Miss Belinda, though we allude to her as such. The texture of those principles which you have instilled into her breast, is of no such weak material as to give way to the first petty breeze that blows. Paula's house will stand, while mine—"

He paused and gave way to a momentary struggle, but that over, he set his lips firmly together and the last vestige of irresolution vanished. Sitting down by her side, he turned his face upon her, and for the first time she realized the power which with one exception he had always exerted over the minds of others. "Miss Belinda," said he, "I am going to give you an evidence of my trust; I am going to leave with you the responsibility of Paula's future. She shall go with me, and learn, if she can, to love me and mine, but she shall also be under obligations to open her heart to you on all matters that concern her life and happiness in my house, and the day you see any falling off in her pure and upright spirit, you shall demand her return, and though it tears the heart from my breast, I will yield her up without question or parley as I am a gentleman and a Christian. Does that content you?"

"It certainly ought to, sir. No one could ask more, I am sure," returned the other in a voice somewhat unsteady for her.

"It is opening my house to the gaze of a stranger," said he, "for I desire you to command Paula to withhold nothing that seriously affects her; but my confidence in you is unbounded and I am sure that whatever you may learn in this way, will be held as sacred by you as though it were buried in a tomb."

"It certainly will, sir."

"As for the dearer hope which I have mentioned, time and the condition of things must decide for us. Meanwhile I shall strive to win a father's place in her heart, if only to build myself a refuge for the days that are to come. You see I speak frankly, Miss Belinda; will you give me some token that you are not altogether dissatisfied with the result of this conversation?"

With the straightforward if somewhat blunt action that characterized all her movements, she stretched out her hand, which he took with something more than his usual high-bred courtesy. "With you at the wheel," said she, "I think I may trust my darling, even to the whirl and follies of such a society as I know Ona loves. A man who can so command himself, ought to be a safe guide to pioneer others."

And the considerate gentleman bowed; but the frank smile that hailed her genial clasp had somehow vanished, and from the sudden cloud that at that moment swept over the roseate heavens, fell a shadow that left its impress on his lip long after the cloud itself had departed.

An hour or so had passed. The fire was burning brightly on the hearthstone, illumining with a steady glow the array of stuffed birds, worsted samplers and old-fashioned portraits with which the walls were adorned, but reserving its richest glow and fullest irradiation for the bended head of Paula, who seated on a little stool in the corner of the hearth, was watching the rise and fall of the flickering flames.

She had packed her little trunk, had said good-bye to all her neighboring friends and was now sitting on the old hearthstone, musing upon the new life that was about to open before her. It was a happy musing, as the smile that vaguely dimpled her cheeks and brightened her eyes beneath their long lashes, amply testified. As Mr. Sylvester watched her from the opposite side of the hearth where he was sitting alone with his thoughts, he felt his heart sink with apprehension at the fervor of anticipation with which she evidently looked forward to the life in the new home. "The young wings think to gain freedom," thought he, "when they are only destined to the confinement of a gilded cage."

He was so silent and looked so sad, Paula with a certain sort of sensitiveness to any change in the emotional atmosphere surrounding her, which was one of her chief characteristics, hastily looked up and meeting his eye fixed on her with that foreboding glance, softly arose and came and sat down by his side. "You look tired," murmured she; "the long ride after a day of business care has been too much for you."

It was the first word of sympathy with his often over-wearied mind and body, that had greeted his ears for years. It made his eyes moisten.

"I have been a little overworked," said he, "for the last two months, but I shall soon be myself again. What were you thinking of, Paula?"

"What was I thinking of?" repeated she, drawing her chair nearer to his in her loving confidence. "I was thinking what wonders of beauty and art lay in that great kernel which you call the city. I shall see lovely faces and noble forms. I shall wander through halls of music, the echo of whose songs may have come to me in the sob of the river or the sigh of the pines, but whose notes in all their beauty and power have never been heard by me even in my dreams. I shall look on great men and touch the garments of thoughtful women. I shall see life in its fullness as I have felt nature in its mightiness, and my heart will be satisfied at last."

Mr. Sylvester drew a deep breath and his eyes burned strangely in the glow of the fire-light. "You expect high things," said he; "did you ever consider that the life in a great city, with its ceaseless rush and constant rivalries, must be often strangely petty in despite of its artistic and social advantages?"

"All life has its petty side," said she, with a sweet arch look. "The eagle that cleaves the thunder-cloud, must sometimes stop to plume its wings. I should be sorry to lose the small things out of existence. Even we in the face of that great sunset appealing to us from the west, have to pile up the firewood on the hearth and set the table for supper."

"But fashion, Paula," he pursued, concealing his wonder at the maturity of mind evinced by this simple child of nature, "that inexorable power that rules the very souls of women who once step within the magic circle of her realm! have you never thought of her and the demands that she makes on the time and attention even of the worshippers of the good and the true?"

"Yes, sometimes," she returned with a repetition of her arch little smile, "when I put on a certain bonnet I have, which Aunt Abby modeled over from one of my grandmother's. Fashion is a sort of obstinate step-dame I imagine, whom it is less trouble to obey than to oppose. I don't believe I shall quarrel with Fashion if she will only promise to keep her hands off my soul."

"But if—" with a pause, "she asks your all, what then?"

"I shall consider that I am in a country of democratic principles," she laughed, "and beg to be excused from acceding to the tyrannical demands of any autocrat male or female."

"You have been listening to Miss Belinda," said he; "she is also opposed to all and any tyrannical measures." Then with a grave look from which all levity had fled, he leaned toward the young girl and gently asked, "Do you know that you are a very beautiful girl, Paula?"

She flushed, looked at him in some surprise and slowly drooped her head. "I have been told I looked like my father," said she, "and I know that means something very kind."

"My child," said he, with gentle insistence, "God has given you a great and wonderful gift, a treasure-casket of whose worth you scarcely realize the value. I tell you this myself, first because I prize your beauty as something quite sacred and pure, and secondly because you are going where you will hear words of adulation, whose folly and bluntness will often offend your ears, unless you carry in your soul some talisman to counteract their effect."

"I understand," said she, "I know what you mean. I will remember that the most engaging beauty is nothing without a pure mind and a good heart."

"And you will remember too," continued he, "that I blessed your innocent head to-night, not because it is circled by the roses of a youthful and fresh loveliness, but because of the pure mind and good heart I see shining in your eyes." And with a fond but solemn aspect he reached out his hand and laid it on her ebon locks.

She bowed her head upon her breast. "I will never forget," said she, and the fire-light fell with a softening glow on the tears that trembled from her eye-lashes.

XIII.

THE END OF MY LADY'S PICTURE.

"Heaven from all creatures tides the book of Fate."—Pope.

Mrs. Sylvester was spending an evening at home. This was something so unusual for this august lady of fashion to indulge in, that she found it difficult not to fall asleep in the huge crimson-backed chair in which she had chosen to ensconce herself. Not that she had desisted from making every effort known to mortal woman to keep herself awake and if possible amused till the expected travellers should arrive. She had played with her bird till the spoiled pet had himself protested, ducking his head under his wing and proceeding without ceremony to make up his little feather bed, as cunning Geraldine used to call the round, fluffy ball into which he rolled himself at night. More than that, she had looked over her ornaments and taken out such articles as she thought could be spared for Paula, to say nothing of playing a bar or so from the last operatic sensation, and laboriously cutting open the leaves of the new magazine. But it was all of no use, and the heavy white lids were slowly falling, when the bell rang and Mr. Bertram Mandeville was announced, or rather Bertram Sylvester as he now chose to be called.

It was a godsend to her as she politely informed him upon his entrance; and though in his secret heart he felt anything but God sent—he was not of a make to appreciate his uncle's wife at her very evident value—he consented to remain and assist her in disposing of the evening till Mr. Sylvester should return.

"He is going to bring a pretty girl with him," remarked she, in a tone of some interest, "a cousin of mine from Grotewell. I should like to have you see her."

"Thank you," replied he, his mind roaming off at the suggestion, into the region of a certain plain little music-room where the clock on the mantel ticked to the beating of his own heart. And for ten minutes Mrs. Sylvester had the pleasure of filling the room with a stream of easy talk, in which Grotewell, dark beauties, the coming Seventh Regiment reception, the last bit of gossip from London, and the exact situation of the Madison Bank formed the principal topics.

To the one last mentioned, it having taken the form of a question, he was forced to reply; but the simple locality having been learned, she rambled easily on, this time indulging him with a criticism upon the personal appearance of certain business gentlemen who visited the house, ending with the somewhat startling declaration:

"If Edward were not the fine appearing gentleman that he undoubtedly is, I should feel utterly out of place in these handsome parlors. Anything but to see an elegant and modern home, decorated with the costliest works of art, and filled with *bijouterie* of the most exquisite delicacy, presided over by a plain and common-place woman or a bald-headed and inferior-looking man. The contrast is too vivid; works of the highest art do not need such a startling comparison to bring out their beauty. Now if Edward stood in the throne-room of a palace, he would somehow make it seem to others as a handsome set off to his own face and figure."

This was all very wife-like if somewhat unnecessary, and Bertram could have listened to it with pleasure, if she had not cast the frequent and side-long glances at the mirror, which sufficiently betrayed the fact that she included herself in this complacent conclusion; as indeed she may have considered herself justified in doing, husband and wife being undoubtedly of one flesh. As it was, he maintained an immovable countenance, though he admired his uncle as much as she did, and the conversation gradually languished till the white somnolent lids of the lady again began to show certain premonitory signs of drooping, when suddenly they were both aroused by the well known click of a latch-key in the door, and in another moment Mr. Sylvester's voice was heard in the hall, saying, in tones whose cheery accents made his wife's eyes open in surprise—

"Welcome home, my dear."

"They have come," murmured Mrs. Sylvester rising with a look of undeniable expectation. Had Paula not been a beauty she would have remained seated.

"Yes, we have come," was heard in hearty tones from the door-way, and Mr. Sylvester with a proud look which Bertram long remembered, ushered into their presence a young girl whose simple cloak and bonnet in no wise prevented Mrs. Sylvester from recognizing the somewhat uncommon beauty she had been led to expect.

"Paula, this is your cousin Ona, and—Ah, Bertram, glad to see you—this is my only nephew, Mr. Sylvester."

The young girl, lost in the sudden glamour of numerous lights, shining upon splendors such as she may have dreamed of over the pages of Irving's Alhambra, but certainly had never before seen, blushed with very natural embarrassment, but yet managed to bestow a pretty enough greeting upon the elegant woman and handsome youth, while Ona after the first moment of almost involuntary hesitation, took in hers the two trembling hands of her youthful cousin and actually kissed her cheek.

"I am not given to caresses as you know," she afterwards explained in a somewhat apologetic tone to her husband; "and anything like an appeal for one on the part of a child or an inferior, I detest; but her simple way of holding out her hand disarmed me, and then such a face demands a certain amount of homage, does it not?" And her husband in his surprise, was forced to acknowledge to himself, that as closely as he had studied his wife's nature for ten years, there were certain crooks and turns in it which even he had never penetrated.

"You look dazzled," that lady exclaimed, gazing not unkindly into the young girl's face; "the sudden glare of so much gas-light has bewildered you."

"I do not think it is that," returned Paula with a frank and admiring look at the gorgeous room and the circle of pleasant faces about her. "Sudden lights I can bear, but I have come from a little cottage on the hillside and the magnificence of nature does not prepare you for the first sudden view of the splendors of art."

Mrs. Sylvester smiled and cast a side glance of amusement at Bertram. "You admire our new hangings I see," remarked she with an indulgence of the other's *näiveté* that greatly relieved her husband.

But in that instant a change had come across Paula; the simple country maid had assimilated herself with the surroundings, and with a sudden grace and dignity that were unstudied as they were charming, dropped her eyes from her cousin's portrait— that for some reason seemed to shine with more than its usual insistence—and calmly replied, "I admire all beautiful color; it is my birthright as a Walton, to do so, I suppose."

Mrs. Sylvester was a Walton also and therefore smiled; but her husband, who had marked with inward distrust, the sudden transformation in Paula, now stepped forward with a word or two of remark concerning his appetite, a prosaic allusion that led to the rapid disappearance of the ladies upstairs and a short but hurried conversation between the two gentlemen.

"I have brought you a sealed envelope from the office," said Bertram, who, in accordance with his uncle's advice, had already initiated himself into business by assuming the position of clerk in the office of the wealthy speculator.

"Ah," returned his uncle hastily opening it. "As I expected, a meeting has been held this day by the board of Directors of the Madison Bank, a vote was cast, my proxy did his duty and I am duly elected President. Bertram, we know what that means," smiled he, holding out his hand with an affectionate warmth greatly in advance of the emotion displayed by him on a former occasion.

"I hope so indeed," young Bertram responded. "An increase of fortune and honor for you, though you seem to have both in the fullest measure already, and a start in the new life for me to whom fortune and honor mean happiness."

A smile younger and more full of hope than any he had seen on his uncle's face for years, responded to this burst. "Bertram," said he, "since our conversation of a couple of weeks ago something has occurred which somewhat alters the opinions I then expressed. If you have patience equal to your energy, and a self-control that will not put to shame your unbounded trust in women, I think I can say God-speed to your serious undertaking, with something like a good heart. Women are not all frivolous and foolish-minded; there are some jewels of simple goodness and faith yet left in the world."

"Thank God for your conversion," returned his nephew smiling, "and if this lovely girl whom you have just introduced to me, is the cause of it, then thank God for her also."

His uncle bowed with a gravity almost solemn, but the ladies returning at this moment, he refrained from further reply. After supper, to which unusual meal Mr. Sylvester insisted upon his nephew remaining, the two gentlemen again drew apart.

"If you have decided upon buying the shares I have mentioned," said the former, "you had better get your money in a position to handle at once. I shall wish to present you to Mr. Stuyvesant to-morrow, and I should like to be able to mention you as a future stockholder in the bank."

"Mr. Stuyvesant!" exclaimed Bertram, ignoring the rest of the sentence.

"Yes," returned his uncle with a smile, "Thaddeus Stuyvesant is the next largest stockholder to myself in the Madison Bank, and his patronage is not an undesirable one."

"Indeed—I was not aware—excuse me, I should be happy," stammered the young man. "As for the money, it is all in Governments and is at your command whenever you please."

"That is good, I'll notify you when I'm ready for the transfer. And now come," said he, with a change from his deep business tone to the lighter one of ordinary social converse, "forget for a half hour that you have discarded the name of Mandeville, and give us an aria or a sonata from Mendelssohn before those hands have quite lost their cunning."

"But the ladies," inquired the youth glancing towards the drawing-room where Mrs. Sylvester was giving Paula her first lesson in ceramics.

"Ah, it is to see how the charm will act upon my shy country lassie, that I request such a favor."

"Has she never heard Mendelssohn?"

"Not with your interpretation."

Without further hesitation the young musician proceeded to the piano, which occupied a position opposite to my lady's picture in this anomalous room denominated by courtesy the library. In another instant, a chord delicate and ringing, disturbed the silence of the long vista, and one of Mendelssohn's most exquisite songs trembled in all its delicious harmony through these apartments of sensuous luxury.

Mr. Sylvester had seated himself where he could see the distant figure of Paula, and leaning back in his chair, watched for the first startled response on her part. He was not disappointed. At the first note, he beheld her spirited head turn in a certain wondering surprise, followed presently by her whole quivering form, till he could perceive her face, upon which were the dawnings of a great delight, flush and pale by turns, until the climax of the melody being reached, she came slowly down the room, stretching out her hands like a child, and breathing heavily as if her ecstacy of joy in its impotence to adequately express itself, had caught an expression from pain.

"O Mr. Sylvester!" was all she said as she reached that gentleman's side; but Bertram Mandeville recognized the accents of an unfathomable appreciation in that simple exclamation, and struck into a grand old battle-song that had always made his own heart beat with something of the fire of ancient chivalry under its breastplate of modern broadcloth.

"It is the voice of the thunder clouds when they marshal for battle!" exclaimed she at the conclusion. "I can hear the cry of a righteous struggle all through the sublime harmony."

"You are right; it is a war-song ancient as the time of battle-axes and spears," quoth Bertram from his seat at the piano.

"I thought I detected the flashing of steel," returned she. "O what a world lies in those simple bits of ivory!"

"Say rather in the fingers that sweep them," uttered Mr. Sylvester. "You will not hear such music often."

"I am glad of that," she cried simply, then in a quick conscious tone explained, "I mean that the hearing of such music makes an era in our life, a starting-point for thoughts that reach away into eternity; we could not bear such experiences often, it would confuse the spirit if not deaden its enjoyment. Or so it seems to me," she added naively, glancing at her cousin who now came sweeping in from the further room, where she had been trying the effect of a change in the arrangement of two little pet monstrosities of Japanese ware.

"What seems to you?" that lady inquired. "O, Mr. Mandeville's playing? I beg pardon, Sylvester is the name by which you now wish to be addressed I suppose. Fine, isn't it?" she rambled on all in the same tone while she cautiously hid an unfortunate gape of her rosy mouth behind the folds of her airy handkerchief. "Mr. Turner says the hiatus you have made in the musical world by leaving the concert room for the desk, can never be repaired," she went on, supposedly to her nephew though she did not look his way, being at that instant engaged in sinking into her favorite chair.

"I am glad," Bertram politely returned with a frank smile, "to have enjoyed the approval of so cultivated a critic as Mr. Turner. I own it occasions me a pang now and then," he remarked to his uncle over his shoulder, "to think I shall never again call up those looks of self-forgetful delight, which I have sometimes detected on the faces of certain ones in my audience."

And he relapsed without pause into a solemn anthem, the very reverse of the stirring tones which he had previously accorded them.

"Now we are in a temple!" whispered Paula, subduing the sudden interest and curiosity which this young man's last words had awakened. And the awe which crept over her countenance was the fittest interpretation to those noble sounds, which the one weary-hearted man in that room could have found.

"I have something to tell you, Ona," remarked Mr. Sylvester shortly after this, as the music being over, they all sat down for a final chat about the fireside. "I have received notice that the directors of the Madison Bank have this day elected me their president. I thought you might like to know it to-night."

"It is a very gratifying piece of news certainly. President of the Madison Bank sounds very well, does it not, Paula?"

The young girl with her soul yet ringing with the grand and solemn harmonies of Mendelssohn and Chopin, turned at this with her brightest smile. "It certainly does and a little awe-inspiring too;" she added with her arch glance.

"Your congratulations are also requested for our new assistant cashier. Arise, Bertram, and greet the ladies."

With a blush his young nephew arose to his feet.

"What! are you going into the banking business?" queried Mrs. Sylvester. "Mr. Turner will be more shocked than ever: he chooses to say that bankers, merchants and such are the solid rock of his church, while the lighter fry such as artists, musicians, and let us hope he includes us ladies, are its minarets, and steeples. Now to make a foundation out of a steeple will quite overturn his methodical mind I fear."

Mr. Sylvester looked genially at his wife; she was not accustomed to attempt the facetious; but Paula seemed to have the power of bringing out unexpected lights and shadows from all with whom she came in contact.

"A clergyman who rears his church on the basis of wealth must expect some overturning now and then," laughed he.

"If by means of it he turns a fresh side to the sun, it will do him no harm," chimed in Paula.

Seldom had there been so much simple gaiety round that fireside; the very atmosphere grew lighter, and the brilliance of my lady's picture became less oppressive.

"We ought to have a happy winter of it," spoke up Mr. Sylvester with a glance around him. "Life never looked more cheerful for us all, I think; what do you say, Bertram my boy."

"It certainly looks promising for me."

"And for me," murmured Paula.

The complacent way with which Mrs. Sylvester smoothed out the feathers of her fan with her jewelled right hand,—she always carried a fan winter and summer, some said for the purpose of displaying those same jewelled fingers—was sufficient answer for her.

At that moment there was a hush, when suddenly the small clock on the mantel-piece struck eleven, and instantly as if awaiting the signal, there came a rush and a heavy crash which drew every one to their feet, and the brilliant portrait of my lady fell from the wall, and toppling over the cabinet beneath, slid with the various articles of bronze and china thereon, almost to the very chair in which its handsome prototype had been sitting.

It was a startling interruption and for an instant no one spoke, then Paula with a look towards her cousin breathed to herself rather than said, "Pray God it be not an omen!" And the pale countenances of the two gentlemen standing face to face on either side of that fallen picture, showed that the shadow of the same superstition had insensibly crossed their own minds.

Mrs. Sylvester was the only one who remained unmoved. "Lift if up," cried she, "and let us see if it has sustained any injury."

Instantly Bertram and her husband sprang forward, and in a moment its glowing surface was turned upward. Who could read the meaning of the look that crossed her husband's face as he perceived that the sharp spear of the bronze horseman, which had been overturned in the fall, had penetrated the rosy countenance of the portrait and destroyed that importunate smile forever.

"I suppose it is a judgment upon me for putting all the money you had allowed me for charitable purposes, into that exquisite bit of bronze," observed Mrs. Sylvester, stooping above the overturned horseman with an expression of regret she had not chosen to bestow on her own ruined picture. "Ah he is less of a champion than I imagined; he has lost his spear in the struggle."

Paula glanced at her cousin in surprise. Was this pleasantry only a veil assumed by this courtly lady to hide her very natural regret over the more serious accident? Even her husband turned toward her with a certain puzzled inquiry in his troubled countenance. But her expression of unconcern was too natural; evidently the destruction of the picture had awakened but small regret in her volatile mind.

"She is less vain than I thought," was the inward comment of Paula.

Ah simple child of the woods and streams, it is the extent of her vanity not the lack of it, that has produced this effect. She has begun to realize that ten years have elapsed since this picture was painted, and that people are beginning to say as they examine it, "Mrs. Sylvester has not yet lost her complexion, I see."

A break necessarily followed this disturbance, and before long Bertram took his leave, not without a cordial pressure from his uncle's hand and a look of kindly interest from the stranger lassie, upon whose sympathetic and imaginative mind the hints let fall as to his former profession, had produced a deep impression. With his departure Mrs. Sylvester's weariness returned, and ere long she led the way to her apartments up stairs. As Paula was hastening to follow Mr. Sylvester stopped her.

"You will not allow this unfortunate occurrence," he said, with a slight gesture towards the picture now standing with its face against the wall, "to mar your first sleep under my roof, will you Paula, my child?"

"No, not if you say that you think Cousin Ona will not be likely to connect it with my appearance here."

"I do not think she will; she is not superstitious and besides does not seem to greatly regret the misfortune."

"Then I will forget it all and only remember the music."

"It was all you anticipated?"

"It was more."

"Sometime I will tell you about the player and the sweet young girl he loves."

"Does he—" she paused, blushing; love was a subject upon which she had never yet spoken to any one.

"Yes he does," Mr. Sylvester returned smiling.

"I thought there was a meaning in the music I did not quite understand. Good night, uncle,"—he had requested her to address him thus though he was in truth her cousin, "and many, many thanks."

But he stopped her again. "You think you will be happy in these rooms," said he; "you love splendor."

She was not yet sufficiently acquainted with his voice to detect the regret underlying its kindly tone, and answered without suspicion. "I did not know it before, but I fear that I do. It dazzled at first, but now it seems as if I had reached a home towards which I had always been journeying. I shall dream away hours of joy before each little ornament that adorns your parlors. The very tiles that surround the fireplace will demand a week of attention at least."

She ended with a smile, but unlike formerly he did not seem to catch the infection. "I had rather you had cared less," said he, but instantly regretted the seeming reproach, for her eyes filled with tears and the tones of her voice trembled as she replied,

"Do you think the beauty I have seen has made me forget the kindness that has brought me here? I love fine and noble objects, glory of color and harmony of shape, but more than all these do I love a generous soul without a blot on its purity, or a flaw in its integrity."

She had meant to utter something that would show her appreciation of his goodness and the universal esteem in which he was held, but was quite unprepared for the start that he gave and the unmistakable deepening of the shadow on his sombre face. But before she could express her regret at the offence, whatever it was, he had recovered himself, and it was with a fatherly tenderness that he laid his hand upon hers while he said, "Such a soul may yours ever continue, my child," and then stood watching her as she glided up the stairs, her charming face showing every now and then as she leaned on her winding way to the top, to bestow upon him the tender little smile she had already learned was his solace and delight.

It was the beginning of happier days for him.

BOOK II.

LIFE AND DEATH.

XIV.

MISS BELINDA HAS A QUESTION TO DECIDE.

"I pray you in your letters,

Speak of me as I am; nothing extenuate,Nor set down aught in malice."—Othello.

Miss Belinda sitting before her bedroom fire on a certain windy night in January, presented a picture of the most profound thought. A year had elapsed since, with heavy heart and moistened eye, she had bidden good-bye to the child of her care, and beheld her drift away with her new friend into a strange and untried life. And now a letter had come from that friend, in which with the truest appreciation for the feelings of herself and sister, he requested their final permission to adopt Paula as his own child and the future occupant of his house and heart.

Yes, after a year of increased comfort, Mrs. Sylvester, who would never have consented to receive as her own any child demanding care or attention, had decided it was quite a different matter to give place and position to a lovely girl already grown, whose beauty was sufficiently pronounced to do credit to the family while at the same time it was of a character to heighten by contrast her own very manifest attractions. So the letter, destined to create such a disturbance in the stern and powerful mind of Miss Belinda, had been written and dispatched.

And indeed it was matter for the gravest reflection. To accede to this important request was to yield up all control over the dear young girl whose affection had constituted the brightness of this somewhat disappointed life, while to refuse an offer made with such evident love and anxiety, was to bring a pang of regret to a heart she hesitated to wound. The question of advantage which might have swayed others in their decision, did not in the least affect Miss Belinda. Now that Paula had seen the world and gained an insight into certain studies beyond the reach of her own attainments, any wishes in which she might have indulged on that score were satisfied, and mere wealth with its concomitant of luxuriant living, she regarded with distrust, and rather in the light of a stumbling-block to the great and grand end of all existence.

Suddenly with that energy which characterized all her movements, she rose from her seat, and first casting a look of somewhat cautious inquiry at the recumbent figure of her sister, asleep in the heavy old fashioned bed that occupied one corner of the room, she proceeded to a bureau drawer and took out a small box which she unlocked on the table. It was full of letters; those same honest epistles, which, as empowered by Mr. Sylvester, she had requested Paula to send her from week to week. Some of them were a year old, but she read them all carefully through, while the clock ticked on the shelf and the wind soughed in the chimney. Certain passages she marked, and when she had finished the pile, she took up the letters again and re-read those passages. They were necessarily desultory in their character, but they all had, in her mind at least, a bearing upon the question on hand, and as such, I give them to my readers.

"O aunty, I have made a friend, a sweet girl friend who I have reason to hope will henceforth be to me as my other eye and hand. Her name is Stuyvesant—a name by the way that always calls up a certain complacent smile on Cousin Ona's countenance—and she is the daughter of one of the directors of Mr. Sylvester's bank. I met her in a rather curious way. For some reason Ona had expressed a wish for me to ride horseback. She is rather too large for the exercise herself, but thought it looked well, she said, to see a lady and groom ride from the front of the house; moreover it would keep me in color by establishing my health. So Mr. Sylvester who denies her nothing, promised us horses and the groom, and as a preparation for acquitting myself with credit, has sent me to one of the finest riding academies in the city. It was here I met Miss Stuyvesant. She is a small interesting-looking girl whose chief beauty lies in her expression which is certainly very charming. I was conscious of a calm and satisfied feeling the moment I saw her. Her eyes which are raised with a certain appeal to your face, are blue, while her lips that break into smiles only at rare moments, are rosy and delicately curved. In her riding-habit she looks like a child, but when dressed for the street she surprises you with the reserved and womanly air with which she carries her proud head. Altogether she is a sweet study to me, alluring me with her glance yet awing me by her dainty ladyhood, a ladyhood too unconscious to be affected and yet so completely a part of her whole delicate being, that you could as soon dissociate the bloom from the rose, as the air of highborn reserve, from this sweet scion of one of New York's oldest families.

"I was mounting my horse when our eyes first met, and I never shall forget her look of delighted surprise. Did she recognize in me the friend I now hope to become? Later we were introduced by Mr. Sylvester who had been so kind as to accompany me that day. The way in which he said to her, 'This is Paula,' proved that I was no new topic of conversation between them, and indeed she afterwards explained to me that she had been forewarned of my arrival during an afternoon call at his house. There was in this first interview none of the unnecessary gush which you have so often reprobated as childish; indeed Miss Stuyvesant is not a person with whom one would presume to be familiar, nor was it till we had met several times that any acknowledgement was made of the mutual interest with which we found ourselves inspired. Cousin Ona to whom I had naturally spoken of the little lady, wished me to cultivate her acquaintance more assiduously, but I knew that if I had excited in her the same interest she had awakened in me, this would not be necessary; our friendship would grow of itself and blossom without any hot-house forcing. And so it did. One day she came to the riding-school with her eyes like stars and her cheeks like the oleanders in your sitting-room. Her brightness was so contagious, I stepped up to her. But she greeted me with almost formal reserve, and mounting her horse, proceeded to engage in her usual exercise. I was not hurt; I recognized the presence of some thought or feeling which made a barrier around her sensitive nature, and duly respected it. Mounting my own horse, I rode around the ring which is the somewhat limited field of my present equestrian efforts, and waited. For I knew from the looks which she cast me every now and then, that the flower of our friendship was outgrowing its sheath and would soon burst into the bud of perfect understanding. At the end of the lesson we approached each other. I do not know how it was done, but we walked home together, or rather I accompanied her to the stoop of her house, and before we parted we had exchanged those words which give emphasis to a sentiment long cherished but now for the first time avowed. Miss Stuyvesant and I are friends, and I feel as though a new stream of enjoyment had opened in my breast.

"The fact that I still call her by this formal title instead of her very pretty name of Cicely, proves the nature of the respect she inspires even in the breasts of her girlish associates."

"Why is it that I frequently hesitate as I go up the stairs and look about me with a vague feeling of apprehension? The bronze figure of Luxury that adorns the landing, wears no semblance of terror to the wildest imagination, and yet I often find myself seized by an inexplicable shudder as I hurry past it; and once I actually looked behind me with the same sensation as if some one had plucked me by the sleeve.

"It is a folly; for recording which, I make my excuses."

"Cousin Ona has decided that I must never wear colors. 'Soft grays, my dear, dead blacks and opaque whites are all that you need to bring out the fine contrast of your hair and complexion; the least hint of blue or pink would destroy it.' So she says and so I must believe, for who else has made such a study of the all important subject of dress. Behold me, then, arrayed for my first reception in a colorless robe of rich silk to which Ona after long consideration allowed me to add some ornaments of plain gold with which Mr. Sylvester has kindly presented me. But I think more of the people I am going to meet than of anything else, though I enjoy the home-feeling which a pretty dress gives me, as well as a violet does its bright blue coat."

"I have heard a great preacher! What shall I say? At first it seems as if nothing could express my joy and satisfaction. The sapling that is shaken to its root by the winds of heaven, keeps silence I imagine. But O Aunty, if my smallness makes me quake, it also makes me feel. What gates of thought have been opened to me! What shining tracks of inquiry pointed out! I feel as if I had been shown a path where angels walked. Can it be that such words have been uttered every week of my life and I in ignorance of them? It is like the revelation of the ocean to unaccustomed eyes. Henceforth small things must seem like pebble stones above which stretch innumerable heavenly vistas. It is not so much that new things have been revealed to me as that old things have been made strangely eloquent. The voice of a daisy on the hill side, the breath of thunder in the mountain gorges, the blossoming of a child's smile under its mother's eye, the fact that golden portals are opened in every life for the coming and going of the messengers of God, all have been made real to me, real as the voice of the Saviour to his disciples as they walked in the fields or started back awe-stricken from the stupendous vision of the cross. It is a solemn thing to see one's humble thoughts caught by the imagination of a great mind and carried on and up into regions you never realized existed.

"I was so burdened with joy that I could not forbear asking Mr. Sylvester if he did not feel as if the whole face of the world had changed since we entered those holy doors. He did not respond with the glad 'Yes' for which I hoped, and though his smile was very kind, I could not help wondering what it was that sometimes fell between us like a veil."

"O Aunty, how my heart does yearn towards Mr. Sylvester at times! As I see him sitting with clouded brow in the midst of so much that ought to charm and enliven him, I ask myself if the advantages of wealth compensate for all this care and anxiety. But I notice he is much more cheerful now than when I first came. Ona says he is in danger of losing the air of melancholy reserve which made him look so distinguished, but I think we can spare a little of such doubtful distinguishment for the sake of the smiles with which he now and then indulges us."

"I feel as if a hand had gripped my throat. Cousin Ona spoke to Mr. Sylvester this morning in a way that made my very heart stand still. And yet it was only a simple, 'Follow your own judgment, Mr. Sylvester.' But how she said it! Do these languid women carry venom in their tongues? I had always thought she was of too easy a disposition to feel anger or display it; but the spring of a serpent is all the deadlier for his long silent basking in the sun. O pardon me for making such a frightful allusion.

But if you had seen her and heard Mr. Sylvester's sigh as he turned and left the room!"

"Mr. Bertram Sylvester has awakened my deepest interest. His uncle has told me his story, which alone of all the things I have heard in this house, I do not feel at liberty to repeat, and it has aroused in me strange thoughts and very peculiar emotions. He is devoted to some one we do not know, and the idea surrounds him in my eyes with a sort of halo that you would perhaps call fanciful, but which I am nevertheless bound to reverence. He does not know that I am acquainted with his story. I wish he did and would let me speak the words that rise to my lips whenever I see him or hear him play."

"There are moments when I long to flee back to Grotewell. It is when Cousin Ona comes in from shopping with a dozen packages to be opened and commented upon, or when Mrs. Fitzgerald has been here or some other of her ultra-fashionable acquaintances. The atmosphere of the house for hours after either of the above occurrences is too heavy for breathing. I have to go away and clear my brain by a brisk walk or a look into Knœdler's or Schaus'."

"The panel where Cousin Ona's picture used to hang, has been filled by one of Meissonier's most interesting studies; and though I never thought Mr. Sylvester particularly fond of the French style of art, he seems very well satisfied with the result. I cannot understand how Cousin Ona can regard the misfortune to her portrait so calmly. I think it would break my heart to see a husband look with complacency on any picture, no matter how exquisite, that took the place of my own, especially if like her's, it was painted in my bridal days. I sometimes wonder if those days are as sacred to the memory of husband and wife as I have always imagined them to be."

"Why does Cousin Ona never speak of Grotewell, and why, if by chance I mention the name, does she drop her eyes and a shadow cross the countenance of Mr. Sylvester?"

"There is a word Mr. Sylvester uses in the most curious way; it is *fuss*. He calls everything a fuss that while insignificant in size or character has power either to irritate or please. A fly is a fuss; so is a dimple in a girl's cheek or a figure that goes wrong in accounts. I have even heard him call a child, 'That dear little fuss.' Bertram unconsciously imitates his uncle in this peculiar mannerism and is often heard alluding to this or that as a *fuss of fusses*. Indeed they say this use of the word is a peculiarity of the Sylvester family."

"I think from the way Mr. Sylvester spoke yesterday, that he must have experienced some dreadful trouble in his life. We were walking in the wards of a hospital—that is,

Miss Stuyvesant, Mr. Sylvester and myself—when some one near us gave utterance to the trite expression, 'O it will heal, but the scar will always remain.' 'That is a common saying,' remarked Mr. Sylvester, 'but how true a one no one realizes but he who carries the scar.'"

"It may be imagination or simply the effect of increased appreciation on my part, but it does seem as if Miss Stuyvesant grew lovelier and more companionable each time that I meet her. She makes me think of a temple in which a holy lamp is burning. Her very silences are eloquent, and yet she is never *distraite* but always cheerful and frequently the brightest of the company. But it is a brightness without glitter, a gentle lustre that delights you but never astonishes. I meet many sweet girls in the so-called heartless circles of society, but none like her. She is my white lily on which a moonbeam rests."

"This house contains a mystery, as Ona is pleased to designate the room at the top of the house to which Mr. Sylvester withdraws when he desires to be alone. And indeed it is a sort of Bluebeard's chamber, in that he keeps it rigidly under lock and key, allowing no one to enter it, not even his wife. The servants declare that no one but himself has ever crossed its threshold, but I can scarcely believe that. Ona has not, but there must surely be some trusty person to whom he allots the care of its furniture. Am I only proving myself to be a true member of my sex when I allow that I cannot hinder my own curiosity from hovering about a spot so religiously guarded? Yet what should we see if its doors were thrown open? A study surrounded with books it displeases him to see misplaced, or a luxurious apartment fitted with every appointment necessary to rest and comfort him when he comes home tired from business."

"I never saw Mr. Sylvester angry till to-day. By some inadvertence he went down town without locking the door of his private room, and though he returned immediately upon missing the key from his pocket, he was barely in time to prevent Cousin Ona from invading the spot he has always kept so sacred from intrusion. I was not present and of course did not hear what was said, but I caught a glimpse of his face as he left the house, and found it quite sufficient to assure me of his dissatisfaction. As for Ona, she declares he pulled her back as if she had been daring the plague. 'I do not expect to find five beautiful wives hanging up there by their necks,' concluded she with a forced laugh, 'but I shall yet see the interior of that room, if only to establish my prerogative as the mistress of this house.'

"I do not now feel as if I wished to see it."

"There is one thing that strikes me as peculiar in Miss Stuyvesant, and that is, that as much pleasure as she seems to take in my society when we meet, she never comes to see me in Mr. Sylvester's house. For a long time I wondered over this but said nothing, but one day upon receiving a second invitation to visit her, I mentioned the fact as delicately as I could, and was quite distressed to observe how seriously she took the rebuke, if rebuke it could be called. 'I cannot explain myself,' she murmured in some embarrassment; 'but Mr. Sylvester's house is closed against me. You must not ask me to seek you there or expect me to do myself the pleasure of attending Mrs. Sylvester's receptions. I cannot. Is that enough for me to say to my dearest friend?' I hardly knew what to reply, but finally ventured to inquire if she was restrained by any fact that would make it undignified in me to seek her society and enjoy the pleasures she is continually offering me. And she answered with such a cheerful negative I was quite reassured. And so the matter is settled. Our friendship is to be emancipated from the bonds of etiquette and I am to enjoy her company whenever I can. To-morrow we are going to take our first ride in the park. The horses have been bought, and much to Cousin Ona's satisfaction, the groom has been hired."

"I was told something the other day, of a nature so unpleasant that I should not think of repeating it, if you had not expressly commanded me to confide to you everything that for any reason produced an effect upon me in my new home. My informant was Sarah, the somewhat gossiping woman whom Ona has about her as seamstress and maid. She said—and she had spoken before I could prevent her—that the way Mrs. Sylvester took on about her mourning at the time of little Geraldine's death was enough to wear out the patience of Job. She even went so far as to tell the dressmaker that if she could not have her dress made to suit her she would not put on mourning at all! Aunty, can you wonder that Mr. Sylvester looks so bitterly sombre whenever mention is made of his child? He loved it, and its own mother could worry over the fit of a dress while his bereaved heart was breaking! I confess I can never feel the same indulgence towards what I considered the idiosyncrasies of a fashionable beauty again. Her smooth white skin makes me tremble; it has never flushed with delight over the innocent smiles of her firstborn."

"Mr. Sylvester is very polite to Cousin Ona and seems to yield to her wishes in everything. But if I were she I think my heart would break over that very politeness. But then she is one who demands formality even from the persons of her household. I have never seen him stoop for a kiss or beheld her even so much as lay her hand on his shoulder. But I have observed him wait on her at moments when he was pale from weariness and she flushed with long twilight reclinings before her sleepy boudoir fire."

"There are times when I would not exchange my present opportunities for any others which might be afforded me. General —— dined here to-day, and what a vision of a great struggle was raised up before me by his few simple words in regard to Gettysburg. I did not know which to admire most, the military bearing and vivid conversation of the great soldier, or the ease and dignity with which Mr. Sylvester met his remarks and answered each glowing sentence. General —— spoke a few words to me. How gentle these lion-like men can be when they stoop their tall heads to address little children or young women!"

"What a noble-hearted man Mr. Sylvester is! Mr. Turner in speaking of him the other night, declared there is no one in his congregation who in a quiet way does so much for the poor. 'He is especially interested in young men,' said he, 'and will leave his own affairs at any time to aid or advise them.' I knew Mr. Sylvester was kind, but Mr. Turner's enthusiasm was uncommon. He evidently admires Mr. Sylvester as much as every one else loves him. And he is not alone in this. Almost every day I hear some remark made of a nature complimentary to my benefactor's character or ability. Even Mr. Stuyvesant who so seldom appears to notice us girls, once interrupted a conversation between Cicely and myself to inquire if Mr. Sylvester was quite well. 'I thought he looked pale to-day,' remarked he, in his dry but not unkindly way, and then added, 'He must not get sick; he is too valuable to us.' This was a great deal for Mr. Stuyvesant to say, and it caused a visible gratification to Mr. Sylvester when I related it to him in the evening. 'I had rather satisfy that man than any other I know,' declared he. 'He is of the stern old-fashioned sort, and it is an honor to any one to merit his approval. I did not tell him that I had also heard Mr. Stuyvesant observe in a conversation with some business friend of his, that Edward Sylvester was the only speculator he knew in whom he felt implicit confidence. Somehow it always gives me an uncomfortable feeling to hear Mr. Sylvester alluded to as a speculator. Besides since he has entered the Bank, he has I am told, entirely restricted himself to what are called legitimate operations."

"Mr. Sylvester came home with a dreadful look on his face to-day. We were standing in the hall at the time the door opened, and he went by us without a nod, almost as if he did not see us. Even Ona was startled and stood gazing after him with an anxiety such as I had never observed in her before, while I was conscious of that sick feeling I have sometimes experienced when he came upon me suddenly from his small room above, or paused in the midst of the gayest talk, to ask me some question that was wholly irrelevant and most frequently sad.

"'He has met with some heavy loss,' murmured his wife, glancing down the handsome parlors with a look such as a mother might bestow upon the face of a sick child. But I was sure she had not sounded his trouble, and in my impetuosity was about to fly to his side when we saw him pause before the image of Luxury that stands on the stair, look at it for a moment with a strange intentness, then suddenly and with a gesture of irrepressible passion, lift his arm as if he would fell it from its place. The action was so startling, Ona clutched my sleeve in terror, but he passed on and in another moment we heard him shut the door of his room.

"Would he be down to dinner? that was the next question. Ona thought not; I did not dare to think. Nevertheless it was a great relief to me when I saw him enter the dining-room with that set immovable look he sometimes wears when Ona begins one of her long and rambling streams of fashionable gossip. 'It is nothing,' flashed from his wife's eyes to mine, and she lapsed at once into her most graceful self, but she nevertheless hastened her meal and I was quite prepared to observe her follow him, as with the polite excuse of weariness, he left the table before desert. I could not hear what she asked him, but his answer came distinctly to my ears from the midst of the library to which they had withdrawn. 'It is nothing in which you have an interest, Ona. Thank heaven you do not always know the price with which the splendors you so love are bought.' And she did not cry out, 'O never pay such a price for any joy of mine! Sooner than cost you so dear I would live on crusts and dwell in a garret.' No, she kept silence, and when in a few minutes later I joined her in the library, it was to find on her usually placid lips, a thin cool smile that struck like ice to my heart, and made it impossible for me to speak.

"But the hardest trial of the day was to hear Mr. Sylvester come in at eleven o'clock—he went out again immediately after dinner—and go up stairs without giving me my usual good-night. It was such a grief to me I could not keep still, but hurried to the foot of the stairs in the hopes he would yet remember me and come back. But instead of that, he no sooner saw me than he threw out his hand almost as if he would push me back, and hastened on up the whole winding flight till he reached the refuge of that mysterious room of his at the top of the house.

"I could not go back to Ona after that—she had been to make a call somewhere with a young gentleman friend of hers;—yes on this very night had been to make a call—but I took advantage of the late hour to retire to my own room where for a long time I lay awake listening for his descending step and seeing, as in a vision, the startling picture of his lifted arm raised against the unconscious piece of bronze on the stair. Henceforth that statue will possess for me a still more dreadful significance."

"It is the twenty-fifth of February. Why should I feel as if I must be sure of the exact date before I slept?"

The next extract followed close on this and was the last which Miss Belinda read.

"Mr. Sylvester seems to have recovered from his late anxiety. He does not shrink from me any more with that half bitter, half sad expression that has so long troubled and bewildered me, but draws me to his side and sits listening to my talk until I feel as if I were really of some comfort to this great and able man. Ona does not notice the change; she is all absorbed in preparing for the visit to Washington, which Mr. Sylvester has promised her."

Miss Belinda calmly folded up the letters and locked them again in the little mahogany box, after which she covered up the embers and quietly went to bed. But next morning a letter was despatched to Mr. Sylvester which ran thus:

"Dear Mr. Sylvester:

"For the present at least you may keep Paula with you. But I am not ready to say that I think it would be for her best good to be received and acknowledged as your daughter—yet. Hoping you will appreciate the motives that actuate this decision,

"I remain, respectfully yours,

"Belinda Ann Walton."

XV.

AN ADVENTURE—OR SOMETHING MORE.

"Bliss was it in that dawn to be alive,But to be young was very heaven."—
Wordsworth.

Oph.—What means this, my lord?

Ham.—Marry, this is the miching mallecho; it means mischief."—Hamlet.

A ride in the Central Park is an every-day matter to most people. It signifies an indolent bowling over a smooth road all alive with the glitter of passing equipages, waving ribbons and fluttering plumes, and brightened now and then by the sight of a well known face amid the general rush of old and young, plain and handsome, sad and gay countenances that flash by you in one long and brilliant procession.

But to Paula and her friend Miss Stuyvesant starting out in the early freshness of a fair April morning, it meant new life, reawakening joy, the sparkle of young leaves just loosed from the bonds of winter, the sweetness and promise of spring airs, and all the budding glory of a new year with its summer of countless roses and its autumn of incalculable glories. Not the twitter of a bird was lost to them, not the smile of an opening flower, not the welcome of a waving branch. Youth, joy, and innocence lived in their hearts and showed them nothing in the mirror of nature that was not equally young, joyous and innocent. Then they were alone, or sufficiently so. The stray wanderers whom they met sitting under the flowering trees, were equally with themselves lovers of nature or they would not be seated in converse with it at this early hour; while the laugh of little children startled from their play by the prance of their high-stepping horses, was only another expression of the sweet but unexpressed delight that breathed in all the radiant atmosphere.

"We are two birds who have escaped thralldom and are taking our first flight into our natural ether," cried Miss Stuyvesant gaily.

"We are two pioneers lit by the spirit of adventure, who have left the cosy hearth of wintry-fires to explore the domains of the frost king, and lo, we have come upon a Paradise of bloom and color!" responded the ringing voice of Paula.

"I feel as if I could mount that little white cloud we see over there," continued Cicely with a quick lively wave of her whip. "I wonder how Dandy would enjoy an empyrean journey?"

"From the haughty bend of his neck I should say he was quite satisfied with his present condition. But perhaps his chief pride is due to the mistress he carries."

"Are you attempting to vie with Mr. Williams, Paula?"

Mr. Williams was the meek-eyed, fair complexioned gentleman, whose predilection for compliment was just then a subject of talk in fashionable circles.

"Only so far as my admiration goes of the most charming lady I see this morning. But who is this?"

Miss Stuyvesant looked up. "Ah, that is some one with whom there is very little danger of your falling in love."

Paula blushed. The gentleman approaching them upon horseback was conspicuous for long side whiskers of a decidedly auburn tinge.

"His name is—" But she had not time to finish, for the gentleman with a glance of astonished delight at Paula, bowed to the speaker with a liveliness and grace that demanded some recognition.

Instantly he drew rein. "Do I behold Miss Stuyvesant among the nymphs!" cried he, in those ringing pleasant tones that at once predispose you towards their possessor.

"If you allude to my friend Miss Fairchild, you certainly do, Mr. Ensign," the wicked little lady rejoined with a waiving of her usual ceremony that astonished Paula.

Mr. Ensign bestowed upon them his most courtly bow, but the flush that mounted to his brow—making his face one red, as certain of his friends were malicious enough to observe on similar occasions—indicated that he had been taken a little more at his word than perhaps suited even one of his easy and proverbially careless temperament. "Miss Fairchild will understand that I am not a Harvey Williams—at least before an introduction," said he with something like seriousness.

But at this allusion to the gentleman whose name had been upon their lips but a moment before, both ladies laughed outright.

"I have just been accused of attempting the rôle of that gentleman myself," exclaimed Paula. "If the fresh morning air will persist in painting such roses on ladies' cheeks," continued she, with a loving look at her pretty companion "what can one be expected to do?"

"Admire," quoth the red bannered cavalier with a glance, however, at the beautiful speaker instead of the demure little Cicely at her side.

Miss Stuyvesant perceived this look and a curious smile disturbed the corners of her rosy lips. "What a fortunate man to be able to do the right thing at the right time," laughed she, gaily touching up her horse that was beginning to show symptoms of restlessness.

"If Miss Stuyvesant will put that in the future tense and then assure us she has been among the prophets, I should be singularly obliged," said he with a touch of his hat and a smiling look at Paula that was at once manly and gentle, careless and yet respectful.

"Ah, life is too bright for prophesies this morning. The moment is enough."

"Is it Miss Fairchild?" queried Mr. Ensign looking back over his shoulder.

She turned just a bit of her cheek towards him. "What Miss Stuyvesant declares to be true, that am I bound to believe," said she, and with the least little ripple of a laugh, rode on.

"It is a pity you have such a dislike for whiskers," Cicely presently remarked with an air of great gravity.

Paula gave a start and cast a glance of reproach at her companion. "I did not notice his whiskers after the first word or two," said she, fixing her eyes on a turn of the road before them. "Such cheerfulness is infectious. I was merry before, but now I feel as if I had been bathed in sunshine."

Cicely's eyes flashed wide with surprise and her face grew serious in earnest. "Mr. Ensign is a delightful companion," observed she; "a room is always brighter for his entrance; and with all that, he is the only young man I know, who having come into a large fortune, feels any of the responsibilities of his position. The sunshine is the result of a good heart and pure living, and that is what makes it infectious, I suppose."

"Let us canter," said Paula. And so the glad young things swept on, life breaking in bubbles around them and rippling away into unfathomable wells of feeling in one of their pure hearts at least. Suddenly a hand seemed to swoop from heaven and dash them both back in dismay. They had reached one of those places where the foot path crosses the equestrian and they had run over and thrown down a little child.

"O heaven!" cried Paula leaping from her horse, "I had rather been killed myself." The groom rode up and she bent anxiously over the child.

It was a boy of some seven or eight years, whose misfortune—he was lame, as the little crutch fallen at his side sufficiently denoted—made appear much younger. He had been struck on his arm and was moaning with pain, but did not seem to be otherwise hurt. "Are you alone?" cried Paula, lifting his head on her arm and glancing hurriedly about.

The little fellow raised his heavy lids and for a moment stared into her face with eyes so deeply blue and beautiful they almost startled her, then with an effort pointed down the path, saying,

"Dad's over there in the long tunnel talking to some one. Tell him I got hurt. I want Dad."

She gently lifted him to his feet and led him out of the road into the apparently deserted path where she made him sit down. "I am going to find his father," said Paula to Cicely, "I will be back in a moment."

"But wait; you shall not go alone," authoritatively exclaimed that little damsel, leaping in her turn to the ground. "Where does he say his father is?"

"In the tunnel, by which I suppose he means that long passage under the bridge over there."

Holding up the skirts of their riding-habits in their trembling right hands, they hurried forward. Suddenly they both paused. A woman had crossed their path; a woman whom to look at but once was to remember with ghastly shrinking for a lifetime. She was wrapped in a long and ragged cloak, and her eyes, startling in their blackness, were fixed upon the pain-drawn countenance of the poor little hurt boy behind them, with a gleam whose feverish hatred and deep malignant enjoyment of his very evident sufferings, was like a revelation from the lowest pit to the two innocent-minded girls hastening forward on their errand of mercy.

"Is he much hurt?" gasped the woman in an ineffectual effort to conceal the evil nature of her interest. "Do you think he will die?" with a shrill lingering emphasis on the last word as if she longed to roll it like a sweet morsel under her tongue.

"Who are you?" asked Cicely, shrinking to one side with dilated eyes fixed on the woman's hardened countenance and the white, too white hand with which she had pointed as she spoke of the child.

"Are you his mother?" queried Paula, paling at the thought but keeping her ground with an air of unconscious authority.

"His mother!" shrieked the woman, hugging herself in her long cloak and laughing with fiendish sarcasm: "I look like his mother, don't I? His eyes—did you notice his eyes? they are just like mine, aren't they? and his body, poor weazen little thing, looks as if it had drawn sustenance from mine, don't it? His mother! O heaven!"

Nothing like the suppressed force of this invocation seething as it was with the worst passions of a depraved human nature, had ever startled those ears before. Clasping Cicely by the hand, she called out to the groom behind them, "Guard that child as you would your life!" and then flashing upon the wretched creature before her with all the force of her aroused nature, she exclaimed, "If you are not his mother, move aside and let us pass, we are in search of assistance."

For an instant the woman stood awe-struck before this vision of maidenly beauty and indignation, then she laughed and cried out with shrill emphasis:

"When next you look like that, go to your mirror, and when you see the image it reflects, say to yourself, 'So once looked the woman who defied me in the Park!'"

With a quick shudder and a feeling as if the noisome cloak of this degraded being had somehow been dropped upon her own fair and spotless shoulders, Paula clasped the hand of Cicely more tightly in her own, and rushed with her down the steps that led into the underground passage towards which they had been directed.

There were but two persons in it when they entered. A short thickset man and another man of a slighter and more gentlemanly build. They were engaged in talking, and the latter was bringing down his right hand upon the palm of his left with a gesture almost foreign in its expressive energy.

"I tell you," declared he, with a voice that while low, reverberated through the hollow vault above him with strange intensity, "I tell you I've got my grip on a certain rich man in this city, and if you will only wait, you shall see strange things. I don't know his name and I don't know his face, but I do know what he has done, and a thousand dollars down couldn't buy the knowledge of me."

"But if you don't know his name and don't know his face, how in the name of all that's mischievous are you going to know your man?"

"Leave that to me! If I once meet him and hear him talk, one more rich man goes down and one more poor devil goes up, or I've not the wit that starvation usually teaches."

The nature of these sentences together with the various manifestations of interest with which they were received, had for a moment deterred the two girls in their hurried advance, but now they put away every thought save that of the poor little creature awaiting his Dad, and lifting up her voice, Paula said,

"Are either of you the father of a little lame lad—"

Instantly and before she could conclude, the taller of the two, who had also been the chief speaker in the above conversation, turned, and she saw his hand begrimed though it was with dirt and dark with many a disgraceful trick, go to his heart in a gesture too natural to be anything but involuntary.

"Is he hurt?" gasped he, but in how different a tone from that of the woman who had used the same words a few minutes before. Then seeing that the persons who addressed him were ladies and one of them at least a very beautiful one, took off his hat with an easy action, that together with what they had heard, proved him to be one of that most dangerous class among us, a gentleman who has gone thoroughly and irretrievably to the bad.

"I am afraid he is, sir," said Paula. "He was attempting to cross the road, and a horse advancing hurriedly, struck him." She had not courage to say her horse in face of the white and trembling dismay that seized him at these words.

"Where is he?" cried he. "Where's my poor boy?" And he bounded up the steps, his hat still in his hand, his long unkempt locks flying, and his whole form expressive of the utmost alarm.

"Down by the carriage road," called out Paula, finding it impossible for them to keep up with such haste.

"But is he much injured?" cried a smooth voice at their side.

They turned; it was the short thickset man who had been the other's companion in the conversation above recorded.

"We trust not," answered Cicely; "his arm received the blow, and he suffers very much, but we hope it is not serious;" and they hurried on.

They found the father seated on the grass holding the little fellow in his arms. The look on his once handsome but now thoroughly corrupt and dissipated face, made their hearts melt within them. However wicked he might be—and that sly treacherous eye, that false impudent lip, that settling of the whole face into the mould which Vice applies to all her votaries, left no doubt of his complete depravity—he dearly loved his child, and love, no matter how it is expressed, or in what garb it appears, is a sacred and beautiful thing, and ennobles for the time being any creature who displays it.

"'Twas a hard knock up, Dad," came from the white lips of the child as he felt his father's trembling hand feel up and down his arm, "but I guess the 'little fellar' can stand it." "Little feller" was evidently the name by which his father was accustomed to address him.

"There are no bones broken," said the father. "To be lame and maimed too would be—"

He did not finish, for a delicately gloved hand was here laid on his sleeve, and a gentle voice whispered, "Money cannot pay for an injury like that, but please accept this;" and Paula thrust a purse into his hand.

He clutched it eagerly, but at her next request that he should tell her where he lived that they might inquire after the boy, he shook his head with a return of his old emphasis.

"The haunts of bats and jackals are not for ladies." Then as he caught sight of her pitiful face bending in farewell over the little urchin, some remembrance perhaps of the days when he had a right to stoop to the ear of beautiful women and walk unrebuked at their side, returned to him from the past, and respectfully lowering his voice, he asked her name.

She gave it and he seemed to lay it away in his mind; then as the ladies turned to remount their horses, rose and began carrying the little fellow off. As he vanished in the turn of the path that led towards the main entrance, they perceived a tall dark figure arise from a seat in the distance and stand looking after him, with a leer on its face and a malicious hugging of itself in a long black cloak, that proclaimed her to be the same ominous being who had before so grievously startled them.

XVI.

THE SWORD OF DAMOCLES.

"And my imaginations are as foulAs Vulcan's smithy."—Hamlet.

"Why, all the souls that were, were forfeit once;

And He that might the vantage best have tookFound out the remedy."—Measure for Measure.

Mrs. Sylvester reclining on the palest of blue couches, in the slanting sunlight of an April afternoon, is a study for a painter. Not that such inspiring loveliness breathed from her person, conspicuous as it was for its rich and indolent grace, but because in every attitude of her large and well formed limbs, in every raise of the thick white lids from eyes whose natural brightness was obscured by the mist of aimless fancies, she presented such an embodiment of luxurious ease, one might almost imagine they were gazing upon the favorite Sultana of some eastern court, or, to be for once poetical as the subject demands, a full blown Egyptian lotos floating in hushed enjoyment on the placid waters of its native stream. Indeed for all the blonde character of her beauty, there was certainly something oriental about the physique of this favored child of fortune. Had the tint of her skin been richened to a magnolia bloom instead of reminding you of that description accorded to the complexion of one of Napoleon's sisters, that it looked like white satin seen through pink glass, she would have passed in any Eastern market, for a rare specimen of Circassian beauty.

But Mr. Sylvester coming home fatigued and harassed, cared little for Circassian beauties or Oriental odalisques. It was a welcome that he desired, and such refreshment as a quick eye and ready hand can bestow when guided by a tender and loving heart; or so thought the watchful Paula as she glided from her room at the sound of his step in the hall, and met him coming weary and disheartened from the side of Ona's couch. The sight of her revived him at once.

"Well, little one, what have you been doing to-day?"

Instantly a shade fell over her countenance. "I hardly know how to tell you. It has been a day of great experiences to me. I am literally shaken with them. I have been wanting to talk to Ona about what I have seen and heard, but thought I had best wait till you came home, for I could not repeat the story twice."

"What! you look pale. Nothing has happened to frighten you I hope," exclaimed he, leading her back to Ona's side, who stirred a little, and presently deigned to take an upright position.

"I do not know if it is fear or horror," cried Paula, shuddering; "I have seen a fearful woman—But first I ought to tell you that I took a ride with Miss Stuyvesant in the Park this morning—"

"Yes, and persisted in going for that lady on horseback instead of sending the groom after her, and all starting from the front of our house," murmured Mrs. Sylvester with lazy chagrin.

Paula smiled, but otherwise took no notice of this standing topic of disagreement.

"It was a beautiful day," she proceeded, "and we enjoyed it very much, but we were so unfortunate as to run over a little boy, at that place where the equestrian road crosses the foot path; a lame child, Mr. Sylvester, who could not get out of our way; poor too, with a ragged jacket on which seemed to make it all the worse."

Ona gave a shrug with her white shoulders, that seemed to question this. "Did you injure him very much?" queried she, with a show of interest; not sufficient however to impair her curiosity as to the cut of one of her nails.

"I cannot say; his little arm was struck, and when I went to pick him up, he lay back in my lap and moaned till I thought my heart would break. But that was not the worst that happened. As we went hurrying up the walk to find the child's father, we were met by a woman wrapped in a black cloak whose long and greasy folds seemed like the symbol of her own untold depravity. Her glance as she encountered the child writhing in pain at my feet, made my heart stand still. It was more than malignant, it was actually fiendish. 'Is he hurt?' she asked, and it seemed as if she gloated over the question; she evidently longed to hear that he was, longed to be told that he would die; and when I inquired if she was his mother, she broke into a string of laughter, that seemed to darken the daylight. 'His mother! O yes, we look alike, don't we!' she exclaimed, pointing with a mocking gesture frightful to see, first at his eyes which were very blue and beautiful, and then at her own which were dark as evil thoughts could make them. I never saw anything so dreadful. Malignancy! and towards a little lame child! what could be more horrible!"

Mr. Sylvester and his wife exchanged looks, then the former asked, "Did she follow you, Paula?"

"No; after telling me that I—But I cannot repeat what she said," exclaimed the young girl with a quick shudder. "Since I came home," she musingly continued, "I have looked and looked at my face in the glass, but I cannot believe that what she declared is true. There is no similarity between us, could never have been any: I will not have it that she ever saw in all the days of her life such a picture as that in her glass." And with a sudden gesture Paula started up and pointed to herself as she stood reflected in one of the tall mirrors with which Ona's boudoir abounded.

"And did she dare to make any comparison between you and her own degraded self?" exclaimed Mr. Sylvester, with a glance at the exquisite vision of pure girlhood thus doubly presented to his notice.

"Yes, what I am, she was once, or so she said. And it may be true. I have never suffered sorrow or experienced wrong, and cannot measure their power to carve the human face with such lines as I beheld on that woman's countenance to-day. But do not let us talk of her any more. She left us at last, and we found the child's father. Mr. Sylvester," she suddenly asked, "are there to be found in this city, men occupying honorable positions and as such highly esteemed, who like Damocles of old, may be said to sit under the constant terror of a falling sword in the shape of some possible disclosure, that if made, would ruin their position before the world forever?"

Mr. Sylvester started as if he had been shot. "Paula!" cried he, and instantly was silent again. He did not look at his wife, but if he had, he would have perceived that even her fair skin was capable of blanching to a yet more startling whiteness, and that her sleepy eyes could flash open with something like expression in their lazy depths.

"I mean," dreamily continued Paula, absorbed in her own remembrance, "that if what we overheard said by the father of that child to-day is true, some one of our prominent men, whose life is not all it appears, is standing on the verge of possible exposure and shame; that a hound is on his track in the form of a starving man; and that sooner or later he will have to pay the price of an unprincipled creature's silence, or fall into public discredit like some others of whom we have lately read." Then as silence filled the room, she added, "It makes me tremble to think that a man of means and seeming honor should be placed in such a position, but worse still that we may know such a one and be ignorant of his misery and his shame."

"It is getting time for me to dress," murmured Ona, sinking back on her pillow and speaking in her most languid tone of voice. "Could you not hasten your story a little Paula?"

But Mr. Sylvester with a hurried glance at the closing eyes of his wife, requested on the contrary that she would explain herself more definitely. "Ona will pardon the delay," said he, with a set, strained politeness that called up the least little quiver of suppressed sarcasm about the rosy infantile lips that he evidently did not consider it worth his while to notice.

"But that is all," said Paula. However she repeated as nearly as she could just what the boy's father had said. At the conclusion Mr. Sylvester rose.

"What kind of a looking man was he?" said that gentleman as he crossed to the window.

"Well, as nearly as I can describe, he was tall, dark and seedy, with a shock of black hair and a pair of black whiskers that floated on the wind as he walked. He was evidently of the order of decayed gentleman, and his manner of talking, especially in the profuse use he made of his arms and hands, was decidedly foreign. Yet his speech was pure and without accent."

Mr. Sylvester's face as he asked the next question was comparatively cheerful. "Was the other man with whom he was talking, as dark and foreign as himself?"

"O no, he was round and jovial, a little too insinuating perhaps, in his way of speaking to ladies, but otherwise a a well enough appearing man."

Mr. Sylvester bowed and looked at his watch. (Why do gentlemen always consult their watches even in the face of the clock?) "Ona, you are right," said he, "it is time you were dressing for dinner." And concluding with a word or two of sympathy as to the peculiar nature of Paula's adventures as he called them, he hastened from the room and proceeded to his little refuge above.

"He has not asked me what became of the child," thought Paula, with a certain pang of surprise. "I expected him to say, 'Shall we not try and see the little fellow, Paula?' if only to allow me to explain that the child's father would not tell me where they lived. But the later affair has evidently put the child out of his head. And indeed it is only natural that a business man should be more interested in such a fact as I have related, than in the sprained arm of a wretched creature's 'little feller.'" And she turned to assist Ona, who had arisen from her couch and was now absorbed in the intricacies of an uncommonly elaborate toilet.

"Those men did not mention any names?" suddenly queried that lady, looking with an expression of careful anxiety, at the twist of her back hair, in the small hand-mirror she held over her shoulder.

"No," said Paula, dropping a red rose into the blonde locks she was so carefully arranging. "He expressly said he did not know the name of the person to whom he alluded. It was a strange conversation for me to overhear, was it not?" she remarked, happy to have interested her cousin in anything out of the domains of fashion.

"I don't know—certainly—of course—" returned Mrs. Sylvester with some incoherence. "Do you think red looks as well with this black as the lavender would do?" she rambled on in her lightest tone, pulling out a box of feathers.

Paula gave her a little wistful glance of disappointment and decided in favor of the lavender.

"I am bound to look well to-night if I never do so again," said Ona. They were all going to a public reception at which a foreign lord was expected to be present. "How fortunate I am to have a perfect little hairdresser in my own family, without being obliged to send for some gossipy, fussy old Madame with her stories of how such and such a one looked when dressed for the Grand Duke's ball, or how Mrs. So and So always gave her more than her price because she rolled up puffs so exquisitely." And stopping to aid the deft girl in substituting the lavender feather for the red rose in her hair—she forgot to ask any more questions.

"Ona," remarked her husband, coming into the room on his way down to dinner—Mrs. Sylvester never dined when she was going to any grand entertainment; it made her look flushed she said—"I am not in the habit of troubling you about your family matters, but have you heard from your father of late?"

Mrs. Sylvester turned from her jewel-casket and calmly surveyed his face. It was fixed and formal, the face he turned to his servants and sometimes—to his wife. "No," said she, with a light little gesture as though she were speaking of the most trivial matter. "In one respect at least, papa is like an angel, his visits are few and far between."

Mr. Sylvester's eye-brows drew heavily together. For a man with a smile of strange sweetness, he could sometimes look very forbidding. "*When* was he here last?" he inquired in a tone more commanding than he knew.

She did not appear to resent it. "Let me see," mused she. "When was it I lost my diamond ear-ring? O I remember, it was on the eve of New Year's day a year ago; I recollect because I had to wear pearls with my garnet brocade," she pettishly sighed. "And papa came the next week, after you had given me the money for a new pair. I have reason to remember *that*, for not a dollar did he leave me."

"Ona!" exclaimed her husband, shrinking back in uncontrollable surprise, while his eyes flashed inquiringly to her ears in which two noble diamonds were brilliantly shining.

"O," she cried, just raising one snowy hand to those sparkling ornaments, while a faint blush, the existence of which he had sometimes doubted, swept over her careless face. "I was enabled to procure them in time; but for a whole two months I had to go without diamonds." She did not say that she had bartered her wedding jewels to make up the sum she needed, but he may have understood that without being told.

"And that is the last time you have seen him?" He held her eyes with his, she could not look away.

"The very last, sir; strange to say."

His glance shifted from her face and he turned with a bow towards the door.

"May I ask," she slowly inquired as he moved across the floor, "what is the reason of this sudden interest in poor papa?"

"Certainly," said he, pausing and looking back, not without some emotion of pity in his glance. "I am sometimes struck with a sense of the duty I owe you, in helping you to bear the burden of certain secret responsibilities which I fear may sometimes prove too heavy for you."

She gave a little rippling laugh that only sounded hollow to the image listening in the glass. "You choose strange times in which to be struck," said she, holding up two dresses for his inspection, with a lift of her brows evidently meant as an inquiry as to which he thought the most becoming.

"Conscience is the chooser, not I," declared he, for once allowing himself to ignore the weighty question of dress thus propounded.

His wife gave a little toss of her head and he left the room.

"I should like Edward very much," murmured she in a burst of confidence to her own reflection in the glass, "if only he would not bother himself so much about that same disagreeable conscience."

"You look unhappy," said Mr. Sylvester to Paula as they came from the dining-room. "Have the adventures of the day made such an impression upon you that you will not be able to enjoy the evening's festivities?"

She lifted her face and the quick smile came.

"I do not like to see your brow so clouded," continued he, smoothing his own to meet her searching eye. "Smiles should sit on the lips of youth, or else why are they so rosy."

"Would you have me smile in face of my first glimpse of wickedness," asked she, but in a gentle tone that robbed her words of half their reproach. "You must remember that I have had but little experience with the world. I have lived all my life in a town of wholesome virtues, and while here I have been kept from contact with anything low or base. I have never known vice, and now all in a moment I feel as if I have been bathed in it."

He took her by the hand and drew her gently towards him. "Does your whole being recoil so from evil, my Paula? What will you do in this wicked world? What will you say to the sinner when you meet him—as you must?"

"I don't know; it's a problem I have never been brought to consider. I feel as if launched on a dismal sea for which I have neither chart nor compass. Life was so joyous to me this morning—" a flush swept over her cheek but he did not notice it— "I held, or seemed to hold, a cup of white wine in my hand, but suddenly as I looked at it, it turned black and—"

Ah, the outreach, the dismal breaking away of thought into the unfathomable, that lies in the pause of an *and*!

"And do you refuse to drink a cup across which has fallen a shadow," murmured Mr. Sylvester, his eyes fixed on her face, "the inevitable shadow of that great mass of human frailty and woe which has been accumulating from the foundation of the world?"

"No, no, I cannot, and retain my humanity. If there is such evil in the world, its pressure must drive it across the path of innocence."

"And you accept the cup?"

"I must; but oh, my vanished beliefs! This morning the wine of my life was pure and white, now it is black and befouled. What will make it clean again?"

With a sigh Mr. Sylvester dropped her hand and turned towards the mantle-piece. It was April as I have said, and there was no fire in the grate, but he posed his foot on the fender and looked sadly down at the empty hearthstone.

"Paula," said he after a space of pregnant silence, "it had to come. The veil of the temple must be rent in every life. Evil is too near us all for us to tread long upon the flowers without starting up the adders that hide beneath them. You had to have your first look into the cells of darkness, and perhaps it is best you had it here and now. The deeps are for men's eyes as well as the starry heavens."

"Yes, yes."

"There are some persons," he went on slowly, "you know them, who tread the ways of life with their eyelids closed to everything but the strip of velvet lawn on which they choose to walk. Earth's sighs and deep-drawn groans are nothing to them. The world may swing on in its way to perdition; so long as their pathway feels soft, they neither heed nor care. But you do not desire to be one of these, Paula! With your great soul and your strong heart, you would not ask to sit in a flowery maze, while the rest of the world went sliding on and down into wells of destruction, you might have made pools of healing by the touch of your womanly sympathy."

"No, no."

"I cannot tell you, I dare not tell you," he went on in a strange pleading voice that tore at the very roots of her heart, and rung in her memory forever, "what evil underlies the whole strata of life! At home and abroad, on our hearthstones and within our offices, the mocking devil sits. You can scarcely walk a block, my little one, without encountering a man or brushing against the dress of a woman across whose soul the black shadow lies heavier than any words of his or hers could tell. What the man you saw to-day, said of one unhappy being in this city, is true, God help us all, of many. Dark spots are easier acquired than blotted out, my Paula. In business as in society, one needs to carry the white shield of a noble purpose or a self-forgetting love, to escape the dripping of the deadly upas tree that branches above all humanity. I have walked its ways, my darling, and I know of what I speak. Your white robe is spotless but—"

"O there is where the pain comes in," she cried; "there, just there, is where the dagger strikes. She says she was once like me. O, could any temptation, any suffering, any wrong or misfortune that might befall me, ever bring me to where she is! If it could—"

"Paula!" This time his voice came authoritatively. "You are making too much of a frenzied woman's impulsive exclamation. To her darkened and despairing eyes any young woman of a similar style of beauty would have called forth the same remark. It was a sign that she was not entirely given up to evil, that she could remember her youth. Instead of feeling contaminated by her words, you ought to feel, that unconsciously to yourself, your fresh young countenance with its innocent eyes did an angel's work to-day. They made her recall what she was in the days of her own innocence; and who can tell what may follow such a recollection."

"O Mr. Sylvester," said she, "you fill me with shame. If I could think that—"

"You can, nothing appeals to the heart of crime like the glance of perfect innocence. If evil walks the world, God's ministers walk it also, and none can tell in what glance of the eye or what touch of the hand, that ministry will speak."

It was her turn now to take his hand in hers. "O how good, how thoughtful you are; you have comforted me and you have taught me. I thank you very much."

With a look she did not perceive, he drew his hand away. "I am glad I have helped you, Paula; there is but one thing more to say, and this I would emphasize with every saddened look you have ever met in all your life. Great sins make great sufferers. Side by side came the two dreadful powers of vice and retribution into the world, and side by side will they keep till they sink at last into the awful deeps of the bottomless pit. When you turn your back on a man who has committed a crime, one more door shuts in his darkened spirit."

The tears were falling from Paula's eyes now. He looked at them with strange wistfulness and involuntarily his hand rose to her head, smoothing her locks with fatherly touches. "Do not think," said he, "that I would lessen by a hair's breadth your hatred of evil. I can more easily bear to see the shadow upon your cup of joy than upon the banner of truth you carry. These eyes must lose none of their inner light in glancing compassionately on your fellow-men. Only remember that divinity itself has stooped to rescue, and let the thought make your contact with weary, wicked-hearted humanity a little less trying and a little more hopeful to you. And now, my dear, that is enough of serious talk for to-day. We are bound for a reception, you know, and it is time we were dressing. Do you want me to tell you a secret?" asked he in a light mysterious tone, as he saw her eyes still filling.

She glanced up with sudden interest.

"I know it is treason," resumed he, "I am fully aware of the grave nature of my offence; but Paula I hate all public receptions, and shall only be able to enjoy myself

114 | P a g e

to-night just so much as I see that you are doing so. Life has its dark portals and its bright ones. This is one that you must enter with your most brilliant smiles."

"And they shall not be lacking," said she. "When a treasure-box of thought is given us, we do not open it and scatter its contents abroad, but lay it away where the heart keeps its secrets, to be opened in the hush of night when we are alone with our own souls and God."

He smiled and she moved towards the door. "None the less do we carry with us wherever we go, the remembrance of our hidden treasure," she smilingly added, looking back upon him from the stair.

And again as upon the first night of her entrance into the house, did he stand below and watch her as she softly went up, her lovely face flashing one moment against the dark background of the luxurious bronze, towering from the platform behind, then glowing with faint and fainter lustre, as the distance widened between them and she vanished in the regions above.

She did not see the toss of his arm with which he threw off the burden that rested upon his soul.

XVII.

GRAVE AND GAY.

"No scandal about Queen Elizabeth I hope."—Sheridan.

"Stands Scotland where it did?"—Macbeth.

"Who is that talking with Miss Stuyvesant?" asked Mr. Sylvester, approaching his wife during one of the lulls that will fall at times upon vast assemblies.

Mrs. Sylvester followed the direction of his glance and immediately responded, "O that is Mr. Ensign, one of the best *partis* of the season. He evidently knows where to pay his court."

"I inquired because he has just requested me to honor him with a formal introduction to Paula."

"Indeed! then oblige him by all means; it would be a great match for her. To say nothing of his wealth, he is *haut ton*, and his red whiskers will not look badly beside Paula's dark hair."

Mr. Sylvester frowned, then sighed, but in a few minutes Paula observed him approaching with Mr. Ensign. At once her hitherto pale cheek flushed, but the young gentleman did not seem to object to that, and after the formal introduction which he had sought was over, he exclaimed in his own bright ringing tones,

"The fates have surely forgotten their usual rôle of unpropitiousness. I did not dare hope to meet you here to-night, Miss Fairchild. Was the ride all that your fancy painted?"

"O," said she, speaking very low and glancing around, "do not allude to it here. We had an adventure shortly after you parted from us."

"An adventure! and no cavalier at your side! If I could but have known! Was it so serious?" he inquired in a moment, seeing her look grave.

"Ask Miss Stuyvesant;" said she. "I cannot talk about it any more to-night. Besides the music carries off one's thoughts. It is like a joyous breeze that whirls away the thistle-down whether it will or no."

He gave her a short quick look grave enough in its way, but responded with his usual graceful humor, "The thistle-down is too vicious a sprite to be beguiled away so easily. If I were to give my opinion on the subject, I should say there was method in its madness. If you have been brought up in the country, as I suspect from your remark, you must know that the white floating ball is not as harmless as it would lead you to imagine. It is a meddlesome nobody, that's what it is, and like some country gossips I know, launches forth from a pure love of mischief to establish his prickers in his neighbor's field."

"*His!* I thought it must be feminine at least to fulfill the conditions you mention. A male gossip, O fie! I shall never have patience with a thistle-ball after this."

"Well," laughed he, "I did start with the intention of making it feminine, but I caught a glimpse of your eyes and lost my courage. I did what I could," added he with a mirthful glance.

"So do the thistles," cried she. Then while both voices joined in a merry laugh, she continued, "But where have we strayed? For a moment it seemed as if we were on the hills at Grotewell; I could almost see the blue sky."

"And I," said he, with his eyes on her face.

"I am sure the brooks bubbled."

"I distinctly heard a bird singing."

"It was a whippowill."

"But my name is Clarence?"

And here both being young and without a care in the world, they laughed again. And the crowded perfumed room seemed to freshen as with a whiff of mountain air.

"You love the country, Miss Fairchild?"

"Yes;" and her smile was the reflection of the summer-lands that arose before her at the word. "With the right side of my heart do I love the spot where nature speaks and man is dumb."

"And with the left?"

"I love the place where great men congregate to face their destiny and control it."

"The latter is the deeper love," said he.

She nodded her head and then said, "I need both to make me happy. Sometimes as I walk these city streets, I feel as if my very longing to escape to the heart of the hills, would carry me there. I remember when I was a child, I was one day running through a meadow, when suddenly a whole flock of birds flew up from the grass and surrounded my head. I was not sure but what I should be caught up and carried away by the force of their flight; and when they rose to mid heaven, something in my breast seemed to follow them. So it is often with me here, only that it is the rush of my thoughts that threatens such a Hegira. Yet if I were to be transported to my native hills, I know I should long to be back again."

"The mountain lassie has wandered into the courts of the king. The perfume of palaces is not easily forgotten."

Her eye turned towards Mr. Sylvester standing near them upright and firm, talking to a group of attentive gentlemen every one of whom boasted a name of more than local celebrity. "Without a royal heart to govern, there would be no palace;" said she, and blushed under a sudden sense of the possible interpretation he might give to her words, till the rose in her hand looked pallid.

But he had followed her glance and understood her better than she thought. "And Mr. Sylvester has such a heart, so a hundred good fellows have told me. You are fortunate to see the city from the loop-hole of such a home as his."

"It is more than a loop-hole," said she.

"Of that I shall never be satisfied till I see it?"

And being content with the look he received, he took her on his arm and led her into the midst of the dancers.

Meanwhile in a certain corner not far off, two gentlemen were talking.

"Sylvester shows off well to-night."

"He always does. With such a figure as that, a man needs but to enter a room to make himself felt. But then he's a good talker too. Ever heard him speak?"

"No."

"Fine voice, true snap, right ring. Great favorite at elections. The fact is, Sylvester is a remarkable man."

"Hum, ha, so I should judge."

"And so fortunate! He has never been known to run foul in a great operation. Put your money in his hand and whew!—your fortune is as good as made."

The other, a rich man, connected heavily with the mining business in Colorado, smiled with that bland overflow of the whole countenance which is sometimes seen in large men of great self-importance.

"It's a pity he's gone out of Wall Street," continued his companion. "The younger fry feel now something like a flock of sheep that has lost its bell-wether."

"They straggle—eh?" returned his portly friend with an increase of his smile that was not altogether pleasant. "So Sylvester has left Wall Street?"

"He closed his last enterprise two weeks before accepting the Presidency of the Madison Bank. Stuyvesant is down on speculation, and well—It looks better you know; the Madison Bank is an old institution, and Sylvester is ambitious. There'll be no reckless handling of funds *there*."

"No!" What was there in that *no* that made the other look up? "I'm not acquainted with Sylvester myself. Has he much family?"

"A wife—there she is, that handsome woman talking with Ditman,—and a daughter, niece or somebody who just now is setting all our young scapegraces by the ears. You can see her if you just crane your neck a little."

"Humph, ha, very pretty, very pretty. How much do you suppose Mrs. Sylvester is worth as she stands, diamonds you know, and all that?"

"Well I should say some where near ten thousand; that sprig in her hair cost a clean five."

"So, so. They live in a handsome house I suppose?"

"A regular palace, corner of Fifth Avenue and ——"

"All his?"

"Nobody's else I reckon."

"Sports horses and carriage I suppose?"

"Of course."

"Yacht, opera box?"

"No reason why he shouldn't."

"What is his salary?"

"A nominal sum, five or ten thousand perhaps."

"Owns good share of the bank's stock I presume?"

"Enough to control it."

"Below par though?"

"A trifle, going up, however."

"And *don't* speculate?"

The way this man drawled his words was excessively disagreeable.

"Not that any one knows of. He's made his fortune and now asks only to enjoy it."

The man from the West strutted back and looked at his companion knowingly. "What do you think of my judgment, Stadler?"

"None better this side of the Pacific."

"Pretty good at spying out cracks, eh?"

"I wouldn't like to undertake the puttying up that would deceive you."

"Humph! Well then, mark this. In two months from to-day you will see Mr. Sylvester rent his house and go south for his health, or the pretty one over there will marry one of the scapegraces you mention, who will lend the man *who don't engage in any further ventures*, more than one or two hundred thousand dollars."

"Ha, you know something."

"I own mines in Colorado and I have my points."

"And Mr. Sylvester?"

"Will find them too sharp for him."

And having made his joke, he yielded to the other's apparent restlessness, and they sauntered off.

They did not observe a pale, demure, little lady that sat near them abstractedly nodding her dainty head to the remarks of a pale-whiskered youth at her side, nor notice the emotion with which she suddenly rose at their departure and dismissed her chattering companion on some impromptu errand. It was only one of the ordinary group of dancers, a pretty, plainly dressed girl, but her name was Stuyvesant.

Rising with a decision that gave a very attractive color to her cheeks, she hastily looked around. A trio of young gentlemen started towards her but she gave them no encouragement; her eye had detected Mr. Sylvester's tall figure a few feet off and it was to him she desired to speak. But at her first movement in his direction, her glance encountered another face, and like a stream that melts into a rushing torrent, her purpose seemed to vanish, leaving her quivering with a new emotion of so vivid a character she involuntarily looked about her for a refuge.

But in another instant her eyes had again sought the countenance that had so moved her, and finding it bent upon her own, faltered a little and unconsciously allowed the lilies she was carrying to drop from her hand. Before she realized her loss, the face before her had vanished, and with it something of her hesitation and alarm.

With a hasty action she drew near Mr. Sylvester. "Will you lend me your arm for a minute?" she asked, with her usual appealing look rendered doubly forcible by the experience of a moment before.

"Miss Stuyvesant! I am happy to see you."

Never had his face looked more cheerful she thought, never had his smile struck her more pleasantly.

"A little talk with a little girl will not hinder you too much, will it?" she queried, glancing at the group of gentlemen that had shrunk back at her approach.

"Do you call that hindrance which relieves one from listening to quotations of bank stock at an evening reception?"

She shook her head with a confused movement, and led him up before a stand of flowering exotics.

"I want to tell you something," she said eagerly but with a marked timidity also, the tall form beside her looked so imposing for all its encouraging bend. "I beg your pardon if I am doing wrong, but papa regards you with such esteem and—Mr. Sylvester do you know a man by the name of Stadler?"

Astonished at such a question from lips so young and dainty, he turned and surveyed her for a moment with quick surprise. Something in her aspect struck him. He answered at once and without circumlocution. "Yes, if you refer to that spry keen-faced man, just entering the supper-room."

"Do you know his companion?" she proceeded; "the portly, highly pompous-looking gentleman with the gold eye-glasses? Look quickly."

"No." There was an uneasiness in his tone however that struck her painfully.

"He is a stranger in town; has not the honor of your acquaintance he says, but from the questions he asked, I judge he has a great interest in your affairs. He spoke of being connected with mines in Colorado. I was sitting behind a curtain and overheard what was said."

Mr. Sylvester turned pale and regarded her attentively. "Might I be so bold," he inquired after a moment, "as to ask you what that was?"

"Yes, sir, certainly, but it is even harder for me to repeat than it was for me to hear. He inquired about your domestic concerns, your home and your income," she murmured blushing; "and then said, in what I thought was a somewhat exulting tone, that in two months or so we should see you go South for your health or—Is not that enough for me to tell you, Mr. Sylvester?"

He gave her a short stare, opened his lips as if to speak, then turned abruptly aside and began picking mechanically at the blossoms before him.

"I, of course, do not know what men mean when they talk of possessing points. But the leer and side glance which accompanies such talk, have a universal language we all understand, and I felt that I must warn you of that man's malice if only because papa regards you so highly."

He shrank as if touched on a sore place, but bowed and answered the wistful appeal of her glance with a shadow of his usual smile, then he turned, and looking towards the door through which the two men had disappeared, made a movement as if he would follow. But remembering himself, escorted her to a seat, saying as he did so:

"You are very kind, Miss Stuyvesant; please say nothing of this to Paula."

She bowed and a flitting smile crossed her upturned countenance. "I am not much of a gossip, Mr. Sylvester, or I should have been tempted to have carried my information to my father instead of to you."

He understood the implied promise in this remark and gave the hand on his arm a quick pressure, before relinquishing her to the care of the pale-complexioned youth who by this time had returned to her side.

In another moment Paula came up on the arm of a black-whiskered gentleman all shirt front and eye-glasses. "O Cicely," she cried, (she called Miss Stuyvesant, Cicely now) "is it not a delightful evening?"

"Are you enjoying yourself so much?" inquired that somewhat agitated little lady, with a glance at the countenance of her friend's attendant.

"I fear it would scarcely seem consistent in me now to say no," returned the radiant girl, with a laughing glance towards the same gentleman.

But when they were alone, the gentleman having departed on some of the innumerable errands with which ladies seem to delight in afflicting their attendant cavaliers at balls or receptions, she atoned for that glance by remarking,

"I do not find the average partner that falls to one's lot in such receptions all that fancy paints." And then finding she had repeated a phrase of Mr. Ensign's, blushed, though no one stood near her but Cicely.

"Fancy's brush would need to be dipped in but two colors to present to our eye the mass of them," was Cicely's laughing reply. "A streak of black for the coat, and a daub of white for the shirt front. *Voila tout.*"

"With perhaps a dash of red in some cases," murmured a voice over their shoulders.

They turned with hurried blushes. "Ah, Mr. Ensign," quoth Cicely in unabashed gaiety, "we reserve red for the exceptions. We did not intend to include our acknowledged friends in our somewhat sweeping assertion."

"Ah, I see, the black streak and the white daub are a symbol of, 'Er—Miss Stuyvesant—very warm this evening! Have an ice, do. *I* always have an ice after dancing; so refreshing, you know.'"

The manner in which he imitated the usual languid drawl of certain of the young scapegraces heretofore mentioned, was irresistible. Paula forgot her confusion in her mirth.

"You are blessed with a capacity for playing both rôles, I perceive," cried Cicely with unusual abandon. "Well, it is convenient, there is nothing like scope."

"Unless it is hope," whispered Mr. Ensign so low that only Paula could hear.

"But I warn you," continued Cicely, with a sweet soft laugh that seemed to carry her heart far out into the passing throng, "that we have no fondness for the model beau of the period. A dish of milk makes a very good supper but it looks decidedly pale on the dinner table."

"Yes," said Paula, eying the various young men that filed up and down before them, some pale, some dark, some handsome, some plain, but all smiling and dapper, if not debonair, "some men could be endured if only they were not *men*."

Mr. Ensign gave her a quick look, and while he laughed at the paradox, straightened himself like one who could be a man if the occasion called. She saw the action and blushed.

But their conversation was soon interrupted. Mr. Sylvester was seen returning from the supper-room, looking decidedly anxious, and while Paula was ignorant of what had transpired to annoy him, her ready spirit caught the alarm, and she was about to rush up to him and address him, when one of the waiters approached, and murmuring a few words she did not hear, handed him a card upon which she descried nothing but a simple circle. Instantly a change crossed his already agitated countenance, and advancing to the ladies with a word or two that while seemingly cheerful, struck Paula as somewhat forced, excused himself with the information that a business friend had been so inconsiderate as to importune him for an interview in the hall. And with just a nod towards Mr. Ensign, who had drawn back at his advance, left them and disappeared in the crowd about the door.

"I do not like these interruptions from business friends in a time of pleasure," cried Paula, looking after him with anxious eyes. "Did you notice how agitated he seemed, Cicely? And half an hour ago he was the picture of calm enjoyment."

"Business is beyond our comprehension, Paula," returned her friend evasively. "It is something like a neuralgic twinge, it takes a man when he least expects it. Have you told Mr. Ensign of our adventure?"

"No, but I informed Mr. Sylvester, and he said such good, true words to me, Cicely. I can never forget them."

"And I told papa; but he only frowned and made some observation about the degeneracy of the times, and the number of scamps thrown to the top by the modern methods of acquiring instantaneous fortunes."

"Your papa is sometimes hard, is he not, Cicely?"

With a flush Miss Stuyvesant allowed her eye to rest for a moment on the crowd shifting before her. "He was dug from a quarry of granite, Paula. He is both hard and substantial; capable of being hewn but not of being moulded. Of such stuff are formed monuments of enduring beauty and solidity. You must do papa justice."

"I do, but I sometimes have a feeling as if the granite column would fall and crush me, Cicely."

"You, Paula?"

Before she could again reply, Mr. Sylvester returned. His face was still pale, but it had acquired an expression of rigidity even more alarming to Paula than its previous aspect of forced merriment. Lifting her by the hand, he drew her apart.

"I shall have to leave you somewhat abruptly," said he. "An important matter demands my instant attention. Bertram is somewhere here, and will see that you and Ona arrive home in safety. You won't allow your enjoyment to be clouded by my hasty departure, will you?"

"Not if it will make you anxious. But I would rather go home with you now. I am sure Cousin Ona would be willing."

"But I am not going home at present," said he; and she ventured upon no further remonstrance.

But her enjoyment was clouded; the sight of suffering or anxiety on that face was more than she could bear; and ere long she said good-night to Cicely, and accepting the arm of Mr. Ensign, who was never very far from her side, proceeded to search for her cousin.

She found her standing in the midst of an admiring throng to whom her diamonds, if not her smiles, were an object of undoubted interest. She was in the full tide of one of her longest and most widely rambling speeches, and to Paula, with that stir of anxiety at her breast, was an image of self-satisfied complacency from which she was fain to drop her eyes.

"Mrs. Sylvester shares the honors with her husband," remarked Mr. Ensign as they drew near.

"But not the trials, or the pain, or the care?" was Paula's inward comment.

Mrs. Sylvester was not easily wooed away from a circle in which she found herself creating such an impression, but at length she yielded to Paula's importunities, and consented to accept young Mr. Sylvester's attendance to their home. The next thing was to find Bertram. Mr. Ensign engaged to do this. Leaving Paula with her cousin, who may or may not have been pleased at this sudden addition to her circle, he sought for the young man who as Mr. Mandeville was not unknown to any of the fashionable men and women of the day. It was no easy task, nor did he find him readily, but at last he came upon him leaning out of a window and gazing at a white lily which he held in his hand. Without preamble, Mr. Ensign made known his errand, and Bertram at once prepared to accompany him back to the ladies.

"By Jove! I didn't know the fellow was so handsome!" thought the former, and frowned he hardly knew why. Bertram was not handsome, but then Clarence Ensign was plain, which Bertram certainly was not.

It was to Mr. Ensign's face however that Paula's eyes turned as the two came up, and he with the ready vivacity of his natural temperament observed it, and took courage.

"I shall soon wish to measure that loop-hole of which I have spoken," said he.

And the soft look in her large dark eye as she responded, "It is always open to friends," filled up the measure of his cup of happiness; a cup which unlike hers, had not been darkened that day by the falling of earth's most dismal shadows.

XVIII.

IN THE NIGHT WATCHES.

"Shall I not take mine ease in mine inn?"—Hen. iv.

"What doth gravity out of his bed at midnight?"—Hen. iv.

"It has been the most delightful evening I have ever passed," said Mrs. Sylvester, as she threw aside her rich white mantle in her ample boudoir. "Sarah, two loops on that dolman to-morrow; do you hear? I thought my arms would freeze. Such an elegant gentleman as the Count de Frassac is! He absolutely went wild over you, Paula, but not understanding a word of English—O there, if that horrid little wretch didn't drop his spoon on my dress after all! He swore it never touched a thread of it, but just look at that spot, right in the middle of a pleating too. Paula, your opinion in regard to the lavendar was correct. I heard Mrs. Forsyth Jones whisper behind my back that lavendar always made blondes look *fade*. Of course I needed no further evidence to convince me that I had entirely succeeded in eclipsing her pale-faced daughter. Her daughter!" and the lazy gurgle echoed softly through the room, "As if every white-haired girl in the city considered herself entitled to be called a blonde!" She stopped to listen, examining herself in the glass near by. "I thought I heard Edward. It was very provoking in him to leave us in the cavalier manner in which he did. I was just going to introduce him to the count, not that he would have esteemed it much of an honor, Edward I mean, but when one has a good-looking husband—Sarah, that curtain over there hangs crooked, pull it straight this instant. Did you try the oysters, Paula? They were perfection, I shall have to dismiss Lorenzo without ceremony and procure me a cook that can make an oyster fricassee. By the way did you notice—" and so on and on for five minutes additional. Presently she burst forth with—"I do believe I know what it is to be thoroughly satisfied at last. The consideration which one receives as the wife of the president of the Madison bank is certainly very gratifying. If I had known I would feel such a change in the social atmosphere, I would have advocated Edward's dropping speculation long ago. Beauty and wealth may help one up the social ladder, but only a settled position such as he has now obtained, can carry you safely over the top. I feel at last as if we had reached the pinnacle of my ambition and had seen the ladder by which we mounted thrown down behind us. If I get my costume from Worth in time, I shall give a German next month."

Paula from her stand at the door—for some minutes she had been endeavoring to escape to her room—surveyed her cousin in wonder. She had never seen her look as she did at that moment. Any one who speaks from the heart, acquires a certain eloquence, and Ona for once was speaking from her heart. The unwonted emotion made her cheeks burn, and even her diamonds, ten thousand dollars worth as we have heard declared, were less brilliant than her eyes. Paula left her station on the door-sill and glided rapidly back to her side. "O Ona," said she, "if you would only look like that when—" she paused, what right had she to venture upon giving lessons to her benefactor.

"When what?" inquired the other, subsiding at once into her naturally languid manner. Then with a total forgetfulness of the momentary curiosity that had prompted the question, held out her head to the attendant Sarah, with a command to be relieved of her ornaments. Paula sighed and hastened to her room. She could not bring herself to mention her anxiety in regard to the still absent master of the house, to this lazily-smiling thoroughly satisfied woman.

But none the less did she herself sit up in the moonlight, listening with bended head for the sound of his step on the walk beneath. She could not sleep while he was absent; and yet the thoughts that disturbed her and kept her from her virgin pillow could not have been entirely for him, or why those wandering smiles that ever and anon passed flitting over her cheek, awakening the dimples that slumbered there, until she looked more like a dreamy picture of delight than a wakeful vision of apprehension. Not entirely for him—yet when somewhere towards three o'clock, she heard the long delayed step upon the stoop, she started up with eager eyes and a nervous gesture that sufficiently betrayed how intense was her interest in her benefactor's welfare and happiness. "If he goes to Ona's room it is all right," thought she; "but if he keeps on upstairs, I shall know that something is wrong and that he needs a comforter."

He did not stop at Ona's room; and struck with alarm, Paula opened wide her door and was about to step out to meet him, when she caught a sight of his face, and started back. Here was no anxiety, that she could palliate! The very fact that he did not observe her slight form standing before him in the brilliant moonlight, proved that a woman's look or touch was not what he was in search of; and shrinking sensitively to one side, she sat down on the edge of her dainty bed, dropping her cheek into her hand with a weary troubled gesture from which all the delight had fled and only the apprehension remained. Suddenly she started alertly up; he was coming down again, this time with a gliding muffled tread. Sliding past her door, he descended to the floor below. She could hear the one weak stair in the heavy staircase creak, and—What! he has passed Ona's room, passed the bronze figure of Luxury on the platform beneath, is on his way to the front door, has opened it, shut it softly behind him and gone out again into the blank midnight streets. What did it mean? For a moment she thought she would run down and awaken Ona, but an involuntary remembrance of how those lazy eyes would open, stare peevishly and then shut again, stopped her on the threshold of her door; and sitting down again upon the side of her bed, she waited, this time with opened eyes eagerly staring before her, and quivering form that started at each and every sound that disturbed the silence of the great echoing house. At six o'clock she again rose; he had just re-entered and this time he stopped at Ona's room.

XIX.

A DAY AT THE BANK.

"There's a divinity that shapes our ends,Rough-hew them how we will."—Hamlet.

There are days when the whole world seems to smile upon one without stint or reservation. Bertram Sylvester wending his way to the bank on the morning following the reception, was a cheerful sight to behold. Youth, health, hope spake in every lineament of his face and brightened every glance of his wide-awake eye. His new life was pleasant to him. Bach, Beethoven and Chopin were scarcely regretted now by the ambitious assistant cashier of the Madison Bank, with a friend in each of its directors and a something more than that in the popular president himself. Besides he had developed a talent for the business and was in the confidence of the cashier, a somewhat sickly man who more than once had found himself compelled to rely upon the rapidly maturing judgment of his young associate, in matters oftentimes of the utmost importance. The manner in which Bertram found himself able to respond to these various calls, convinced him that he had been correct in his opinion of his own nature, when he informed his uncle that music was his pleasure rather than his necessity.

Entering the building by way of Pearl Street, he was about to open the door leading into the bank proper, when he heard a little piping voice at his side, and turning, confronted the janitor's baby daughter. She was a sweet and interesting child, and with his usual good nature Bertram at once stopped to give her a kiss.

"I likes you," prattled she as he put her down again after lifting her up high over his head, "but I likes de oder one best."

"I hope the other one duly appreciates your preference," laughed he, and was again on the point of entering the bank when he felt or thought he felt a hand laid on his arm. It was the janitor himself this time, a worthy man, greatly trusted in the bank, but possessed of such an extraordinary peculiarity in the way of a pair of protruding eyes, that his appearance was always attended by a shock.

"Well, Hopgood, what is it?" cried Bertram, in his cheery tone.

The janitor drew back and mercifully shifted his gaze from the young man's face. "Nothing sir; did I stop you? Beg pardon," he continued, half stammering, "I'm dreadful awkward sometimes." And with a nod he sidled off towards his little one whom he confusedly took up in his arms.

Now Bertram was sure the man had touched him and that, too, with a very eager hand, but being late that morning and consequently in somewhat of a hurry, he did not stop to pursue the matter. Hastening into the Bank, he assisted the teller in opening the safe, that being his especial duty, and was taking out such papers as he himself required, when he was surprised to catch another sight of those same extraordinary organs of which I have just spoken, peering upon him from the door by which he had previously entered. They vanished as soon as he encountered them, but more than once during the morning he perceived them looking upon him from various quarters of the bank, till he felt himself growing seriously annoyed, and sending for the man, asked him what he meant by this unusual surveillance. The janitor seemed troubled, flushed painfully and fixed his eyes in manifest anxiety on the cashier who, engaged in some search of his own, was just handling over the tin boxes that lined the vault before them. Not till he had seen him shove them back into their place and leave the spot, did he venture upon his reply. "I'm sure, sir, I'm very sorry if I have annoyed you, but do you think Mr. Sylvester will be down at the usual hour?"

"I know of no reason why he should not," returned Bertram.

"I have something to say to him when he comes in," stammered the man, evidently taken aback by Bertram's look of surprise. "Will you be kind enough to ring the bell the first moment he seems to be at leisure? I don't know as it is a matter of any importance but—" He stopped, evidently putting a curb upon himself. "Can I rely on you, sir?"

"Yes, certainly, I will tell my uncle when he comes in that you want to speak to him. He will doubtless send for you at once."

The man looked embarrassed. "Excuse me, sir, but that's just what I'd rather you wouldn't do. Mr. Sylvester is always very busy and he might think I wished to annoy him about some matters of my own, sir, as indeed I have not been above doing at odd times. If you would ring when he comes in, that is all I ask."

Bertram thought this a strange request, but seeing the man so anxious, gave the required promise, and the janitor hurried off. "Curious!" muttered Bertram. "Can anything be wrong?" And he glanced about him with some curiosity as he went to his desk. But every one was at his post as usual and the countenances of all were equally undisturbed.

It was a busy morning and in the rush of various matters Bertram forgot the entire occurrence. But it was presently recalled to him by hearing some one remark, "Mr. Sylvester is late to-day," and looking up from some papers he was considering, he found it was a full hour after the time at which his uncle was in the habit of appearing. Just then he caught still another sight of the protruding eyes of Hopgood staring in upon him from the half-opened door at the end of the bank.

"The fellow's getting impatient," thought he, and experienced a vague feeling of uneasiness.

Another half hour passed. "What can have detained Mr. Sylvester?" cried Mr. Wheelock the cashier, hastily approaching Bertram.

"There is to be an important meeting of the Directors to-day, and some of the gentlemen are already coming in. Mr. Sylvester is not accustomed to keep us waiting."

"I don't know, I am sure," returned Bertram, remembering with an accession of uneasiness, the abruptness with which his uncle had left the entertainment the evening before.

"Shall I telegraph to the house?"

"No, that is not necessary. Besides Folger says he passed him on Broadway this morning."

"Going down street with a valise in his hand," that gentlemen quietly put in. Folger was the teller. "He was looking very pale and didn't see me when I nodded."

"What time was that?" asked Bertram.

"About twelve; when I went out to lunch."

A quick gasp sounded at their side, followed by a hurried cough. Turning, Bertram encountered for the fifth time the eyes of Hopgood. He had entered unperceived by the small door that separated the inner inclosure from the outer, and was now standing very close to them, eying with side-long looks the safe at their back, the faces of the gentleman speaking, yes, and even the countenances of the clerks, as they bent busily over their books.

"Did you ring, sir?" asked he, catching Bertram's look of displeasure.

"No."

The man seemed to feel the rebuke implied in this short response, and ambled softly away. But in another moment he was stopped by Bertram.

"What is the matter with you to-day, Hopgood? Can you have anything of real importance on your mind; anything connected with my uncle?"

The janitor started, and looked almost frightened. "Be careful what you say," whispered he; then with a keen look at Mr. Wheelock just then on the point of entering the directors' room, he was turning to escape by the little door just mentioned, when it opened and Mr. Stuyvesant came in. With a look almost of terror the janitor recoiled, throwing himself as it were between the latter and the door of the safe; but recovering himself, surveyed the keen quiet visage of the veteran banker with a rolling of his great eyes absolutely painful to behold. Mr. Stuyvesant, who was somewhat absorbed in thought, did not appear to notice the agitation he had caused, and with just a hurried nod followed Mr. Wheelock into the Directors' room. Instantly the janitor drew himself up with an air of relief, and shortly glancing at the clock which lacked a few minutes yet of the time fixed for the meeting, slided hastily away from Bertram's detaining hand, and disappeared in the crowd without. In another moment Bertram saw him standing at the outer door, looking anxiously up and down the street.

"Something *is* wrong," murmured Bertram. "What?" And for a moment he felt half tempted to return Mr. Stuyvesant's friendly bow with a few words expressive of his uneasiness, but the emphasis with which Hopgood had murmured the words, "Be careful what you say," unconsciously deterred him, and concealing his nervousness as best he might, he entered the Directors' office.

It was now time for the meeting to open, and the gentlemen were all seated around the low green baize table that occupied the centre of the room. Impatience was written on all their countenances. Mr. Stuyvesant especially was looking at the heavy gold watch in his hand, with a frown on his deeply wrinkled brow that did not add to its expression of benevolence. The empty seat at the head of the table stared upon Bertram uncompromisingly.

"My wife gives a reception to-day," ventured one gentleman to his neighbor.

"And I have an engagement at five that won't bear postponement."

"Sylvester has always been on hand before."

"We can't proceed without him," was the reply.

Mr. Wheelock looked thoughtful.

With a nod of his head towards such gentlemen as met his eye, Bertram hastened to a little cupboard devoted to the use of himself and uncle. Opening it, he looked within, took down a coat he saw hanging before him, and unconsciously uttered an exclamation. It was a dress-coat such as had been worn by Mr. Sylvester the evening before.

"What does this mean! My uncle has been here!" were the words that sprang to his lips; but he subdued his impulse to speak, and hastily hanging up the coat, relocked the door. Proceeding at once to the outer room, he asked two or three of the clerks if they were sure Mr. Sylvester had not been in during the day. But they all returned an unequivocal "no," and that too with a certain stare of surprise that at once convinced him he was betraying his agitation too plainly.

"I will telegraph whether Wheelock considers it necessary or not," thought he, and was moving to summon a messenger boy when he caught sight of Hopgood slowly making his way in from the street. He was very pale and walked with his eyes fixed on the ground, ominously shaking his great head in a way that bespoke an inner struggle of no ordinary nature. Bertram at once sauntered out to meet him.

"Hopgood," said he, "your evident anxiety is infectious. What has happened to make my uncle's detention a matter of such apparent import? If you do not wish to confide in me, his nephew almost his son, speak to Mr. Wheelock or to one of the directors, but don't keep anything to yourself which concerns his welfare or—What are you looking at?"

The man was gazing as if fascinated at the keys in Bertram's hand.

"Nothing sir, nothing. You must not detain me; I have nothing to say. I will wait ten minutes," he muttered to himself, glancing again at the clock. Suddenly he saw the various directors come filing out of the inner room, and darted for the second time from Bertram's detaining hand.

"I hope nothing has happened to Mr. Sylvester," exclaimed one gentleman to another as they filed by.

"If he were given to a loose ends' sort of business it would be another thing."

"He looked exceedingly well at the reception last night," exclaimed another; "but in these days—"

Suddenly there was a hush. A telegraph boy had just entered the door and was asking for Mr. Bertram Sylvester.

"Here I am," said Bertram, hastily taking the envelope presented him. Slightly turning his back, he opened it. Instantly his face grew white as chalk.

"Gentlemen," said he, "you will have to excuse my uncle to-day; a great misfortune has occurred to him." Then with a slow and horror-stricken movement, he looked about him and exclaimed, "*Mrs. Sylvester is dead.*"

A confused murmur at once arose, followed by a hurried rush; but of all the faces that flocked out of the bank, none wore such a look of blank and helpless astonishment as that of Hopgood the janitor, as with bulging eyes and nervously working hands, he slowly wended his way to the foot of the stairs and there sat down gazing into vacancy.

XX.

THE DREGS IN THE CUP.

"O eloquent, just and mightie death! whom none could advise, thou hast persuaded; what none hath dared, thou hast done; and whom all the world hath flattered, thou only hast cast out of the world and despised: thou hast drawn together all the farre stretched greatnesses; all the pride, crueltie and ambition of man and covered it all over with these two narrow words, *Hic jacet*."—Sir Walter Raleigh.

Bertram's hurried ring at his uncle's door was answered by Samuel the butler.

"What is this I hear?" cried the young man, entering with considerable agitation, "Mrs. Sylvester dead?"

"Yes sir," returned the old and trusty servant, with something like a sob in his voice. "She went out riding this morning behind a pair of borrowed horses—and being unused to Michael's way of driving, they ran away and she was thrown from the carriage and instantly killed."

"And Miss Fairchild?"

"She didn't go with her. Mrs. Sylvester was alone."

"Horrible, horrible! Where is my uncle, can I see him?"

"I don't know, sir," the man returned with a strange look of anxiety. "Mr. Sylvester is feeling very bad, sir. He has shut himself up in his room and none of his servants dare disturb him, sir."

"I should, however, like him to know I am here. In what room shall I find him?"

"In the little one, sir, at the top of the house. It has a curious lock on the door; you will know it by that."

"Very well. Please be in the hall when I come down; I may want to give you some orders."

The old servant bowed and Bertram hastened with hushed steps to ascend the stairs. At the first platform he paused. What is there in a house of death, of sudden death especially, that draws a veil of spectral unreality over each familiar object! Behind that door now inexorably closed before him, lay without doubt the shrouded form of her who but a few short hours before, had dazzled the eyes of men and made envious the hearts of women with her imposing beauty! No such quiet then reigned over the spot filled by her presence. As the vision of a dream returns, he saw her again in all her splendor. Never a brow in all the great hall shone more brightly beneath its sparkling diamonds; never a lip in the whole vast throng curled with more self-complacent pride, or melted into a more alluring smile, than that of her who now lay here, a marble image beneath the eye of day. It was as if a flowery field had split beneath the dancing foot of some laughing siren. One moment your gaze is upon the swaying voluptuous form, the half-shut beguiling eye, the white out-reaching arms upon whose satin surface a thousand loves seem perching; the next you stare horror-stricken upon the closing jaws of an awful pit, with the flash of something bright in your eyes, and the sense of a hideous noiseless rush in which earth and heaven appear to join, sink and be swallowed! Bertram felt his heart grow sick. Moving on, he passed the bronze image of Luxury lying half asleep on its bed of crumpled roses. Hideous mockery! What has luxury to do with death? She who was luxury itself has vanished from these halls. Shall the mute bronze go on smiling over its wine cup while she who was its prototype is carried by without a smile on the lips once so vermeil with pride and tropical languors!

Arrived at the top of the house, Bertram knocked at the door with the strange lock, and uttering his own name, asked if there was anything he could do here or elsewhere to show his sympathy and desire to be of use in this great and sudden bereavement. There was no immediate reply and he began to fear he would be obliged to retire without seeing his uncle, when the door was slowly opened and Mr. Sylvester came out. Instantly Bertram understood the anxiety of the servant. Not only did Mr. Sylvester's countenance exhibit the usual traces of grief and horror incident to a sudden and awful calamity, but there were visible upon it the tokens of another and still more unfathomable emotion, a wild and paralyzed look that altered the very contour of his features, and made his face almost like that of a stranger.

"Uncle, what is it?" sprang involuntarily to his lips. But Mr. Sylvester betraying by a sudden backward movement an instinctive desire to escape scrutiny, he bethought himself, and with hasty utterance offered some words of consolation that sounded strangely hollow and superficial in that dim and silent corridor. "Is there nothing I can do for you?" he finally asked.

"Everything is being done," exclaimed his uncle in a strained and altered voice; "Robert is here." And a silence fell over the hall, that Bertram dared not break.

"I have help for everything but—" He did not say what, it seemed as if something rose up in his throat that choked him.

"Bertram," said he at last in a more natural tone, "come with me."

He led him into an adjoining room and shut the door. It was a room from which the sunshine had not been excluded and it seemed as if they could both breathe more easily.

"Sit down," said his uncle, pointing to a chair. The young man did so, but Mr. Sylvester remained standing. Then without preamble, "Have you seen her?"

There was no grief in the question, only a quiet respect. Death clothes the most volatile with a garment of awe. Bertram slowly shook his head. "No," said he, "I came at once up stairs."

"There is no mark on her white body, save the least little discolored dent here," continued his uncle, pointing calmly to his temple. "She had one moment of fear while the horses ran, and then——" He gave a quick shudder and advancing towards Bertram, laid his hand on his nephew's shoulder in such a way as to prevent him from turning his head. "Bertram," said he, "I have no son. If I were to call upon you to perform a son's work for me; to obey and ask no questions, would you comply?"

"Can you ask?" sprang from the young man's lips; "you know that you have only to command for me to be proud to obey. Anything you can require will find me ready."

The hand on his shoulder weighed heavier. "It seems a strange time to talk about business, Bertram, but necessity knows no law. There is a matter in which you can afford me great assistance if you will undertake to do immediately what I ask."

"Can you doubt——"

"Hush, it is this. On this paper you will find a name; below it a number of addresses. They are all of places down town and some of them not very reputable I fear. What I desire is for you to seek out the man whose name you here see, going to these very places after him, beginning with the first, and continuing down the list until you find him. When you come upon him, he will ask you for a card. Give him one on which you will scrawl before his eyes, a circle, so. It is a token which he should instantly understand. If he does, address him with freedom and tell him that your employer—you need make use of no names—re-demands the papers made over to him this morning. If he manifests surprise or is seen to hesitate, tell him your orders are imperative. If he declares ruin will follow, inform him that you are not to be frightened by words; that your employer is as fully aware of the position of affairs as he. Whatever he says, bring the papers."

Bertram nodded his head and endeavored to rise, but his uncle's hand rested upon him too heavily.

"He is a small man; you need have no dread of him physically. The sooner you find him and acquit yourself of your task, the better I shall be pleased." And then the hand lifted.

On his way down stairs Bertram encountered Paula. She was standing in the hall and accosted him with a very trembling tone in her voice. All her questions were in regard to Mr. Sylvester.

"Have you seen him?" she asked. "Does he speak—say anything? No one has heard him utter a word since he came in from down town and saw her lying there."

"Yes, certainly; he spoke to me; he has been giving me some commissions to perform. I am on my way now to attend to them."

She drew a deep breath. "O!" she cried, "would that he had a son, a daughter, a child, some one!"

This exclamation following what had taken place above struck Bertram forcibly. "He has a son in me, Paula. Love as well as duty binds me to him. All that a child could do will I perform with pleasure. You can trust me for that."

She threw him a glance of searching inquiry. "His need is greater than it seems," whispered she. "He was deeply troubled before this terrible accident occurred. I am afraid the arrow is poisoned that has made this dreadful wound. I cannot explain myself," she went on hurriedly, "but if you indeed regard him as a father, be ready with any comfort, any help, that affection can bestow, or his necessities require. Let me feel that he has near him some stay that will not yield to pressure."

There was so much passion in this appeal that Bertram involuntarily bowed his head. "He has two friends," said he, "and here is my hand that I will never forsake him."

"I do not need to offer mine," she returned, "He is great and good enough to do without my assistance." But nevertheless she gave her hand to Bertram and with a glow of her lip and eye that made her beauty, supreme at all times, something almost supernatural in its character.

"I dared not tell him," she whispered to herself as the front door closed with the dull slow thud proper to a house of mourning. "I dare not tell any one, but—"

What lay beyond that but?

When Mr. Sylvester came in at six o'clock in the morning, Paula had risen from the bed on which she had been sitting, but not to make preparation for rest, for she could not rest. The vague shadow of some surrounding evil or threatened catastrophe was upon her, and though she forced herself to change her dress for a warmer and more suitable one, she did not otherwise break her vigil, though the necessity for it seemed to be at an end. It was a midwinter morning and the sun had not yet risen, so being chilly as well as restless, she began to pace the floor, stopping now and then to glance out of the window, in the hopes of detecting some signs of awakening day in the blank and solemn east. Suddenly as she was thus consulting the horizon, a light flashed up from below, and looking down upon the face of the extension that ran along at right angles to her window, she perceived that the shades were up in Mrs. Sylvester's boudoir. They had doubtless been left so the evening before, and Mr. Sylvester upon turning up the gas had failed to observe the fact. Instantly she felt her heart stand still, for the house being wide and the extension narrow, all that went on in that boudoir, or at least in that portion of it which Mr. Sylvester at present occupied, was easily observable from the window at which she stood; and that something was going on of a serious and important nature, was sufficiently evident from the expression of Mr. Sylvester's countenance. He was standing with his face bent towards some one seated out of sight, his wife undoubtedly, though what could have called her from her dreams—and was busily engaged in talking. The subject whatever it was, absorbed him completely. If Paula had allowed herself the thought, she would have described him as pleading and that with no ordinary vehemence. But suddenly while she gazed half fascinated and but little realizing what she was doing, he started back and a fierce change swept over his face, a certain incredulity, that presently gave way to a glance of horror and repugnance, which the quick action of his out-thrown palm sufficiently emphasized. He was pushing something from him, but what? A suggestion or a remembrance? It was impossible to determine.

The countenance of Mrs. Sylvester who that moment appeared in sight sailing across the floor in her azure wrapper, offered but little assistance in the way of explanation. Immovable under most circumstances, it was simply at this juncture a trifle more calm and cold than usual, presenting to Paula's mind the thought of a white and icy barrier, against which the most glowing of arrows must fall chilled and powerless.

"O for a woman's soul to inform that breast if but for a moment!" cried Paula, lost in the passion of this scene, while so little understanding its import. When as if in mockery to this invocation, the haughty form upon which she was gazing started rigidly erect, while the lip acquired a scorn and the eye a menace that betrayed the serpent ever in hiding under this white rose.

Paula could look no longer. This last revelation had awakened her to the fact that she was gazing upon a scene sacred to the husband and wife engaged in it. With a sense of shame she rushed to the bed and threw herself upon it, but the vision of what she had beheld would not leave her so easily. Like letters of fire upon a black ground, the panorama of looks and gestures to which she had just been witness, floated before her mind's eye, awakening a train of thought so intense that she did not know which was worse, to be there in the awful dawn dreaming over this episode of the night, or to rise and face again the reality. The fascination which all forbidden sights insensibly exert over the minds of the best of us, finally prevailed, and she slowly crept to the window to catch a parting glimpse of Mr. Sylvester's tall form hurrying blindly from the boudoir followed by his wife's cold glance. The next minute the exposed condition of the room seemed to catch that lady's attention, and with an anxious look into the dull gray morn, Mrs. Sylvester drew down the shades, and the episode was over.

Or so Paula thought; but when she was returning up stairs after her solitary breakfast—Mrs. Sylvester was too tired and Mr. Sylvester too much engaged to eat, as the attentive Samuel informed her—the door of Ona's room swung ajar, and she distinctly heard her give utterance to the following exclamation:

"What! give up this elegant home, my horses and carriage, the friends I have had such difficulty in obtaining, and the position which I was born to adorn? I had rather die!" And Paula feeling as if she had received the key to the enigma of the last night's unaccountable manifestations, was about to rush away to her own apartment, when the door swayed open again and she heard his voice respond with hard and bitter emphasis,

"And it might be better that you should. But since you will probably live, let it be according to your mind. I have not the courage—"

There the door swung to.

An hour from that Mr. Sylvester left the house with a small valise in his hand, and Mrs. Sylvester dressed in her showiest costume, entered her carriage for an early shopping excursion.

And so when Paula whispered to herself, "I did not dare to tell him; I did not dare to tell any one, but—" she thought of those terrible words, "Die? It might be better, perhaps, that you should!" and then remembered the ghastly look of immeasurable horror with which a few hours later, he staggered away from that awful burden, whose rigid lines would never again melt into mocking curves, and to whom the morning's wide soaring hopes, high reaching ambitions and boundless luxuries were now no more than the shadows of a vanished world; life, love, longing, with all their demands, having dwindled to a noisome rest between four close planks, with darkness for its present portion and beyond—what?

XXI.

DEPARTURE.

"Forever and forever, farewell Cassius.If we do meet again, why we shall smile;If not, why then, this parting was well made."—Julius Cæsar.

Samuel had received his orders to admit Mr. Bertram Sylvester to his uncle's room, at whatever hour of the day or night he chose to make his appearance. But evening wore away and finally the night, before his well-known face was seen at the door. Proceeding at once to the apartment occupied by Mr. Sylvester, he anxiously knocked. The door was opened immediately.

"Ah, Bertram, I have been expecting you all night." And from the haggard appearance of both men, it was evident that neither of them had slept.

"I have sat down but twice since I left you, and then only in conveyances. I have been obliged to go to Brooklyn, to—"

"But you have found him?"

"Yes, I found him."

His uncle glanced inquiringly at his hands; they were empty.

"I shall have to sit down," said Bertram; his brow was very gloomy, his words came hesitatingly. "I had rather have knocked my head against the wall, than have disappointed you," he murmured after a moment's pause. "But when I did find him, it was too late."

"Too late!" The tone in which this simple phrase was uttered was indescribable. Bertram slowly nodded his head.

"He had already disposed of all the papers, and favorably," he said.

"But—"

"And not only that," pursued Bertram. "He had issued orders by telegraph, that it was impossible to countermand. It was at the Forty Second Street depôt I found him at last. He was just on the point of starting for the west."

"And has he gone?"

"Yes sir."

Mr. Sylvester walked slowly to the window. It was raining drearily without, but he did not notice the falling drops or raise his eyes to the leaden skies.

"Did you meet any one?" he asked at length. "Any one that you know, I mean, or who knows you?"

"No one but Mr. Stuyvesant."

"Mr. Stuyvesant!"

"Yes sir," returned Bertram, dropping his eyes before his uncle's astonished glance. "I was coming out of a house in Broad Street when he passed by and saw me, or at least I believed he saw me. There is no mistaking him, sir, for any one else; besides it is a custom of his I am told, to saunter through the down town streets after the warehouses are all closed for the night. He enjoys the quiet I suppose, finds food for reflection in the sleeping aspect of our great city." There was gloom in Bertram's tone; his uncle looked at him curiously.

"What house was it from which you were coming when he passed you?"

"A building where Tueller and Co. do business, shady operators in paper, as you know."

"And you believed he recognized you?"

"I cannot be sure, sir. It was dark, but I thought I saw him look at me and give a slight start."

Ah, how desolate sounds the drip, drip of a ceaseless rain, when conversation languishes and the ear has time to listen!

"I will explain to Mr. Stuyvesant when I see him, that you were in search of a man with whom I had pressing business," observed Mr. Sylvester at last.

"No," murmured Bertram with effort, "it might emphasize the occurrence in his mind; let the matter drop where it is."

There was another silence, during which the drip of the rain on the window-ledge struck on the young man's ears like the premonitory thud of falling earth upon a coffin-lid. At length his uncle turned and advanced rapidly towards him.

"Bertram," said he, "you have done me a favor for which I thank you. What you have learned in the course of its accomplishment I cannot tell. Enough perhaps to make you understand why I warned you from the dangerous path of speculation, and set your feet in a way that if adhered to with steadfast purpose, ought to lead you at last to a safe and honorable prosperity. Now—No, Bertram," he bitterly interrupted himself as the other opened his lips, "I am in need of no especial commiseration, my affairs seem bound to prosper whether I will or not—now I have one more commission to give you. Miss Fairchild—" his voice quavered and he leaned heavily on the chair near which he was standing. "Have you seen her, Bertram? Is the poor child quite prostrated? Has this frightful occurrence made her ill, or does she bear up with fortitude under the shock of this sudden calamity?"

"She is not ill, but her suffering is undoubted. If you could see her and say a few words to relieve her anxiety in regard to yourself, I think it would greatly comfort her. Her main thought seems to be for you, sir."

Mr. Sylvester frowned, raised his hand with a repelling gesture, and hastily opened his lips. Bertram thought he was about to utter some passionate phrase. But instead of that he merely remarked, "I am sorry I cannot see her, but it is quite impossible. You must stand between me and this poor child, Bertram. Tell her I send her my love; tell her that I am quite well; anything to solace her and make these dark days less dreary. If she wants a friend with her, let a messenger be sent for whomever she desires. I place no restrictions upon anything you choose to do for her comfort or happiness, but let me be spared the sight of any other face than yours until this is all over. After the funeral—it nay sound ungracious, but I am far from feeling so—I shall wish to be left alone for awhile. If she can be made to understand this—"

"I think her instincts, sir, have already led her to divine your wishes. If I am not mistaken, she is even now making preparations to return to her relatives."

Mr. Sylvester gave a start. "What, so soon!" he murmured, and the sadness of his tone smote Bertram to the heart. But in another moment he recovered himself and shortly exclaimed, "Well! well! that is as it should be. You will watch over her Bertram, and see that she is kindly cared for. It would be a grief to me to have her go away with any more than the necessary regret at losing one who was always kind to *her*."

"I will look after her as after a sister," returned Bertram. "She shall miss no attention which I can supply."

With a look Mr. Sylvester expressed his thanks. Then while Bertram again attempted to speak, he gave him a cordial pressure of the hand, and withdrew once more to his favorite spot.

And the rain beat, beat, and it sounded more and more like the droppings of earth upon a nailed down coffin-lid.

The funeral was a large one. The largest some said that had ever been seen in that quarter of the city. If Mrs. Sylvester's position had not been what it was, the sudden and awful nature of her death, would have been sufficient to draw together a large crowd. Among those who thus endeavored to show their respect was Miss Stuyvesant.

"I could not join you here in your pleasures," she whispered to Paula in the short interview they had upstairs, preparatory to the services, "but I cannot keep away in the dark hours!" And from her look and the clasp of her hand, Paula gained fresh courage to endure the slow pressure of anxiety and grief with which she was secretly burdened.

Moreover she had the pleasure of introducing her beloved friend to Mr. Bertram Sylvester, a pleasure which she had long promised herself whenever the opportunity should arrive, as Miss Stuyvesant was somewhat of an enthusiast as regards music. She did not notice particularly then, but she remembered afterwards, with what a blushing cheek and beautiful glance the dainty young girl received his bow, and responded to his few respectful words of pleasure at meeting the daughter of a man whom he had learned to regard with so much respect.

Mr. Sylvester was in a room by himself. The few glimpses obtained of him by his friends, convinced them all, that this trouble touched him more deeply than those who knew his wife intimately could have supposed. Yet he was calm, and already wore that fixed look of rigidity which was henceforth to distinguish the expression of his fine and noble features.

In the ride to Greenwood he spoke little. Paula who sat in the carriage with him did not receive a word, though now and then his eye wandered towards her with an expression that drove the blood to her heart, and made the whole day one awful memory of incomprehensible agony and dim but terrible forebodings. The ways of the human soul, in its crises of grief or remorse were so new to her. She had passed her life beside rippling streams and in peaceful meadows, and now all at once, with shadow on shadow, the dark pictures of life settled down before her, and she could not walk without stumbling upon jagged rocks, deep yawning chasms and caves of impenetrable gloom.

The sight of the grave appalled her. To lay in such a bed as that, the fair and delicate head that had often found the downy pillows of its azure couch too hard for its languid pressure. To hide in such a dismal, deep, dark gap, a form so white and but a little while before, so imposing in its splendor and so commanding in its requirements. The thought of heaven brought no comfort. The beauty they had known lay here; soulless, inert, rigid and responseless, but here. It was gifted with no wings with which to rise. It owned no attachment to higher spheres. Death had scattered the leaves of this white rose, but from all the boundless mirror of the outspread heavens, no recovered semblance of its perfected beauty, looked forth to solace Paula or assuage the misery of her glance into this gloomy pit. Ah, Ona, the social ladder reaches high, but it does not scale the regions where your poor soul could find comfort now.

Bertram saw the white look on Paula's face and silently offered his arm. But there are moments when no mortal help can aid us; instants when the soul stands as solitary in the universe, as the ship-wrecked mariner on a narrow strip of rock in a boundless sea. Life may touch, but eternity enfolds us; we are single before God and as such must stand or fall.

Upon their return to the house, Mr. Sylvester withdrew with a few intimate friends to his room, and Paula, lonely beyond expression, went to her own empty apartment to finish packing her trunks and answer such notes as had arrived during her absence. For attention from outsiders was only too obtrusive. Many whom she had never met save in the most formal intercourse, flooded her now with expressions of condolence, which if they had not been all upon one pattern and that the most conventional, might have afforded her some relief. Two or three of the notes were precious to her and these she stowed safely away, one contained a deliberate offer of marriage from a wealthy old stock-broker; this she as deliberately burned after she had written a proper refusal. "He thinks I have no home," she murmured.

And had she? As she paced through the silent halls and elaborately furnished rooms on her way to her solitary dinner, she asked herself if any place would ever seem like home after this. Not that she was infatuated by its elegance. The lofty walls might dwindle, the gorgeous furniture grow dim, the works of beauty disappear, the whole towering structure contract to the dimensions of a simple cottage or what was worse, a seedy down-town house, if only the something would remain, the something that made return to Grotewell seem like the bending back of a towering stalk to the ground from which it had taken its root. "If?" she cried—and stopped there, her heart swelling she knew not why. Then again, "I thought I had found a father!" Then after a longer pause, a wild uncontrollable; "Bless! bless! bless!" which seemed to re-echo in the room long after her lingering step had left it.

"Will he let me go without a word?"

It was early morning and the time had come for Paula's departure. She was standing on the threshold of her room, her hands clasped, her eyes roving up and down the empty halls. "Will he let me go without a word?"

"O Miss Paula, what do you think?" cried Sarah, creeping slowly towards her from the spectral recesses of a dim corner. "Jane says Mr. Sylvester was up all last night too. She heard him go down stairs about midnight and he went through all the rooms like a gliding spectre and into *her* room too!" she fearfully whispered; "and what he did there no one knows, but when he came out he locked the door, and this morning the cook heard him give orders to Samuel to have the trunks that were ready in Mrs. Sylvester's room taken away. O Miss, do you think he can be going to give all those beautiful things to you?"

Paula recoiled in horror. "Sarah!" said she, and could say no more. The vision of that tall form gliding through the desolate house at midnight, bending over the soulless finery of his dead wife, perhaps stowing it away in boxes, came with too powerful a suggestion to her mind.

"Shure, I thought you would be pleased," murmured the girl and disappeared again into one of the dim recesses.

"Will he let me go without a word?"

"Miss Paula, Mr. Bertram Sylvester is waiting at the door in a carriage," came in low respectful tones to her ears, and Samuel's face full of regret appeared at the top of the stairs.

"I am coming," murmured the sad-hearted girl, and with a sob which she could not control, she took her last look of the pretty pink chamber in which she had dreamed so many dreams of youthful delight, and perhaps of youthful sorrow also, and slowly descended the stairs. Suddenly as she was passing a door on the second floor, she heard a low deep cry.

"Paula!"

She stopped and her hand went to her heart, the reaction was so sudden. "Yes," she murmured, standing still with great heart-beats of joy, or was it pain?

The door slowly opened. "Did you think I could let you go without a blessing, my Paula, my little one!" came in those deep heart-tones which always made her tears start. And Mr. Sylvester stepped out of the shadows beyond and stood in the shadows at her side.

"I did not know," she murmured. "I am so young, so feeble, such a mote in this great atmosphere of anguish. I longed to see you, to say good-bye, to thank you, but—" tears stopped her words; this was a parting that rent her leader heart.

Mr. Sylvester watched her and his deep chest rose spasmodically. "Paula," said he, and there was a depth in his tone even she had never heard before, "are these tears for me?"

With a strong effort she controlled herself, looked up and faintly smiled. "I am an orphan," she gently murmured; "you have been kind and tender to me beyond words; I have let myself love you as a father."

A spasm crossed his features, the hand he had lifted to lay upon her head fell at his side, he surveyed her with eyes whose despairing fondness told her that her love had been more than met by this desolate childless man. But he did not reply as seemed natural, "Be to me then as a child. I can offer you no mother to guide or watch over you, but one parent is better than none. Henceforth you shall be known as my daughter." Instead of that he shook his head mournfully, yearningly but irrevocably, and said, "To be your father would have been a dear position to occupy. I have sometimes hoped that I might be so blessed as to call it mine, but that is all past now. Your father I can never be. But I can bless you," he murmured brokenly, "not as I did that day in your aunt's little cottage, but silently and from afar as God always meant you should be blessed by me. Good-bye, Paula."

Then all the deeps in her great nature broke up. She did not weep, but she looked at him with her large dark eyes and the cry in them smote his heart. With a struggle that blanched his face, he kept his arms at his side, but his lips worked in agony, and he slowly murmured, "If after a time your heart loves me like this, and you are willing to bear shadow as well as sunshine with me, come back with your aunt and sit at my hearthstone, not as my child but as a dear and honored guest. I will try and be worthy—" He paused, "Will you come, Paula?"

"Yes, yes."

"Not soon, not now," he murmured, "God will show you when."

And with nothing but a look, without having touched her or so much as brushed her garments with his, he retired again into his room.

XXII.

HOPGOOD.

"Give it an understanding but no tongue."—Hamlet.

Hopgood was a man who could keep a secret, but who made so much ado in the process that he reminded one of the placard found posted up somewhere out west which reads, "A treasure of gold concealed here; don't dig!" Or so his wife used to say, and she ought to know, for she had lived with him five years, three of which he had spent in the detective service.

"If he would only trust the wife of his bosom with whatever he's got on his mind, instead of ambling around the building with his eyes rolling about like peas in a caldron of boiling water, one might manage to take some comfort in life, and not hurt anybody either. For two days now, ever since the wife of Mr. Sylvester died and Mr. Sylvester has been away from the bank, he's acted just like a lunatic. Not that that has anything to do with his gettin up of nights and roamin down five pair of stairs to see if the watchman is up to his duty, or with his askin a dozen times a day if I remembers how Mr. Sylvester found him and me, well nigh starvin in Broad Street, and gave him the good word which got him into this place? O no! O no, of course not! But *something* has, and while he persists in shutting out from his breast the woman he swore to love, honor, and cherish, that woman is not bound to bear the trials of life with patience. Every time he jumps out of his chair at the sound of Mr. Sylvester's name, and some one is always mentionin' it, I plumps me down on mine with an expression of my views regarding a kitchen stove that does all its drawin' when the oven's empty."

So spake Mrs. Hopgood to her special crony and constant visitor, Mrs. Kirkshaw of Water Street, pursing up a mouth that might have been good-natured if she had ever given it an opportunity. But Mrs. Kirkshaw who passed for a gossip with her neighbors, was a philosopher in the retirement of the domestic circle and did not believe in the blow for blow system.

"La!" quoth she, with a smoothing out of her apron suggestive of her employment as laundress, "show a dog that you want his bone and you'll never get it. Husbands is like that very stove you've been a slanderin of. Rattle on coal when the fire's low and you put it out entirely; but be a bit patient and drop it on piece by piece, coaxing-like, and you'll have a hot stove afore you know it."

Which suggestion struck Mrs. Hopgood like a revelation, and for a day and night she resorted to the coaxing system; the result of which was to send Mr. Hopgood out of the room to sit on the stairs in mortal terror, lest his good nature should get the better of his discretion. His little daughter, Constantia Maria—so named and so called from two grandmothers, equally exacting in their claims and equally impecunious as regards their resources—was his sole solace in this long vigil. Her pretty innocent prattle scarcely disturbed his meditation, while it soothed his nerves, and with no one by but this unsuspecting child, he could roll his great eyes to his heart's content without fear of her descrying anything in them, but the love with which her own little heart abounded.

On the morning after the funeral, however, Constantia Maria was restored to his wife's arms on the plea that she did not seem quite well, and Hopgood went out and sat alone. In a few minutes, however, he returned, and ambling restlessly up and down the room, stopped before his persistently smiling wife and said somewhat tremulously:

"If Mr. Sylvester takes a notion to come up and see Constantia Maria to-day, I hope you'll take the opportunity to finish your ironing or whatever else it is you may have to do. I've noticed he seems a little shy with the child when you are around."

"Shy with the child when I am around! well I do declare!" exclaimed she, forgetting her late rôle in her somewhat natural indignation. "And what have I ever done to frighten Mr. Sylvester? Nothing but putting on of a clean apron, when he comes in and a dustin' of the best chair for his use. It's a trick of yours to get a chance of speakin' to him alone, and I'll not put up with it. As if it wasn't bad enough to have a kettle with the nozzle dangling, without living with a man who has a secret he won't share with his own wife and the mother of his innocent babe."

With a start the worthy man stared at her till he grew red in the face, probably with the effort of keeping his eyes steady for so long a time. "Who told you I had a secret?" said he.

"Who told me?" and then she laughed, though in a somewhat hysterical way, and sat down in the middle of the floor and shook and shook again. "Hear the man!" she cried. And she told him the story of the placard out west and then asked him, "if he thought she didn't remember how he used to act when he was a chasin' up of a thief in the days when he was on the police force."

"But," he cried, quite as pale now as he had been florid the moment before, "I'm not in the police force now and you are acting quite silly and I've no patience with you." And he was making for the door, presumably to sit upon the stairs, when with a late repentance she seized him by the arm and said:

"La now," an expression she had caught from Mrs. Kirkshaw, "I didn't mean nothin' by my talk. Come back, John; Constantia Maria is not well, and if Mr. Sylvester comes up to see her, I'll just slip out and leave you alone."

And upon that he told her she was a good wife and that if he had any secret from her it was only because he was a poor man. "Honesty and prudence are all the treasures I possess to keep us three from starving. Shall I part with either of them just to satisfy your curiosity?" and being a good woman at heart, she said "no," though she secretly concluded that prudence in his case involved trust in one's wife first, and disbelief in the rest of the world afterward; and took her future resolutions accordingly.

"Well, Hopgood, you look anxious; do you want to speak to me?"

The janitor eyed the changed and melancholy face of his patron, with an expression in which real sympathy for his trouble, struggled with the respectful awe which Mr. Sylvester's presence was calculated to inspire.

"If you please," said he, speaking very low, for more or less of the bank employees were moving busily to and fro, "Constantia Maria is not well and she has been asking all day for the *dear man*, as she insists upon calling you, sir, with many apologies for the freedom."

Mr. Sylvester smiled with a faint far-away look in his dark eye that made Hopgood stare uneasily out of the window. "Sick! why then I must go up and see her," he returned in a matter-of-fact way that proved his visits in that direction were of no uncommon occurrence. "A moment more and I shall be at liberty."

Hopgood bowed and renewed his stare out of the window, with an intensity happily spared from serious consequences to the passers-by, by the merciful celerity with which Mr. Sylvester procured his overcoat, put such papers in his pocket as he required, and joined him.

"Constantia Maria, here is Mr. Sylvester come to see you."

It was a pleasure to observe how the little thing brightened in her mother's arms, where but a moment before she had lain quite pale and still, and slipping to the ground rushed up to meet the embrace of this stern and melancholy-faced man. "I am so glad you have come," she cried over and over again; and her little arms went round his neck, and her soft cheek nestled against his, with a content that made the mother's eyes sparkle with pleasure, as obedient to her promise, she quietly left the room.

And Mr. Sylvester? If any one had seen the abandon with which he yielded to her caresses and returned them, he would have understood why this child should have loved him with such extraordinary affection. He kissed her forehead, he kissed her cheek, and seemed never weary of smoothing down her bright and silky curls. She reminded him of Geraldine. She had the same blue eyes and caressing ways. From the day he had come upon his old friend Hopgood in a condition of necessity almost of want, this blue-eyed baby had held its small sceptre over his lonely heart, and unbeknown to the rest of the world, had solaced many a spare five minutes with her innocent prattle. The Hopgoods understood the cause of his predilection and were silent. It was the one thing Mrs. Hopgood never alluded to in her gossips with Mrs. Kirkshaw. But to-day the attentions of Mr. Sylvester to the little one seemed to make the janitor restless. He walked up and down the narrow room uneasily surveying the pair out of the corner of his great glassy eyes, till even Mr. Sylvester noticed his unusual manner and put the child down, observing with a sigh, "You think she is not well enough for any excitement?"

"No sir, it is not that," returned the other uneasily, with a hasty look around him. "The fact is, I have something to say to you, sir, about—a discovery—I made the other day." His words came very slowly, and he looked down with great embarrassment.

Mr. Sylvester frowned slightly, and drew himself up to the full height of his very imposing figure. "A discovery," repeated he, "when?"

"The day you paid that early visit to the bank, sir, the day Mrs. Sylvester died."

The frown on Mr. Sylvester's brow grew deeper. "The day—" he began, and stopped.

"Excuse me, sir," exclaimed Hopgood with a burst. "I ought not to have mentioned it, but you asked me *when*, and I—"

"What was this discovery?" inquired his superior, imperatively.

"Nothing much," murmured the other now all in a cold sweat. "But I felt as if I ought to tell you. You have been my benefactor, sir, I can never forget what you have done for me and mine. If I saw death or bereavement between me and any favor I could do for you, sir, I would not hesitate to risk them. I am no talker, sir, but I am true and I am grateful." He stopped, choked, and his eyes rolled frightfully. Mr. Sylvester looked at him, grew a trifle pale, and put the little child away that was nestling up against his knee.

"You have not told me what you have discovered," said he.

"Well, sir, only this." And he took from his pocket a small roll of paper which he unfolded and held out in his hand. It contained a gold tooth-pick somewhat bent and distorted.

A flush dark and ominous crept over Mr. Sylvester's cheek. He glanced sternly at the trembling janitor, and uttered a short, "Well?"

"I found it on the floor of the bank just after you went out the other morning," the other pursued well-nigh inaudibly. "It was lying near the safe. As it was not there when you went in, I took it for granted it was yours. Am I right, sir?"

The anxious tone in which this last question was uttered, the studied way in which the janitor kept his eyes upon the floor could not have been unnoticed by Mr. Sylvester, but he simply said,

"I have lost mine, that may very possibly be it."

The janitor held it towards him; his eyes did not leave the floor. "The responsibility of my position here is sometimes felt by me to be very heavy," muttered the man in a low, unmodulated tone. It was his duty in those days previous to the Manhattan Bank robbery, to open the vault in the morning, procure the books that were needed, and lay them about on the various desks in readiness for the clerks upon their arrival. He had also the charge of the boxes of the various customers of the bank who chose to entrust their valuables to its safe keeping; which boxes were kept, together with the books, in that portion of the vault to which he had access. "I should regret my comfortable situation here, but if it was necessary, I would go without a murmur, trusting that God would take care of my poor little lamb."

"Hopgood, what do you mean?" asked Mr. Sylvester somewhat sternly. "Who talks about dismissing you?"

"No one," responded the other, turning aside to attend to some trivial matter. "But if ever you think a younger or a fresher man would be preferable in my place, do not hesitate to make the change your own necessities or that of the Bank may seem to require."

Mr. Sylvester's eye which was fixed upon the janitor's face, slowly darkened.

"There is something underlying all this," said he, "what is it?"

At once and as if he had taken his resolution, the janitor turned. "I beg your pardon," said he, "I ought to have told you in the first place. When I opened the vaults as usual on the morning of which I speak, I found the boxes displaced; that was nothing if you had been to them, sir; but what did alarm me and make me feel as if I had held my position too long was to find that one of them was unlocked."

Mr. Sylvester fell back a step.

"It was Mr. Stuyvesant's box, sir, and I remember distinctly seeing him lock it the previous afternoon before putting it back on the shelf."

The arms which Mr. Sylvester had crossed upon his breast tightened spasmodically. "And it has been in that condition ever since?" asked he.

The janitor shook his head. "No," said he, taking his little girl up in his arms, possibly to hide his countenance. "As you did not come down again on that day, I took the liberty of locking it with a key of my own when I went to put away the books and shut the vault for the night." And he quietly buried his face in his baby's floating curls, who feeling his cheek against her own put up her hand and stroked it lovingly, crying in her caressing infantile tones,

"Poor papa! poor tired papa."

Mr. Sylvester's stern brow contracted painfully. The look with which his eye sought the sky without, would have made Paula's young heart ache. Taking the child from her father's clasp, he laid her on the bed. When he again confronted the janitor his face was like a mask.

"Hopgood," said he, "you are an honest man and a faithful one; I appreciate your worth and have had confidence in your judgment. Whom have you told of this occurrence beside myself?"

"No one, sir."

"Another question; if Mr. Stuyvesant had required his box that day and had found it in the condition you describe, what would you have replied to his inquiries?"

The janitor colored to the roots of his hair in an agony of shame Mr. Sylvester may or may not have appreciated, but replied with the straightforward earnestness of a man driven to bay, "I should have been obliged to tell him the truth sir; that whereas I had no personal knowledge of any one but myself, having been to the vaults since the evening before, I was called upon early that morning to open the outside door to you, sir, and that you came into the bank," (he did not say looking very pale, agitated and unnatural, but he could not help remembering it) "and finding no one on duty but myself,—the watchman having gone up stairs to take his usual cup of coffee before going home for the day—you sent me out of the room on an errand, which delayed me some little time, and that when I came back I found you gone, and every thing as I had left it except that small pick lying on the floor."

The last words were nearly inaudible but they must have been heard by Mr. Sylvester, for immediately upon their utterance, the hand which unconsciously had kept its hold upon the tooth-pick, opened and with an uncontrollable gesture flung the miserable tell-tale into the stove near by.

"Hopgood," said the stately gentleman, coming nearer and holding him with his eyes till the poor man turned pale and cold as a stone, "has Mr. Stuyvesant had occasion to open his box since you locked it?"

"Yes sir, he called for it yesterday afternoon."

"And who gave it to him?"

"I sir."

"Did he appear to miss anything from it?"

"No, sir."

"Do you believe, Hopgood, that there was anything missing from it?"

The janitor shrank like a man subjected to the torture. He fixed his glance on Mr. Sylvester's face and his own gradually lightened.

"No sir!" said he at last, with a gasp that made the little one lift her curly head from her pillow and shake it with a slow and wistful motion strange to see in a child of only two years.

The proud man bowed, not with the severity however that might have been expected; indeed his manner was strangely shadowed, and though his lip betrayed no uneasiness and his eye neither faltered or fell, there was a vague expression of awe upon his countenance, which it would take more than the simple understanding of the worthy but not over subtle man before him, to detect much less to comprehend.

"You may be sure that Mr. Stuyvesant will never complain of any one having tampered with his effects while you are the guardian of the vaults," exclaimed Mr. Sylvester in clear ringing tones. "As for his box being open, it is right that I should explain that it was the result of a mistake. I had occasion to go to a box of my own in

156 | P a g e

a hurry that morning, and misled by the darkness and my own nervousness perhaps, took up his instead of my own. Not till I had opened it—with the tooth-pick, Hopgood, for I had been to a reception and did not have my keys with me—did I notice my mistake. I had intended to explain the matter to Mr. Stuyvesant, but you know what happened that day, and since then I have thought nothing of it."

The janitor's face cleared to its natural expression. "You are very kind, sir, to explain yourself to me," said he; "it was not necessary." But his lightened face spoke volumes. "I have been on the police force and I know how to hold my tongue when it is my duty, but it is very hard work when the duty is on the other side. Have you any commands for me?"

Mr. Sylvester shook his head, and his eye roamed over the humble furniture and scanty comforts of this poor man's domicile. Hopgood thought he might be going to offer him some gift or guerdon, and in a low distressed tone spoke up:

"I shall not try to ask your pardon, sir, for anything I have said. Honesty that is afraid to show itself, is no honesty for me. I could not meet your eye, knowing that I was aware of any circumstance of which you supposed me ignorant. What I know, you must know, as long as I remain in the position you were once kind enough to procure for me. And now that is all I believe, sir."

Mr. Sylvester dropped his eyes from the bare walls over which they had been restlessly wandering, and fixed them for a passing moment on the countenance of the man before him. Then with a grave action he lifted his hat from his head, and bowed with the deference he might have shown to one of his proudest colleagues, and without another look or word, quietly left the room.

Hopgood in his surprise stared after him somewhat awe-struck. But when the door had quite closed, he caught up his child almost passionately in his arms, and crushing her against his breast, asked, while his eye roamed round the humble room that in its warmth and comfort was a palace to him, "Will he take the first opportunity to have me dismissed, or will his heart forgive the expression of my momentary doubts, for the sake of this poor wee one that he so tenderly fancies?"

The question did not answer itself, and indeed it was one to which time alone could reply.

BOOK III.

THE JAPHA MYSTERY.

XXIII.

THE POEM.

"I've shot my arrow o'er the houseAnd hurt my brother."—Hamlet.

When Miss Belinda first saw Paula, she did not, like her sister, remark upon the elegance of her appearance, the growth of her beauty, or the evidences of increased refinement in the expression of her countenance and the carriage of her form, but with her usual penetration noted simply, the sadness in her eye and the tremulous motion of her lip.

"You had then become fond of your cousin?" queried she with characteristic bluntness.

Paula not understanding the motive of this remark, questioned her with a look.

"Young faces do not grow pale or bright eyes become troubled without a cause. Grief for your cousin might explain it, but if you have suffered from no grief—"

"My cousin was very kind to me," hurriedly interrupted Paula. "Her death was very sudden and very heart-rending."

"So it was;" returned Miss Belinda, "and I expected to see you look worn and sad but not restless and feverish. You have a living grief, Paula, what is it?"

The young girl started and looked down. For the first time in her life she wished to avoid that penetrating glance. "If I have, I cannot talk of it," she murmured. "I have experienced so much this past week; my coming away was so unexpected, that I hardly understand my own feelings, or realize just what it is that troubles me most. All that I know is, that I am very tired and so sad, it seems as if the sun would never shine again."

"There is then something you have not written me?" inquired the inexorable Miss Belinda.

"The experiences of this last week could never be written,—or told," returned Paula with a droop of her head. "Upon some things our better wisdom places a stone which only the angels can roll away. The future lies all open before us; do not let us disturb the past."

And Miss Belinda was forced to be content lest she should seem to be over anxious.

Not so the various neighbors and friends to whom the lengthened sojourn of one of their number in an atmosphere of such wealth and splendor, possessed something of the charm of a forbidden romance. For months Paula was obliged to endure questions, that it required all her self-control to answer with calmness and propriety. But at length the most insatiable gossip amongst them was satisfied; Paula's figure was no longer a novelty in their streets; curiosity languished and the young girl was allowed to rest.

And now could those who loved her, discern that with the lapse of time and the daily breathings of her native air, the sad white look had faded from her face, leaving it a marvel of freshness and positive, if somewhat spiritualized, beauty. The print of deeper thoughts and holier yearnings was there, but no sign of blighted hopes or uncomprehended passions. A passing wind had blown the froth from off the cup, but had not disturbed the sparkle of the wine. She had looked in the face of grief, but had not as yet been clasped in her relentless arms. Only two things could vitally disturb her; a letter from Cicely, or a sudden meeting in the village streets with that elderly lady who haunted the Japha mansion. The former because it recalled a life around which her fancies still played with dangerous persistency, and the latter because it aroused vain and inexplicable conjectures as to that person's strange and lingering look in her direction. Otherwise she was happy; finding in this simple village-life a meaning and a purpose which her short but passionate outlook on a broader field, had taught her, perhaps, both to detect and comprehend. She no longer walked solitary with nature. The woods, the mountains with all their varying panoply of exuberant verdure, had acquired a human significance. At her side went the memories of beloved faces, the thoughts of trusted friends. From the clouds looked forth a living eye, and in the sound of rustling leaf and singing streamlet, spake the voices of human longing and human joy.

Her aunts had explained their position to Paula and she had responded by expressing her determination to be a teacher. But they would not hear of that at present, and while she waited their pleasure in the matter, she did what she could to assist them in their simple home-life and daily duties, lending her beauty to tasks that would have made the eyes of some of her quondam admirers open with surprise, if only they could have followed the action of her hands, after having once caught a glimpse of the face that brightened above them. And so the summer months went by and September came.

There was to be an entertainment in the village and Paula was to assist. The idea had come from her aunt and was not to be rejected. In one of the strange incomprehensible moods which sometimes came upon her at this time, she had written a poem, and nothing would do but that she mast read it before the assembled company of neighbors and friends, that were to be gathered at the Squire's house on this gala evening. She did not wish to do it. The sacred sense of possession passes when we uncover our treasure to another's eyes, giving way to a lower feeling not to be courted by one of Paula's sensitive nature. Besides she would rather have poured this first outburst of secret enthusiasm into other ears than these; but she had given her word and the ordeal must be submitted to. There are many who remember how she looked on that night. She had arrayed herself for the occasion, in the prettiest of her dresses, and mindful of Ona's injunction, did not mar the effect of its soft and uniform gray with any hint of extraneous color. The result was that they saw only her beauty; and what beauty! A very old man, an early settler in the village, who had tottered out to enjoy a last glimpse of life before turning his aged face to the wall, said it made the thought of heaven a little more real. "I can go home and think how the angels look," said he in his simple, half-childish way. And no one contradicted him, for there was a still light on her face that was less of earth than heaven, though why it should rest there to-night she least of all could have told, for her poem had to do with earth and its deepest passions and its wildest unrest. It was a clarion blast, not a dreaming rhapsody, that lay coiled up in the paper she held in her hand.

My readers must pardon me if I give them Paula's poem, for without it they would not understand its effect and consequent result. It was called, "The Defence of the Bride," and was of the old ballad order. As she rose to read, many of the younger ones in the audience began cautiously to move to one side, but at the first words, young as well as old paused and listened where they stood, for her voice was round and full, and the memory of clashing spears and whirling battle-axes that informed the war-song which she had heard Bertram play, was with her, to give color to her tones and fire to her glance.

THE DEFENCE OF THE BRIDE.

He was coming from the altar when the tocsin rang alarm,With his fair young wife beside him, lovely in her bridal charm;But he was not one to palter with a duty, or to slightThe trumpet-call of honor for his vantage or delight.

Turning from the bride beside him to his stern and martial train,From their midst he summoned to him the brothers of Germain;At the word they stepped before him, nine strong warriors brave and true,From the youngest to the eldest, Enguerrand to mighty Hugh.

"Sons of Germain, to your keeping do I yield my bride to-day.Guard her well as you do love me; guard her well and holily.Dearer than mine own soul to me, you will hold her as your life,'Gainst the guile of seeming friendship and the force of open strife."

"We will guard her," cried they firmly; and with just another glanceOn the yearning and despairing in his young wife's countenance,Gallant Beaufort strode before them down the aisle and through the door,And a shadow came and lingered where the sunlight stood before.

Eight long months the young wife waited, watching from her bridal roomFor the coming of her husband up the valley forest's gloom.Eight long months the sons of Germain paced the ramparts and the wall,With their hands upon their halberds ready for the battle-call.

Then there came a sound of trumpets pealing up the vale below,And a dozen floating banners lit the forest with their glow,And the bride arose like morning when it feels the sunlight nigh,And her smile was like a rainbow flashing from a misty sky.

But the eldest son of Germain lifting voice from off the wall,Cried aloud, "It is a stranger's and not Sir Beaufort's call;Have you ne'er a slighted lover or a kinsman with a heartBase enough to seek his vengeance at the sharp end of the dart?"

"There is Sassard of the Mountains," answered she without guile,"While I wedded at the chancel, he stood mocking in the aisle;And my maidens say he swore there that for all my plighted vow,They would see me in his castle yet upon Morency's brow."

"It is Sassard and no other then," her noble guardian cried;"There is craft in yonder summons," and he rung his sword beside."To the walls, ye sons of Germain! and as each would hold his lifeFrom the bitter shame of falsehood, let us hold our master's wife."

"Can you hold her, can you shield her from the breezes that await?"Cried the stinging voice of Sassard from his stand beside the gate."If you have the power to shield her from the sunlight and the wind,You may shield her from stern Sassard when his falchion is untwined."

"We can hold her, we can shield her," leaped like fire from off the wall,And young Enguerrand the valiant, sprang out before them all."And if breezes bring dishonor, we will guard her from their breath,Though we yield her to the keeping of the sacred arms of Death."

And with force that never faltered, did they guard her all that day,Though the strength of triple armies seemed to battle in the fray,The old castle's rugged ramparts holding firm against the foe,As a goodly dyke resisteth the whelming billow's flow.

But next morning as the sunlight rose in splendor over all,Hugh the mighty, sank heart-wounded in his station on the wall,At the noon the valiant Raoul of the merry eye and heart,Gave his beauty and his jestings to the foeman's jealous dart.

Gallant Maurice next sank faltering with a death wound 'neath his hair,But still fighting on till Sassard pressed across him up the stair.Generous Clement followed after, crying as his spirit passed,"Sons of Germain to the rescue, and be loyal to the last!"

Gentle Jaspar, lordly Clarence, Sessamine the doughty brand,Even Henri who had yielded ne'er before to mortal hand;One by one they fall and perish, while the vaunting foemen pourThrough the breach and up the courtway to the very turret's door.

Enguerrand and Stephen only now were left of all that nine,To protect the single stairway from the traitor's fell design;But with might as 'twere of thirty, did they wield the axe and brand,Striving in their desperation the fierce onslaught to withstand.

But what man of power so godlike he can stay the billow's wrack,Or with single-handed weapon hold an hundred foemen back!As the sun turned sadly westward, with a wild despairing cry,Stephen bowed his noble forehead and sank down on earth to die.

"Ah ha!" then cried cruel Sassard with his foot upon the stair,"Have I come to thee, my boaster?" and he whirled his sword in air."Thou who pratest of thy power to protect her to the death,What think'st thou now of Sassard and the wind's aspiring breath?"

"What I think let this same show you," answered fiery Enguerrand,And he poised his lofty battle-ax with sure and steady hand;"Now as Heaven loveth justice, may this deathly weapon fallOn the murderer of my brothers and th' undoer of us all."

With one mighty whirl he sent it; flashing from his hand it came,Like the lightning from the heavens in a whirl of awful flame,And betwixt the brows of Sassard and his two false eyeballs passed,And the murderer sank before it, like a tree before the blast.

"Now ye minions of a traitor if you look for vengeance, come!"And his voice was like a trumpet when it clangs a victor home.But a cry from far below him rose like thunder upward, "Nay!Let them turn and meet the *husband* if they hunger for the fray."

O the yell that sprang to heaven as that voice swept up the stair,And the slaughter dire that followed in another moment there!From the least unto the greatest, from the henchman to the lord,Not a man on all that stairway lived to sheath again his sword.

At the top that flame-bound forehead, at the base that blade of fire—'Twas the meeting of two tempests in their potency and ire.Ere the moon could falter inward with its pity and its woe,Beaufort saw the path before him unencumbered of the foe.

Saw his pathway unencumbered and strode up and o'er the floor,Even to the very threshold of his lovely lady's door,And already in his fancy did he see the golden beamOf her locks upon his shoulder and her sweet eyes' happy gleam:

When behold a form upstarting from the shadows at his side.That with naked sword uplifted barred the passage to his bride;It was Enguerrand the dauntless, but with staring eyes and hairBlowing wild about a forehead pale as snow in moonlit glare.

"Ah my master, we have held her, we have guarded her," he said,"Not a shadow of dishonor has so much as touched her head.Twenty wretches lie below there with the brothers of Germain,Twenty foemen of her honor that I, Enguerrand, have slain.

"But one other foe remaineth, one remaineth yet," he cried,"Which it fits this hand to punish ere you cross unto your bride.It is I, Enguerrand!" shrieked he; "and as I have slain the rest,So I smite this foeman also!"—and his sword plunged through his breast.

O the horror of that moment! "Art thou mad my Enguerrand?"Cried his master, striving wildly to withdraw the fatal brand.But the stern youth smiling sadly, started back from his embrace,While a flash like summer lightning, flickered direful on his face.

"Yes, a traitor worse than Sassard;" and he pointed down the stair,"For my heart has dared to love her whom my hand defended there.While the others fought for honor, I by passion was made strong,Set your heel upon my bosom for my soul has done you wrong.

"But," and here he swayed and faltered till his knee sank on the floor,Yet in falling turned his forehead ever toward that silent door;"But your warrior hand my master, may take mine without a stain,For my hand has e'er been loyal, and your enemy is slain."

A short silence followed the last word, then a burst of applause testified to the appreciation of her audience, and Paula crept away to hide her blushing cheeks in the comparative darkness of a little vine-covered balcony that jutted out from the ante-room. What were her thoughts as she leaned there! In the subsidence of any great emotion—and Paula had felt every word she uttered—there is more or less of shock and tumult. She did not think, she only felt. Suddenly a hand was laid on her arm and a low voice whispered in her ear,

"Did you write that poem yourself?"

Turning, she encountered the shadowy form of a woman leaning close at her side and appearing in the dim light that shone on her from the lamps beyond, an eager image of expectancy.

"Yes," returned Paula, "why do you ask?"

The woman, whoever she was, did not answer. "And you believe in such devotion as that!" she murmured. "You can understand a man, aye, or a woman either, risking happiness and fame, life and death, for the sake of a trust! Such things are not folly to you! You could see a heart spill itself drop by drop through a longer vigil than the eight months watching on the ramparts, and not sneer at a fidelity that could not falter because it had given its word? Speak; you write of faithfulness with a pen of fire, is your heart faithful too?"

There was something in these words, spoken as they were in a tone of suppressed passion, that startled and aroused Paula. Leaning forward, she endeavored to see the face of the woman who thus forcibly addressed her, but the light was too dim. The outline of a brow covered by some close headgear was all she could detect.

"You speak earnestly," said Paula, "but that is what I like. Fidelity to a cause, or fidelity to a trust, demands the sympathy and admiration of all honest and generous hearts. If I am ever called upon to maintain either, I hope that my enthusiasm will not have all been expended in words."

"You please me," murmured the woman, "you please me; will you come and see me and let me tell you a story to mate the poem you have given us to-night?"

The trembling eagerness of her tone it would be impossible to describe. Paula was thrilled by it. "If you will tell me who you are," said Paula, "I certainly will try and come. I should be glad to hear anything you have to relate to me."

"I thought every one knew who I was," returned the woman; and drawing Paula back into the ante-room, she turned her face upon her. "Any one will tell you where Margery Hamlin lives," said she. "Do not disappoint me, and do not keep me waiting long." And with a nod and a deep strange smile that made her aged face almost youthful, she entered the crowd and disappeared from Paula's sight.

It was the woman whose nightly visits to the deserted home of the Japhas had once been the talk and was still the unsolved mystery of the town.

XXIV.

THE JAPHA MANSION.

"Ah what a warning for a thoughtless man,Could field or grove, could any spot on earthShow to his eye an image of the pangsWhich it has witnessed; render back an echoOf the sad steps by which it hath been trod.—Wordsworth.

Unexplained actions if long continued, lose after awhile their interest if not their mystery. The aged lady who now for many years had been seen at every night-fall to leave her home, traverse the village streets, enter the Japha mansion, remain there an hour and then re-issue with tremulous steps and bowed head, had become so common a sight to the village eye, that even the children forgot to ask what her errand was, or why she held her head so hopefully when she entered, or looked so despondent when she came forth.

But to Paula, for reasons already mentioned, this secret and persistent vigil in a forsaken and mysterious dwelling, was fraught with a significance which had never lost its power either to excite her curiosity or to arouse her imagination. Many a time had she gone home from some late encounter with the aged lady, to brood by the hour upon the expression of that restless eye which in its wanderings never failed to turn upon her own youthful face and linger there in the manner I have already noted. She thought of it by night, she thought of it by day. She felt herself drawn to that woman's suffering heart as by invisible cords. To understand the feelings of this desolate being, she had even studied the face of that old house, until she knew it under its every aspect. Often in shutting her eyes at night, she would perceive as in a mirror a vision of its long gray front, barred door and sealed windows shining in the moon, save where the deep impenetrable shadows of its two guardian poplars lay black and dismal upon its ghostly surface. Again she would behold it as it reared itself dark and dripping in a blinding storm, its walls plastered with leaves from the immovable poplars, and its neglected garden lying sodden and forlorn under the flail of the ceaseless storm. Then its early morning face would strike her fancy. The slow looming of its chimney-tops against a brightening sky; the gradual coming out of its forsaken windows and solemn looking doors from the mystery of darkness into the no less mystery of day; the hint of roselight on its barren boards; the gleam of sunshine on its untrodden threshold; a sunshine as pure and sweet as if a bride stood there in her beauty, waiting for admission into the deserted halls beyond. All and everything that could tend to invest the house and its constant visitor with an atmosphere of awe and interest, had occurred to this young girl in her daily reveries and nightly dreams. It was therefore with a thrill deep as her expectation and vivid as her sympathy, that she recognized in her eager interlocutor and proposed confident, the woman about whose life and actions rested for her such a veil of impenetrable mystery. The thought moved her, excited her, and made the rest of the evening pass like a dream. She was anxious for the next day to come, that she might seek this Mrs. Hamlin in her home, and hear from her lips the tale of devotion that should mate her own simple but enthusiastic poem.

When the next day did come, it rained, rained bitterly, persistent and with a steady drive from the north east, that made her going out impossible. The day following she was indisposed, and upon the succeeding afternoon, she was engaged in duties that precluded all thought of visiting. The next day was Sunday, and Monday had its own demands which she could not slight. It was therefore well nigh a week from the night of the entertainment, before the opportunity offered for which she was so anxious. Her curiosity and expectation had thus time to grow, and it was with a determination to allow nothing to stand in her way, that she set out from home in a flood of mild September sunshine, to visit Mrs. Hamlin. But alas, for resolutions made in a country village prior to the opening of a church fair! She had scarcely gone a dozen steps before she was accosted by one of the managers, a woman who neither observes your haste, nor pays any attention to your possible preoccupation. Do what she could, she found it impossible to escape from this persistent individual until she had satisfied her upon matters which it took a full half hour to discuss, and when at last she succeeded in doing so, it was only to fall into the hands of an aged deacon of the church, whose protecting friendship it were a sin to wound, while his garrulous tongue made it no ordinary trial of patience to stand and listen. In short the best part of the afternoon was gone before she found herself at the door of Mrs. Hamlin's house. But she was not to be deterred by further hesitation from the pursuit of her object. Rapping smartly on the door, she listened. No stir came from within. Again she rapped and again she listened. No response came to assure her that her summons had been heard. Surprised at this, for she had been told Mrs. Hamlin was always at home during the afternoon, she glanced up at the church clock in plain view from the doorstep, and blushed to observe that it was six o'clock, the hour at which this mysterious woman always left her house, to accomplish her vigil at the Japha mansion.

"What have I done?" thought Paula, and felt a strange thrill as she realized that even at that moment, the woman with the eager but restless eyes, was shut within the precincts of that deserted dwelling, engaged in prayer, perhaps wet with tears, who knows? The secret of what she did in that long and quiet twilight hour had never been revealed. Leaving the little brown house behind, Paula found herself insensibly taking the road to the Japha mansion. If she could not enter it and share the watch of the devoted woman who had promised her her confidence, she could at least observe if the windows were open or the blinds raised. To be sure she ought to be at home, but Miss Belinda was indulgent and did not question her comings and goings too closely. An irresistible force drew her down the street, and she did not hesitate to follow the lead of her impulse. No one accosted her now, it was the tea hour in most of these houses and the streets were comparatively deserted. The only house whose chimneys lacked the rising smoke, was the one towards which her footsteps were tending. She could descry it from afar. Its gaunt walls from which the paint had long ago faded, stared uncompromisingly upon her in the autumn sunshine. There was no welcome in its close shutters with their broken slats from which hung tangled strips of old rags—the remnants of some boy's kite. The stiff and solemn poplars rose grim and forbidding at the gate once swung wide to the fashion and gallantry of proud ladies and stalwart gentlemen, but now pushed aside solely by the hand of a tremulous old woman, or the irreverent palm of some daring school-boy. From the tangled garden looked forth neither flower nor blossoming shrub. Beauty and grace could not thrive in this wilderness of decay. A dandelion would have felt itself out of place beneath the eye of that ghostly door, with the sinister plank nailed across it, like the separating line between light and darkness, right and wrong, life and death. What loneliness! what a monument of buried passions outliving death itself!

Paula paused as she reached the gate; but remembering that Mrs. Hamlin was accustomed to enter the house by a side door, hurried around the corner and carefully surveyed the windows from that quarter. One of the shutters was open, allowing the flame of the setting sun to gild the panes like gold. She did not know then nor has she been able to explain since, what it was that came over her at the sight, but almost before she realized it, she had returned to the gate, opened it, threaded the overgrown garden, reached the door which she had so frequently beheld the aged woman enter and knocked.

Instantly she was seized with a consciousness of what she had done, and frightened at her temerity, meditated an immediate escape. Drawing the folds of her mantle about her form and face, she prepared to fly, when she remembered the look of entreaty with which this woman had said on that night of their conversation, "Do not disappoint me! Do not keep me long in suspense!" and moved by a fresh impulse, turned and inflicted another resounding knock on the door.

The result was unlooked-for and surprising. To the sound from within of a quick passionate cry, there came a hurried movement, followed by a deep silence, then another hasty stir succeeded by a longer silence, then a rush which seemed to bring all things with it, and the door opened and Mrs. Hamlin appeared before her with a countenance so pallid with expectancy, that Paula instinctively felt that in some unconscious way, she had loosened the bonds of an uncontrollable emotion, and was drawing back, when the woman with a quick look in her shrouded face, exultantly caught her hand in hers, and drawing her over the threshold, gasped out in a delirium of incomprehensible joy:

"I knew you would come! I knew that God would not let you forget! Fifteen years have I waited, Jacqueline! fifteen long, tedious, suffering years! But they all seem like nothing now! You have come, you have come, and all that I ask, is that God will not let me die till I realize my joy!"

The emotion with which she uttered these strange words was so overpowering, and her body seemed so weak to stand the strain, that Paula instinctively put forth her hand to sustain her. The action loosened her cloak. Instantly the eyes that had been fixed upon her with such delirious rapture grew blank with dismay, a frightful shudder ran through the woman's aged frame; she tore at the cloak that still enveloped the young girl's shoulders, and pulling it off, took one view of the fresh and beautiful countenance before her, and without uttering a word, fell back in a deep and deadly swoon upon the floor.

"O what have I done?" cried Paula, flinging herself down beside that pale and rigid figure; but instantly remembering herself she leaped to her feet and looked about for some means to resuscitate the sufferer. There was a goblet of water on a table near by. Seizing it, she bathed the face and hands of the woman before her, moaning aloud in her grief and dismay, "Have I killed her! O what is this mystery that brings such a doom of anguish to this poor heart?"

But from those pallid lips came no response, and feeling greatly alarmed, Paula was about to rush from the house for assistance, when she felt a tremulous pull upon her skirt, and turning, saw that the glassy eyes had opened at last and were now gazing upon her with mute but eloquent appeal.

She instantly returned. "O I am so sorry," she murmured, sinking again upon her knees beside the suffering woman. "I did not know, could not realize that my presence here would affect you so deeply. Forgive me and tell me what I can do to make you forget my presumption."

The woman shook her head, her lips moved and she struggled vainly to rise. Paula immediately lent her the aid of her strong young hand and in a few minutes, Mrs. Hamlin was on her feet. "O God!" were her first words as she sank into the chair which Paula hastily drew forward, "that I should taste the joy and she be still unsaved!"

Seeing her so absorbed, Paula ventured to glance around her. She found herself in a large square room sparsely but comfortably furnished in a style that bespake it as the former sitting-room of the dead and buried Japhas. From the walls above hung a few ancient pictures. A large hair-cloth sofa of a heavy antique shape, confronted the eye from one side of the room, an equally ancient book-case from the other. The carpet was faded and so were the curtains, but they had once been of an attractive hue and pattern. Conspicuous in the midst stood a large table with a well-trimmed lamp upon it, and close against it an easy chair with an upright back. This last as well as everything else in the room, was in a condition of neatness that would have surprised Paula if she had not been acquainted with the love and devotion of this woman, who in her daily visits to this house, probably took every pains to keep things freshened and in order.

Satisfied with her survey, she again directed her attention to Mrs. Hamlin, and started to find that person's eyes fixed upon her own with an expression of deep, demanding interest.

"You are looking at the shadows of things that were," exclaimed the old lady in thrilling tones. "It is a fearful thought to be shut up with the ghost of a vanished past, is it not? That chair by your side has not been sat in since Colonel Japha rose from it twelve years ago to totter to the bed where he breathed his last. It is waiting, everything is waiting. I thought the end had come to-night, that the vigil was over, the watch finished, but God in his wisdom says, 'No,' and I must wait a little longer. Alas in a little while longer the end will be here indeed!"

The despondency with which she uttered these last words showed where her thoughts were tending, and to comfort her, Paula drew up a chair and sat down by her side. "You were going to tell me the story of a great love and a great devotion. Cannot you do so now?"

The woman started, glanced hastily around, and let her eyes travel to Paula's face where they rested with something of their old look of secret longing and doubt.

"You are the one who wrote the poem," she murmured; "I remember." Then with a sudden feverish impulse, leaned forward, and stroking back the waving locks from Paula's brow, exclaimed hurriedly, "You look like her, you have the same dark hair and wonderful eyes, more beautiful perhaps, but like her, O so like her! That is why I made such a mistake." She shuddered, with a quick low sob, but instantly subdued her emotion and taking Paula's hand in hers continued, "You are young, my daughter; youth does not enjoy carrying burdens; can I, a stranger ask you to assist me with mine?"

"You may," returned Paula. "If it will give you any relief I will help you bear it willingly."

"You will! Has heaven then sent me the aid my failing spirits demand? Can I count on you, child? But I will ask for no promise till you have heard my story. To no one have I ever imparted the secret of my life, but from the first moment I saw your fair young face, I felt that through you would come my help, if help ever came to make my final moments easier and my last days less bitter." And rising up, she led Paula to a door which she solemnly opened. "I am glad that you are here," said she. "I could never have asked you to come, but since you have braved the dead and crossed this threshold, you must see and know the whole. You will understand my story better."

Taking her through a dark passage, she threw wide another door, and the parlors of the vanished Japhas opened before them. It was a ghostly vision. A weird twilight scene of clustered shadows brooding above articles of musty grandeur. In spite of the self-command learned by her late experiences, Paula recoiled, saying,

"It is too sad, too lonesome!" But the woman without heeding her, hurried her on over the worm-eaten carpet and between the time-worn chairs and heavy-browed cabinets, to the hall beyond.

"I have not been here, myself, for a year," said Mrs. Hamlin, glancing fearfully up and down the dusky corridor. "It is not often I can brave the memories of this spot." And she pointed with one hand towards the darkened door at its end, whose spacious if not stately panels gave no hint to the eye of the dread bar that crossed it like a line of doom upon the outside, and then turning, let her eye fall with still heavier significance upon the broad and imposing staircase that rose from the centre of the hall to the duskier and more dismal regions above.

"A brave, old fashioned flight of steps is it not! But the scene of a curse, my child." And unheeding Paula's shudder, she drew her up the stairs.

"See," continued her panting guide as they reached a square platform near the top, from which some half dozen or more steps branched up on either side. "They do not build like this nowadays. But Colonel Japha believed in nothing new, and thought more of his grand old hall and staircase, than he did of all the rest of his house. He little dreamed of what a scene it would be the witness. But come, it is getting late and you must see her room."

It was near the top of the staircase and was fully as musty, faded and dismal as the rest. Yet there was an air of expectancy about it, too, that touched Paula deeply. From between the dingy hangings of the bed, looked forth a pair of downy pillows, edged with yellowed lace, and beneath them a neatly spread counterpane carefully turned back over comfortable-looking blankets, as one sees in a bed that only awaits its occupant; while on the ancient hearth, a pile of logs stood heaped and ready for the kindling match.

"It is all waiting you see," said the old lady in a trembling voice, "like everything else, just waiting."

There was an embroidery frame in one corner of the room, from which looked a piece of faded and half completed work. The needle was hanging from it by a thread, and a skein of green worsted hung over the top, Paula glanced at it inquiringly.

"It is just as she left it! He never entered the room after she went and I would never let it be touched. It is just the same with the piano below. The last piece she played is still standing open on the rack. I loved her so, and I thought then that a few months would bring her back! See, here is her bible. She never used to read it, but she prized it because it was her mother's. I have placed it on the pillow where she will see it when she comes to lay her poor tired head down to rest." And with a reverent hand the aged matron drew the curtains back from the open bed, and disclosed the little bible lying thick with dust in the centre of the nearest pillow.

"O who was this you loved so well? And why did she leave you?" cried Paula with the tears in her eyes, at sight of this humble token.

The aged lady seized her hand and hurried her back into the room below. "I will tell you where I have waited and watched so long. Only be patient till I light the lamp. It is getting late and any chance wanderer going by and seeing all dark, might think I had forgotten my promise and was not here."

XXV.

JACQUELINE.

"The cold in clime are cold in blood,And love as scarce deserves the name,But mine is like the lava floodThat burns in Etna's breast of flame."—Byron.

"There are some men that have the appearance of being devoid of family affection, who in reality cherish it in the deepest and most passionate degree. Such a man was Colonel Japha. You have doubtless heard from your cradle what the neighbors thought of this stately, old fashioned gentleman. He was too handsome in his youth, too proudly reticent in his manhood, too self-contained and unrelenting in his age, not to be the talk of any town that numbered him among its inhabitants. But only from myself, a relative of the family and his housekeeper for years, can you learn with what undeviating faith and love he clung to the few upon whom he allowed his heart to fasten in affection. When he married Miss Carey, the world said, 'He has chosen a beauty, because fine manners and a pretty face look well behind the Japha coffee-urn!' But we, that is, this same young wife and myself, knew that in marrying her he had taken unto himself his other half, the one sweet woman for whom his proud heart could beat and before whom his stately head could bow. When she died, the world exclaimed, 'He will soon fill her place!' But I who watched the last look that passed between them in the valley of the shadow of that death, knew that the years would come and the years would go without seeing Colonel Japha marry again.

"The little babe whom she left to his care, took all the love which he had left. From the moment it began to speak, he centered in its tiny life all the hope and all the pride of his solitary heart. And the Japha pride was nearly as great as the Japha heart. She was a pretty child; not a beauty like her mother or like you, my dear, who however so nearly resemble her. But for all that, pretty enough to satisfy the eyes of her secretly doting father, and her openly doting nurse and cousin. I say secretly doting father. I do not mean by that that he regarded her with an affection which he never displayed, but that it was his way to lavish his caresses at home and in the privacy of her little nursery. He never made a parade of anything but his pride. If he loved her, it was enough for her to know it. In the street and the houses of their friends, he was the strict, somewhat severe father, to whom her childish eyes lifted at first with awe, but afterwards with a quiet defiance, that when I first saw it, made my heart stand still with unreasoning alarm.

"She was so reserved a child and yet so deeply passionate. From the beginning I felt that I did not understand her. I loved her; I have never loved any mortal as I did her—and do; but I could not follow her impulses or judge of her feelings by her looks.

"When she grew older it was still worse. She never contradicted her father, or appeared in any open way to disobey his commands, or thwart him in his plans. Yet she always did what she pleased, and that so quietly, he frequently did not observe that matters had taken any other direction, than that which he had himself ordained. 'It is her mother's tact,' he used to say. Alas it was something more than that; it was her father's will united to the unscrupulousness of some forgotten ancestor.

"But with the glamour of her eighteen years upon me, I did not recognize this then, any more than he. I saw her through the magic glasses of my own absorbing love, and tremble as I frequently would in the still scorn of her unfathomable passion, I never dreamed she could do anything that would seriously offend her father's affection or mortify his pride. The truth is, that Jacqueline did not love us. Say what you will of the claims of kindred, and the right of every father to his childrens' regard, Jacqueline Japha accepted the devotion that was lavished upon her, but she gave none in return. She could not, perhaps. Her father was too cold in public and too warm in his home-bursts of affection. I was plain and a widow; no mate for her in age, condition or estate. She could neither look up to me nor lean upon me. I had been her nurse in childhood and though a relative, was still a dependent; what was there in all that to love! If her mother had lived—But we will not dwell on possibilities. Jacqueline had no mother and no friend that was dear enough to her, to teach her unwilling soul the great lesson of self-control and sacrifice.

"You will say that is strange. That situated as she was, she ought to have found friends both dear and congenial; but that would be to declare that Jacqueline was like others of her age and class, whereas she was single and alone; a dark-browed girl, who allured the gaze of both men and women, but who cared but little for any one till—But wait, child. I shall have to speak of matters that will cause your cheeks to blush. Lay your head down on my knee, for I cannot bear the sight of blushes upon a cheek more innocent than hers."

With a gentle movement she urged Paula to sit upon a little stool at her feet, pressed the young girl's head down upon her lap, and burying the lovely brow beneath her aged hands, went hurriedly on.

"You are young, dear, and may not know what it is to love a man. Jacqueline was young also, but from the moment she returned home to us from a visit she had been making in Boston, I perceived that something had entered her life that was destined to make a great change in her; and when a few weeks later, young Robert Holt from Boston, came to pay his respects to her in her father's house, I knew, or thought I did, what that something was. We were sitting in this room I remember, when the servant-girl came in, and announced that Mr. Holt was in the parlor. Jacqueline was lying on the sofa, and her father was in his usual chair by the table. At the name, Holt, the girl rose as if it had suddenly thundered, or the lightning had flashed. I see her now. She was dressed in white—though it was early fall she still clung to her summer dresses—her dark hair was piled high, and caught here and there with old-fashioned gold pins, a splendid red rose burned on her bosom, and another flashed crimson as blood from her folded hands.

"'Holt?' repeated the Colonel without turning his head, 'I know no such man.'

"'He said he wished to see Miss Jacqueline,' simpered the servant.

"'Oh,' returned the Colonel indifferently. He never showed surprise before the servants—and went on with his book, still without turning his head.

"I thought if he had turned it, he would scarcely sit there reading so quietly; for Jacqueline who had not stirred from her alert and upright position, was looking at him in a way no father, least of all a father who loved his child as he did her, could have beheld without agitation. It was the glance of a tigress waiting for the sight of an inconsiderate move, in order to spring. It was wild unconstrainable joy, eying a possible check and madly defying it. I shuddered as I looked at her eye, and sickened as I perceived a huge drop of blood ooze from her white fingers, where they unconsciously clutched a thorn, and drop dark and disfiguring upon her virgin garments. At the indifferent exclamation of her father, her features relaxed, and she turned haughtily towards the girl, with a veiling of her secret delight that already bespoke the woman of the world.

"'Tell Mr. Holt that I will see him presently,' said she, and was about to follow the girl from the room when I caught her by the sleeve.

"'You will have to change your dress,' said I, and I pointed to the ominous blot disfiguring its otherwise spotless white.

"She started and gave me a quick glance.

"'I have a skin like a spider's web,' cried she. 'I should never meddle with roses.' But I noticed she did not toss the blossom away.

"'Who is this Mr. Holt?' now asked the Colonel suddenly turning, the servant having left the room.

"'He is a gentleman I met in Boston,' came from his daughter's lips, in her usual light and easy tones. 'He is probably passing through our town on his way to Providence, where I was told he did business. His call is no more than a formality, I presume.' And with an indifferent little smile and nod, she vanished from the room, that a moment before had been filled with the threat of her silent passion. The Colonel gave a short sigh but returned undisturbed to his book.

"In the course of a few minutes Jacqueline came back. She had changed her dress for one as summerlike as the other, but still finer and more elaborate. She looked elegant, imperious, but the joy had died out from her eyes, and in its place was another expression incomprehensible to me, but fully as alarming as any that had gone before. 'Mr. Holt finds himself obliged to remain in town over night, and would like to pay his respects to you,' said she to her father.

"The Colonel immediately rose, looking very grand as he turned and surveyed his daughter with his clear penetrating eye.'

"'You have a lover, have you not?' he asked, laying his hand on her bare and beautifully polished shoulder.

"An odd little smile crossed her lip. She looked at her hands on which never a ring shone, and coquettishly tossed her head. 'Let the gentleman speak for himself,' said she, 'I give no man his title until he has earned it.'

"Her father laughed. A lover was not such a dreadful thing in his eyes provided he were worthy. And Jacqueline would not choose unworthily of course—a Japha and his daughter! 'Well then,' said he, 'let us see if he can make good his title; Holt is not a bad name and Boston is not a poor place to hail from.' And without more ado, they hurried from the room. But the light had all died out from her face! What did it mean?

"At tea time I met the gentleman. He had evidently made his title good. I was not only favorably impressed with him but actually struck. Of all the high-bred, clear-eyed, polished and kindly gentlemen who had sat about the board since I first came into the family in Mrs. Japha's lifetime, here was surely the finest, the handsomest and the best; and surprised in more ways than one, I was giving full play to my relief and exhilaration, when I caught sight of Jacqueline's eye, and felt again the cold shudders of secret doubt and apprehension. Smile upon him as she would, coquet with him as she did, the flame and the glory that drew her like an inspiration to her feet when his name was announced, had fled, and left not a shadow behind. Had he failed in his expressions of devotion? Was he hard or cold or severe, under all that pleasant and charming manner? Had the hot soul of our motherless child rushed upon ice, and in the shock of the dreadful chill, fallen inert? No, his looks bespake no coldness; they dwelt upon Jacqueline's lovely but inscrutable face, with honest fervor and boundless regard. He evidently loved her most passionately, but she—if it had not been for that first moment of unconscious betrayal, I should have decided that she cared for him no more than she did for the few others who had adored her, in the short space of her incomprehensible life.

"The mystery was not cleared up when she came to me that night with a short, 'How do you like my lover, Margery?' I was forty years her senior, but she always called me Margery.

"'I think he is the finest, most agreeable man I ever met,' said I. 'Is he your lover, Jacqueline? Are you going to marry him?'

"She turned about from the vase which she was denuding of its flowers, and gave me one of her sphinx-like looks. 'You must ask papa,' said she. 'He holds the destinies of the Japhas in his hand, does he not?'

"'Does he?' I involuntarily whispered to myself; following the steady poise of her head and the assured movements of her graceful form, with a glance of doubt, but loving her all the same, O loving her all and ever the same!

"'Your father is not the man to cross you when the object of your affections is as worthy as this gentleman. He loved your mother too fondly.'

"'He did?' She had turned quick as a flash and was looking me straight in the eyes.

"'I never saw such union!' I exclaimed, vaguely remembering that her mother's name had always seemed to have power to move her. 'There was no parade of it before the world; but here at their own fireside, it was heart to heart and soul to soul. It was not love it was assimilation.'

"The young girl rose upon me like a flame; her very eyes seemed to dart fire; her lips looked like living coals; she was almost appalling in her terrible beauty and superhuman passion. 'Not love!' she exclaimed, her every word falling like a burning spark, 'not love but assimilation! Yet do you suppose if I told my father that my soul had found its mate; my heart its other half; that this, *this* nature,' here she struck her breast as she would a stone, 'had at last found its master; that the wayward spirit of which you have sometimes been afraid, was become a part of another's life, another's soul, another's hope, do you suppose he would listen? Hush!' she cried, seeing me about to speak. 'You talk of love, what do you know of it, what does he know of it, who saw his young wife die, yet himself consented to live? Is love a sitting by the fire with hand locked in hand while the winter winds rage and the droning kettle sings? Love is a going through the fire, a braving of the winter winds, a scattering of the soul in sparks that the night and the tempest lick up without putting out the germ of the eternal flame. Love!' she half laughed; 'O, it takes a soul that has never squandered its treasure upon every passing beggar, to know how to love! Do you see that star?' It was night as I have said and we were standing near an open window. 'It has lost its moorings and is falling; when it descries the ocean it will plunge into it; so with some natures, they soar high and keep their orbit well, till an invisible hand turns them from their course and they fall, to be swallowed up, aye swallowed up, lost and buried in the great sea that has awaited them so long.'

"'And you love—like this—' I murmured, quailing before the power of her passion.

"'Would it not be strange if I did not,' she asked in an altered voice. 'You say he is everything noble, handsome and attractive.'

"'Yes, yes,' I murmured, 'but—'

"She did not wait to hear what lay behind that but. Picking up her flowers, she hastily crossed the room. 'Did my young mother shriek from joy, when my father's horses ran away with them along that deadly precipice at the side of the Southmore road? To lie for a few maddening moments on the breast of the man you love, earth reeling beneath you, heaven swimming above you, and then with a cry of bliss to fall heart to heart, down the hideous gap of some awful gulf, and be dashed into eternity with the cry still on your lips, that is what I call love and that is what I—'

"She paused, turned upon me the whole splendor of her face, seemed to realize to what an extent her impetuosity had lifted the veil with which she usually shrouded her bitterly suppressed nature, and calming herself with a sudden quick movement, gave me a short mocking courtesy and left the room.

"Do you wonder that for half the night I sat up brooding and alive to the faintest sounds!

"Next day Mr. Holt called again, and a couple of weeks after—long enough to enable Colonel Japha to make whatever inquiries he chose as to his claims as a gentleman of means and position—sent a formal entreaty for Jacqueline's hand. I had never seen Colonel Japha more moved. His admiration for the young man was hearty and sincere. From a worldly point of view, as well as from all higher standpoints, the match was one of which he could be proud; and yet to speak the word that would separate from him the only creature that he loved, was hard as the cutting off an arm or the plucking out of an eye. 'Do you think she loves him?' asked he of me with a rare condescension of which he was not often guilty. 'You are a woman and ought to understand her better than I. Do you think she loves him?'

"After the words I had heard her speak, what could I reply but, 'Yes, sir; she is of a reserved nature and controls her feelings in his presence, but she loves him for all that, with the intensest fervor and passion.'

"He repeated again, 'You are a woman and you ought to know.' And then called his daughter to him.

"I cannot tell what passed between them, but the upshot of it was, that the Colonel despatched an answer to the effect that the father's consent would not be lacking, provided the daughter's could be obtained. I learned this from Jacqueline herself who brought me the letter to post.

"'You see then, that your father understands,' said I.

"Her rich red lip curled mockingly, but she did not reply.

"Naturally Mr. Holt answered to this communication in person. Jacqueline received him with a fitful coquetry that evidently puzzled him, for all the distinguishing charm which it added to a beauty apt to be too reserved and statue-like. She however took his ring which blazed on her finger like a drop of ice on congealed snow. 'I am engaged,' she murmured as she passed by my door, 'and to a Holt!' The words rang long in my ears; why?

"She desired no congratulations; she permitted nothing to be said about her engagement, among the neighbors. She had even taken off her ring which I found lying loose in one of her bureau drawers. And no one dared to remonstrate, not even her father, punctillious as he was in all matters of social etiquette. The fact is, Jacqueline was not the same girl she had been before she gave her promise to Mr. Holt. From the moment he bade her good-bye, with the remark that he was going away to get a golden cage for his bride, she began to reveal a change. The cold reserve gave way to feverish expectancy. She trod these rooms as if there were burning steels in the floors, she looked from the windows as if they were prison bars; night and day she gazed from them yet she never went out. The letters she received from him were barely read and tossed aside; it was his coming for which she hungered. Her father noticed her restless and eager gaze, and frequently sighed. I felt her strange removed manner and secretly wept. 'If he does not amply return this passion,' thought I, 'my darling will find her life a hell!'

"But he did return it; of that I felt sure. It was my only comfort.

"Suddenly one day the restlessness vanished. Her beauty burst like a flame from smoke; she trod like a spirit that hears invisible airs. I watched her with amazement till she said 'Mr. Holt comes to-night,' then I thought all was explained and went smiling about my work. She came down in the afternoon clad as I had never seen her before. She wore one of her Boston dresses and she looked superb in it. From the crown of her head to the sole of her foot, she dazzled like a moving picture; but she lacked one adornment; there was no ring on her finger. 'Jacqueline!' cried I, 'you have forgotten something.' And I pointed towards her hand.

"She glanced at it, blushed a trifle as I thought, and pulled it out of her pocket. 'I have it,' said she, 'but it is too large,' and she thrust it carelessly back.

"At three o'clock the train came in. Then I saw her eye flash and her lip burn. In a few minutes later two gentlemen appeared at the gate.

"'Mr. Holt and his brother!' were the words I heard whispered through the house. But I did not need that announcement to understand Jacqueline at last."

XXVI.

A MAN'S JUSTICE AND A WOMAN'S MERCY.

"Fair is foul and foul is fair."—Macbeth.

"Have you ever seen a man whose instantaneous effect upon you was electrical; in whose expression, carriage, or manner, there was concealed a charm that attracted and interested you, apart from his actual worth and beauty? Such a one was Mr. Roger Holt, the gentleman I now discerned entering the gate with Jacqueline's lover. It was not that he was handsome. He could not for one moment bear any comparison with his brother in substantial attraction, and yet when they were both in the room, you looked at him in preference to the other, and was vexed with yourself for doing so. He seemed to be the younger as he was certainly the smaller; yet he took the lead, even in coming up the walk. Why had he not taken it in the deeper and more important matter? Was it because he did not love her?

"I was not present when Jacqueline greeted her guests and presented Mr. Roger Holt to her father. But later in the day I spent a half hour with them and saw enough to be able to satisfy myself as to the falsity of my last supposition. Never had I seen on a human countenance the evidences of a wilder passion than that which informed his features, as he sat in the further window of the parlor, presumably engaged in admiring the autumn landscape, but really occupied in casting short side-long glances at Jacqueline, who sat listening with a superb nonchalence, but with a restless gleam in her wandering eye, to the genial talk between her acknowledged lover and the Colonel. I half feared he would rise from his seat, and flinging himself before her, demand then and there an explanation of her engagement.

"But beyond the impatience of those short burning glances, he controlled himself well, and it was Jacqueline who moved at last.

"I saw the purpose growing in her eyes long before she stirred. The face which had been a mystery to me from her cradle, was in the presence of this man, like an open page which all might read. Its letters were flame, but that did not make them any less clear. I felt her swaying towards him, before an eyelash trembled or a quiver shook her tall form.

He may have understood her purpose also, for his eye wandered towards the open piano. She rose like a queen.

"'Mr. Roger Holt is a singer,' said she in passing her father, 'I am going to ask him to give us one of the old ballads you profess to like so much.'

"The conversation at once ceased. The Colonel who made no secret of his fondness for music, turned at once towards the stranger, with an expression of great courtesy. Instantly that gentleman rose, and meeting the request of his hostess with a profound bow, proceeded at once to the piano. 'He will not leave it till he has spoken to her,' thought I. Nor did he, for that very moment as they stood turning her music over, I perceived his lips move in a hurried question, to which she as briefly responded, whereupon he caught up a sheet of music from the pile, and flinging back his head with a victorious smile, began to sing.

"Had I known what lay behind his words, I would have braved everything rather than have allowed him to utter a note in that room which had once rung with the carols of Jacqueline's mother. But what could I guess of the possible evil underlying the natural ebullition of unrestrained passion that from some cause of pride or pique, had met with a strange inexplicable check. So I sat still, shuddering perhaps, but quiet in my corner; while the haunting tones of his strange and thrilling voice, rose and fell in the most uncanny of Scottish love songs. Nor did I do more than wonder with all my agitated soul, when at the conclusion Jacqueline came back, and pausing beside the man to whom she had given her troth, looked down in his beaming face and smiled with that overflow of delight, which she dared not bestow upon his brother.

"Another little incident of that hour remains engraven upon my memory. She had been showing to the gentlemen a rare plant that stood in the front parlor window, and was dilating upon its marvels, when Mr. Robert Holt, her accepted lover, took in his clasp the small white hand wandering so invitingly among the leaves of the huge palm, and glancing at the finger which should have worn his ring, looked inquiringly into her face.

"'O,' said she, interrupting her little speech to draw away her hand, 'you miss your diamond? I have it, sir. It lies very safe in my pocket; it is a beautiful gem, but *your ring does not fit me.*'

"The way she said those words and the air with which she tossed back her head, must have made one heart in that room beat joyously, but it did not reassure me or subdue my secret apprehension.

"'Not fit!' her lover responded; and begged her to allow him to try it on and see, but she shook her head with wilful coquetry, and turning to the piano, commenced singing a gay little song that was like silver bells, shaken by a sudden and mighty tempest.

"Even the Colonel felt the change in his daughter, though he never guessed the cause, and came and went during the evening that followed, with certain odd sighs that made my heart ache with strange forebodings. Only her lover was unconscious, or if he felt the new and wayward force and fire in her manner, attributed it to his own presence and unspeakable devotion. Mr. Roger Holt, on the contrary, thoroughly understood it. Though he was strangely calm, as calm now as he had previously been alert and fiery, he never lost a gleam of her eye in his direction, or a turn of her form towards the chair where he sat. But the smile with which he contemplated her was not pleasant to me. It was informed with self-consciousness, and a certain hard triumph, that made it almost sinister. 'She has given her hand to the true man,' I mused, 'wherever her heart may be. But had she given it?' I began to doubt as I began to muse. With that uncontrollable will of hers, she was capable of anything; did she intend to break with Robert, now that she had seen Roger? I detected no signs of it beyond the evident delight they took in each other's presence. They were guilty of no further conversation of a secret or intimate character, and when with the striking of the clock at ten, Mr. Robert Holt rose to leave, his brother followed without any demur, even preceding him in his departure and limiting his farewell to a short brotherly pressure of Jacqueline's fair hand.

"But much may be conveyed in a pressure, or so I began to think as I heard the low laugh that rippled from Jacqueline's lips as she turned to go up to her room; and if I had been her mother—

"But that is not what you want to hear. Enough that I did not follow her, that I did not even acquaint Colonel Japha with my fears, that indeed I did nothing but lie awake, praying and asking what I ought to do. There had been so little said; there had been so little done. A word, a sentence between them, the interchange of a couple of songs, and—What else that I could communicate to another?

"A week, two weeks passed, and her look of wilful happiness did not fly. She was flooded with notes from her accepted lover, whose handwriting I had learned by this time to distinguish, but not one, so far as I could learn, from any other source; yet her feet tripped lightly through the house, and her form had a rich grace in its every movement, that bespoke a mind settled in some deep joy or quiet determination. I felt the impenetrability of a secretly cherished hope, whenever I looked at her. If I had not known to the contrary, I should have said that her prospective marriage had become to her a dream of unfathomable delight. Whence then came this rapture? Through what communication was born this secret hope? I could not guess, I could only watch and wait.

"Meanwhile some random guesses at the truth had been made by the neighbors. Jacqueline had a lover. That lover was a gentleman; but the Colonel was critical; he had refused his consent and the young people had parted. Such was the talk, begotten perhaps by the persistency with which Jacqueline remained in the house, and the almost severe look with which Colonel Japha trod the streets of his native village, which he soon felt would lose all their charm in the departure of his only child. I scarcely ventured out more than Jacqueline; for I have but little control over my feelings and did not know what I would do, if any one should closely press me with questions.

"The unexpected discovery that our pretty young servant girl was in the habit of stealing into Jacqueline's room late at night, was the first thing that startled me into asking whether or not my supposition was true, that Jacqueline received no messages from Mr. Robert Holt. And scarcely had I become certain that a clandestine correspondence was being carried on between them through the medium of this girl, then the climax came, and knowledge on my part and secrecy on hers availed no longer.

"It was a day in October. The stoves had been put up in the house, and seeing Jacqueline roaming about the halls, in a renewed fit of that strange restlessness which had affected her the day before Mr. Roger Holt's visit, I went into her room to light a fire, and make everything look cheerful before dusk. I found the atmosphere warm, and going to the stove, discovered that a fire had been already kindled there, but had gone out for want of fuel. I at once commenced to rake away the ashes, in order to make preparations for a new one, when I came upon several scraps of half burned paper.

"Jacqueline had been burning letters. Do you blame me for picking out those scraps and hastening with them to another room, when I tell you they were written in a marked and characteristic hand that bore little or no resemblance to that of her accepted lover, and that the words which flashed first upon my eye were those ominous ones of *my wife*!

"They were three in number, and while more or less discolored and irregular, were still legible. Think child with what a thrill of horror and sharp motherly anguish, I read such words as 'Love you! I would press you in my arms if you were plague-stricken! The least turn of your head makes my blood cringe, as if a flame had touched me. I would follow you on my knees, if you led me round the world. Let me see Robert take your hand again and I will—'

"'Forget you! Do we forget the dagger that has struck us? I am another man since—'

"'I will have you if Robert goes mad and your father kills me. That I am burdened with a wife, is nothing. What is a wife that I do not—' 'You shall be my true wife, my—'

184 | P a g e

"'To-night then, be ready; I will wait for you at the gate. A little resolution on your part, and then—'

"I could read no further. The living, burning truth had forced itself upon me, that Jacqueline, our darling, our pride, the soul of our life, stood tottering upon the brink of a gulf horrible as the mouth of hell. For I never doubted for an instant what her answer would be to this entreaty. In all her past life, God pity us, there had been no tokens of that immovable hold on virtue, that would save her in such an extremity as this. Nevertheless, to make all sure, I flew back to her room, and tearing open bureau drawers and closet doors, discovered that her prettiest things had been sent away. She was going, then, and on that very night! and her father did not even know she was untrue to her betrothed lover. The horror of the situation was too much for me; I faltered as I left her room, her dainty, maidenly room, and actually crouched against the wall like a guilty thing, as I heard the sound of her voice singing some maddening strain in the parlors below. What should I do? Appeal to her, or warn her father of the frightful peril in which his honor and happiness stood? Alas, any appeal to her would be useless. In the glare of this awful revelation I had come to a full comprehension of her nature. But her father was a man; he could command as well as entreat, could even force obedience if all other methods failed. To him, then, must I go; but I had rather have gone to the rack. He was so proud a man! Had owned to such undeviating trust in his daughter's honor, as a Japha and his child! The blow would kill him; or daze him so, he might better have been killed. My knees shook under me, as I traversed the hall to his little study over the parlor, and when I came to the door, I rather fell against it than knocked, so great was my own anguish, and so deep my terror of his. He was a ready man and he came to the door at once, but upon seeing me, drew back as if his eye had fallen upon a phantom.

"'Hush!' said I, scarcely knowing what I uttered; and going in, I closed the door and latched it firmly behind me. 'I have come,' said I in a voice that made him start, 'to ask you to save your daughter. She is in deadly peril; she—' a strain of her song came in at that moment from the staircase. She was ascending to her room. He looked at me in a doubt of my sanity.

"'Not physical peril,' I stammered, 'but *moral*. She loves madly, unreasonably, and with a headlong passion that laughs at every obstacle, a man whom neither you nor heaven can look upon with aught but execration. She—'

"'Mrs. Hamlin!'—How well I remember his cool, calm voice, so deliberate in his impressive moments, so deliberate now, when perhaps she was donning hat and shawl for her elopement—'You are laboring under a great mistake. Instead of execrating Mr. Holt, I admire him most profoundly. Since the time has come for me to give up my daughter, I know of no one to whom I would rather surrender her.'

"'But Mr. Holt is not the man,' I cried, half wild in my fear and desperation. 'Do you remember the gentleman who came with him on his last visit? He called him his brother, and he is I believe, but—'

"The way he turned his grand white forehead towards me at that, made every fibre in my being quiver. 'Jacqueline does not love *him*!' exclaimed he. How sharp his voice, how changed his eye! I shrank back, trembling as I bowed my head, thinking of the word yet to be said.

"'But he won't compare—' he went on with a severe intonation. 'Besides her honor is engaged. You are dealing in fancies, Mrs. Hamlin.'

"I tore out of my breast the scraps of paper which had enlightened me so horribly, and held them towards him; then bethought myself, and drew back. 'I have proof,' said I; 'but first I must tell you that Jacqueline is not as good a girl as you have thought her. She is not her mother's child in the qualities of love and honor. She is destined to bring a great woe upon your head. In her passion for this man, she has forgotten your trust in her, the incorruptibility of your name, the honor of your house. Be strong, sir, for God is about to smite you in your tenderest spot.

"Ah, with what pride he towered upon me! this white-haired, stately gentleman before whom I had hitherto held my breath in admiring awe; towered upon me though his face was ghostly pale and his hand trembled like an aspen as he held it out!

"'Give me the papers you hold there,' cried he. 'Either you are gone mad, or else— Who wrote these lines?' he demanded, glancing down upon the hard, firm scrawl that blackened the bits of paper I had given him.

"'Mr. Roger Holt,' I returned unhesitatingly. 'I found those bits in Jacqueline's stove. Her clothes have been sent away, sir,' I continued as I saw his face grow fixed above the scraps he consulted. 'Twilight is coming on and—Mr. Roger Holt is a married man!'

"'What!'

"I never saw such a look flash from a human face as that which darted from his at that terrible moment. I thought he would have fallen, but he only dropped the papers out of his hand. 'Heaven forgive us!' murmured I, calmed by a sight of his misery, into some semblance of of self-control, 'but we have never understood Jacqueline. She is not to be led, sir, by principles or duty. She loves this man, and love with her is a stormy wind, capable of sweeping her into any abyss of contumely or suffering. If you would save her, kill her love; the death of her lover would only transform her into a demon.'

"He looked at me as if I had told him the world had come to an end. 'My Jacqueline!' he murmured in a low, incredulous voice of the tenderest yearning. 'My Jacqueline!'

"'Oh!' I shrieked, torn by my anguish for him and the terror of her escaping while we were yet talking, 'God knows I had rather have died than contaminate her by such words as I have uttered. She is dear to me as my soul; dearer to me than my life. I have a mother's feeling for her, sir. If to fling myself headlong from that window, would delay her feet from going down the stairs to meet her guilty lover, I would gladly do it. It is her danger makes me speak. O sir, realize that danger and hasten before she has taken the irrevocable step.'

"He started like a man pricked by a sudden dart. 'She is going—you believe she is going to meet him?'

"'I do,' said I.

"He gave me a terrible look and started for the door. I hurriedly picked up the scraps that had fallen to the floor, and rushed around by an inner passage-way to my own little room, hiding my head and waiting as for the crash of a falling avalanche. Suddenly a cry rose in the hall.

"There are some sounds that lift you unconsciously to your feet. Dashing out of my room, I detected the face of the servant-girl whom I have before mentioned, looking out of her door some distance down the corridor. Hastening towards her, I uttered some words about her being a busy-body, and thrusting her inside her room, locked the door upon her. Then I hastened with what speed I might to the front of the house, and coming out upon the grand staircase, met a sight that shook me to the very soul. You have been up the stairs; you know how they branch off to left and right from the platform near the top. The left branch led in those days to Colonel Japha's room, the right to the apartments occupied by Jacqueline and myself. Coming upon them, then, as I did from my side of the house, I found myself in full view of the opposite approach, and there on the topmost step I beheld Colonel Japha, standing in an attitude of awful denunciation, while half way down the staircase, I beheld the figure of Jacqueline, hindered in her gliding course towards the front door by the terrible, 'Stop!' whose echo had reached me in my room and caused me to rush quaking and horrified to this spot. I leaned back sick and horror-stricken against the wall. There was no mercy in his voice: he had awakened to a full realization of the situation and the pride of the Japhas had made him steel.

"'You are my child!' he was saying. 'I have loved you and do still; but proceed one step farther towards the man that awaits you at the gate, and the door that opens upon you, *shuts* never to open again!'

"'Colonel!' I exclaimed, starting forward; but he heard me no more than he would a fly buzzing or a bird singing.

"'I desire it to shut; I have no wish to come back!' issued from the set white lips of the girl beneath us. 'There is no such charm for me in this humdrum house, that I should wish to exchange life with the man I adore, for its droning, spiritless existence!' And she lifted her foot to proceed.

"'Jacqueline!' I shrieked, leaning forward in my turn, and holding her by my anguish, as I never believed she could be held by anything, 'Think, child, think what you do! It is not life you are going to but death. A man who can take a young girl from her father's house, from her lover's arms, from her mother's grave, from the shrine of all that is pure and holy, to dash her into a pit of all that is corrupt, loathsome and deadly, is not one with whom you can *live*. You say you adore him: can one adore falsehood, selfishness and depravity? Does hypocrisy win love? Can the embraces of a serpent bring peace? Jacqueline, Jacqueline, you are yet pure; come back to our love and our hearts, before we die here in our shame at the head of the stairs, where your mother was carried out to her grave!'

"She trembled. I saw the hand that clutched the banister loosen its grip; she cast one quick look behind her, and her eyes flashed upon her father's face; it was set like a flint.

"'If you come back,' cried he, leaning towards her, but not advancing a step from where he stood, 'you must come back of your own free will. I will hold no creature prisoner in my house. I must trust you implicitly, or not at all. Speak then, which shall it be?' And he raised his hand above his head, with a supreme and awful gesture, 'a father's blessing or a father's curse?'

"'A father's curse, then! since you command me to choose,' rang out from her lips in a burst of uncontrollable passion. 'I want no blessing that separates me from *him*!' And she pointed towards the door with a look that, defiant as it was, spoke of a terrible love before which all our warnings and entreaties were but as empty air.

"'Curses then upon your head, slayer of a family's honor, a father's love, and a mother's memory! Curses upon you, at home and abroad! in the joy of your first passion and in the agony of your last despair! May you live to look upon that door as the gateway to heaven, and find it shut! May your children, if you are cursed with them, turn in your face, as you are turning now in mine! May the lightning of heaven be your candle, and the blackness of death your daily food and your nightly drink!' And with a look in which all the terrors he invoked, seemed to crash downward from his reeling brain upon her shrinking terror-crouched head, he gave one mighty gasp and fell back stricken to the floor.

"'God!' burst from her lips, and she rushed downwards to the door like a creature hunted to its quarry. I saw her white face gleam marble-like in the fading light that came in from the chinks about the door. I saw her trembling hand fumbling with the knob, and rousing from my stupor, called down to her with all the force of a breaking heart,

"'Jacqueline, beware!'

"She turned once more. There was something in my voice she could not withstand. 'I do not hope to keep you,' cried I, 'but before you go, hear this. In the days to come, when the face that now beams upon you with such longing, shall have learned to turn from you in weariness, if not distaste, when hunger, cold, contumely and disease shall have blasted that fair brow and seared those soft cheeks, know, that although a father can curse, a woman who loves like a mother can forgive. The father cries, 'Once go out of that door and it shuts upon you never to open!' 'Once come to *that* door, say I,' pointing in the direction of the house's other entrance, 'and if I live and if I move, it shall open to you, were you as defiled and wretched and forsaken as Magdalen. Remember! Each day at this hour will I watch for you, kneeling upon its threshold. In sickness or in health, in joy or in sorrow, in cold or in heat. The hour of six is sacred. Some one of them shall see you falling weeping on my breast!'

"She gave me a quick stare out of her wide black eyes, then a mocking smile curled her lips, and murmuring a short, 'You rave!' opened the door, and rushed out into the falling dusk. With a resounding clang like the noise of a stone rolled upon an open grave, the great door swung to, and I was left alone in that desolated house with my stricken master.

XXVII.

THE LONE WATCHER.

"Hark! to the hurried question of Despair,Where is my child?—and Echo answers—
Where?"—Byron.

"Colonel Japha recovered from his shock, but was never the same man again. All that
was genial, affectionate and confiding in his nature, had been turned as by a
lightning's stroke, to all that was hard, bitter and suspicious. He would not allow the
name of Jacqueline to be spoken in his presence; he would listen to no allusion made
to those days when she was the care and perplexity, but also the light and pleasure of
the house. Men are not like women, my child; when they turn, it is at an angle, the
whole direction of their nature changes.

"Perhaps the news that presently came to us from Boston may have had something to
do with this. It was surely dreadful enough; Jacqueline's perfidy had slain her lover.
Mr. Robert Holt, the cultured, noble, high-souled gentleman, had been found lying
dead on the floor of his room, a few days after the events I have just related, with a
lady's diamond ring in his hand and the remnants of a hastily burned letter in the grate
before him. He had burst a blood-vessel, and had expired instantly.

"This sudden and tragic ending of a man of energy and will, was also the reason,
perhaps, why Grotewell never arrived at the truth of Jacqueline's history. Boston was
a long way from here in those days, and the story of her lover's death was not
generally known, while the fact of her elopement was. Consequently she was
supposed to have fled with the man who had been seen to visit her most frequently; a
report which neither the Colonel nor myself had the courage to deny.

"My child, you have a brow like snow, and a cheek like roses; you know little of life's
sorrows and little of life's sins. To you the skies are blue, the woods vernal, the air
balmy; the sad looks upon men's and women's faces, tell but shallow tales of the
ceaseless grinding of grief in their pent up souls. But you are gentle, and you have an
imagination that goes beyond your experience; perhaps if you pause and think, you
can understand what a tale could be told of the weeks and months and years that now
followed, without hint or whisper of the fate of her who had gone out from amongst
us with the brand of her father's curse upon her brow. At first we hoped,
yes, *he* hoped,—I could see it in his eyes when there came a sudden ring at the
bell,—that some sign of her penitence, or some proof of her existence, would come
to relieve the torture of our fears, if not the shame of our memories. But the door that
closed upon her on that fatal eve, had shut without an echo. While we vainly waited,

time had ample leisure to carve the furrows of age as well as of suffering on the Colonel's once smooth brow, and to change my daily vigil into a custom of despair, rather than of hope. Time had also leisure to rob us of much of our worldly goods and to make our continued living in this grand old house, an act that involved constant care and the closest economy. That we were enabled to preserve appearances to the day that beheld the Colonel laid low by the final stroke of his dread disease, was only due to the secret charity of a certain gentleman, who, declaring he was indebted to us, secretly supplied me with means of support.

"But of all this you care little.

"You had rather hear about the evening watch with its hopeful assurance, 'Yet another day and she will be here,' to be followed so soon by the despairing acknowledgement, 'Yet another day and she has not come!' or of those dark hours when the Colonel lay blank and white upon his pillow, with his eyes fixed on the door which would never open to the beating of a daughter's heart, while the gray shadow of an awful resolution deepened upon his immovable face. What that resolution was I could not know, but I feared it, when I saw what a sternness it gave to his eye, what a fixedness to his set and implacable lip; and when in the waning light of a certain December afternoon, the circle of neighbors about his bed gave way to the stiff and forbidding form of Mr. Phelps, I felt a thrill of mortal apprehension and only waited to hear the short, 'It shall be done,' of the lawyer to some slowly whispered command of the colonel, to rise from my far off corner and stand ready to accost Mr. Phelps as he came from the bedside of the dying man.

"'What is it?' I asked, rushing up to him as he issued forth into the hall, and seizing him by the arm, with a woman's unreasoning impetuosity. 'I have nursed his daughter on my knee; tell me, then, what it is he has ordered you to do in this final moment?'

"Mr. Phelps for all his ungainly bearing, is not a hard-hearted man, as you know, and he doubtless saw the depth of the misery that made me forget myself. Giving me a look that was not without its touch of sarcasm, he replied, 'The colonel has made me promise, to see that a plank is nailed across the front door of this house, after his body has been carried out to burial.'

"A board across the front door! His anger then was implacable. The withering curse that had rung in my ears for ten years, was to outlive his death! With a horrified groan, I pressed my hands over my eyes and rushed back. My first glimpse of the Colonel's face showed me that the end was at hand, but that fact only made more imperative my consuming desire to see that curse removed, even though it were done with his final breath. Drawing near his bedside, I leaned down, and waiting till his eye wandered to my face, asked him if there was nothing he wished amended before his strength failed. He understood me. We had not sat for so long, face to face across the chasm of a hideous memory, without knowing something of the workings of each other's mind. Glancing up at his wife's portrait which ever faced him as he lay upon his pillow, his mouth grew severe and he essayed to shake his head. I at once pointed to the portrait.

"'What will you say to her when she meets you on the borders of heaven?' I demanded with the courage of despair.' She will ask, 'Where is my child?' And what will you reply?'

"The fingers that lay upon the coverlid moved spasmodically; he eyed me with a steady deepening stare, awful to meet, fearful to remember. I went on steadily; 'She has gone out of this house with your curse; tell me that if she comes back, she may be greeted with your forgiveness.' Still that awful stare which changed not. 'I have watched and waited for her every day since her departure,' I whispered, 'and shall watch and wait for her, every day until I die. Shall a stranger's love be greater than a father's?' This time his lips twitched and the grey shadow shifted, but it did not rise. 'I had sworn to do it,' I went on. 'When you lay there at the top of the stairs, smitten down by your first shock, I told her, come sickness, come health, I should keep a daily vigil at that door of the house which your severity had not closed upon her; and I have kept my word till now and shall keep it to the end. What will you do for this miserable child of whose being you are the author?'

"With indescribable anxiety I paused and watched him, for his lips were moving. 'Do for her?' he repeated.

"How awful is the voice of the dying! I shivered as I listened, but drew near and nearer, that I might lose no word that came from his stony lips.

"'She will not come,' gasped he, with an effort that raised him up in bed, and deepened that horrible stare, 'but—'

"Who shall say what he might have uttered if Death's hand had delayed a single instant, but the inexorable shadow fell, and he never finished the sentence.

"My child, these are frightful things for you to hear. God knows I would not assail your pure ears with a tale like this, if it were not for the help and sympathy I hope to gain from you. Sin is a hideous thing; the gulf it opens is wide and deep; well may it be said to swallow those who trust themselves above its flower-hung brink. But we who are human, owe something to humanity. Love stops not because of the gulf; love follows the sinner with wilder and more heart-breaking longing, the deeper and deeper he sinks into the illimitable darkness. Ten years have passed since we laid the Colonel away in the burying-place of all the Japhas, and dutiful to his last request, nailed up the front door of his speedily to be forsaken mansion. In all that time my watch has remained unbroken in this house, which by will he had left to me, but which I secretly hold in trust for her. The hour of six has found me at my post, sometimes elate with hope, sometimes depressed with repeated disappointments, but whether hopeful or sad, always trustful that the great God who Himself so loved all sinners, that He gave the life of His Son to rescue them, would ultimately grant me the desire of my heart. But the decrepitude of age is coming upon me, and each morning I leave my bed, with growing fear lest my infirmities will increase until they finally overcome my resolution. Child, if this should happen, if lying in my bed I should some day hear that she had come back, and failing to find the lamp burning and the welcome ready, had gone away again—But the thought is madness. I cannot bear it. A sinner, lost, degraded, suffering, starving, perhaps, is wandering this way. She is hardened and old in guilt; she has drunk the cup of life's passions and found them corrupting poison; all that was lovely and pure and good has withdrawn from her; she stands alone, shut off by her sin, like a wild thing in a circle of flame. What shall touch this soul? The preacher's voice has no charm for her; good men's advice is but empty air. God's love must be mirrored in human love, to strike an eye so unused to looking up. Where shall she find such love? It is all that can rescue her; love as great as her sin, as boundless as her degradation, as persistent as her suffering. Child—"

"I know what you are going to say," suddenly exclaimed Paula, rising up and confronting Mrs. Hamlin with a steady high look of determination. "In the day of your weakness or illness you want some one to unlock the door and light the lamp. You have found her!"

XXVIII.

SUNSHINE ON THE HILLS.

"If I speak to thee in Friendship's name,Thou think'st I speak too coldly;If I mention Love's devoted flame,Thou say'st I speak too boldly."—Moore.

The story told by Mrs. Hamlin had a great effect upon Paula, not only on account of its own interest and the promise it had elicited from her, but because of the remembrances it revived of Mr. Sylvester and her life in New York. Any vision of evil or suffering, any experience that roused the affections or awakened the sensibilities, could not fail to recall to her mind the forcible figure of Mr. Sylvester as he stood that day by his own hearthstone, talking of the temptations that assail humanity; and any reminiscence of him must necessarily bring with it much that charmed and aroused. For a week, then, she felt the effect of a great unsettlement. Her village home appeared a prison; she longed to run, soar—anything to escape; the horizon was full of beckoning hands. A brooding melancholy settled upon her reveries; the prospect of a life spent in the narrow circle to which she had endeavored to re-accustom herself, became unendurable.

Thus it is with us. We slide in a groove and seem happy, when suddenly a book we read, a story we hear, an experience we encounter, shakes us out of our content, and makes continuance in the old course a violation of the most demanding instincts of our nature.

In the full tide of this unrest, Paula went out for a solitary walk on the hills. Nature can soothe if she cannot satisfy. Then the day itself was one to make the soul glad and the heart rejoice. As the young girl trod the meadows, she wondered that she could be sad. Earth and air were so full of splendor. Nature seemed to be in league with the angels of light. September stood upon the earth like a goddess of might and glory. Every tint of green that variegated the mountain-side, wooed the eye with suggestions of unfathomable beauty. A bough of scarlet flame lit here and there amid the verdure, served to illuminate the woods as for the passage of a king; and not Solomon in all his glory ever wore an aspect more sumptuous than the flowers that flecked the meadow and fringed the hardy roadside with imperial purple. A wind was blowing, a keen but kindly breeze, laden with sweetness and alert to awaken Æolian airs from the boughs of whistling beech and alder. Even the low field grasses seemed to partake in the general cheer, and nodded to each other with a witching and irresistible abandon. Had a poet been at her side, or any one capable of divining the hidden things of nature, what a commentary to all their united thoughts she would have found in the delicious tremble of the laughing leaves, in the restless music of the runaway brooks, in the lowly crickets with their single song, in the cloud-haunting birds with their trailing melodies, and in all the roll and rumble of earth's commingled noises. Alluring as was the book of nature, she could not read it alone. She felt the lack of a loving hand to turn the page. "Is it that I am lonely!" she murmured.

The thought deepened her trouble. Coming down from the hillside, she entered a skirting of woods that ran along by the river. Here she had always found peace and some of her richest treasures of thought. Through this opaline archway she had walked with her fancies, like Saint Catherine with her lily. It was sacred to all that was sweet and deep and pure within her. "Lonely!" she whispered; "I will not be lonely. To some God gives years of happy companionship; to others but a day. Shall one complain because it has fallen to his portion to have the lesser share? I will remember my one day and be glad."

"My one day!" She caught herself at the utterance and literally started at the suggestion it offered. There was but one person whom she had seen but for a day. Could she have been thinking of him?

With a flush deep as the autumn leaves she carried, she was hurrying on, when suddenly in the opening before her, a shadow fell, and a mellow voice exclaimed in her ear,

"Do I meet Miss Fairchild in her native woods?"

It was Clarence Ensign.

The surprise was very great and it took her a moment to steady herself. She had felt so assured that she should never see him or any other of her New York friends again. Had not Cicely written that he had gone West, soon after her own departure from New York. With a deepening of his voice Mr. Ensign repeated the question.

At once the day seemed to acquire all it had hitherto lacked. Looking up, she met his eye fixed admiringly upon her, and all that was merry, lightsome and gay within her, leaped at once to the surface. Ignoring his question with smiling abandon, she exclaimed,

"What shall be done to the man who delights in surprises and startles timid maidens without a cause?"

"He shall be held in captivity by the hand of his denouncer, until he has sued for pardon and obtained her generous forgiveness," returned he, holding out his palm.

She barely touched it with her own. "I see that your repentance is sincere, so your pardon shall be speedy," laughed she.

"Your discrimination is at fault, I never felt more impenitent in my life. I am a hardened wretch, Miss Fairchild, a hardened wretch! But you do not ask me from what corner of the earth I have come. You take me too much for granted; like the chirrup of a squirrel, let me say, or the whistle of a bullfinch. But perhaps you think I inhabit these woods?"

"No; but a day like this is so full of miracles, why should we be astonished at one more! I suppose you came on the train, but should not be surprised to hear you started, like Pluto, from the earth. Anything seems possible in such a sunshine."

"You are right, and I have sprung from the earth. I have been buried five mortal months in a law-suit out west, or else I should have been here before. I hope my delay has made me none the less welcome."

He was holding back a branch as he spoke, and his eyes were on a level with hers. She felt caught as in a net, and struggled vainly to keep down her color. "No," said she, "welcome is a guest's due, whether he come early or late. I should be sorry to be lacking in the duties of a hostess, though my drawing-room is somewhat more spacious than cosy," she continued, looking around on the fields into which they had emerged, "and my facilities for bespeaking you welcome greater than my power to make you comfortable."

"Comfort is a satisfaction of the mind, rather than of the body. I am not *un*comfortable, Miss Fairchild." Then as he stooped to relieve her of half her burden of trailing leaves and flowers, he exclaimed in a matter-of-fact tone, "Your aunt is a notable woman, Miss Fairchild, I admire her greatly."

"What!" said she, "you have been to the cottage? You have seen Aunt Belinda?"

"Of course," laughed he, "or how should I be here? You have been sent for, Miss Fairchild, and I am the humble bearer of your aunt's commands. But I forget, the practical has nothing to do with such a day. I am supposed to have sprung from the ground, and to know by instinct, just in what nook you were hiding from the sunlight. Very well. I acknowledge that instinct is sometimes capable of going a great way."

But this time her ready answer was lacking. She was wondering what her aunt would think of this sudden appearance of a stranger whose name she had never so much as mentioned.

"It is a pleasant rest to stand and look at a view like that, after a summer of musty labor," said he, gazing up the river with a truly appreciative eye. "I do not wonder you carry the charm of the wild woods in your laugh and glance, if you have been brought up in the sight of such a view as that."

"It has been my meat and drink from childhood," said she, and wondered why she wanted to say no more upon her favorite theme.

"Yet you tell me you love the city?"

"Too much to ever again be happy here."

It was a slip for which her cheek burned and her lids fell, the moment after. She had been thinking of Mr. Sylvester, and unconsciously spake as she might have done, if he had been at her side, instead of this genial-hearted young man. With a woman's instinctive desire to retrieve herself, she hurriedly continued, "Life is so full and large and deep in a great town, if you are only happy enough to meet those who are its blood and brain and sinew. One misses the rush of the great wheel of time in a spot like this. The world moves, but we do not feel it; it is like the quiet sweep of the stars over our heads. But in the city, days, weeks and months make themselves felt. The universe jars under the feet of hurrying masses. The story of the world is being written on pavement, corridor, and dome, so that he who runs may read. One realizes he is alive; the unit is part of the multiple. To those who are tired, God gives the rest of the everlasting hills, but to those who are eager, he holds out the city with its innumerable opportunities and incentives. And I am eager," she said. "The flower blooms on the mountain, and its perfume is sweet, but the chariot sings as it rushes, and the noise of its wheels is music in my ears."

She paused, turned her face to the breeze, and seemed to forget she was not alone. Clarence Ensign eyed her with astonishment; he had never heard her speak like this; the earnest side of her great nature had never been turned towards him before, and he felt himself shrink into insignificance in its presence. What was he that he should pluck a star from the heavens, to buckle on his breast! Wealth and position were a match for beauty great as hers, and a kind heart current coin all the world over, for a gentle disposition and a loving nature; but for this—He turned away and in his abstraction switched his foot with his cane.

"Then it was in New York that I met Cicely," exclaimed Paula.

He shook off his broodings, turned with a manful gesture, and met her sweet unfathomable eye, so brilliant with enthusiasm a moment ago, but at this instant so softly deep and tender.

"And the friendship of Miss Stuyvesant is a precious thing to you?" said he.

"Few things are more so," was her reply.

He bit his lip and his brow grew lighter. After all, great souls frequently cling to those of lesser calibre, provided they are true and unflawed. He would not be discouraged. But his tone when he spoke had acquired a reverence that did not lessen its music. "You are, then, one of the few women who believe in friendship?"

"As I believe in heaven."

Looking at her, he took off his hat. Her eye stole to his serious countenance. "Miss Stuyvesant is to be envied," said he.

"Are friends so rare?"

"Such friends are," said he.

She gave him a bright little look. "Had you been with Miss Stuyvesant, and she had expressed herself as I have done, you would have said, 'Miss Fairchild is to be envied,' and you would have been nearer the truth than now. Cicely's friendship is to mine what an unbroken mirror is to a little racing brook. It reflects but one image, while mine—" She could not go on. How could she explain to this stranger that Cicely's heart was undivided in its regard, while hers owned allegiance to more than her bosom friend.

"If I were with Miss Stuyvesant now," he declared, too absorbed in his own ideas to notice the break in hers, "I should still say in face of this friendship, 'Miss Stuyvesant is to be envied.' I have no mind for more than one thought to-day," exclaimed he, with a look that made her tremble.

There are some men who never know in what field to stay the current of their impetuosity: Clarence Ensign did. He said no more than this of all that was seething in his mind and heart. He felt that he must prove himself a man, before he exercised a man's privilege. Besides, his temperament was mercurial, and never remained long under the bondage of a severe thought, or an impressive tone of mind. He worshipped the lofty, but it was with tabor and cymbal and high-sounding lute. A climb over the stile at the foot of the hill was enough to restore him to himself. It was therefore with merry eyes and laughing lips that they approached the house and entered Miss Belinda's presence.

There are some persons whose prerogative it is to carry sunshine with them wherever they go. Clarence Ensign was one of these. Without an effort, without any display of incongruous hilarity, he always succeeded by the mere joyousness of his own nature, in calling forth all that was bright and enjoyable in others. When therefore they stepped into the quaint old-fashioned parlor, all prepared to receive them, Paula was not surprised to perceive it brighten, and her aunts' faces grow cheerful and smiling. Who could meet Clarence Ensign's laughing eye and not smile? What did astonish her, however, was the sight of an elegant basket of hot-house lowers perched on a table in the centre of the room. It made her pause, and cast looks of inquiry at the demure countenance of Miss Abby, and the quietly satisfied expression of her more thoughtful aunt.

"A remembrance from the city!" said Mr. Ensign gracefully. "I thought it might help to recall some happy hours to you."

With a swelling of the heart which she could not understand, she leaned over the ample cluster of roses and heliotrope. She felt as though she could embrace them; they were more than flowers, they were the visible emblem of all she had missed, and for which she had longed these many months.

"I seem to receive the whole in the part," said she.

He may or may not have understood her, but he saw she was gratified, and that was sufficient. The afternoon flew by on wings of light. Miss Belinda, who was not accustomed to holidays, but who thoroughly appreciated them when they came, entered into the conversation with zest; while Miss Abby's unconscious expressions of pleasure were too *naïve* not to add to, rather than detract from the general enjoyment. The twilight, with its good-bye, came all too soon.

"I have a request to make before I go," said Mr. Ensign. He was standing alone with Paula in the embrasure of the window, a few moments before his departure. "When we see a flower nodding on a ledge above our heads, we long for it; I have heard you talk of friendship, and a great desire has seized me. Miss Fairchild will you be my friend?"

She gave him a startled glance that, however, soon settled into a mellow radiant look of sympathy and pleasure.

"That is asking for something which if I hesitate to accord, it is because the word, 'friend,' carries with it so much," said she, with a sweet seriousness that disarmed her words of any latent sting they might otherwise have contained.

"I know it," he replied, "and I am very bold to ask it upon so slight an acquaintance; but life is short and real treasure is so scarce. You will not deny me, Miss Fairchild?" Then seeing her look down, hastily continued, "I have acquaintances by the score—friends who style themselves thus, by the dozen, but no *friend*. I want one; I want you for that one. Will you be it? I shall be jealous though, I warn you," he went on, with a cropping out of his mirthful nature; "I shall not be pleased to observe the circle widened indefinitely. I shall want my own place and no one else in my place."

"No one else can fill the place once given to a friend. Each one has his own niche."

"And I am to have mine?" His look was firm, his eye steadfast.

"Yes," she breathed.

With a proud stooping of his head, he took her hand and kissed it. The action became him; he was tall and well made, and gallantry induced by feeling, sat well upon him. In spite of herself, she thought of old-time stories of the Norse chivalry; he stood so radiant and bent so low.

"I shall prize my friend at her queenly value," said he; and without more ado, uttered his farewell and took his departure.

"Paula!"

The young girl started from a reverie which had held her for a long time enchained at that fast darkening window, and hastily looking up, perceived her Aunt Belinda standing before her, with her eye fixed upon her face, with a kind but searching glance.

"Yes, aunt."

"You have not told me who this Mr. Ensign is. In all the letters you wrote me you did not mention his name, I think."

"No, aunt. The fact is, I did not meet him until a few days before I left, and then only for an evening, you might say."

"Indeed! that one evening seems to have made its impression. Tell me something about him, Paula."

"His own countenance speaks for him better than I can, aunt. He is good and he is kind; an honest young man, who need fear the eye of no one. He is wealthy, I am informed, and the son of highly respected parents. He was first presented to me by

Miss Stuyvesant, whose friend he is, afterwards by Mr. Sylvester. His coming here was a surprise to me."

Miss Belinda's firm mouth, which had expanded at this dutiful response, twitched with a certain amused expression over this last announcement. Eying her niece with unrelenting inquiry, she pursued, "You have not been happy for the last few weeks, Paula. Our life seems narrow to you; you long to fly away to larger fields and more expansive skies."

With a guilty droop of her head, Paula stole her hand into that of her aunt's.

"I do not wonder," continued Miss Belinda, still watching the flushing cheek and slightly troubled mouth of the lovely girl before her. "I once breathed other air myself, and know well what charms lie beyond these mountains. In giving you up for awhile, I gave you up forever, I fear."

"No, no," whispered the young girl, "I am always yours wherever I go. Not that I am going away," she hastily murmured.

Her aunt smiled and gently stroked her niece's hand. "When the time comes, I shall bid you God speed, Paula. I am no ogress to tie my dove's wings to her nest. Love and the home it provides are the natural lot of women. None feel it more than those who have missed both."

"Aunt!" Paula was shocked and perplexed. A breaking wave full of doubts and possibilities, seemed to dash over her at this suggestion.

"Young men of judgment and principle do not come so many miles to see a youthful maiden, without a purpose," continued her aunt inexorably. "You know that, do you not, Paula?"

"Yes; but the purpose may differ in different cases," returned the young girl hurriedly. "I would not like to believe that Mr. Ensign came here with the one you give him credit for—not yet. You trouble me, aunt," pursued she, glancing tremulously about. "It is like opening a great door flooded with sunshine, upon eyes scarcely strong enough to bear the glimmer sifting through its cracks. I feel humiliated and—" She did not finish, perhaps her thought itself was incomplete.

"If a light comes sifting through the cracks, I am satisfied," said her aunt in a lighter tone than common. And she kissed her niece, and went smiling out of the room, murmuring to herself,

"I have been over-fearful; everything is coming right."

There are moments when life's great mystery overpowers us; when the riddle of the soul flaunts itself before us unexplained, and we can do no more than stand and take the rush of the tide that comes sweeping down upon us. Paula was not the girl she was before she went to New York. Love was no longer a dreamy possibility, a hazy blending of the unknown and the fancied; its tale had been too often breathed in her ear, its reality made too often apparent to her eye. But love to which she could listen, was as new and fresh and strange, as a world into which her foot had never ventured. That her aunt should point to a certain masculine form, no matter how attractive or interesting, and say, "Love and home are the lot of women," made her blood rush back on her heart, like a stream from which a dam has been ruthlessly wrenched away. It was too wild, too sudden; a friend's name was so much easier to speak, or to contemplate. She did not know what to do with her own heart, made to speak thus before its time; its beatings choked her; everything choked her; this was a worse imprisonment than the other. Looking round, her eye fell upon the flowers. Ah, was not their language expressive enough, without this new suggestion? They seemed to lose something in this very gain. She liked them less she thought, and yet her feet drew near, and near, and nearer, to where they stood, exhaling their very souls out in delicious perfume. "I am too young!" came from Paula's lips. "I will not think of it!" quickly followed. Yet the smile with which she bent over the fragrant blossoms, had an ethereal beauty in it, which was not all unmixed with the

"Light that never was on land or sea,The consecration and the poet's dream."

"He has asked to be my friend," murmured she, as she slowly turned away. "It is enough; it must be enough." But the blossom she had stolen from the midst of the fragrant collection, seemed to whisper a merry nay, as it nodded against her hand, and afterwards gushed out its sweet life on her pure young breast.

XXIX.

MIST IN THE VALLEY.

"The true beginning of our end."—Midsummer Night's Dream.

Mr. Ensign was not slow in developing his ideas of friendship. Though he did not venture upon repeating his visit too soon, scarcely a week passed without bringing to Paula a letter or some other testimonial of his increasing devotion. The blindest eye could not fail to remark whither he was tending. Even Paula was forced to acknowledge to herself that she was on the verge of a flowery incline, that sooner or later would bring her up breathless against the dread alternative of a decided yes or no. Friendship is a wide portal, and sometimes admits love; had it served her traitorously in this?

Her aunt who watched her with secret but lynx-eyed scrutiny, saw no reason to alter the first judgment of that mysterious, "It is all coming right," with which she viewed the first symptoms of Paula's girlish appreciation of her lover. If eyes and lips could speak, Paula was happy. The mournful shadows which of late had flitted with more or less persistency over her face, had vanished in a living smile, which if not deep, was cloudlessly radiant; and her voice when not used in speech, was rippling away in song, as glad as a finch's on the mountain side.

Miss Belinda was therefore very much astonished when one day Paula burst into her presence, and flinging herself down on her knees, threw her arms about her waist, crying,

"Take me away, dear aunt, I cannot, dare not stay here another day."

"Paula, what do you mean?" exclaimed Miss Belinda, holding her back and endeavoring to look into her face. But the young girl gently resisted.

"I have just had a letter from Cicely," she returned in a low and muffled voice. "She has seen Mr. Sylvester, and says he looks both wan and ill. He told her, too, that he was lonely, and I know what that means; he wants his child. The time has come for me to go back. He said it would, and that I would know when it came. Take me, aunt, take me to Mr. Sylvester."

Miss Belinda, to whom self-control was one of the cardinal virtues, leaned back in her chair and contemplated the eager, tear-stained face that was now raised to hers, with silent scrutiny. "Paula," said she at last, "is that your only reason for desiring to return to New York?"

A flush, delicate as it was fleeting, swept over the dew of Paula's cheek. She rose to her feet and met her aunt's eye, with a look of gentle dignity. "No," said she, "I wish to test myself. Birds that are prisoned will caress any hand that offers them freedom. I wish to see if the lure holds good when my wings are in mid-heaven."

There was a dreamy cadence to her voice as she uttered that last phrase, that startled her aunt. "Paula," exclaimed she, "Paula, don't you know your own heart?"

"Who does?" returned Paula; then in a sudden rush of emotion threw herself once more at her aunt's side, saying, "It is in order to know it, that I ask you to take me away."

And Miss Belinda, as she smoothed back her darling's locks, was obliged to acknowledge to herself, that time has a way of opening, in the stream of life, unforeseen channels to whose current we perforce must yield, or else hopelessly strand upon the shoals.

BOOK IV.

FROM A. TO Z.

XXX.

MISS BELINDA PRESENTS MR. SYLVESTER WITH A CHRISTMAS GIFT.

"For, O; for, O the hobby horse is forgot."—Hamlet.

It was a clear winter evening. Mr. Sylvester sat in his library, musing before a bright coal fire, whose superabundant heat and blaze seemed to make the loneliness of the great empty room more apparent. He had just said to himself that it was Christmas eve, and that he, of all men in the world, had the least reason to realize it, when the door-bell rang. He was expecting Bertram, whose advancement to the position of cashier in place of Mr. Wheelock, now thoroughly broken down in health, had that day been fully determined upon in a late meeting of the Board of Directors. He therefore did not disturb himself. It was consequently a startling surprise, when a deep, pleasant voice uttered from the threshold of the door, "I have brought you a Christmas present;" and looking up, he saw Miss Belinda standing before him, with Paula at her side.

"My child!" was his involuntary exclamation, and before the young girl knew it, she was folded against his breast with a passionate fervor that more than words, convinced her of the depth of the sacrifice which had held them separate for so long. "My darling! my little Paula!"

She felt her heart stand still. Gently disengaging herself, she looked in his face. She found it thin and wan, but lit by such a pleasure she could not keep back her smile. "You are glad, then, of your little Christmas present?" said she.

He smiled and shook his head; he had no words with which to express a joy like this.

Miss Belinda meanwhile stood with a set expression on her face, that, to one who did not know her, would immediately have proclaimed her to be an ogress of the very worst type. Not a glance did she give to the unusual splendor about her, not a wavering of her eye betokened that she was in any way conscious that she had just stepped from the threshold of a very humble cottage, into a home little short of a palace in size and the splendor of its appointments. All her attention was concentrated on the two faces before her.

"The ride on the cars has made Paula feverish," cried she, in sharp clear tones that rang with unexpected brusqueness through the curtained alcoves of that lordly apartment.

They both started at this sudden introduction of the prosaic into the hush of their happy meeting, but remembering themselves, drew Miss Belinda forward to the fire and made her welcome in this house of many memories.

It was a strange moment to Paula when she first turned to go up those stairs, down which she had come in such grief eight months or more ago. She found herself lingering on its well-remembered steps, and the first sight of the rich bronze image at the top, struck her with a sense of the old-time pleasure, that was not unlinked with the old-time dread. But the aspect of her little room calmed her. It was just as she had left it; not an article had been changed. "It is as if I had gone out one door and come in another," she whispered. All the months that had intervened seemed to float away. She felt this even more when upon again descending, she found Bertram in the library. His frank and interesting face had always been pleasant to her, but in the joy of her return it shone upon her with almost the attraction of a brother's. "I am at home again," she kept whispering to herself, "I am at home."

Miss Belinda was engrossed in conversation with Bertram, so that Paula was left free to take her old place by Mr. Sylvester's side, where she sat with such an aspect of contentment, that her beauty was half forgotten in her happiness.

"You remembered me, then, sometimes in the little cottage in Grotewell?" asked he, after a silent contemplation of her countenance. "I was not forgotten when you left the city streets?"

She answered with a bright little shake of her head, but she was inwardly wondering as she looked at his strong and picturesque face, with its nobly carved features and melancholy smile, if he had been absent from her thoughts for so much as a moment, in all these dreary months of separation.

"I did not believe you would forget," he gently pursued, "but I scarcely dared hope you would lighten my fireside with your face again. It is such a dismal one, and youth is so linked to brightness."

The flush that crossed her cheek, startled him into sudden silence. She recovered herself and slowly shook her head. "It is not a dismal one to me. I always feel brighter and better when I sit beside it. I have missed your counsel," she said; "brightness is nothing without depth."

His eyes which had been fixed on her face, turned slowly away. He seemed to hold an instant's communion with himself; suddenly he said, "And depth is worse than nothing, without it mirrors the skies. It is not from shadowed pools, such bright young lips should drink, but from the waves of an inexhaustible sea, smote upon by all the winds and sunshine of heaven."

In another moment, however, he was all cheerfulness. "You have brought me a Christmas present," cried he, "and we must make it a Christmas holiday indeed. Here is the beginning:" and with one of his old grave smiles, he handed Bertram a little note which had been awaiting him on the library table. "But Paula and Miss Belinda must have their pleasure too. Paula, are you too tired for a ride down town? I will show you New York on a Christmas eve," continued he to Miss Walton, seeing that Paula's attention was absorbed by the expression of sudden and moving surprise which had visited Bertram's face, upon the perusal of his note. "It is a stirring sight. Nothing more cheering can be found the wide world over, for those who have a home and children to make happy."

"I certainly should enjoy a glimpse of holiday cheer," assented Miss Belinda. And Paula recalled to herself by the sound of her aunt's voice, gayly re-echoed her assertion.

So Samuel was despatched for a carriage, and in a few minutes they were all riding down Fifth Avenue, *en route* for Tiffany's, Macy's, and any other store that might offer special attractions. It was a happy company. As they rolled along, Paula felt her heart grow lighter and lighter, Mr. Sylvester was almost gay, while even Aunt Belinda condescended to be merry. Bertram alone was silent, but as Paula caught short glimpses of his face, while speeding past some illuminated corner, she felt that it was that silence which is "the perfectest herald of joy."

"I shall make you get out and mix with the crowd," said Mr. Sylvester. "I want you to feel the throb of the great heart of the city on such a night as this. It is as if all men were brothers—or fathers, I should say. People that ordinarily pass each other without a sign, nod and smile with pleasing recognition of the evening's cheer. Grave and reverend seigniors, are not ashamed to be seen carrying packages by the dozen. Indeed, he who is most laden is considered the best fellow, and he who is so unfortunate as to show nothing but empty arms, feels shy if not ashamed; a condition of mind into which I shall soon fall myself, if we do not presently reach our destination."

Paula never forgot that night. As from the midst of our common-place memories, some one hour stands out distinct and strange, like a sweet foreigner in a crowd of village faces, so to Paula, this ride through the lighted streets, with the ensuing rush from store to store, piloted by Bertram and Miss Belinda, and protected by Mr. Sylvester, was her one weird glimpse into the Arabian Nights' country. Why, she could not have told; why, she did not stop to think. She had been to all these places before, but never with such a heart as this—never, never with such an overflowing heart as this.

"I have washed away my reproach," cried Mr. Sylvester, coming out to the carriage with his arms full of bundles. "Aunt Belinda is to blame for this; she set the example, you see." And with a merry laugh, he tossed one thing after another into Paula's lap, reserving only one small package for himself. "I scarcely know what I have bought," said he. "I shall be as much surprised as any one, when you come to undo the bundles. 'A pretty thing,' was all I waited to hear from the shop girls."

"There is a small printing press for one thing," cried Paula merrily. "I saw the man at Holton's eye you with a certain sort of shrewd humor, and hastily do it up. You paid for it; probably thinking it one of the 'pretty things.' We shall have to make it over to Bertram, as being the only one amongst us who by any stretch of imagination can be said to be near enough the age of boyhood to enjoy it."

"I do not know about that," cried Bertram, with a ringing infectious laugh, "my imagination has been luring me into believing that I am not the only boy in this crowd."

And so they went on, toying with their new-found joy as with a plaything, and hard would it have been to tell in which of those voices rang the deeper contentment.

The opening of the packages on the library-table afforded another season of merriment. Such treasures as came to light! A roll of black silk, which could only have been meant for Miss Belinda. A casket of fretted silver, just large enough to hold Paula's gloves; a scarf-ring, to which no one but Bertram could lay claim; a bundle of confections, a pair of diamond-studded bracelets, a scarf of delicate lace, articles for the desk, and knick-knacks for the toilet table, and last, but not least, in weight at least, the honest little printing-press.

"Oh, I never dreamed of this," said Paula, "when we chose Christmas eve for our journey."

"Nor would you have done right to stay away if you had," returned Mr. Sylvester gayly.

But when the sport was all over, and Paula stood alone with Mr. Sylvester in the library, awaiting his last good-night, the deeper influences of this holy time made themselves felt, and it was with an air of gentle seriousness, he told her that it had been a happy Christmas eve to him.

"And to me," returned Paula. "Bertram too, seemed very happy. Would it be too inquisitive in me to ask what good news the little note contained, to work such wonders?"

A smile such as was seldom seen on Mr. Sylvester's face of late, flashed brightly over it. "It was only a card of invitation to dinner," said he, "but it came from Mr. Stuyvesant, and that to Bertram means a great deal."

The surprise in Paula's eyes made him smile again. "Will it be a great shock to you, if I tell you that the name of the woman for whom Bertram made the sacrifice of his art, was Cicely Stuyvesant?"

"Cicely? my Cicely?" Her astonishment was great, but it was also happy. "Oh, I never dreamed—ah, now I see," she went on naively. "That is the reason she refrained from coming to this house; she was afraid of meeting *him*. But to think I should never have guessed it, and she my dearest friend! Oh, I am very happy; I admire Bertram so much, and it is such a beautiful secret. And Mr. Stuyvesant has invited him to his house! I do not wonder you felt like making the evening a gala one. Mr. Stuyvesant would not do that if he were not learning to appreciate Bertram."

"No; there is method in all that Mr. Stuyvesant does. More than that, if I am not mistaken, he has known this beautiful secret, as you call it, from the first, and would be the last to receive Bertram as a guest to his table, if he did not mean him the best and truest encouragement."

"I believe you are right," said Paula. "I remember now that one day when I was spending the afternoon with Cicely, he came into the room where I was, and finding me for the moment alone, sat down, and in his quaint old-fashioned manner asked me in the most abrupt way what I thought of Bertram Sylvester. I was surprised, but told him I considered him one of the noblest young men I knew, adding that if a fine mind, a kind heart, and a pure life were open to regard, Bertram had the right to claim the esteem of all his friends and associates. The old gentleman looked at me somewhat curiously, but nodded his head as if pleased, and merely remarking, 'It is not necessary to mention we had this conversation, my dear,' got up and proceeded slowly from the room. I thought it was simply a not unnatural curiosity concerning a young man with whom he had more or less business connection; but now I perceive it had a deeper significance."

"He could scarcely have found a more zealous little advocate for Bertram if he had hunted the city over. Bertram may be more obliged to you than he knows. He has been very patient, but the day of his happiness is approaching."

"And Cicely's! I feel as if I could scarcely wait to see her with this new hope in her eyes. She has kept me without the door of her suspense, but she must let me across the threshold of her happiness."

The look with which Mr. Sylvester eyed the fair girl's radiant face deepened. "Paula," said be, "can you leave these new thoughts for a moment to hear a request I have to make?"

She at once turned to him with her most self-forgetful smile.

"I have been making myself a little present," pursued he, slowly taking out of his pocket the single package he had reserved from the rest. "Open it, dear."

With fingers that unconsciously trembled, she hastily undid the package. A little box rolled out. Taking off its cover, she took out a plain gold locket of the style usually worn by gentlemen on their watch-chains. "Fasten it on for me," said he.

Wondering at his tone which was almost solemn, she quietly did his bidding. But when she essayed to lift her head upon the completion of her task, he gently laid his hand upon her brow and so stood for a moment without a word.

"What is it?" she asked, with a sudden indrawing of her breath. "What moves you so, Mr. Sylvester?"

"I have just taken a vow," said he.

She started back agitated and trembling.

"I had reason to," he murmured, "pray at nights when you go to bed, that I may be able to keep it."

"What?" sprang to her lips; but she restrained herself and only allowed her glance to speak.

"Will you do it, Paula?"

"Yes, oh yes!" Her whole heart seemed to rush out in the phrase. She drew back as at the opening of a door in an unexpected spot. Her eye had something of fear in it and something of secret desperation too. He watched her with a gaze that strangely faltered.

"A woman's prayers are a man's best safeguard," murmured he. "He must be a wretch who does not feel himself surrounded by a sacred halo, while he knows that pure lips are breathing his name in love and trust before the throne of the Most High."

"I will pray for you as for myself," she whispered, and endeavored to meet his eyes. But her head drooped and she did not speak as she would have done a few months before; and when a few instants later they parted in their old fashion at the foot of the stairs, she did not turn to give him the accustomed smile and nod with which she used to mount the stairs, spiral by spiral, and disappear in her little room above. Yet he did not grieve at the change, but stood looking up the way she had gone, like a man before whom some vision of unexpected promise had opened.

XXXI.

A QUESTION.

"Think on thy sins."—Othello.

The next morning when Mr. Sylvester came down to breakfast, he found on the library-table an exquisite casket, similar to the one he had given Paula the night before, but larger, and filled with flowers of the most delicious odor.

"For Miss Fairchild," explained Samuel, who was at that moment passing through the room.

With a pang of jealous surprise, that, however, failed to betray itself in his steadily composed countenance, Mr. Sylvester advanced to the side of the table, and lifted up the card that hung attached to the beautiful present. The name he read there seemed to startle him; he moved away, and took up his paper with a dark flush on his brow, that had not disappeared when Miss Belinda entered the room.

"Humph!" was her immediate exclamation, as her eye rested upon the conspicuous offering in the centre of the apartment. But instantly remembering herself, advanced with a cheerful good-morning, which however did not prevent her eyes from wandering with no small satisfaction towards this fresh evidence of Mr. Ensign's assiduous regard.

"Paula is remembered by others than ourselves," remarked Mr. Sylvester, probably observing her glance.

"Yes; she has a very attentive suitor in Mr. Ensign," returned Miss Belinda shortly. "A pleasant appearing young man," she ejaculated next moment; "worthy in many respects of success, I should say."

"Has he—do you mean to say that he has visited you in Grotewell?" asked Mr. Sylvester, his eye upon the paper in his hand.

"Certainly; a few more interviews will settle it."

The paper rustled in Mr. Sylvester's grasp, but his voice was composed if not formal, as he observed, "She regards his attentions then with favor?"

"She wears his flowers in her bosom, and brightens like a flower herself when he is seen to approach. If allowed to go her way unhindered, I have but little doubt as to how it will end. Mr. Ensign is not handsome, but I am told that he has every other qualification likely to make a gentle creature like Paula happy."

"He is a good fellow," exclaimed Mr. Sylvester under his breath.

"And goodness is the first essential in the character of the man who is to marry Paula," inexorably observed Miss Belinda. "An open, cheerful disposition, a clear conscience and a past with no dark pages in its history, must mark him who is to link unto his fate our pure and sensitive Paula. Is it not so, Mr. Sylvester?"

The advertisements in that morning's *Tribune* must have been unusually interesting, judging from the difficulty which Mr. Sylvester experienced in withdrawing his eyes from them. "The man whom Paula marries," said he at last, "can neither be too good, too kind, or too pure. Nor shall any other than a good, kind, and pure man possess her," he added in a tone that while low, effectually hushed even the slow-to-be-intimidated Miss Belinda. In another moment Paula entered.

Oh, the morning freshness of some faces! Like the singing of birds in a prison, is the sound and sight of a lovely maiden coming into the grim, gray atmosphere of a winter breakfast room. Paula was exceptionally gifted with this auroral cheer which starts the day so brightly. At sight of her face Mr. Sylvester dropped his paper, and even Miss Belinda straightened herself more energetically. "Merry Christmas," cried her sweet young voice, and immediately the whole day seemed to grow glad with promise and gaysome with ringing sleigh-bells. "It's snowing, did you know it? A world of life is in the air; the flakes dance as they come down, like dervishes in a frenzy. It was all we lacked to make the day complete; now we have everything."

"Yes," said Miss Belinda, with a significant glance at the table, "everything."

Paula followed her glance, saw the silver box with its wealth of blossoms, and faltered back with a quick look at Mr. Sylvester's grave and watchful countenance.

"Mr. Ensign seems to be possessed of clairvoyance," observed Miss Belinda easily. "How he could know that you were to be in town to-day, I cannot imagine."

"I wrote him in my last letter that in all probability I should spend the holidays with Mr. Sylvester," explained Paula simply, but with a slow and deepening flush, that left the roses she contemplated nothing of which to boast. "I did so, because he proposed to visit Grotewell on Christmas."

There was a short silence in the room, then Mr. Sylvester rose, and remarking with polite composure, "It is a very pretty remembrance," led the way into the dining-room. Paula with a slow drooping of her head quickly followed, while Miss Belinda brought up the rear, with the look of a successful diplomat.

A meal in the Sylvester mansion was always a formal affair, but this was more than formal. A vague oppression seemed to fill the air; an oppression which Miss Belinda's stirring conversation found it impossible to dissipate. In compliance to Mr. Sylvester's request, she sat at the head of the table, and was the only one who seemed able to eat anything. For one thing she had never seen Ona in that post of honor, but Paula and Mr. Sylvester could not forget the graceful form that once occupied that seat. The first meal above a grave, no matter how long it has been dug, must ever seem weighted with more or less unreality.

Besides, with Paula there was a vague unsettled feeling, as if some delicate inner balance had been too rudely shaken. She longed to fly away and think, and she was obliged to sit still and talk.

The end of the meal was a relief to all parties. Miss Belinda went up stairs, thoughtfully shaking her firm head; Mr. Sylvester sat down again to his paper, and Paula advanced towards the dainty gift that awaited her inspection on the library table. But half way to it she paused. A strange shyness had seized her. With Mr. Sylvester sitting there, she dared not approach this delicate testimonial of another's affection. She did not know as she wished to. Her eyes stole in hesitation to the floor. Suddenly Mr. Sylvester spoke:

"Why do you not look at your pretty present, Paula?"

She started, gave him a quick glance, and advanced hurriedly towards the table; but scarcely had she reached it when she paused, turned and hastened over to his side. He was still reading, or appearing to read, but she saw his hand tremble where it grasped the sheet, though his face with its clear cut profile, shone calm and cold against the dark background of the wall beyond.

"I do not care to look at it now," said she, with a hurried interlacing of her restless fingers.

He turned towards her and a quick thrill passed over his countenance. "Sit down, Paula," said he, "I want to talk to you."

She obeyed as might an automaton. Was it the tone of his voice that chilled her, or the studied aspect of his fixed and solemn countenance? He did not speak at once, but when he did, there was no faltering in his voice, that was lower than common, but deep, like still waters that have run into dark channels far from the light of day.

"Paula, I want to ask you a question. What would you think of a man that, with deliberate selfishness, went into the king's garden, and plucking up by the roots the most beautiful flower he could find there, carried it into a dungeon to pant out its exquisite life amid chill and darkness?"

"I should think," replied she, after the first startled moment of silence, "that the man did well, if by its one breath of sweetness, the flower could comfort the heart of him who sat in the dungeon."

The glance with which Mr. Sylvester regarded her, suddenly faltered; he turned with quickness towards the fire. "A moment's joy is, then, excuse for a murder," exclaimed he. "God and the angels would not agree with you, Paula."

There was a quivering in his tone, made all the more apparent by its studied self-possession of a moment before. She trembled where she sat, and opened her lips to speak, but closed them again, awed by his steady and abstracted gaze, now fixed before him in gloomy reverie. A moment passed. The clock ticking away on the mantel-piece seemed to echo the inevitable "Forever! never!" of Longfellow's old song. Neither of them moved. At length, in a low and trembling voice, Paula spoke:

"Is it murder, when the flower loves the dark of the dungeon more than it does the light of day?"

With a subdued but passionate cry he rose hastily to his feet. "Yes," said he, and drew back as if he could not bear the sight of her face or the glance of her eye. "Sunshine is the breath of flowers; sweet wooing gales, their natural atmosphere. He who meddles with a treasure so choice does it at his peril." Then as she hurriedly rose in turn, softened his whole tone, and assuming his usual air of kindly fatherhood, asked her in the most natural way in the world, what he could do to make her happy that day.

"Nothing," replied she, with a droop of her head; "I think I will go and see Cicely."

A short sigh escaped him. "The carriage shall be ready for you," said he. "I hope your friend's happiness will overflow into your own gentle bosom, and make the day a very pleasant one. God bless your young sweet heart, my Paula!"

Her breast heaved, her large, dark, mellow eyes flashed with one quick glance towards his face, then she drew back, and in another moment left his side and quietly glided from the room. His very life seemed to go with her, yet he did not stir; but he sighed deeply when, upon turning towards the library-table, he found that she had carried away with her the silent testimonial of another and more fortunate man's love and devotion.

XXXII.

FULL TIDE.

"A skirmish of wit between them."—Much Ado About Nothing.

Man thinks he is strong, and lays his foundations, raises his walls, and dreams of his completed turrets, without reckoning the force of the gales or the insidious inundating of the waters that may bring low the mounting structure before its time. When with a firm hand, Mr. Sylvester thrust back from his heart the one delight which of all the world could afford, seemed to him at that moment the dearest and the best, he thought the struggle was over and the victory won. It had not even commenced. He was made startlingly alive to this fact at the very next interview he had with Paula. She had just come from Miss Stuyvesant, and the reflection of her friend's scarcely comprehended joy was on her countenance, together with a look he could not comprehend, but which stirred and haunted him, until he felt forced to ask if she had seen any other of her old friends, in the short visit she had paid.

"Yes," said she, with a distressed blush. "Mr. Ensign was unexpectedly there."

It is comparatively easy to restrain your own hand from snatching at a treasure you greatly covet, but it is much more difficult to behold another and a lesser one grasp and carry it away before your eyes. He succeeded in hiding the shadow that oppressed him, but he was constrained to recognize the sharpness of the conflict that was about to be waged in the recesses of his own breast. A conflict, because he knew that a lift of his finger, or a glance of his eye would decide the matter then, while in a week, perhaps, the glamour of a young sunshiny love, would have worked its inevitable result, and the happiness that had so unexpectedly startled upon him in his monotonous and sombre path, would have wandered forever out of his reach. How did he meet its unexpected rush. Sternly at first, but with greater and greater wavering as the days went by, each one revealing fresh beauties of character and deeper springs of feeling in the enchanting girl thus brought in all her varied charm before his eyes. Why should he not be happy? If there were dark pages in his life, had they not long ago been closed and sealed, and was not the future bright with promise? A man of his years was not through with life. He felt at times as he gazed upon her face with its indescribable power of awakening far-reaching thoughts and feelings in callous breasts long unused to the holy influence of either, that he had just begun to live; that the golden country, with its enticing vistas, lay all before him, and that the youth, which he had missed, had somehow returned to his prime, fresh with more than its usual enthusiasm and bright with more than its wonted hopes and projects. With this glorious woman at his side, life would be new indeed, and if new why not pure and sweet and noble? What was there to hinder him from making the existence of this sweet soul a walking amongst gentle duties, satisfied dreams and holy aspirations? A past remorse? Why the gates could be closed on that! A strain of innate weakness for the world's good opinion and applause? Ah! with love in his life such a weakness must disappear; besides had he not taken a vow on her dear head, that ought to hedge him about as with angel's wings in the hour of temptation? Men with his experience do not invoke the protection of innocence to guard a degraded soul. Why, then, all this hesitation? A great boon was being offered to him after years of loneliness and immeasurable longing; was it not the will of heaven, that he should meet and enjoy this unexpected grace? He dared to stop and ask, and once daring to ask, the insidious waters found their way beneath the foundations of his resolution, and the lofty structure he had reared in such self-confidence, began to tremble where it stood, though as yet it betrayed no visible sign of weakness.

Meanwhile, society with its innumerable demands, had drawn the beautiful young girl within its controlling grasp. She must go here, she must go there; she must lend her talents to this, her beauty to that. Before she had decided whether she ought to remain in the city a week, two had flown by, and in all this time Mr. Ensign had been ever at her side, brightening in her own despite, hours which might else have been sad, and surrounding her difficult path with proofs of his silent and wary devotion. A golden net seemed to be closing around her, and, though as yet, she had given no token of a special recognition of her position, Miss Belinda betrayed by the uniform complacence of her demeanor, that she for one regarded the matter as effectually settled.

The success which Bertram had met in his first visit at Mr. Stuyvesant's, was not the least agitating factor in this fortnight's secret history. He was too much a part of the home life at Mr. Sylvester's, not to make the lightest thrill of his frank and sensitive nature felt by all who invaded its precincts. And he was in a state of repressed expectancy at this time, that unconsciously created an atmosphere about him of vague but restless excitement. The hearts of all who encountered his look of concentrated delight, must unconsciously beat with his. A strain sweeter than his old-time music was in his voice. When he played upon the piano, which was but seldom, it was as if he breathed out his soul before the holy images. When he walked, he seemed to tread on air. His every glance was a question as to whether this great joy, for which he had so long and patiently waited, was to be his? Love, living and apotheosized, appeared to blaze before them, and no one can look on love without feeling somewhere in his soul the stir of those deep waters, whose pulsing throb even in the darkness of midnight, proves that we are the children of God.

Cicely was uncommunicative, but her face, when Paula beheld it, was like the glowing countenance of some sculptured saint, from which the veil is slowly being withdrawn.

Suddenly there came an evening when the force of the spell that held all these various hearts enchained gave way. It was the night of a private entertainment of great elegance, to be held at the house of a friend of Miss Stuyvesant. Bertram had received formal permission from the father of Cicely, to act as his daughter's escort, and the fact had transformed him from a hopeful dreamer, into a man determined to speak and know his fate at once. Paula was engaged to take part in the entertainment, and the sight of her daintily-decked figure leaving the house with Mr. Ensign, was the last drop in the slowly gathering tide that was secretly swelling in Mr. Sylvester's breast; and it was with a sudden outrush of his whole determined nature that he stepped upstairs, dressed himself in evening attire, and deliberately followed them to the place where they were going. "The wealth of the Indies is slipping from my grasp," was his passionate exclamation, as he rode through the lighted streets. "I cannot see it go; if she can care more for me than for this sleek, merry-hearted young fellow, she shall. I know that my love is to his, what the mighty ocean is to a placid lake, and with such love one ought to be panoplied as with resisting steel."

A stream of light and music met him, as he went up the stoop of the house that held his treasure. It seemed to intoxicate him. Glow, melody and perfume, were so many expressions of Paula. His friends, of whom there were many present, received him with tokens of respect, not unmingled with surprise. It was the first time he had been seen in public since his wife's death, and they could not but remark upon the cheerfulness of his bearing, and the almost exalted expression of his proud and restless eye. Had Paula accompanied him, they might have understood his emotion, but with the beautiful girl under the care of one of the most eligible gentlemen in town, what could have happened to Mr. Sylvester to make his once melancholy countenance blazon like a star amid this joyous and merrily-laughing throng. He did not enlighten them, but moved from group to group, searching for Paula. Suddenly the thought flashed upon him, "Is it only an hour or so since I smiled upon her in my own hall, and shook my head when she asked me with a quick, pleading look, to come with them to this very spot?" It seemed days, since that time. The rush of these new thoughts, the final making up of this slowly-maturing purpose, the sudden allowing of his heart to regard her as a woman to be won, had carried the past away as by the sweep of a mountain torrent. He could not believe he had ever known a moment of hesitancy, ever looked at her as a father, ever bid her go on her way and leave the prisoner to his fate. He must always have felt like this; such momentum could not have been gathered in an hour; she must know that he loved her wildly, deeply, sacredly, wholly, with the fibre of his mind, his body and his soul; that to call her his in life and in death, was the one demanding passion of his existence, making the past a dream, and the future—ah, he dared not question that! He must behold her face before he could even speculate upon the realities lying behind fate's down-drawn curtain.

Meanwhile fair faces and lovely forms flitted before him, carrying his glance along in their train, but only because youth was a symbol of Paula. If these fresh young girls could smile and look back upon him, with that lingering glance which his presence ever invoked, why not she who was not only sweet, tender, and lovely, but gifted with a nature that responded to the deep things of life, and the stern passions of potent humanity. Could a merry laugh lure her while he stood by? Was the sunshine the natural atmosphere of this flower, that had bloomed under his eye so sweetly and shed out its innocent fragrance, at the approach of his solemn-pacing foot? He began to mirror before his mind's eye the startled look of happy wonder with which she would greet his impassioned glance, when released from whatever duties might be now pressing upon her; she wandered into these rooms, to find him awaiting her, when suddenly there was a stir in the throng, a pleased and excited rush, and the large curtain which he had vaguely noticed hanging at one end of the room, uplifted and— was it Paula? this coy, brilliant, saucy-eyed Florentine maiden, stepping out from a bower of greenery, with finger on her lip, and a backward glance of saucy defiance that seemed to people the verdant walks behind her with gallant cavaliers, eager to follow upon her footsteps? Yes; he could not be mistaken; there was but one face like that in the world. It was Paula, but Paula with youth's merriest glamour upon her, a glamour that had caught its radiant light from other thoughts than those in which he had been engaged. He bowed his head, and a shudder went through him like that which precedes the falling knife of the executioner. Even the applause that greeted the revelation of so much loveliness and alluring charm, passed over him like a dream. He was battling with his first recognition of the possibility of his being too late. Suddenly her voice was heard.

She was speaking aloud to herself, this Florentine maiden who had outstripped her lover in the garden, but the tone was the same he had heard beside his own hearthstone, and the archness that accompanied it had frequently met and encouraged some cheerful expression of his own. These are the words she uttered. Listen with him to the *naïve*, half tender, half pettish voice, and mark with his eyes the alternate lights and shadows that flit across her cheek as she broodingly murmurs:

He is certainly a most notable gallant. His "Good day, lady!" and his "Good even to you!" are flavored with the cream of perfectest courtesy. But gallantry while it sits well upon a man, does not make him one, any more than a feather makes the cap it adorns. For a Tuscan he hath also a certain comeliness, but then I have ever sworn, in good faith too, that I would not marry a Tuscan, were he the best made man in Italy. Then there is his glance, which proclaims to all men's understandings that he loves me, which same seems overbold; but then his smile!

Well, for a smile it certainly does credit to his wit, but one cannot live upon smiles; though if one could, one might consent to make a trial of his—and starve belike for her pains. (*She drops her cheek into her hand and stands musing.*)

Mr. Sylvester drew a deep breath and let his eyes fall, when suddenly a hum ran through the audience about him, and looking quickly up, he beheld Mr. Ensign dressed in full cavalier costume, standing behind the musing maiden with a half merry, half tender gleam upon his face, that made the thickly beating heart of his rival shrink as if clutched in an iron vise. What followed, he heard as we do the words of a sentence read to us from the judge's seat. The cavalier spoke first and a thousand dancing colors seemed to flash in the merry banter that followed.

Martino.—She muses, and on no other than myself, as I am ready to swear by that coy and tremulous glance. I will move her to avow it. (*Advances.*) Fair lady, greeting! A kiss for your sweet thoughts.

Nita. (*With a start*).—A kiss, Signior Martino? You must acknowledge that were but a sorry exchange for thoughts like mine, so if it please you, I will keep my thoughts and you your kiss; and lest it should seem ungracious in me to give nothing upon your asking, I will bestow upon you my most choice good day, and so leave you to your meditations. (*Curtseys and is about to depart.*)

Martino.—You have the true generosity, lady; you give away what it costs you the dearest to part from. Nay, rumple not your lip; it is the truth for all your pretty poutings! Convince me it is not.

Nita.—Your pardon, but that would take words, and words would take time, and time given to one of your persuasion would refute all my arguments on the face of them. (*Still retreating.*)

Martino.—Well, lady, since it is your pleasure to be consistent, rather than happy, adieu. Had you stayed but as long as the bee pauses on an oleander blossom, you would have heard—

Nita.—Buzzing, signior?

Martino.—Yes, if by that word you would denominate vows of constancy and devotion. For I do greatly love you, and would tell you so.

Nita.—And for that you expect me to linger! as though vows were new to my ears, and words of love as strange to my understanding as tropical birds to the eyes of a Norseman.

Martino.—If you do love me, you will linger.

Nita.—Yet if I do, (*Slowly advancing*) be assured it is from some other motive than love.

Martino.—So it be not from hate I am contented.

Nita.—To be contented with little, proves you a man of much virtue.

Martino.—When I have you, I am contented with much.

Nita.—That *when* is a wise insertion, signior; it saves you from shame and me from anger.—Hark! some one calls.

Martino.—None other but the wind; it is a kindly breeze, and grieves to hear how harsh a pretty maiden can be to the lover who adores her.

Nita.—Please your worship, I do not own a lover.

Martino.—Then mend your poverty, and accept one.

Nita.—I am no beggar to accept of alms.

Martino.—In this case, he who offers is the beggar.

Nita.—I am too young to wear a jewel of so much pretension.

Martino.—Time is a cure for youth, and marriage a happy speeder of time.

Nita.—But youth needs no cure, and if marriage speedeth time, I'll live a maid and die one. The days run swift enough without goading, Signior Martino.

Martino.—But lady—

Nita..—Nay, your tongue will outstrip time, if you put not a curb upon it. In faith, signior, I would not seem rude, but if in your courtesy you would consent to woo some other maiden to-day, why I would strive and bear it.

Martino.—When I stoop to woo any other lady than thee, the moon shall hide its face from the earth, and shine upon it no more.

Nita.—Your thoughts are daring in their flight to-day.

Martino.—They are in search of your love.

Nita.—Alack, your wings will fail.

Martino.—Ay, when they reach their goal.

Nita.—Dost think to reach it?

Martino.—Shall I not, lady?

Nita.—'Tis hard to believe it possible, yet who can tell? You are not so handsome, signior, that one would die for you.

Martino.—No, lady; but what goes to make other men's faces fair, goes to make my heart great. The virtue of my manhood rests in the fact that I love you.

Nita.—Faith! so in some others. 'Tis the common fault of the gallants, I find. If that is all—

Martino.—But I will always love you, even unto death.

Nita.—I doubt it not, so death come soon enough.

Martino. (*Taps his poiniard with his hand.*)—Would you have it come now, and so prove me true to my word?

Nita. (*Demurely*).—I am no judge, to utter the doom that your presumption merits.

Martino.—Your looks speak doom, and your sweet lips hide a sword keener than that of justice.

Nita.—Have you tried them, signior, that you speak so knowingly concerning them? (*Retreating.*) Your words, methinks, are somewhat like your kisses, all breath and no substance.

Martino.—Lady! sweet one! (*Follows her.*)

Nita.—Nay, I am gone. (*Exit.*)

Martino.—I were of the fools' fold, did I fail to follow at a beck so gentle. (*Exit.*)

That was not all, but it was all that Mr. Sylvester heard. Hastily retreating, he went out into the corridor and ere long found himself in the conservatory. He felt shaken; felt that he could not face all this unmoved. He knew he had been gazing at a play; that because this Florentine maiden looked at her lover with coyness, gentleness, tenderness perhaps, it did not follow that she, his Paula, loved the real man behind this dashing cavalier. But the possibility was there, and in his present frame of mind could not be encountered without pain. He dared not stay where men's eyes could follow him, or women's delicate glances note the heaving of his chest. He had in the last three hours given himself over so completely to hope. He realized it now though he would not have believed it before. With man's usual egotism he had felt that it was only necessary for him to come to a decision, to behold all else fall out according to his mind. He had forgotten for the nonce the power of a youthful lover, eager to serve, ready to wait, careful to press his way at every advantage. He could have cursed himself for the folly of his delay, as he strode up and down among the flowering shrubs in the solitude which the attractions of the play created. "Fool! fool!" he muttered between his teeth, "to halt on the threshold of Paradise till the door closed in my face, when a step would have carried me where—" He grew dizzy as he contemplated. The goal looks never so fair as when just within reach of a rival's hand.

A vigorous clapping, followed by a low gush of music, woke him at last to the realization that the little drama had terminated. With a hasty movement he was about to return to the parlors, when he heard the low murmur of voices, and on looking up, saw a youthful couple advancing into the conservatory, whom at first glance he recognized for Bertram and Miss Stuyvesant. They were absorbed in each other, and believing themselves alone, came on without fear, presenting such a picture of love and deep, unspeakable joy, that Mr. Sylvester paused and gazed upon them as upon the sudden embodiment of a cherished vision of his own imaginings. Bertram was speaking ordinary words no doubt, words suited to the occasion and the time, but his voice was attuned to the beatings of his long repressed heart, while the bend of his proud young head and the glance of his yearning eye were more eloquent than speech, of the leaning of his whole nature in love and protection towards the dainty, flushing creature at his side. It was a sight to make old hearts young and a less happy lover sick with envy. In spite of his gratification at his nephew's success, Mr. Sylvester's brow contracted, and it was with difficulty he could subdue himself into the appearance of calm benevolence necessary to pass them with propriety. Had it been Paula and Mr. Ensign!

He did not know how it was that he managed to find her at last. But just as he was beginning to realize that wisdom demanded his departure from this scene, he suddenly came upon her sitting with her face turned toward the crowd and waiting—for whom? He had never seen her look so beautiful, possibly because he had never before allowed himself to gaze upon her with a lover's eyes. She had exchanged her piquant Roman costume for the pearl gray satin in which Ona had delighted to array her, and its rich substance and delicate neutral tint harmonized well with the amber brocade of the curtain against which she sat.

Power, passion and purity breathed in her look, and lent enchantment to her form. She was poetry's unique jewel, and at this moment, thought rather than merriment sat upon her lips, and haunted her somewhat tremulous smiles. He approached her as a priest to his shrine, but once at her side, once in view of her first startled blush, stooped passionately, and forgetting everything but the suspense at his heart, asked with a look and tone such as he had never before bestowed upon her, if the play which he had seen that evening had been real, or only the baseless fabric of a dream.

She understood him and drew back with a look almost of awe, shaking her head and replying in a startled way, "I do not know, I dare not say, I scarcely have taken time to think."

"Then take it," he murmured in a voice that shook her body and soul, "for *I* must know, if *he* does not." And without venturing another word, or supplying by look or gesture any explanation of his unexpected appearance, or as equally unexpected departure, he bowed before her as if she had been a queen instead of the child he had been wont in other days to regard her, and speedily left her side.

But he had not taken two steps before he paused. Mr. Ensign was approaching.

"Mr. Sylvester! you are worse than the old woman of the tale, who declaring she would not, that nothing could ever induce her to—*did*."

"You utter a deeper truth than you realize," returned that gentleman, with a grave emphasis meant rather for her ears than his. "It is the curse of mortals to overrate their strength in the face of great temptations. I am no exception to the rule." And with a second bow that included this apparently triumphant lover within its dignified sweep, he calmly proceeded upon his way, and in a few moments had left the house.

Mr. Ensign, who for all his careless disposition, was quick to recognize depths in others, stared after his commanding figure until he had disappeared, then turned and looked at Paula. Why did his heart sink, and the lights and joy and promise of the evening seem to turn dark and shrivel to nothing before his eyes!

XXXIII.

TWO LETTERS.

"I have no other but a woman's reason,I think him so, because I think him so."—Two Gentlemen of Verona.

A woman who has submitted to the undivided attentions of a gentleman for any length of time, feels herself more or less bound to him, whether any special words of devotion have passed between them or not, particularly if from sensitiveness of nature, she has manifested any pleasure in his society. Paula therefore felt as if her wings had been caught in a snare, when Mr. Ensign upon leaving her that evening, put a small note in her hand, saying that he would do himself the pleasure of calling for his reply the next day. She did not need to open it. She knew intuitively the manly honest words with which he would be likely to offer his heart and life for her acceptance; yet she did open it almost as soon as she reached her room, sitting down in her outside wraps for the purpose. She was not disappointed. Every line was earnest, ardent, and respectful. A true love and a happy cheerful home awaited her if—the stupendous meaning latent in an *if!*

With folded hands lying across the white page, with glance fixed on the fire always kept burning brightly in the grate, she sat querying her own soul and the awful future. He was such a charming companion; life had flashed and glimmered with a thousand lights and colors since she knew him; his very laugh made her want to sing. With him she would move in sunshiny paths, open to the regard of all the world, giving and receiving good. Life would need no veils and love no check. A placid stream would bear her on through fields of smiling verdure. Dread hopes, strange fears, uneasy doubts and vague unrests, would not disturb the heart that rested its faith upon his frank and manly bosom. A breeze blew through his life that would sweep all such evils from the path of her who walked in trust and love by his side. In trust and love; ah! that was it. She trusted him, but did she love him? At one time she had been convinced that she did, else these past few weeks would have owned a different history. He came upon her so brightly amid her gloom; filled her days with such genial thoughts, and drew the surface of her soul so unconsciously after him. It was like a zephyr sweeping over the sea; every billow that leaps to follow seems to own the power of that passing wind. But could she think so now, since she had found that the mere voice and look of another man had power to awaken depths such as she could not name and scarcely as yet had been able to recognize? that though the billows might flow under the genial smile of her young lover, the tide rose only at the call of a deeper voice and a more imposing presence?

She was a thinking spirit and recoiled from yielding too readily to any passing impulse. Love was a sacrament in her eyes; something entirely too precious to be accepted in counterfeit. She must know the secret of her inclinations, must weigh the influence that swayed her, for once given over to earth's sublimest passion, she felt that it would have power to sweep her on to an eternity of bliss or suffering.

She therefore forced herself to probe deep into the past, and pitilessly asked her conscience, what her emotions had been in reference to Mr. Sylvester before she positively knew that love for her as a woman had taken the place of his former fatherly regard. Her blushing cheek seemed to answer for her. Right or wrong, her life had never been complete away from his presence. She was lonesome and unsatisfied. When Mr. Ensign came she thought her previous unrest was explained, but the letter from Cicely describing Mr. Sylvester as sick and sorrowful, had withdrawn the veil from the delusion, and though it had settled again with Mr. Sylvester's studied refusal to accept her devotion, was by this evening's betrayal utterly wrenched away and trampled into oblivion. By every wild throb of her heart at the sound of his voice in her ear, by every out-reaching of her soul to enter into his every mood, by the deep sensation of rest she felt in his presence, and the uneasy longing that absorbed her in his absence, she knew that she loved Mr. Sylvester as she never could his younger, blither, and perhaps nobler rival. Each word spoken by him lay treasured in her heart of hearts. When she thought of manly beauty, his face and figure started upon her from the surrounding shadows, making all romance possible and poetry the truest expression of the human soul. While she lived, he must ever seem the man of men to charm the eye, affect the heart, and move the soul. Yet she hesitated. Why?

There is nothing so hard to acknowledge to ourselves as the presence of a blemish in the character of those we love and long to revere. It was like giving herself to the rack to drag from its hiding-place and confront in all its hideous deformity, the doubt which, unconfessed perhaps, had of late mingled with her great reverence and admiring affection for this not easily to be comprehended man. But in this momentous hour she had power to do it. Conscience and self-respect demanded that the image before which she was ready to bow with such abandon, should be worthy her worship. She was not one who could carry offerings to a clouded shrine. She must see the glory shining from between the cherubim. "I must worship with my spirit as well as with my body, and how can I do that if there is a spot on his manhood, or a false note in his heart. If I did but know the secret of his past; why the prisoner sits in the dungeon! He is gentle, he is kindly, he loves goodness and strives to lead me in the paths of purity and wisdom, and yet something that is not good or pure clings to him, which he has never been able to shake loose. I perceive it in his melancholy glance; I catch its accents in his uneven tones; it rises upon me from his most thoughtful words, and makes his taking of a vow fearfully and warningly significant. Yet how much he is honored by his fellow-men, and with what reliance they look up to him for guidance and support. If I only knew the secrets of his heart!" thought she.

It was a trembling scale that hung balancing in that young girl's hand that night. On one side, frankness, cheerfulness, manly worth, honest devotion, and a home with every adjunct of peace and prosperity; on the other, love, gratitude, longing, admiration, and a dark shadow enveloping all, called doubt. The scale would not adjust itself. It tore her heart to turn from Mr. Sylvester, it troubled her conscience to dismiss the thought of Mr. Ensign. The question was yet undecided when she rose and began putting away her ornaments for the night.

What was there on her dressing-table that made her pause with such a start, and cast that look of half beseeching inquiry at her own image in the glass? Only another envelope with her name written upon it. But the way in which she took it in her hand, and the half guilty air with which she stole back with it to the fire, would have satisfied any looker-on I imagine, that conscience or no conscience, debate or no debate, the writer of these lines had gained a hold upon her heart, which no other could dispute.

It was a compactly written note and ran thus:

"A man is not always responsible for what he does in moments of great suspense or agitation. But if, upon reflection, he finds that he has spoken harshly or acted unwisely, it is his duty to remedy his fault; and therefore it is that I write you this little note. Paula, I love you; not as I once did, with a fatherly longing and a protective delight, but passionately, yearningly, and entirely, with the whole force of my somewhat disappointed life; as a man loves for whom the world has dissolved leaving but one creature in it, and that a woman. I showed you this too plainly to-night. I have no right to startle or intimidate your sweet soul into any relation that might hereafter curb or dissatisfy you; if you can love me freely, with no back-lookings to any younger lover left behind, know that naught you could bestow, can ever equal the world of love and feeling which I long to lavish upon you from my heart of hearts. But if another has already won upon your affections too much for you to give an undivided response to my appeal, then by all the purity and innocence of your nature, forget I have ever marred the past or disturbed the present by any word warmer than that of a father.

"I shall not meet you at breakfast and possibly not at dinner to-morrow, but when evening comes I shall look for my soul's dearer and better half, or my childless manhood's nearest and most cherished friend, as God pleaseth and your own heart and conscience shall decree.

"Edward Sylvester."

Miss Belinda was very much surprised to be awakened early the next morning, by a pair of loving arms clasped yearningly about her neck.

Looking up, she descried Paula kneeling beside her bed in the faint morning light, her cheeks burning, and her eyelids drooping; and guessing perhaps how it was, started up from her recumbent position with an energy strongly suggestive of the charger, that smells the battle afar off.

"What has happened?" she asked. "You look as if you had not slept a wink."

For reply Paula pulled aside the curtain at the head of her bed, and slipped into her hand Mr. Ensign's letter. Miss Belinda read it conscientiously through, with many grunts of approval, and having finished it, laid it down with a significant nod, after which she turned and surveyed Paula with keen but cautious scrutiny. "And you don't know what answer to give," she asked.

"I should," said Paula, "if—Oh aunt, you know what stands in my way! I have seen it in your eyes for some time. There is some one else—"

"But he has not spoken?" vigorously ejaculated her aunt.

Without answering, Paula put into her hand, with a slow reluctance she had not manifested before, a second little note, and then hid her head amid the bedclothes, waiting with quickly beating heart for what her aunt might say.

She did not seem in haste to speak, but when she did, her words came with a quick sigh that echoed very drearily in the young girl's anxious ears. "You have been placed by this in a somewhat painful position. I sympathize with you, my child. It is very hard to give denial to a benefactor."

Paula's head drew nearer to her aunt's breast, her arms crept round her neck. "But must I?" she breathed.

Miss Belinda knitted her brows with great force, and stared severely at the wall opposite. "I am sorry there is any question about it," she replied.

Paula started up and looked at her with sudden determination. "Aunt," said she, "what is your objection to Mr. Sylvester?"

Miss Belinda shook her head, and pushing the girl gently away, hurriedly arose and began dressing with great rapidity. Not until she was entirely prepared for breakfast did she draw Paula to her, and prepare to answer her question.

"My objection to him is, that I do not thoroughly understand him. I am afraid of the skeleton in the closet, Paula. I never feel at ease when I am with him, much as I admire his conversation and appreciate the undoubtedly noble instincts of his heart. His brow is not open enough to satisfy an eye which has accustomed itself to the study of human nature."

"He has had many sorrows!" Paula faintly exclaimed, stricken by this echo of her own doubts.

"Yes," returned her aunt, "and sorrow bows the head and darkens the eye, but it does not make the glance wavering or its expression mysterious."

"Some sorrows might," urged Paula tremulously, arguing as much with her own doubts as with those of her aunt. "His have been of no ordinary nature. I have never told you, aunt, but there were circumstances attending Cousin Ona's death that made it especially harrowing. He had a stormy interview with her the very morning she was killed; words passed between them, and he left her with a look that was almost desperate. When he next saw her, she lay lifeless and inert before him. I sometimes think that the shadow that fell upon him at that hour will never pass away."

"Do you know what was the subject of their disagreement?" asked Miss Belinda anxiously.

"No, but I have reason to believe it had something to do with business affairs, as nothing else could ever arouse Cousin Ona into being at all disagreeable."

"I don't like that phrase, *business affairs*; like charity, it covers entirely too much. Have you never had any doubts yourself about Mr. Sylvester?"

"Ah, you touch me to the quick, aunt. I may have had my doubts, but when I look back on the past, I cannot see as they have any very substantial foundation. Supposing, aunt, that he has been merely unfortunate, and I should live to find that I had discarded one whose heart was darkened by nothing but sorrow? I should never forgive myself, nor could life yield me any recompense that would make amends for a sacrifice so unnecessary."

"You love him, then, very dearly, Paula?"

A sudden light fell on the young girl's face. "Hearts cannot tell their love," said she, "but since I received this letter from him, it has seemed as if my life hung balancing on the question, as to whether he is worthy of a woman's homage. If he is not, I would give my life to have him so. The world is only dear to me now as it holds him."

Miss Belinda picked up Mr. Ensign's letter with trembling fingers. "I thought you were safe when the younger man came to woo," said she. "Girls, as a rule, prefer what is bright to what is sombre, and Mr. Ensign is truly a very agreeable as well as worthy young man."

"Yes, aunt, and he came very near stealing my heart as he undoubtedly did my fancy, but a stronger hand snatched it away, and now I do not know what to do or how to act, so as to awaken in the future no remorse or vain regrets."

Miss Belinda opened the letters again and consulted their contents in a matter-of-fact way. "Mr. Ensign proposes to come this afternoon for his answer, while Mr. Sylvester defers seeing you till evening. What if I seek Mr. Sylvester this morning and have a little conversation with him, which shall determine, for once and all, the question which so troubles us? Would you not find it easier to meet Mr. Ensign when he comes?"

"You talk to Mr. Sylvester, and upon such a topic! Oh, I could not bear that. Pardon me, aunt, but I think I am more jealous of his feelings than of my own. If his secret can be learned in a half-hour's talk, it must be listened to by no one but myself. And I believe it can," she murmured reverently; "he is so tender of me he would never let me go blindfold into any path, concerning which I had once expressed anxiety. If I ask him whether there is any good reason before God or man why I should not give him my entire faith and homage, he will answer honestly, though it be the destruction of his hopes to do so?"

"Have you such trust as that in his uprightness as a lover, and the guardian of your happiness?"

"Have not you, aunt?"

And Miss Belinda remembering his words on the occasion of his first proposal to adopt Paula, was forced to acknowledge that she had.

So without further preliminaries, it was agreed upon that Paula should refrain from making a final decision until she had eased her heart by an interview with Mr. Sylvester.

"Meantime, you can request Mr. Ensign to wait another day for his answer," said Miss Belinda.

But Paula with a look of astonishment shook her head. "Is it you who would counsel me to such a piece of coquetry as that?" said she. "No, dear aunt, my heart is not with Mr. Ensign, as you know, and it is impossible for me to encourage him. If Mr. Sylvester should prove unworthy of my affection, I must bear, as best I may, the loss which must accrue; but till he does, let me not dishonor my womanhood by allowing hope to enter, even for a passing moment, the breast of his rival."

Miss Belinda blushed, and drew her niece fondly towards her. "You are right," said she, "and my great desire for your happiness has led me into error. Honesty is the noblest adjunct of all true love, and must never be sacrificed to considerations of selfish expediency. The refusal which you contemplate bestowing upon Mr. Ensign, must be forwarded to him at once."

And with a final embrace, in which Miss Belinda allowed herself to let fall some few natural tears of disappointment, she dismissed the young girl to her task.

XXXIV.

PAULA MAKES HER CHOICE.

"Good fortune then,To make me bless't or cursed'st among men."—Merchant of Venice.

It was evening in the Sylvester mansion. Mr. Sylvester who, according to his understanding with Paula, had been absent from his home all day, had just come in and now stood in his library waiting for the coming footfall that should decide whether the future held for him any promise of joy.

He had never looked more worthy of a woman's regard than he did that night. A matter that had been troubling him for some time had just been satisfactorily disposed of, and not a shadow, so far as he knew, lay upon his business outlook. This naturally brightened his cheek and lent a light to his eye. Then, hope is no mean beautifier, and this he possessed notwithstanding the disparity of years between himself and Paula. It was not, however, of sufficiently assured a nature to prevent him from starting at every sound from above, and flushing with quite a disagreeable sense of betrayal when the door opened and Bertram entered the room, instead of the gentle and exquisite being he had expected.

"Uncle, I am so full of happiness, I had to stop and bestow a portion of it upon you. Do you think any one could mistake the nature of Miss Stuyvesant's feelings, who saw her last night?"

"Hardly," was the smiling reply. "At all events I have not felt like wasting much but pleasant sympathy upon you. Your pathway to happiness looks secure, my boy."

His nephew gave him a wistful glance, but hid his thought whatever it was. "I am going to see her to-night," remarked he. "I am afraid my love is something like a torrent that has once burst its barrier; it cannot rest until it has worked its channel and won its rightful repose."

"That is something the way with all love," returned his uncle. "It may be dallied with while asleep, but once aroused, better meet a lion in his fury or a tempest in its rush. Are you going to test your hope, to-night?"

The young man flushed. "I cannot say." But in another moment gayly added, "I only know that I am prepared for any emergency."

"Well, my boy, I wish you God-speed. If ever a man has won a right to happiness, you are that man; and you shall enjoy it too, if any word or action of mine can serve to advance it."

"Thank you!" replied Bertram, and with a bright look around the apartment, prepared to take his leave. "When I come back," he remarked, with a touch of that manly *naïveté* to which I have before alluded, "I hope I shall not find you alone."

Ignoring this wish which was re-echoed somewhat too deeply within his own breast for light expression, Mr. Sylvester accompanied his nephew to the front door.

"Let us see what kind of a night it is," observed he, stepping out upon the stoop. "It is going to rain."

"So it is," returned Bertram, with a quick glance overhead; "but I shall not let such a little fuss as that deter me from fulfilling my engagement." And bestowing a hasty nod upon his uncle, he bounded down the step.

Instantly a man who was loitering along the walk in front of the house, stopped, as if struck by these simple words, turned, gave Bertram a quick look, and then with a sly glance back at the open door where Mr. Sylvester still stood gazing at the lowering heavens, set himself cautiously to follow him.

Mr. Sylvester, who was too much pre-occupied to observe this suspicious action, remained for a moment contemplating the sky; then with an aimless glance down the avenue, during which his eye undoubtedly fell upon Bertram and the creeping shadow of a man behind him, closed the door and returned to the library.

The sight of another's joy has the tendency to either unduly depress the spirits or greatly to elate them. When Paula came into the room a few minutes later, it was to find Mr. Sylvester awaiting her with an expression that was almost radiant. It made her duty seem doubly hard, and she came forward with the slow step of one who goes to meet or carry doom. He saw, and instantly the light died out of his face, leaving it one blank of despair. But controlling himself, he took her cold hand in his, and looking down upon her with a tender but veiled regard, asked in those low and tremulous tones that exerted such an influence upon her:

"Do I see before me my affectionate and much to be cherished child, or that still dearer object of love and worship, which it shall be the delight of my life to render truly and deeply happy?"

"You see," returned she, after a moment of silent emotion, "a girl without father or brother to advise her; who loves, or believes she does, a great and noble man, but who is smitten with fear also, she cannot tell why, and trembles to take a step to which no loving and devoted friend has set the seal of his approval."

The clasp with which Mr. Sylvester held her hand in his, tightened for an instant with irrepressible emotion, then slowly unloosed. Drawing back, he surveyed her with eyes that slowly filled with a bitter comprehension of her meaning.

"You are the only man," continued she, with a glance of humble entreaty, "that has ever stood to me for a moment in the light of a relation. You *have* been a father to me in days gone by, and to you it therefore seems most natural for me to appeal when a question comes up that either puzzles or distresses me. Mr. Sylvester, you have offered me your love and the refuge of your home; if you say that in your judgment the counsel of all true friends would be for me to accept this love, then my hand is yours and with it my heart; a heart that only hesitates because it would fain be sure it has the smile of heaven upon its every prompting."

"Paula!"

The voice was so strange she looked up to see if it really was Mr. Sylvester who spoke. He had sunk back into a chair and had covered his face with his hands. With a cry she moved towards him, but he motioned her back.

"Condemned to be my own executioner!" he muttered. "Placed on the rack and bid to turn the wheel that shall wrench my own sinews! My God, 'tis hard!"

She did not hear the words, but she saw the action. Slowly the blood left her cheek, and her hand fell upon her swelling breast with a despairing gesture that would have smitten Miss Belinda to the heart, could she have seen it. "I have asked too much," she whispered.

With a start Mr. Sylvester rose. "Paula," said he, in a stern and different tone, "is this fear of which you speak, the offspring of your own instincts, or has it been engendered in your breast by the words of another?"

"My Aunt Belinda is in my confidence, if it is she to whom you allude," rejoined she, meeting his glance fully and bravely. "But from no lips but yours could any words proceed capable of affecting my estimate of you as the one best qualified to make me happy."

"Then it is my words alone that have awakened this doubt, this apprehension?"

"I have not spoken of doubt," said she, but her eyelids fell.

"No, thank God!" he passionately exclaimed. "And yet you feel it," he went on more composedly. "I have studied your face too long and closely not to understand it."

She put out her hands in appeal, but for once it passed unheeded.

"Paula," said he, "you must tell me just what that doubt is; I must know what is passing in your mind. You say you love me—" he paused, and a tremble shook him from head to foot, but he went inexorably on—"it is more than I had a right to expect, and God knows I am grateful for the precious and inestimable boon, far as it is above my deserts; but while loving me, you hesitate to give me your hand. Why? What is the name of the doubt that disturbs that pure breast and affects your choice? Tell me, I must know."

"You ask me to dissect my own heart!" she cried, quivering under the torture of his glance; "how can I? What do I know of its secret springs or the terrors that disturb its even beatings? I cannot name my fear; it has no name, or if it has—Oh, sir!" she cried in a burst of passionate longing, "your life has been one of sorrow and disappointment; grief has touched you close, and you might well be the melancholy and sombre man that all behold. I do not shrink from grief; say that the only shadow that lies across your dungeon-door is that cast by the great and heart-rending sorrows of your life, and without question and without fear I enter that dungeon with you—"

The hand he raised stopped her. "Paula," cried he, "do you believe in repentance?"

The words struck her like a blow. Falling slowly back, she looked at him for an instant, then her head sank on her breast.

"I know what your hatred of sin is," continued he. "I have seen your whole form tremble at the thought of evil. Is your belief in the redeeming power of God as great as your recoil from the wrong that makes that redemption necessary?"

Quickly her head raised, a light fell on her brow, and her lips moved in a vain effort to utter what her eyes unconsciously expressed.

"Paula, I would be unworthy the name of a man, if with the consciousness of possessing a dark and evil nature, I strove by use of any hypocrisy or specious pretense at goodness, to lure to my side one so exceptionally pure, beautiful and high-minded. The ravening wolf and the innocent lamb would be nothing to it. Neither would I for an instant be esteemed worthy of your regard, if in this hour of my wooing there remained in my life the shadow of any latent wrong that might hereafter rise up and overwhelm you. Whatever of wrong has ever been committed by me—and it is my punishment that I must acknowledge before your pure eyes that my soul is not spotless—was done in the past, and is known only to my own heart and the God who I reverently trust has long ago pardoned me. The shadow is that of remorse, not of fear, and the evil, one against my own soul, rather than against the life or fortunes of other men. Paula, such sins can be forgiven if one has a mind to comprehend the temptations that beset men in their early struggles. I have never forgiven myself, but—" He paused, looked at her for an instant, his hand clenched over his heart, his whole noble form shaken by struggle, then said—"forgiveness implies no promise, Paula; you shall never link yourself to a man who has been obliged to bow his head in shame before you, but by the mercy that informs that dear glance and trembling lip, do you think you can ever grow to forgive me?"

"Oh," she cried, with a burst of sobs, violent as her grief and shame, "God be merciful to me, as I am merciful to those who repent of their sins and do good and not evil all the remaining days of their life."

"I thought you would *forgive* me," murmured he, looking down upon her, as the miser eyes the gold that has slipped from his paralyzed hand. "Him whom the hard-hearted sinner and the hypocrite despise, God's dearest lambs regard with mercy. I learned to revere God before I knew you, Paula, but I learned to love Him in the light of your gentleness and your trust. Rise up now and let me wipe away your tears—my daughter."

She sprang up as if stung. "No, no," she cried, "not that; I cannot bear that yet. I must think, I must know what all this means," and she laid her hand upon her heart. "God surely does not give so much love for one's undoing; if I were not destined to comfort a life so saddened, He would have bequeathed me more pity and less—" The lifted head fell, the word she would have uttered, stirred her bosom, but not her lips.

It was a trial to his strength, but his firm man's heart did not waver. "You do comfort me," said he; "from early morning to late night your presence is my healing and my help, and will always be so, whatever may befal. A daughter can do much, my Paula."

She took a step back towards the door, her eyes, dark with unfathomable impulses, flashing on him through the tears that hung thickly on her lashes.

"Is it for your own sake or for mine, that you make use of that word?" said she.

He summoned up his courage, met that searching glance with all its wild, bewildering beauty, and responded, "Can you ask, Paula?"

With a lift of her head that gave an almost queenly stateliness to her form, she advanced a step, and drawing a crumpled paper from her pocket, said, "When I went to my room last night, it was to read *two* letters, one from yourself, and one from Mr. Ensign. This is his, and a manly and noble letter it is too; but hearts have right to hearts, and I was obliged to refuse his petition." And with a reverent but inexorable hand, she dropped the letter on the burning coals of the grate at their side, and softly turned to leave the room.

"Paula!" With a bound the stern and hitherto forcibly repressed man, leaped to her side. "My darling! my life!" and with a wild, uncontrollable impulse, he caught her for one breathless moment to his heart; then as suddenly released her, and laying his hand in reverence on her brow, said softly, "Now go and pray, little one; and when you are quite calm, an hour hence or a week hence whichever it may be, come and tell me my fate as God and the angels reveal it to you." And he smiled, and she saw his smile, and went out of the room softly, as one who treadeth upon holy ground.

Mr. Sylvester was considered by his friends and admirers as a proud man. If a vote had been cast among those who knew him best, as from what especial passion common to humanity he would soonest recoil, it would have been unanimously pronounced shame, and his own hand would have emphasized the judgment of his fellows. But shame which is open to the gaze of the whole world, differs from that which is sacred to the eyes of one human being, and that the one who lies nearest the heart.

As Paula's retreating footsteps died away on the stairs, and he awoke to the full consciousness that his secret was shared by her whose love was his life, and whose good opinion had been his incentive and his pride, his first sensation was one of unmitigated anguish, but his next, strange to say, that of a restful relief. He had cast aside the cloak he had hugged so closely to his breast these many years, and displayed to her shrinking gaze the fox that was gnawing at his vitals; and Spartan though he was, the dew that had filled her loving eyes was balm to him. And not only that; he had won claim to the title of true man. Her regard, if regard it remained, was no longer an airy fabric built upon a plausible seeming, but a firm structure with knowledge for its foundation. "I shall not live to whisper, 'If she knew my whole life, would she love me so well?'"

His first marriage had been so wholly uncongenial and devoid of sympathy, that his greatest longing in connection with a fresh contract, was to enjoy the full happiness of perfect union and mutual trust; and though he could never have summoned up courage to take her into his confidence, unsolicited, now that it had been done he would not have it undone, no, not if by the doing he had lost her confidence and affection.

But something told him he had not lost it. That out of the darkness and the shock of this very discovery, a new and deeper love would spring, which having its birth in human frailty and human repentance, would gain in the actual what it lost in the ideal, bringing to his weary, suffering and yearning man's nature, the honest help of a strong and loving sympathy, growing trust, and sweetest because wisest encouragement.

It was therefore, with a growing sense of deep unfathomable comfort, and a reverent thankfulness for the mercies of God, that he sat by the fire idly watching the rise and fall of the golden flames above the fluttering ashes of his rival's letter, and dreaming with a hallowing sense of his unworthiness, upon the possible bliss of coming days. Happiness in its truest and most serene sense was so new to him, it affected him like the presence of something strangely commanding. He was awe-struck before it, and unconsciously bowed his head at its contemplation. Only his eyes betrayed the peace that comes with all great joy, his eyes and perhaps the faint, almost unearthly smile that flitted across his mouth, disturbing its firm line and making his face for all its inevitable expression of melancholy, one that his mother would have loved to look upon. "Paula!" came now and then in a reverent, yearning accent from between his lips, and once a low, "Thank God!" which showed that he was praying.

Suddenly he rose; a more human mood had set in, and he felt the necessity of assuring himself that it was really he upon whom the dreary past had closed, and a future of such possible brightness opened. He walked about the room, surveying the rich articles within it, as the possible belongings of the beautiful woman he adored; he stood and pictured her as coming into the door as his wife, and before he realized what he was doing, had planned certain changes he would make in his home to adapt it to the wants of her young and growing mind, when with a strange suddenness, the door upon which he was gazing flew back, and Bertram Sylvester entered just as he had come from the street. He looked so haggard, so wild, so little the picture of himself as he ventured forth a couple of hours before, that Mr. Sylvester started, and forgetting his happiness in his alarm, asked in a tone of dismay:

"What has happened? Has Miss Stuyvesant—"

Bertram's hand went up as if his uncle had touched him upon a festering wound. "Don't!" gasped he, and advancing to the table, sat down and buried his face for a moment in his arms, then rose, and summoning up a certain manly dignity that became him well, met Mr. Sylvester's eye with forced calmness, and inquired:

"Did you know there was a thief in our bank, Uncle Edward?"

XXXV.

THE FALLING OF THE SWORD.

"Foul deeds will rise,Though all the world o'erwhelm them, to men's eyes."—
Hamlet.

Mr. Sylvester towered on his nephew with an expression such as few men had ever seen even on his powerful and commanding face.

"What do you mean?" asked he, and his voice rang like a clarion through the room.

Bertram trembled and for a moment stood aghast, the ready flush bathing his brow with burning crimson. "I mean," stammered he, with difficulty recovering himself, "that when Mr. Stuyvesant came to open his private box in the bank to-day, that he not only found its lock had been tampered with, but that money and valuables to the amount of some twelve hundred dollars were missing from among its contents."

"What?"

The expression which had made Mr. Sylvester's brow so terrible had vanished, but his wonder remained.

"It is impossible," he declared. "Our vaults are too well watched for any such thing to occur. He has made some mistake; a robbery of that nature could not take place without detection."

"It would seem not, and yet the fact remains. Mr. Stuyvesant himself informed me of it, to-night. He is not a careless man, nor reckless in his statements. Some one has robbed the bank and it remains with us to find out who."

Mr. Sylvester, who had been standing all this while, sat down like a man dazed, the wild lost look on Bertram's face daunting him with a fearful premonition. "There are but four men who have access to the vault where the boxes are kept," said he: then quickly, "Why did Mr. Stuyvesant wait till to-night to speak to you? Why did he not notify us at once of a loss so important for us to know?"

The flush on Bertram's brow slowly subsided, giving way to a steady pallor. "He waited to be sure," said he. "He had a memorandum at home which he desired to consult; he was not ready to make any rash statement: he is a thinking man and more considerate than many of his friends are apt to imagine. If the lock had not been found open he would have thought with you that he had made some mistake; if he had not missed from the box some of its contents, he would have considered the condition of the lock the result of some oversight on his own part or of some mistake on the part of another, but the two facts together were damning and could force upon him but one conclusion. Uncle," said he, with a straightforward look into Mr. Sylvester's countenance, "Mr. Stuyvesant knows as well as we do who are the men who have access to the vaults. As you say, the opening of a box during business hours and the abstracting from it of papers or valuables by any one who has not such access, would be impossible. Only Hopgood, you and myself, and possibly Folger, could find either time or opportunity for such a piece of work; while after business hours, the same four, minus Folger who contents himself with knowing the combination of the inner safe, could open the vaults even in case of an emergency. Now of the four named, two are above suspicion. I might almost say three, for Hopgood is not a man it is easy to mistrust. One alone, then, of all the men whom Mr. Stuyvesant is in the habit of meeting at the Bank, is open to a doubt. A young man, uncle, whose rising has been rapid, whose hopes have been lofty, whose life may or may not be known to himself as pure, but which in the eyes of a matured man of the world might easily be questioned, just because its hopes are so lofty and its means for attaining them so limited."

"Bertram!" sprang from Mr. Sylvester's white lips.

But the young man raised his hand with almost a commanding gesture. "Hush," said he, "no sympathy or surprise. Facts like these have to be met with silent endurance, as we walk up to the mouth of the cannon we cannot evade, or bare our breast to the thrust of the bayonet gleaming before our eyes.—I would not have you think," he somewhat hurriedly pursued, "that Mr. Stuyvesant insinuated anything of the kind, but his daughter was not present in the parlor, and—" A sigh, almost a gasp finished the sentence.

"Bertram!" again exclaimed his uncle, this time with some authority in his voice. "The shock of this discovery has unnerved you. You act like a man capable of being suspected. That is simply preposterous. One half hour's conversation with Mr. Stuyvesant on my part will convince him, if he needs convincing, which I do not believe, that whoever is unworthy of trust in our bank, you are not the man."

Bertram raised his head with a gleam of hope, but instantly dropped it again with a despairing gesture that made his uncle frown.

"I did not know that you were inclined to be so pusillanimous," cried Mr. Sylvester; "and in presence of a foe so unsubstantial as this you have conjured up almost out of nothing. If the bank has been robbed, it cannot be difficult to find the thief. I will order in detectives to-morrow. We will hold a board of inquiry, and the culprit shall be unmasked; that is, if he is one of the employees of the bank, which it is very hard to believe."

"Very, and which, if true, would make it unadvisable in us to give the alarm that any public measures taken could not fail to do."

"The inquiry shall be private, and the detectives, men who can be trusted to keep their business secret."

"How can any inquiry be private? Uncle, we are treading on delicate ground, and have a task before us requiring great tact and discretion. If the safe had only been assaulted, or there were any evidences of burglary to be seen! But we surely should have heard of it from some one of the men, if anything unusual had been observed. Hopgood would have spoken at least."

"Yes, Hopgood would have spoken."

The tone in which this was uttered made Bertram look up. "You agree with me, then, that Hopgood is absolutely to be relied upon?"

"Absolutely." A faint flush on Mr. Sylvester's face lent force to this statement.

"He could not be beguiled or forced by another man to reveal the combination, or to relax his watch over the vaults entrusted to his keeping?"

"No."

"He is alone with the vaults where the boxes are kept for an hour or two in the early morning!"

"Yes, and has been for three years. Hopgood is honesty itself."

"And so are Folger and Jessup and Watson," exclaimed Bertram emphatically.

"Yes," his uncle admitted, with equal emphasis.

"It is a mystery," Bertram declared; "and one I fear that will undo me."

"Nonsense!" broke forth somewhat impatiently from Mr. Sylvester's lips; "there is no reason at this time for any such conclusion. If there is a thief in the bank he can be found; if the robbery was committed by an outsider, he may still be discovered. If he is not, if the mystery rests forever unexplained, you have your character, Bertram, a character as spotless as that of any of your fellows, whom we regard as above suspicion. A man is not going to be condemned by such a judge of human nature as Mr. Stuyvesant, just because a mysterious crime has been committed, to which the circumstances of his position alone render it possible for him to be party. You might as well say that Jessup and Folger and Watson—yes, or myself, would in that case lose his confidence. They are in the bank, and are constantly in the habit of going to the vaults."

"None of those gentlemen want to marry his daughter," murmured Bertram. "It is not the director I fear, but the father. I have so little to bring her. Only my character and my devotion."

"Well, well, pluck up courage, my boy. I have hopes yet that the whole matter can be referred to some mistake easily explainable when once it is discovered. Mistakes, even amongst the honest and the judicious, are not so uncommon as one is apt to imagine. I, myself, have known of one which if providence had not interfered, might have led to doubts seemingly as inconsistent as yours. To-morrow we will consider the question at length. To-night—Well, Bertram, what is it?"

The young man started and dropped his eyes, which during the last words of his uncle had been fixed upon his face with strange and penetrating inquiry. "Nothing," said he, "that is, nothing more;" and rose as if to leave.

But Mr. Sylvester put out his hand and stopped him. "There *is* something," said he. "I have seen it in your face ever since you entered this room. What is it?"

The young man drew a deep breath and leaned back in his chair. Mr. Sylvester watched him with growing pallor. "You are right," murmured his nephew at last; "there is something more, and it is only justice that you should hear it. I have had two adventures to-night; one quite apart from my conversation with Mr. Stuyvesant. Heaven that watches above us, has seen fit to accumulate difficulties in my path, and this last, perhaps, is the least explainable and the hardest to encounter."

"What do you allude to?" cried his uncle, imperatively; "I have had an evening of too much agitation to endure suspense with equanimity. Explain yourself."

"It will not take long," said the other; "a few words will reveal to you the position in which I stand. Let me relate it in the form of a narrative. You know what a dark portion of the block that is in which Mr. Stuyvesant's house is situated. A man might hide in any of the areas along there, without being observed by you unless he made some sound to attract your attention. I was, therefore, more alarmed than surprised when, shortly after leaving Mr. Stuyvesant's dwelling, I felt a hand laid on my shoulder, and turning, beheld a dark figure at my side, of an appearance calculated to arouse any man's apprehension. He was tall, unkempt, with profuse beard, and eyes that glared even in the darkness of his surroundings, with a feverish intensity. 'You are Mr. Sylvester,' said he, with a look of a wild animal ready to pounce upon his prey. 'Yes,' said I, involuntarily stepping back, 'I am Mr. Sylvester.' 'I want to speak to you,' exclaimed he, with a rush of words as though a stream had broken loose; 'now, at once, on business that concerns you. Will you listen?'

"I thought of the only business that seemed to concern me then, and starting still farther back, surveyed him with surprise. 'I don't know you,' said I; 'what business can you have with me?' 'Will you step into some place where it is warm and find out?' he asked, shivering in his thin cloak, but not abating a jot of his eagerness. 'Go on before me,' said I, 'and we will see.' He complied at once, and in this way we reached Beale's Coffee-Room, where we went in. 'Now,' said I, 'out with what you have to say and be quick about it. I have no time to listen to nonsense and no heart to attend to it.' His eye brightened; he did not cast a glance at the smoking victuals about him, though I knew he was hungry as a dog. 'It is no nonsense,' said he, 'that I have to communicate to you.' And then I saw he had once been a gentleman. 'For two years and a half have I been searching for you,' he went on, 'in order that I might recall to your mind a little incident. You remember the afternoon of February, the twenty-fifth, two years ago?'

"'No,' said I, in great surprise, for his whole countenance was flushed with expectancy. 'What was there about that day that I should remember it?' He smiled and bent his face nearer to mine. 'Don't you recollect a little conversation you had in a small eating-house in Dey Street, with a gentleman of a high-sounding voice to whom you were obliged continually to say 'hush!''" I stared at the man, as you may believe, with some notion of his being a wandering lunatic. 'I have never taken a meal in any eating-house in Dey Street,' I declared, motioning to a waiter to approach us. The man observing it, turned swiftly upon me. 'Do you think I care for any such petty *fuss* as that?' asked he, indicating the rather slightly built man I had called to my rescue, while he covertly studied my face to observe the effect of his words.

"I started. I could not help it; this use of an expression almost peculiar to myself, assured me that the man knew me better than I supposed. Involuntarily I waved the waiter back and turned upon the man with an inquiring look.

"'I thought you might consider it worth your while to listen,' said he, smiling with the air of one who has or thinks he has a grip upon you. Then suddenly, 'You are a rich man, are you not? a proud man and an honored one. You hold a position of trust and are considered worthy of it; how would you like men to know that you once committed a mean and dirty trick; that those white hands that have the handling of such large funds at present, have in days gone by been known to dip into such funds a little too deeply; that, in short, you, Bertram Sylvester, cashier of the Madison Bank, and looking forward to no one knows what future honors and emoluments, have been in a position better suited to a felon's cell than the trusted agent of a great and wealthy corporation?'

"I did not collar him; I was too dumb-stricken for any such display of indignation. I simply stared, feeling somewhat alarmed as I remembered my late interview with Mr. Stuyvesant, and considered the possibility of a plot being formed against me. He smiled again at the effect he had produced, and drew me into a corner of the room where we sat down. 'I am going to tell you a story,' said he, 'just to show you what a good memory I have. One day, a year and more ago, I sauntered into an eating-house on Dey Street. I have not always been what you see me now, though to tell you the truth, I was but little better off at the time of which I speak, except that I did have a dime or so in my pocket, and could buy a meal of victuals—if I wished.' And his eyes roamed for the first time to the tables stretching out before him down the room. 'The proprietor was an acquaintance of mine, and finding I was sleepy as well as hungry, let me go into a certain dark pantry, where I curled up amid all sorts of old rubbish and went to sleep. I was awakened by the sound of voices talking very earnestly. The closet in which I was hidden was a temporary affair built up of loose boards, and the talk of a couple of men seated against it was easy enough to be heard. Do you want to know what that conversation was?'

"My curiosity was roused by this time and I said yes. If this was a plot to extort money from me, it was undeniably better for me to know upon just what foundations it rested. I thought the man looked surprised, but with an aplomb difficult to believe assumed, he went on to say, 'The voices gave me my only means of judging of the age, character, or position of the men conversing, but I have a quick ear, and my memory is never at fault. From the slow, broken, nervously anxious tone of one of the men, I made up my mind that he was elderly, hard up, and not over scrupulous; the other voice was that of a gentleman, musical and yet pronounced, and not easily forgotten, as you see, sir. The first words I heard aroused me and convinced me it was worth while to listen. They were uttered by the gentleman. 'You come to me with such a dirty piece of business! What right have you to suppose I would hearken to you for an instant!' 'The right,' returned the other, 'of knowing you have not been above doing dirty work in your life time.' The partition creaked at that, as though one of the two had started forward, but I didn't hear any reply made to this strange accusation. 'Do you think,' the same voice went on, 'that I do not know where the five thousand dollars came from which you gave me for that first speculation? I knew it when I took it, and if I hadn't been sure the operation would turn out fortunately, you would never have been the man you are to-day. It came out of funds entrusted to you, and was not the gift of a relative as you would have made me believe.' 'Good heaven!' exclaimed the other, after a silence that was very expressive just then and there, 'and you let me—' 'Oh we won't go into that,' interrupted the less cultivated voice. 'All you wanted was a start, to make you the successful man you have since become. I never worried much about morals, and I don't worry about them now, only when you say you won't do a thing likely to make my fortune, just because it is not entirely free from reproach, I say, remember what I know about you, and don't talk virtue to me.'

"'I am rightly punished,' came from the other, in a tone that proved him to be a man more ready to do a wrong thing than to face the accusation of it. 'If I ever did what you suppose, the repentance that has embittered all my success, and the position in which you have this day placed me, is surely an ample atonement.' 'Will you do what I request?' inquired the other, giving little heed to this expression of misery, of which I on the contrary took special heed. 'No,' was the energetic reply; 'because I am not spotless it is no sign that I will wade into filth. I will give you money as I have done scores of times before, but I will lend my hand to no scheme which is likely to throw discredit on me or mine. Were you not connected to me in the way in which you are—' 'You would pursue the scheme,' interrupted the other; 'it is because you know that I cannot talk, that you dare repudiate it. Well I will go to one—' 'You shall not,' came in short quick tones, just such tones as you used to me, sir, when we first entered this room. 'You shall leave the country before you do anything more, or say anything more, to compromise me or yourself. I may have done wrong in my day, but that is no reason why I should suffer for it at your hands, tempter of youth, and deceiver of your own flesh and blood! *You* shall never bring back those days to me again; they are buried, and have been stamped out of sight by many an honest dealing since, and many as I trust before God, good and sterling action. I have long since begun a new life; a life of honor, and pure, if successful, dealing. Not only my own happiness, but that of one who should be considered by you, depends upon my maintaining that life to the end, unshadowed by unholy remembrances, and unharrassed by any such proffers as you have presumed to make to me here to-day. If you want a few thousand dollars to leave the country, say so, but never again presume to offend my ears, or those of any one else we may know, with any such words as you have made use of to-day.' And the spiritless creature subsided, sir, and said no more to that rich, honored, and successful man who was so sensitive to even the imputation of guilt.

"But I am not spiritless and just where he dropped the affair, I took it up. 'Here is a chance for me to turn an honest penny,' thought I, and with a deliberation little to be expected of me, perhaps, set myself to spot that man and make the most out of the matter I could. Unfortunately I lost the opportunity of seeing his face. I was too anxious to catch every word they uttered, to quit my place of concealment till their conversation was concluded, and then I was too late to be sure which of the many men leaving the building before me was the one I was after. The waiters were too busy to talk, and the proprietor himself had taken no notice. Happily as I have before said, I never forget voices; moreover one of the two speakers had made use of a phrase peculiar enough to serve as a clue to his identity. It was in answer to some parting threat of the older man, and will remind you of an expression uttered by yourself an hour or so ago. 'Do you suppose I will let such a little fuss as that deter me?' It was the cue to his speech, by which I intended to hunt out my man from amongst the rich, the trusted and the influential persons of this city, and when found, to hold him.'

"'And you think you have done this?' said I, too conscious of the possible net about my feet to be simply angry. 'I know it,' said he; 'every word you have uttered since we have been here has made me more and more certain of the fact. I could swear to your voice, and as to your use of that tell-tale word, it was not till I thought to inquire of a certain wide-awake fellow down town, who amongst our business men were in the habit of using that expression, and was told Mr. Sylvester of the Madison Bank, that I was enabled to track you. I know I have got my hand on my man at last and—' He looked down at his thread-bare coat and around at the tables with their smoking dishes, and left me to draw my own conclusion.

"Uncle, there are crises in life which no former experience teaches you how to meet. I had arrived at such a one. Perhaps you can understand me when I say I was well nigh appalled. Denial of what was imputed to me might be wisdom and might not. I felt the coil of a deadly serpent about me, and knew not whether it was best to struggle or to simply submit. The man noted the effect he had made and complacently folded his arms. He was of a nervous organization and possessed an eye like a hungry wolf, but he could wait. 'This is a pretty story,' said I at last, and I reject it altogether. 'I am an honest man and have always been so; you will have to give up your hopes of making anything out of me.' 'Then you are willing,' said he, 'that I should repeat this story to one of the directors of your bank, whom I know?'

"I looked at him; he returned my gaze with a cold nonchalence more suggestive of a deep laid purpose, than even his previous glance of feverish determination. I immediately let my eye run over his scanty clothing and loose flowing hair and beard. 'Yes,' said I, with as much sarcasm as I knew how to assume, 'if you dare risk the consequences, I think I may.' He at once drew himself up. 'You think,' said he, 'that you have a common-place adventurer to deal with; that my appearance is going to testify in your favor; that you have but to deny any accusation which such a hungry-looking, tattered wretch as I, may make, and that I shall be ignominiously kicked out of the presence into which I have forced myself; that in short I have been building my castle in the air. Mr. Sylvester, I am a poor devil but I am no fool. When I left Dey Street on the twenty-fifth of February two years ago, it was with a sealed paper in my pocket, in which was inscribed all that I had heard on that day. This I took to a lawyer's office, and not being, as I have before said, quite as impecunious in those days as at present, succeeded in getting the lawyer, whom I took care should be a most respectable man, to draw up a paper to the effect that I had entrusted him with this statement—of whose contents he however knew nothing—on such a day and hour, to which paper a gentleman then present, consented at my respectful solicitation to affix his name as witness, which gentleman, strange to say, has since proved to be a director of the bank of which you are the present cashier, and consequently the very man of all others best adapted to open the paper whose seal you profess to be so willing to see broken.'

'"His name!' It was all that I could say. 'Stuyvesant,' cried the man, fixing me with his eye in which I in vain sought for some signs of secret doubt or unconscious wavering. I rose; the position in which I found myself was too overwhelming for instant decision. I needed time for reflection, possibly advice—from you. A resolution to brave the devil must be founded on something more solid than impulse, to hold its own unmoved. I only stopped to utter one final word and ask one leading question. 'You are a smart man,' said I, 'and you are also a villain. Your smartness would give you food and drink, if you exercised it in a manner worthy of a man, but your villainy if persisted in, will eventually rob you of both, and bring you to the prison's cell or the hangman's gallows. As for myself, I persist in saying that I am now and always have been an honest man, whatever you may have overheard or find yourself capable of swearing to. Yet a lie is an inconvenient thing to have uttered against you at any time, and I may want to see you again; if I do, where shall I find you?' He thrust his hand into his pocket and drew out a small slip of folded paper, which he passed to me with a bow that Chesterfield would have admired. 'You will find it written within,' said he 'I shall look for you any time to-morrow, up to seven o'clock. At that hour the lawyer of whom I have spoken, sends the statement which he has in his possession to Mr. Stuyvesant.' I nodded my assent, and he moved slowly towards the door. As he did so, his eyes fell upon a roll of bread lying on a counter. I at once stepped forward and bought it. Vile as he was, and deadly as was the snare he contemplated drawing about me, I could not see that wolfish look of hunger, and not offer him something to ease it. He took the loaf from my hands and bit greedily into it but suddenly paused, and shook his head with a look like self-reproach, and thrusting the loaf under his arm, turned towards the door with the quick action of one escaping. Instantly, and before he was out of sight or hearing, I drew the attention of the proprietor to him. 'Do you see that man?' I asked. 'He has been attempting a system of blackmail upon me.' And satisfied with thus having provided a witness able of identifying the man, in case of an emergency, I left the building.

"And now you know it all," concluded he; and the silence that followed the utterance of those simple words, was a silence that could be felt.

"Bertram?"

The young man started from his fixed position, and his eyes slowly traversed toward his uncle.

"Have you that slip of paper which the man gave you before departing?"

"Yes," said he.

"Let me have it, if you please."

The young man with an agitated look, plunged his hand into his pocket, drew out the small note and laid it on the table between them. Mr. Sylvester let it lie, and again there was a silence.

"If this had happened at any other time," Bertram pursued, "one could afford to let the man have his say; but now, just as this other mystery has come up—"

"I don't believe in submitting to blackmail," came from his uncle in short, quick tones.

Bertram gave a start. "You then advise me to leave him alone?" asked he, with unmistakable emotion.

His uncle dropped the hand which till now he had held before his face, and hastily confronted his nephew. "You will have enough to do to attend to the other matter without bestowing any time or attention upon this. The man that robbed Mr. Stuyvesant's box, can be found and must. It is the one indispensable business to which I now delegate you. No amount of money and no amount of diligence is to be spared. I rely on you to carry the affair to a successful termination. Will you undertake the task?"

"Can you ask?" murmured the young man, with a shocked look at his uncle's changed expression.

"As to this other matter, we will let it rest for to-night. To-morrow's revelations may be more favorable than we expect. At all events let us try and get a little rest now; I am sure we are both in a condition to need it."

Bertram rose. "I am at your command," said he, and moved to go. Suddenly he turned, and the two men stood face to face. "I have no wish," pursued he, "to be relieved of my burden at the expense of any one else. If it is to be borne by any one, let it be carried by him who is young and stalwart enough to sustain it." And his hand went out involuntarily towards his uncle.

Mr. Sylvester took that hand and eyed his nephew long and earnestly. Bertram thought he was going to speak, and nerved himself to meet with fortitude whatever might be said. But the lips which Mr. Sylvester had opened, closed firmly, and contenting himself with a mere wring of his nephew's hand, he allowed him to go. The slip of paper remained upon the table unopened.

That night as Paula lay slumbering on her pillow, a sound passed through the house. It was like a quick irrepressible cry of desolation, and the poor child hearing it, started, thinking her name had been called. But when she listened, all was still, and believing she had dreamed, she turned her face upon her pillow, and softly murmuring the name that was dearest to her in all the world, fell again into a peaceful sleep.

But he whose voice had uttered that cry in the dreary emptiness of the great parlors below, slept not.

XXXVI.

MORNING.

"Two maidens by one fountain's joyous brink,And one was sad and one had cause for sadness."

Cicely Stuyvesant waiting for her father at the foot of the stairs, on the morning after these occurrences, was a pretty and a touching spectacle. She had not slept very well the night before, and her brow showed signs of trouble and so did her trembling lips. She held in her hand a letter which she twirled about with very unsteady fingers. The morning was bright, but she did not seem to observe it; the air was fresh, but it did not seem to invigorate her. A rose-leaf of care lay on the tremulous waters of her soul, and her sensitive nature thrilled under it.

"Why does he not come?" she whispered, looking again at the letter's inscription.

It was in Mr. Sylvester's handwriting, and ought not to have occasioned her any uneasiness, but her father had intimated a wish the night before, that she should not come down into the parlor if Bertram called, and—Her thoughts paused there, but she was anxious about the letter and wished her father would hasten.

Let us look at the little lady. She had been so bright and lovesome yesterday at this time. Never a maiden in all this great city of ours had shown a sweeter or more etherial smile. At once radiant and reserved, she flashed on the eye and trembled from the grasp like some dainty tropical creature as yet unused to our stranger clime. Her father had surveyed her with satisfaction, and her lover—oh, that we were all young again to experience that leap of the heart with which youth meets and recognizes the sweet perfections of the woman it adores! But a mist had obscured the radiance of her aspect, and she looks very sad as she stands in her father's hall this morning, leaning her cheek against the banister, and thinking of the night when three years ago, she lingered in that very spot, and watched the form of the young musician go by her and disappear in the darkness of the night, as she then thought forever. Joy had come to her by such slow steps and after such long waiting. Hope had burst upon her so brilliantly, and with such a speedy promise of culmination. She thrilled as she thought how short a time ago it was, since she leaned upon Bertram's arm and dropped her eyes before his gaze.

The appearance of her father at length aroused her. Flushing slightly, she held the letter towards him.

"A letter for you, papa. I thought you might like to read it before you went out."

Mr. Stuyvesant, who for an hour or more had been frowning over his morning paper with a steady pertinacity that left more than the usual amount of wrinkles upon his brow, started at the wistful tone of this announcement from his daughter's lips, and taking the letter from her hand, stepped into the parlor to peruse it. It was, as the handwriting declared, from Mr. Sylvester, and ran thus:

"Dear Mr. Stuyvesant:

"I have heard of your loss and am astounded. Though the Bank is not liable for any accident to trusts of this nature, both Bertram and myself are determined to make every effort possible, to detect and punish the man who either through our negligence, or by means of the opportunities afforded him under our present system of management, has been able to commit this robbery upon your effects. We therefore request that you will meet us at the bank this morning at as early an hour as practicable, there to assist us in making such inquiries and instituting such measures, as may be considered necessary to the immediate attainment of the object desired.

"Respectfully yours,

"Edward Sylvester."

"Is it anything serious?" asked his daughter, coming into the parlor and looking up into his face with a strange wistfulness he could not fail to remark.

Mr. Stuyvesant gave her a quick glance, shook his head with some nervousness and hastily pocketed the epistle. "Business," mumbled he, "business." And ignoring the sigh that escaped her lips, began to make his preparations for going at once down town.

He was always an awkward man at such matters, and it was her habit to afford him what assistance she could. This she now did, lending her hand to help him on with his overcoat, rising on tip-toe to tie his muffler, and bending her bright head to see that his galoshes were properly fastened; her charming face with its far-away look, shining strangely sweet in the dim hall, in contrast with his severe and antiquated countenance.

He watched her carefully but with seeming indifference till all was done and he stood ready to depart, then in an awkward enough way—he was not accustomed to bestow endearments—drew her to him and kissed her on the forehead; after which he turned about and departed without a word to season or explain this unwonted manifestation of tenderness.

A kiss was an unusual occurrence in that confiding but undemonstrative household, and the little maiden trembled. "Something is wrong," she murmured half to herself, half to the dim vista of the lonely parlor, where but a night or so ago had stood the beloved form of him, who, bury the thought as she would, had become, if indeed he had not always been, the beginning and the ending of all her maidenly dreams: "what? what?" And her young heart swelled painfully as she realized like many a woman before her, that whatever might be her doubts, fears, anguish or suspense, nothing remained for her but silence and a tedious waiting for others to recognize her misery and speak.

Meanwhile how was it with her dearest friend and confident, Paula? The morning, as I have already declared, was bright and exceptionally beautiful. Sunshine filled the air and freshness invigorated the breeze. Cicely was blind to it all, but as Paula looked from her window preparatory to going below, a close observer might have perceived that the serenity of the cloudless sky was reflected in her beaming eyes, that peace brooded above her soul and ruled her tender spirit. She had held a long conversation with Miss Belinda, she had prayed, she had slept and she had risen with a confirmed love in her heart for the man who was at once the admiration of her eyes and the well-spring of her deepest thoughts and wildest longings. "I will show him so plainly what the angels have told me," whispered she, "that he will have no need to ask." And she wound her long locks into the coil that she knew he best liked and fixed a rose at her throat, and so with a smile on her lip went softly down stairs. O the timid eager step of maidenhood when drawing toward the shrine of all it adores! Could those halls and lofty corridors have whispered their secret, what a story they would have told of beating heart and tremulous glance, eager longings, and maidenly shrinkings, as the lovely form, swaying with a thousand hopes and fears, glided from landing to landing, carrying with it love and joy and peace. And trust! As she neared the bronze image that had always awakened such vague feelings of repugnance on her part, and found its terrors gone and its smile assuring, she realized that her breast held nothing but faith in him, who may have sinned in his youth, but who had repented in his manhood, and now stood clear and noble in her eyes. The assurance was too sweet, the flood of feeling too overwhelming. With a quick glance around her, she stopped and flung her arms about the hitherto repellant bronze, pressing her young breast against the cold metal with a fervor that ought to have hallowed its sensuous mould forever. Then she hurried down.

Her first glance into the dining-room brought her a disappointment. Mr. Sylvester had already breakfasted and gone; only Aunt Belinda sat at the table. With a slightly troubled brow, Paula advanced to her own place at the board.

"Mr. Sylvester has urgent business on hand to-day," quoth her aunt. "I met him going out just as I came down."

Her look lingered on Paula as she said this, and if it had not been for the servants, she would doubtless have given utterance to some further expression on the matter, for she had been greatly struck by Mr. Sylvester's appearance and the sad, firm, almost lofty expression of his eye, as it met hers in their hurried conversation.

"He is a very busy man," returned Paula simply, and was silent, struck by some secret dread she could not have explained. Suddenly she rose; she had found an envelope beneath her plate, addressed to herself. It was bulky and evidently contained a key. Hastening behind the curtains of the window, she opened it. The key was to that secret study of his at the top of the house, which no one but himself had ever been seen to enter, and the words that enwrapped it were these:

"If I send you no word to the contrary, and if I do not come back by seven o'clock this evening, go to the room of which this is the key, open my desk, and read what I have prepared for your eyes.

"E. S."

XXXVII.

THE OPINION OF A CERTAIN NOTED DETECTIVE.

"But still there clungOne hope, like a keen sword on starting threads uphung."—Revolt of Islam.

"Facts are stubborn things."—Elliott.

Meanwhile Mr. Stuyvesant hasted on his way down town and ere long made his appearance at the bank. He found Mr. Sylvester and Bertram seated in the directors' room, with a portly smooth-faced man whose appearance was at once strange and vaguely familiar.

"A detective, sir," explained Mr. Sylvester rising with forced composure; "a man upon whose judgment I have been told we may rely. Mr. Gryce, Mr. Stuyvesant."

The latter gentleman nodded, cast a glance around the room, during which his eye rested for a moment on Bertram's somewhat pale countenance, and nervously took a seat.

"A mysterious piece of business, this," came from the detective's lips in an easy tone, calculated to relieve the tension of embarrassment into which the entrance of Mr. Stuyvesant seemed to have thrown all parties. "What were the numbers of the bonds found missing, if you please?"

Mr. Stuyvesant told him.

"You are positively assured these bonds were all in the box when you last locked it?"

"I am."

"When was that, sir? On what day and at what hour of the day, if you please?"

"Tuesday, at about three o'clock, I should say."

"The box was locked by you? There is no doubt about that fact?"

"None in the least."

"Where were you standing at the time?"

"In front of the vault door. I had taken out the box myself as I am in the habit of doing, and had stepped there to put it back."

"Was any one near you then?"

"Yes. The cashier was at his desk and the teller had occasion to go to the safe while I stood there. I do not remember seeing any one else in my immediate vicinity."

"Do you remember ever going to the vaults and not finding some one near you at the time or at least in full view of your movements?"

"No."

"I have informed Mr. Gryce," interposed Mr. Sylvester, with a ring in his deep voice that made Mr. Stuyvesant start, "that our chief desire at present is to have his judgment upon the all important question, as to whether this theft was committed by a stranger, or one in the employ and consequently in the confidence of the bank."

Mr. Stuyvesant bowed, every wrinkle in his face manifesting itself with startling distinctness as he slowly moved his eyes and fixed them on the inscrutable countenance of the detective.

"You agree then with these gentlemen," continued the latter, who had a way of seeming more interested in everything and everybody present than the person he was addressing, "that it would be difficult if not impossible for any one unconnected with the bank, to approach the vaults during business hours and abstract anything from them without detection?"

"And do these gentleman both assert that?" queried Mr. Stuyvesant, with a sharp look from uncle to nephew.

"I believe they do," replied the detective, as both the gentlemen bowed, Bertram with an uncontrollable quiver of his lip, and Mr. Sylvester with a deepening of the lines about his mouth, which may or may not have been noticed by this man who appeared to observe nothing.

"I should be loth to conclude that the robbery was committed by any one but a stranger," remarked Mr. Stuyvesant; "but if these gentlemen concur in the statement you have just made, I am bound to acknowledge that I do not myself see how the theft could have been perpetrated by an outsider. Had the box itself been missing, it would be different. I remember my old friend Mr. A—, the president of the police department, telling me of a case where a box containing securities to the amount of two hundred thousand dollars, was abstracted in full daylight from the vaults of one of our largest banks; an act requiring such daring, the directors for a long time refused to believe it possible, until a detective one day showed them another box of theirs which he had succeeded in abstracting in the same way.[1] But the vaults in that instance were in a less conspicuous portion of the bank than ours, besides to approach an open vault, snatch a box from it and escape, is a much simpler matter than to remain long enough to open a box and choose from its contents such papers as appeared most marketable. If a regular thief could do such a thing, it does not seem probable that he would. Nevertheless the most acute judgment is often at fault in these matters, and I do not pretend to have formed an opinion."

The detective who had listened to these words with marked attention, bowed his concurrence and asked if the bonds mentioned by Mr. Stuyvesant were all that had been found missing from the bank. If any of the other boxes had been opened, or if the contents of the safe itself had ever been tampered with.

"The contents of the safe are all correct," came in deep tones from Mr. Sylvester. "Mr. Folger, my nephew and myself went through them this morning. As for the boxes I cannot say, many of them belong to persons travelling; some of them have been left here by trustees of estates, consequently often lie for weeks in the vaults untouched. If however any of them have been opened, we ought to be able to see it. Would you like an examination made of their condition?"

The detective nodded.

Mr. Sylvester at once turned to Mr. Stuyvesant. "May I ask you to mention what officer of the bank you would like to have go to the vaults?"

That gentleman started, looked uneasily about, but meeting Bertram's eye, nervously dropped his own and muttered the name of Folger.

Mr. Sylvester suppressed a sigh, sent for the paying-teller, and informed him of their wishes. He at once proceeded to the vaults. While he was gone, Mr. Gryce took the opportunity to make the following remark.

"Gentlemen," said he, "let us understand ourselves. What you want of me, is to tell you whether this robbery has been committed by a stranger or by some one in your employ. Now to decide this question it is necessary for me to ask first, whether you have ever had reason to doubt the honesty of any person connected with the bank?"

"No," came from Mr. Sylvester with sharp and shrill distinctness. "Since I have had the honor of conducting the affairs of this institution, I have made it my business to observe and note the bearing and character of each and every man employed under me, and I believe them all to be honest."

The glance of the detective while it did not perceptibly move from the large screen drawn across the room at the back of Mr. Sylvester, seemed to request the opinions of the other two gentlemen on this point.

Bertram observing it, subdued the rapid beatings of his heart and spoke with like distinctness. "I have been in the bank the same length of time as my uncle," said he, "and most heartily endorse his good opinion of the various persons in our employ."

"And Mr. Stuyvesant?" the immovable glance seemed to say.

"Men are honest in my opinion till they are proved otherwise," came in short stern accents from the director's lips.

The detective drew back in his chair as if he considered that point decided, and yet Bertram's eye which had clouded at Mr. Stuyvesant's too abrupt assertion, did not clear again as might have been expected.

"There is one more question I desire to settle," continued the detective, "and that is, whether this robbery could have been perpetrated after business hours, by some one in collusion with the person who is here left in charge?"

"No;" again came from Mr. Sylvester, with impartial justice. "The watchman—who by the way has been in the bank for twelve years—could not help a man to find entrance to the vaults. His simple duty is to watch over the bank and give alarm in case of fire or burglary. It would necessitate a knowledge of the combination by which the vault doors are opened, to do what you suggest, and that is possessed by but three persons in the bank."

"And those are?"

"The cashier, the janitor, and myself."

He endeavored to speak calmly and without any betrayal of the effort it caused him to utter those simple words, but a detective's ear is nice and it is doubtful if he perfectly succeeded.

Mr. Gryce however limited himself to a muttered, humph! and a long and thoughtful look at a spot on the green baize of the table before which he sat.

"The janitor lives in the building, I suppose?"

"Yes, and is, as I am sure Mr. Stuyvesant will second me in asserting, honesty to the back-bone."

"Janitors always are," observed the detective; then shortly, "How long has *he* been with you?"

"Three years."

Another "humph!" and an increased interest in the ink spot.

"That is not long, considering the responsibility of his position."

"He was on the police force before he came to us," remarked Mr. Sylvester.

Mr. Gryce looked as if that was not much of a recommendation.

"As for the short time he has been with us," resumed the other, "he came into the bank the same winter as my nephew and myself, and has found the time sufficient to earn the respect of all who know him."

The detective bowed, seemingly awed by the dignity with which the last statement had been uttered; but any one who knew him well, would have perceived that the film of uncertainty which had hitherto dimmed the brightness of his regard was gone, as if in the other's impressive manner, if not in the suggestion his words had unconsciously offered, the detective had received an answer to some question which had been puzzling him, or laid his hand upon some clue which had till now eluded his grasp. The inquiries which he made haste to pursue, betrayed, however, but little of the tendency of his thoughts.

"The janitor, you say, knows the combination by which the vault doors are opened?"

"The *vault doors*," emphasized Mr. Sylvester. "The safe is another matter; that stands inside the vault and is locked by a triple combination which as a whole is not known to any one man in this building, not even to myself."

"But the boxes are not kept in the safe?"

"No, they are piled up with the books in the vaults at the side of the safe, as you can see for yourself, if you choose to join Mr. Folger."

"Not necessary. The janitor, then, is the only man besides yourselves, who under any circumstances or for any reason, could get at those boxes after business hours?"

"He is."

"One question more. Who is the man to attend to those boxes? I mean to ask, which of the men in your employ is expected to procure a box out of the vaults when it is called for, and put it back in its place when its owner is through with it?"

"Hopgood usually does that business, the janitor of whom we have just been speaking. When he is upstairs or out of the way, any one else whom it may be convenient to call."

"The janitor, then, has free access to the boxes at all times, night and day?"

"In one sense, yes, in another, no. Should he unlock the vaults at night, the watchman would report upon his proceedings."

"But there must be time between the closing and opening of the bank, when the janitor is alone with the vaults?"

"There is a space of two hours after seven in the morning, when he is likely to be the sole one in charge. The watchman goes home, and Hopgood employs himself in sweeping out the bank and preparing it for the business of the day."

"Are the watchman and the janitor on good terms with one another?"

"Very, I believe."

The detective looked thoughtful. "I should like to see this Hopgood," said he.

But just then the door opened and Mr. Folger came in, looking somewhat pale and disturbed. "We are in a difficulty," cried he, stepping up to the table where they sat. "I have found two of the boxes unlocked; that belonging to Hicks, Saltzer and Co., and another with the name of Harrington upon it. The former has been wrenched apart, the latter opened with some sort of instrument. Would you like to see them, sir?" This to Mr. Sylvester.

With a start that gentleman rose, and as suddenly reseated himself. "Yes," returned he, carefully avoiding his nephew's eye; "bring them in."

"Hicks, Saltzer and Co., is a foreign house," remarked Mr. Stuyvesant to the detective, "and do not send for their box once a fortnight, as I have heard Mr. Sylvester declare. Mr. Harrington is on an exploring expedition and is at present in South America." Then in lower tones, whose sternness was not unmixed with gloom, "The thief seems to have known what boxes to go to."

Bertram flushed and made some passing rejoinder; Mr. Sylvester and the detective alone remained silent.

The boxes being brought in, Mr. Gryce opened them without ceremony. Several papers met his eye in both, but as no one but the owners could know their rightful contents, it was of course impossible for him to determine whether anything had been stolen from them or not.

"Send for the New York agent of Hicks, Saltzer and Co.," came from Mr. Sylvester, in short, business-like command.

Bertram at once rose. "I will see to it," said he. His agitation was too great for suppression, the expression of Mr. Stuyvesant's eye, that in its restlessness wandered in every direction but his own, troubled him beyond endurance. With a hasty move he left the room. The cold eye of the detective followed him.

"Looks bad," came in laconic tones from the paying teller.

"I had hoped the affair begun and ended with my individual loss," muttered Mr. Stuyvesant under his breath.

The stately president and the inscrutable detective still maintained their silence.

Suddenly the latter moved. Turning towards Mr. Sylvester, he requested him to step with him to the window. "I want to have a look at your several employees," whispered he, as they thus withdrew. "I want to see them without being seen by them. If you can manage to have them come in here one by one upon some pretext or other, I can so arrange that screen under the mantel-piece, that it shall not only hide me, but give me a very good view of their faces in the mirror overhead."

"There will be no difficulty about summoning the men," said Mr. Sylvester.

"And you consent to the scheme?"

"Certainly, if you think anything is to be gained by it."

"I am sure that nothing will be lost. And sir, let the cashier be present if you please; and sir," squeezing his watch chain with a complacent air, as the other dropped his eyes, "talk to them about anything that you please, only let it be of a nature that will necessitate a sentence or more in reply. I judge a man as much by his voice as his expression."

Mr. Sylvester bowed, and without losing his self-command, though the short allusion to Bertram had greatly startled him, turned back to the table where Mr. Folger was still standing in conversation with the director.

"I will not detain you longer," said he to the paying teller. "Your discretion will prevent you from speaking of this matter, I trust." Then as the other bowed, added carelessly, "I have something to say to Jessup; will you see that he steps here for a moment?"

Mr. Folger again nodded and left the room. Instantly Mr. Gryce bustled forward, and pulling the screen into the position he thought best calculated to answer his requirements, slid rapidly behind it. Mr. Stuyvesant looked up in surprise.

"I am going to interview the clerks for Mr. Gryce's benefit," exclaimed Mr. Sylvester. "Will you in the meantime look over the morning paper?"

"Thank you," returned the other, edging nervously to one side, "my note-book will do just as well," and sitting down at the remote end of the table, he took out a book from his pocket, above which he bent with very well simulated preoccupation. Mr. Sylvester called in Bertram and then seated himself with a hopeless and unexpectant look, which he for the moment forgot would be reflected in the mirror before him, and so carried to the eye of the watchful detective. In another instant Jessup entered.

What was said in the short interview that followed, is unimportant. Mr. Jessup, the third teller, was one of those clear eyed, straightforward appearing men whose countenance is its own guarantee. It was not necessary to detain him or make him speak. The next man to come in was Watson, and after he had gone, two or three of the clerks, and later the receiving teller and one of the runners. All stopped long enough to insure Mr. Gryce a good view of their faces, and from each and all did Mr. Sylvester succeed in eliciting more or less conversation in response to the questions he chose to put.

With the disappearance of the last mentioned individual, Mr. Gryce peeped from behind the screen. "A set of as honest-looking men as I wish to see!" uttered he with a frank cordiality that was scarcely reflected in the anxious countenances about him. "No sly-boots among them; how about the janitor, Hopgood?"

"He shall be summoned at once, if you desire it," said Mr. Sylvester, "I have only delayed calling him that I might have leisure to interrogate him with reference to his duties, and this very theft. That is if you judge it advisable in me to tamper with the subject unassisted?"

"Your nephew can help you if necessary," replied the imperturbable detective. "I should like to hear what the man, Hopgood, has to say for himself," and he glided back into his old position.

But Mr. Sylvester had scarcely reached out his hand to ring the bell by which he usually summoned the janitor, when the agent of Hicks, Saltzer & Co. came in. It was an interruption that demanded instant attention. Saluting the gentleman with his usual proud reserve, he drew his attention to the box lying upon the table.

"This is yours, I believe, sir," said he. "It was found in our vaults this morning in the condition in which you now behold it, and we are anxious to know if its contents are all correct."

"They have been handled," returned the agent, after a careful survey of the various papers that filled the box, "but nothing appears to be missing."

Three persons at least in that room breathed more easily.

"But the truth is," the gentleman continued, with a half smile towards the silent President of the bank, "there was nothing in this box that would have been of much use to any other parties than ourselves. If there had been a bond or so here, I doubt if we should have come off so fortunately, eh? The lock has evidently been wrenched open, and that is certainly a pretty sure sign that something is not right hereabouts."

"Something is decidedly wrong," came from Mr. Sylvester sternly; "but through whose fault we do not as yet know." And with a few words expressive of his relief at finding the other had sustained no material loss, he allowed the agent to depart.

He had no sooner left the room than Mr. Stuyvesant rose. "Are you going to question Hopgood now?" queried he, nervously pocketing his note-book.

"Yes sir, if you have no objections."

The director fidgeted with his chair and finally moved towards the door.

"I think you will get along better with him alone," said he. "He is a man who very easily gets embarrassed, and has a way of acting as if he were afraid of me. I will just step outside while you talk to him."

But Mr. Sylvester with a sudden dark flush on his brow, hastily stopped him. "I beg you will not," said he, with a quick realization of what Hopgood might be led to say in the forthcoming interview, if he were not restrained by the presence of the director.

"Hopgood is not so afraid of you that he will not answer every question that is put to him with straightforward frankness." And he pushed up a chair, with a smile that Mr. Stuyvesant evidently found himself unable to resist. The screen trembled slightly, but none of them noticed it; Mr. Sylvester at once rang for Hopgood.

He came in panting with his hurried descent from the fifth story, his face flushed and his eyes rolling, but without any of the secret perturbation Bertram had observed in them on a former occasion. "He cannot help us," was the thought that darkened the young man's brow as his eyes left the janitor, and faltering towards his uncle, fell upon the table before him.

Everything was reflected in the mirror.

"Well, Hopgood, I have a few questions to put to you this morning," said Mr. Sylvester in a restrained, but not unkindly tone.

The worthy man bowed, bestowed a salutatory roll of his eyes on Mr. Stuyvesant, and stood deferentially waiting.

"No, he cannot help us," was again Bertram's thought, and again his eyes faltered to his uncle's face, and again fell anxiously before him.

"It has not been my habit to trouble you with inquiries about your management of matters under your charge," continued Mr. Sylvester, stopping till the janitor's wandering eyes settled upon his own. "Your conduct has always been exemplary, and your attention to duty satisfactory; but I would like to ask you to-day if you have observed anything amiss with the vaults of late? anything wrong about the boxes kept there? anything in short, that excited your suspicion or caused you to ask yourself if everything was as it should be?"

The janitor's ruddy face grew pale, and his eye fell with startled inquiry on Mr. Harrington's box that still occupied the centre of the table. "No, sir," he emphatically replied, "has anything—"

But Mr. Sylvester did not wait to be questioned. "You have attended to your duties as promptly and conscientiously as usual; you have allowed no one to go to the vaults day or night, who had no business there? You have not relaxed your accustomed vigilance, or left the bank alone at any time during the hours it is under your charge?"

"No sir, not for a minute, sir; that is—" He stopped and his eye wandered towards Mr. Stuyvesant. "Never for a minute, sir," he went on, "without I knew some one was in the bank, who was capable of looking after it."

"The watchman has been at his post every night up to the usual hour?"

"Yes sir."

"There has been no carelessness in closing the vault doors after the departure of the clerks?"

"No sir."

"And no trouble," he continued, with a shade more of dignity, possibly because Hopgood's tell-tale face was beginning to show signs of anxious confusion, "and no trouble in opening them at the proper time each morning?"

"No sir."

"One question more—"

But here Bertram was called out, and in the momentary stir occasioned by his departure, Hopgood allowed himself to glance at the box before him more intently than he had hitherto presumed to do. He saw it was unlocked, and his hands began to tremble. Mr. Sylvester's voice recalled him to himself.

"You are a faithful man," said that gentleman, continuing his speech of a minute before, "and as such we are ready to acknowledge you; but the most conscientious amongst us are sometimes led into indiscretions. Now have you ever through carelessness or by means of any inadvertence, revealed to any one in or out of the bank, the particular combination by which the lock of the vault-door is at present opened?"

"No sir, indeed no; I am much too anxious, and feel my own responsibility entirely too much, not to preserve so important a secret with the utmost care and jealousy."

Mr. Sylvester's voice, careful as he was to modulate it, showed a secret discouragement. "The vaults then as far as you know, are safe when once they are closed for the night?"

"Yes sir." The janitor's face expressed a slight degree of wonder, but his voice was emphatic.

Mr. Sylvester's eye travelled in the direction of the screen. "Very well," said he; and paused to reflect.

In the interim the door opened for a second time. "A gentleman to see Mr. Stuyvesant," said a voice.

With an air of relief the director hastily rose, and before Mr. Sylvester had realized his position, left the room and closed the door behind him. A knell seemed to ring its note in Mr. Sylvester's breast. The janitor, released as he supposed from all constraint, stepped hastily forward.

"That box has been found unlocked," he cried with a wave of his hand towards the table; "some one has been to the vaults, and I—Oh, sir," he hurriedly exclaimed, disregarding in his agitation the stern and forbidding look which Mr. Sylvester in his secret despair had made haste to assume, "you did not want me to say anything about the time you came down so early in the morning, and I went out and left you alone in the bank, and you went to the vaults and opened Mr. Stuyvesant's box by mistake, with a tooth-pick as you remember?"

The mirror that looked down upon that pair, showed one very white face at that moment, but the screen that had trembled a moment before, stood strangely still in the silence.

"No," came at length from Mr. Sylvester, with a composure that astonished himself. "I was not questioning you about matters of a year agone. But you might have told that incident if you pleased; it was very easily explainable."

"Yes sir, I know, and I beg pardon for alluding to it, but I was so taken aback, sir, by your questions; I wanted to tell the exact truth, and I did not want to say anything that would hurt you with Mr. Stuyvesant; that is if I could help it. I hope I did right, sir," he blundered on, conscious he was uttering words he might better have kept to himself, but too embarrassed to know how to emerge from the difficulty into which his mingled zeal and anxiety had betrayed him. "I was never a good hand at answering questions, and if any thing really serious has happened, I shall wish you had taken me at my word and dismissed me immediately after that affair. Constantia Maria would have been a little worse off perhaps, but I should not be on hand to answer questions, and—"

"Hopgood!"

The man started, eyed Mr. Sylvester's white but powerfully controlled countenance, seemed struck with something he saw there, and was silent.

"You make too much now, as you made too much then of a matter that having its sole ground in a mistake, is, as I say, easily explainable. This affair which has come up now, is not so clear. Three of the boxes have been opened, and from one certain valuables have been taken. Can you give me any information that will assist us in our search after the culprit?"

"No sir." The tone was quite humble, Hopgood drew back unconsciously towards the door.

"As for the mistake of a year ago to which you have seen proper to allude, I shall myself take pains to inform Mr. Stuyvesant of it, since it has made such an impression upon you that it trammels your honesty and makes you consider it at all necessary to be anxious about it at this time."

And Hopgood unused to sarcasm from those lips, drew himself together, and with one more agitated look at the box on the table, sidled awkwardly from the room. Mr. Sylvester at once advanced to the screen which he hastily pushed aside. "Well, sir," said he, meeting the detective's wavering eye and forcing him to return his look, "you have now seen the various employees of the bank and heard most of them converse. Is there anything more you would like to inquire into before giving us the opinion I requested?"

"No sir," said the detective, coming forward, but very slowly and somewhat hesitatingly for him. "I think I am ready to say—"

Here the door opened, and Mr. Stuyvesant returned. The detective drew a breath of relief and repeated his words with a business-like assurance. "I think I am ready to say, that from the nature of the theft and the mysterious manner in which it has been perpetrated, suspicion undoubtedly points to some one connected with the bank. That is all that you require of me to-day?" he added, with a bow of some formality in the direction of Mr. Sylvester.

"Yes," was the short reply. But in an instant a change passed over the stately form of the speaker. Advancing to Mr. Gryce, he confronted him with a countenance almost majestic in its severity, and somewhat severely remarked, "This is a serious charge to bring against men whose countenances you yourself have denominated as honest. Are we to believe you have fully considered the question, and realize the importance of what you say?"

"Mr. Sylvester," replied the detective, with great self-possession and some dignity, "a man who is brought every day of his life into positions where the least turning of a hair will sink a man or save him, learns to weigh his words, before he speaks even in such informal inquiries as these."

Mr. Sylvester bowed and turned towards Mr. Stuyvesant. "Is there any further action you would like to have taken in regard to this matter to-day?" he asked, without a tremble in his voice.

With a glance at the half open box of the absent Mr. Harrington, the agitated director slowly shook his head. "We must have time to think," said he.

Mr. Gryce at once took up his hat. "If the charge implied in my opinion strikes you, gentlemen, as serious, you must at least acknowledge that your own judgment does not greatly differ from mine, or why such unnecessary agitation in regard to a loss so petty, by a gentleman worth as we are told his millions." And with this passing shot, to which neither of his auditors responded, he made his final obeisance and calmly left the room.

Mr. Sylvester and Mr. Stuyvesant slowly confronted one another.

"The man speaks the truth," said the former. "You at least suspect some one in the bank, Mr. Stuyvesant?"

"I have no wish to," hastily returned the other, "but facts—"

"Would facts of this nature have any weight with you against the unspotted character of a man never known by you to meditate, much less commit a dishonest action?"

"No; yet facts are facts, and if it is proved that some one in our employ has perpetrated a theft, the mind will unconsciously ask who, and remain uneasy till it is satisfied."

"And if it never is?"

"It will always ask who, I suppose."

Mr. Sylvester drew back. "The matter shall be pushed," said he; "you shall be satisfied. Surveillance over each man employed in this institution ought sooner or later to elicit the truth. The police shall take it in charge."

Mr. Stuyvesant looked uneasy. "I suppose it is only justice," murmured he, "but it is a scandal I would have been glad to avoid."

"And I, but circumstances admit of no other course. The innocent must not suffer for the guilty, even so far as an unfounded suspicion would lead."

"No, no, of course not." And the director bustled about after his overcoat and hat.

Mr. Sylvester watched him with growing sadness. "Mr. Stuyvesant," said he, as the latter stood before him ready for the street, "we have always been on terms of friendship, and nothing but the most pleasant relations have ever existed between us. Will you pardon me if I ask you to give me your hand in good-day?"

The director paused, looked a trifle astonished, but held out his hand not only with cordiality but very evident affection.

"Good day," cried he, "good-day."

Mr. Sylvester pressed that hand, and then with a dignified bow, allowed the director to depart. It was his last effort at composure. When the door closed, his head sank on his hands, and life with all its hopes and honors, love and happiness, seemed to die within him.

He was interrupted at length by Bertram. "Well, uncle?" asked the young man with unrestrained emotion.

"The theft has been committed by some one in this bank; so the detective gives out, and so we are called upon to believe. *Who* the man is who has caused us all this misery, neither he, nor you, nor I, nor any one, is likely to very soon determine. Meantime—"

"Well?" cried Bertram anxiously, after a moment of suspense.

"Meantime, courage!" his uncle resumed with forced cheerfulness.

But as he was leaving the bank he came up to Bertram, and laying his hand on his shoulder, quietly said:

"I want you to go immediately to my house upon leaving here. I may not be back till midnight, and Miss Fairchild may need the comfort of your presence. Will you do it, Bertram?"

"Uncle! I—"

"Hush! you will comfort me best by doing what I ask. May I rely upon you?"

"Always."

"That is enough."

And with just a final look, the two gentlemen parted, and the shadow which had rested all day upon the bank, deepened over Bertram's head like a pall.

It was not lifted by the sight of Hopgood stealing a few minutes later towards the door by which his uncle had departed, his face pale, and his eyes fixed in a stare, that bespoke some deep and moving determination.

XXXVIII.

BLUE-BEARD'S CHAMBER.

"Present fearsAre less than horrible imaginings."—Macbeth.

Clarence Ensign was not surprised at the refusal he received from Paula. He had realized from the first that the love of this beautiful woman would be difficult to obtain, even if no rival with more powerful inducements than his own, should chance to cross his path. She was one who could be won to give friendship, consideration, and sympathy without stint; but from the very fact that she could so easily be induced to grant these, he foresaw the improbability, or at least the difficulty of enticing her to yield more. A woman whose hand warms towards the other sex in ready friendship, is the last to succumb to the entreaties of love. The circle of her sympathies is so large, the man must do well, who of all his sex, pierces to the sacred centre. The appearance of Mr. Sylvester on the scene, settled his fate, or so he believed; but he was too much in earnest to yield his hopes without another effort; so upon the afternoon of this eventful day, he called upon Paula.

The first glimpse he obtained of her countenance, convinced him that he was indeed too late. Not for him that anxious pallor, giving way to a rosy tinge at the least sound in the streets without. Not for him that wandering glance, burning with questions to which nothing seemed able to grant reply. The very smile with which she greeted him, was a blow; it was so forgetful of the motive that had brought him there.

"Miss Fairchild," he stammered, with a generous impulse to save her unnecessary pain, "you have rejected my offer and settled my doom; but let me believe that I have not lost your regard, or that hold upon your friendship which it has hitherto been my pleasure to enjoy."

She woke at once to a realization of his position. "Oh Mr. Ensign," she murmured, "can you doubt my regard or the truth of my friendship? It is for me to doubt; I have caused you such pain, and as you may think, so ruthlessly and with such lack of consideration. I have been peculiarly placed," she blushingly proceeded. "A woman does not always know her own heart, or if she does, sometimes hesitates to yield to its secret impulses. I have led you astray these last few weeks, but I first went astray myself. The real path in which I ought to tread, was only last night revealed to me. I can say no more, Mr. Ensign."

"Nor is it necessary," replied he. "You have chosen the better path, and the better man. May life abound in joys for you, Miss Fairchild."

She drew herself up and her hand went involuntarily to her heart. "It is not joy I seek," said she, "but—"

"What?" He looked at her face lit with that heavenly gleam that visited it in rare moments of deepest emotion, and wondered.

"Joy is in seeing the one you love happy," cried she; "earth holds none that is sweeter or higher."

"Then may that be yours," he murmured, manfully subduing the jealous pang natural under the circumstances. And taking the hand she held out to him, he kissed it with greater reverence and truer affection than when, in the first joyous hours of their intercourse, he carried it so gallantly to his lips.

And she—oh, difference of time and feeling—did not remember as of yore, the noble days of chivalry, though he was in this moment, so much more than ever the true knight and the reproachless cavalier.

For Paula's heart was heavy. Fears too unsubstantial to be met and vanquished, had haunted her steps all day. The short note which Mr. Sylvester had written her, lay like lead upon her bosom. She longed for the hours to fly, yet dreaded to hear the clock tick out the moments that possibly were destined to bring her untold suffering and disappointment. A revelation awaiting her in Mr. Sylvester's desk up stairs? That meant separation and farewell; for words of promise and devotion can be spoken, and the heart that hopes, does not limit time to hours.

With Bertram's entrance, her fears took absolute shape. Mr. Sylvester was not coming home to dinner. Thenceforward till seven o'clock, she sat with her hand on her heart, waiting. At the stroke of the clock, she rose, and procuring a candle from her room, went slowly up stairs. "Watch for me," she had said to Aunt Belinda, "for I fear I shall need your care when I come down."

What is there about a mystery however trivial, that thrills the heart with vague expectancy at the least lift of the concealing curtain! As Paula paused before the door, which never to her knowledge had opened to the passage of any other form than that of Mr. Sylvester, she was conscious of an agitation wholly distinct from that which had hitherto afflicted her. All the past curiosity of Ona concerning this room, together with her devices for satisfying that curiosity, recurred to Paula with startling distinctness. It was as if the white hand of that dead wife had thrust itself forth from the shadows to pull her back. The candle trembled in her grasp, and she unconsciously recoiled. But the next moment the thought of Mr. Sylvester struck warmth and determination through her being, and hastily thrusting the key into the lock, she pushed open the door and stepped across the threshold.

Her first movement was that of surprise. In all her dreams of the possible appearance of this room, she had never imagined it to be like this. Plain, rude and homely, its high walls unornamented, its floor uncovered, its furniture limited to a plain desk and two or three rather uncomfortable-looking chairs, it struck upon her fancy with the same sense of incongruity, as might the sight of a low-eaved cottage in the midst of stately palaces and lordly pleasure-grounds. Setting down her candle, she folded her hands to still their tremblings, and slowly looked around her. This was the spot, then, to which he was accustomed to flee when oppressed by any care or harassed by any difficulty; this cold, bare, uninviting apartment with its forbidding aspect unsoftened by the tokens of a woman's care or presence! To this room, humbler than any in her aunt's home in Grotewell, he had brought all his griefs, from the day his baby lay dead in the rooms below, to that awful hour which saw the wife and mother brought into his doors and laid a cold and pulseless form in the midst of his gorgeous parlors! Here he had met his own higher impulses face to face, and wrestled with them through the watches of the night! In this wilderness of seeming poverty, he had dreamed, perhaps, his first fond dream of her as a woman, and signed perhaps his final renunciation of her as the future companion of his life! What did it mean? Why a spot of so much desolation in the midst of so much that was lordly and luxurious? Her fears might give her a possible interpretation, but she would not listen to fears. Only his words should instruct her. Going to the desk, she opened it. A sealed envelope addressed to herself, immediately met her eyes. Taking it out with a slow and reverent touch, she began to read the long and closely written letter which it contained.

And the little candle burned on, shedding its rays over her bended head and upon the dismal walls about her, with a persistency that seemed to bring out, as in letters of fire, the hidden history of long ago, with its vanished days and its forgotten midnights.

XXXIX.

FROM A. TO Z.

"A naked human heart."—Young.

"My Beloved Child:

"So may I call you in this the final hour of our separation, but never again, dear one, never again. When I said to you, just twenty-four hours ago, that my sin was buried and my future was clear, I spake as men speak who forget the justice of God and dream only of his mercy. An hour's time convinced me that an evil deed once perpetrated by a man, is never buried so that its ghost will not rise. Do as we will, repent as we may, the shadowy phantom of a stained and unrighteous youth is never laid; nor is a man justified in believing it so, till death has closed his eyes, and fame written its epitaph upon his tomb.

"Paula, I am at this hour wandering in search of the being who holds the secret of my life and who will to-morrow blazon it before all the world. It is with no hope I seek him. God has not brought me to this pass, to release me at last, from shame and disgrace. Suffering and the loss of all my sad heart cherished, wait at my gates. Only one boon remains, and that is, your sympathy and the consolation of your regard. These, though bestowed as friends bestow them, are very precious to me; I cannot see them go, and that they may not, I tell you the full story of my life.

"My youth was happy—my early youth, I mean. Bertram's father was a dear brother to me, and my mother a watchful guardian and a tender friend. At fifteen, I entered a bank, the small bank in Grotewell, which you ought to remember. From the lowest position in it, I gradually worked my way up till I occupied the cashier's place; and was just congratulating myself upon my prospects, when Ona Delafield returned from boarding-school, a young lady.

"Paula, there is a fascination, which some men who have known nothing deeper and higher, call love. I, who in those days had cherished but few thoughts beyond the ordinary reach of a narrow and somewhat selfish business mind, imagined that the well-spring of all romance had bubbled up within me, when my eyes first fell upon this regal blonde, with her sleepy, inscrutable eyes and bewildering smile. Ulysses within sound of the siren's voice, was nothing to it. He had been warned of his danger and had only his own curiosity to combat, while I was not even aware of my peril, and floated within reach of this woman's power, without making an effort to escape. She was so subtle in her influence, Paula; so careless in the very exercise of her sovereignty. She never seemed to command; yet men and women obeyed her.

Peculiarities which mar the matron, are often graces in a young, unmarried girl, whose thoughts are a mystery, and whose emotions an untried field. I believed I had found the queen of all beauty and when in an unguarded hour she betrayed her first appreciation of my devotion, I seemed to burst into a Paradise of delights, where every step I took, only the more intoxicated and bewildered me. My first realization of the sensuous and earthly character of my happiness came with the glimpse of your child-face on that never-to-be-forgotten day when we met beside the river. Like a star seen above the glare of a conflagration, the pure spirit that informed your glance, flashed on my burning soul, and for a moment I knew that in you budded the kind of woman-nature which it befitted a man to seek; that in the hands of such a one as you would make, should he trust his honor and bequeath his happiness. But when did a lover ever break the bonds that imprisoned his fancy, at the inspiration of a passing voice. I went back to Ona and forgot the child by the river.

"Paula, I have no time to utter regrets. This is a hard plain tale which I have to relate; but if you love me still—if, as I have sometimes imagined, you have always loved me—think what my life had been if I had heeded the warning which God vouchsafed me on that day, and contrast it with what it is, and what it must be.

"I went back to Ona, then, and the hold which she had upon me from the first, took form and shape. As well as she could love any one, she loved me, and though she had offers from one or two more advantageous sources, she finally decided that she would risk the future and accept me, if her father consented to the alliance. You who are the niece of the man of whom I must now speak, may or may not know what that meant. I doubt if you do; he left Grotewell while you were a child, and any gossip concerning him must ever fall short of the real truth. Enough, then, that it meant, if Jacob Delafield could see in my future any promises of success sufficient to warrant him in accepting me as his son-in-law, no woman living ought to hesitate to trust me with her hand. He was the Squire of the town, and as such entitled to respect, but he was also something more, as you will presently discover. His answer to my plea was:

"'Well, how much money have you to show?'

"Now I had none. My salary as cashier of a small country bank was not large, and my brother's prolonged sickness and subsequent death, together with my own somewhat luxurious habits, had utterly exhausted it. I told him so, but added that I had, somewhere up among the hills, an old maiden aunt who had promised me five thousand dollars at her death; and that as she was very ill at that time—hopelessly so, her neighbors thought—in a few weeks I should doubtless be able to satisfy him with the sight of a sum sufficient to start us in housekeeping, if no more.

"He nodded at this, but gave me no distinct reply. 'Let us wait,' said he.

"But youth is not inclined to wait. I considered my cause as good as won, and began to make all my preparations accordingly. With a feverish impatience which is no sign of true love, I watched the days go by, and waited for, if I did not anticipate, the death which I fondly imagined would make all clear. At last it came, and I went again into Mr. Delafield's presence.

"'My aunt has just died,' I announced, and stood waiting for the short, concise,

"'Go ahead, then, my boy!' which I certainly expected.

"Instead of that, he gave me a queer inexplicable smile, and merely said, 'I want to see the greenbacks, my lad. No color so good as green, not even the black upon white of 'I promise to pay.'

"I went back to my desk in the bank, chagrined. Ona had told me a few days before that she was tired of waiting, that the young doctor from the next town was very assiduous in his attentions, and as there was no question as to his ability to support a wife, why—she did not finish her sentence, but the toss of her head and her careless tone at parting, were enough to inflame the jealousy of a less easily aroused nature than mine. I felt that I was in hourly danger of losing her, and all because I could not satisfy her father with a sight of the few thousands which were so soon to be mine.

"The reading of my aunt's will, which confirmed my hopes, did not greatly improve matters. 'I want to see the money,' the old gentleman repeated; and I was forced to wait the action of the law and the settlement of the estate. It took longer than even he foresaw. Weeks went by and my poor little five thousand seemed as far from my control as on the day the will was read. There was some trouble, I was not told what, that made it seem improbable that I should reap the benefit of my legacy for some time. Meanwhile Ona accepted the attentions of the young doctor, and my chances of winning her, dwindled rapidly day by day. I became morbidly eager and insanely jealous. Instead of pursuing my advantage—for I undoubtedly possessed one in her own secret inclination towards me—I stood off, and let my rival work his way into her affections unhindered. I was too sore to interrupt his play, as I called it, and too afraid of myself to actually confront him in her presence. But the sight of them riding together one day, was more than I could endure even in my spirit of unresistance. 'He shall not have her,' I cried, and cast about in my mind how to bring my own matters into such shape as to satisfy her father and so win her own consent to my suit. My first thought was to borrow the money, but that was impracticable in a town where each man's affairs are known to his neighbor. My next was to hurry up the settlement of the estate by appeal to my lawyer. The result of the latter course was a letter of many promises, in the midst of which a great temptation assailed me.

"Colonel Japha, of whose history you have heard more or less true accounts, was at that time living in the old mansion you took such pains to point out to me in that walk we took together in Grotewell. He had suffered a great anguish in the flight and degradation of his only daughter, and though the real facts connected with her departure were not known in the village, he was so overcome with shame, and so shattered in health, he lived in the utmost seclusion, opening his doors to but few visitors, among whom I, for some unexplained reason, was one. He used to say he liked me and saw in me the makings of a considerable man; and I, because he was Colonel Japha and a strong spirit, returned his appreciation, and spent many of my bitter and unhappy hours in his presence. It was upon one of these occasions the temptation came to which I have just alluded.

"I had been talking about his health and the advisability of his taking a journey, when he suddenly rose and said, 'Come with me to my study.'

"I of course went. The first thing I saw upon entering was a trunk locked and strapped. 'I am going to Europe to-morrow,' said he, 'to be gone six months.'

"I was astonished, for in that town no one presumed to do anything of importance without consulting his neighbors; but I merely bowed my congratulations, and waited for him to speak, for I saw he had something on his mind that he wished to say. At last it came out. He had a daughter, he said, a daughter who had disgraced him and whom he had forbidden his house. She was not worthy of his consideration, yet he could not help but remember her, and while he never desired to see her enter his doors, it was not his wish that she should suffer want. He had a little money which he had laid by and which he wished to put into my hands for her use, provided anything should happen to him during his absence. 'She is a wanderer now,' he cried, 'but she may one day come back, and then if I am dead and gone, you may give it to her.' I was not to enter it in the bank under his name, but regard it as a personal trust to be used only under such circumstances as he mentioned.

"The joy with which I listened to this proposal amounted almost to ecstacy when he went to his desk and brought out five one thousand dollar bills and laid them in my hand. 'It is not much,' said he, 'but it will save her from worse degradation if she chooses to avail herself of it.'

"Not much; oh no, not much, but just the sum that would raise me out of the pit of despondency into which I had fallen, and give me my bride, a chance in the world, and last, but not least, revenge on the rival I had now learned to hate. I was obliged to give the colonel a paper acknowledging the trust, but that was no hindrance. I did not mean to use the money, only to show it; and long before the colonel could return, my own five thousand would be in my hands—and so, and so, and so, as the devil reasons and young infatuated ears listen.

"Colonel Japha thought I was an honest man, nor did I consider myself otherwise at that time. It was a chance for clever action; a bit of opportune luck that it would be madness to discard. On the day the vessel sailed which carried Colonel Japha out of the country, I went to Mr. Delafield and showed him the five crisp bank notes that represented as it were by proxy, the fortune I so speedily expected to inherit. 'You have wanted to see five thousand dollars in my hand,' said I; 'there they are.'

"His look of amazement was peculiar and ought to have given me warning; but I was blinded by my infatuation and thought it no more than the natural surprise incident to the occasion. 'I have been made to wait a long time for your consent to my suit,' said I; 'may I hope that you will now give me leave to press my claims upon your daughter?'

"He did not answer at once, but smiled, eying meanwhile the notes in my hand with a fascinated gaze which instinctively warned me to return them to my pocket. But I no sooner made a move indicative of that resolve, than he thrust out his cold slim hand and prevented me. 'Let me see them,' cried he.

"There was no reason for me to refuse so simple a request to one in Mr. Delafield's position, and though I had rather he had not asked for the notes, I handed them over. He at once seemed to grow taller. 'So this is your start off in life,' exclaimed he.

"I bowed, and he let his eyes roam for a moment to my face. 'Many a man would be glad of worse,' smiled he; then suavely, 'you shall have my daughter, sir.'

"I must have turned white in my relief, for he threw his head back and laughed in a low unmusical way that at any other time would have affected me unpleasantly. But my only thought then, was to get the money back and rush with my new hopes into the room from which came the low ceaseless hum of his daughter's voice. But at the first movement of my hand towards him, he assumed a mysterious air, and closing his fingers over the notes, said:

"'These are yours, to do what you wish with, I suppose?'

"I may have blushed, but if I did, he took no notice. 'What I wish to do with them,' returned I, 'is to shut them up in the bank for the present, at least till Ona is my wife.'

"'Oh no, no, no, you do not,' came in easy, almost wheedling tones from the man before me. 'You want to put them where they will double themselves in two months.' And before I could realize to what he was tempting me, he had me down before his desk, showing me letters, documents, etc., of a certain scheme into which if a man should put a dollar to-day, it would 'come out three and no mistake, before the year was out. It is a chance in a thousand,' said he; 'if I had half a million I would invest it in this enterprise to-day. If you will listen to me and put your money in there, you will be a rich man before ten years have passed over your head.'

"I was dazzled. I knew enough of such matters to see that it was neither a hoax nor a chimera. He did have a good thing, and if the five thousand dollars had been my own—But I soon came to consider the question without that conditional. He was so specious in his manner of putting the affair before me, so masterful in the way he held on to the money, he gave me no time to think. 'Say the word,' cried he, 'and in two months I bring you back ten thousand for your five. Only two months,' he repeated, and then slowly, 'Ona was born for luxury.'

"Paula, you cannot realize what that temptation was. To amass wealth had never been my ambition before, but now everything seemed to urge it upon me. Dreams of unimagined luxury came to my mind as these words were uttered. A vision of Ona clad in garments worthy of her beauty floated before my eyes; the humble home I had hitherto pictured for myself, broadened and towered away into a palace; I beheld myself honored and accepted as the nabob of the town. I caught a glimpse of a new paradise, and hesitated to shut down the gate upon it. 'I will think of it,' said I, and went into the other room to speak to Ona.

"Ah, if some angel had met me on the threshold! If my mother's spirit or the thought of your dear face could have risen before me then and stopped me! Dizzy, intoxicated with love and ambition, I crossed the room to where she sat reeling off a skein of blue silk with hands that were whiter than alabaster. Kneeling down by her side, I caught those fair hands in mine.

"'Ona,' I cried, 'will you marry me? Your father has given his consent, and we shall be very happy.'

"She bestowed upon me a little pout, and half mockingly, half earnestly inquired, 'What kind of a house are you going to put me in? I cannot live in a cottage.'

"'I will put you in a palace,' I whispered, 'if you will only say that you will be mine.'

"'A palace! Oh, I don't expect palaces; a house like the Japhas' would do. Not but what I should feel at home in a palace,' she added, lifting her lordly head and looking beautiful enough to grace a sceptre. Then, archly for her, 'And papa has given his consent?'

"'Yes,' I ardently cried.

"'Then Dr. Burton might as well go,' she answered. 'I will trust my father's judgment, and take the palace—when it comes.'

"After that, it was impossible to disappoint her.

"Paula, in stating all this, I have purposely confined myself to relating bare facts. You must see us as we were. The glamour which an unreasoning passion casts over even a dishonest act, if performed for the sake of winning a beautiful woman, is no excuse in my own soul for the evil to which I succumbed that day, nor shall it seem so to you. Bare, hard, stern, the fact confronts me from the past, that at the first call of temptation I fell; and with this blot on my character, you will have to consider me— unhappy being that I am!

"I did not realize then, however, all that I had done. The operation entered into by Mr. Delafield prospered, and in two months I had, as he predicted, ten thousand dollars instead of five, in my possession. Besides, I had just married Ona, and for awhile life was a dream of delight and luxury. But there came a day when I awoke to an insight of the peril I had escaped by a mere chance of the die. The money which I had expected from my aunt's will, turned out to be amongst certain funds that had been risked in speculation by some agent during her sickness, and irrecoverably lost. The expression of her good-will was all that ever came to me of the legacy upon which I had so confidently relied.

"I was sitting with my young wife in the pretty parlor of our new home, when the letter came from my lawyer announcing this fact, and I never can make you understand what effect it had upon me. The very walls seemed to shrivel up into the dimensions of a prison's cell; the face that only an hour before had possessed every conceivable charm for me, shone on my changed vision with the allurement, but also with the unreality of a will-o'-the-wisp. All that might have happened if the luck, instead of being in my favor, had turned against me, crushed like a thunderbolt upon my head, and I rose up and left the presence of my young wife, with the knowledge at my heart that I was no more nor less than a thief in the eyes of God, if not in that of my fellow-men; a base thief, who if he did not meet his fit punishment, was only saved from it by fortuitous circumstances and the ignorance of those he had been so near despoiling.

"The bitterness of that hour never passed away. The streets in which I had been raised, the house which had been the scene of my temptation, Mr. Delafield's face, and my own home, all became unendurable to me. I felt as if each man I met must know what I had done; and secret as the transaction had been, it was long before I could enter the bank without a tremor of apprehension lest I should hear from some quarter, that my services there would no longer be required. The only comfort I received was in the thought that Ona did not know at what a cost her hand had been obtained. I was still under the glamour of her languid smiles and countless graces, and was fain to believe that notwithstanding a certain unresponsiveness and coldness in her nature, her love would yet prove a compensation for the remorse that I secretly suffered.

"My distaste for Grotewell culminated. It was too small for me. The money I had acquired through the use of my neighbor's funds burned in my pocket. I determined to move to New York, and with the few thousands I possessed, venture upon other speculations. But this time in all honesty. Yes, I swore it before God and my own soul, that never again would I run a risk similar to that from which I had just escaped. I would profit by the money I had acquired, oh yes, but henceforth all my operations should be legitimate and honorable. My wife, who was fast developing a taste for ease and splendor, seconded my plans with something like fervor, while Mr. Delafield actually went so far as to urge my departure. 'You are bound to make a rich man,' said he 'and must go where great fortunes are to be secured.' He never asked me what became of the five thousand dollars I returned to Colonel Japha upon his arrival from Europe.

"So I came to New York.

"Paula, the man who loses at the outset of a doubtful game, is fortunate. I did not lose, I won. As if in that first dishonest deed of mine I had summoned to my side the aid of evil influences, each and every operation into which I entered prospered. It seemed as if I could not make a mistake; money flowed towards me from all quarters; power followed, and I found myself one of the most successful and one of the most unhappy men in New York. There are some things of which a man cannot write even to the one dear heart he most cherishes and adores. You have lived in my home, and will acquit me from saying much about her who, with all her faults and her omissions, was ever kind to you. But some things I must repeat in order to make intelligible to you the change which gradually took place within me as the years advanced. Beauty, while it wins the lover, can never of itself hold the heart of a husband who possesses aspirations beyond that which passion supplies. Reckless, worldly and narrow-minded as I had been before the commission of that deed which embittered my life, I had become by the very shock that followed the realization of my wrong-doing, a hungry-hearted, eager-minded and melancholy-spirited man, asking but one boon in recompense for my secret remorse, and that was domestic happiness and the sympathetic affection of wife and children. Woman, according to my belief, was born to be chiefly and above all, the consoler. What a man missed in the outside world, he was to find treasured at home. What a man lacked in his own nature, he was to discover in the delicate and sublimated one of his wife. Beautiful dream, which my life was not destined to see realized!

"The birth of my only child was my first great consolation. With the opening of her blue eyes upon my face, a well-spring deep as my unfathomable longing, bubbled up within my breast. Alas, that very consolation brought a hideous grief; the mother did not love her child; and another strand of the regard with which I still endeavored to surround the wife of my youth, parted and floated away out of sight. To take my little one in my arms, to feel her delicate cheek press yearningly to mine, to behold her sweet infantile soul develop itself before my eyes, and yet to realize that that soul would never know the guidance or sympathy of a mother, was to me at once rapture and anguish. I sometimes forgot to follow up a fortunate speculation, in my indulgence of these feelings. I was passionately the father as I might have been passionately the husband and the friend. Geraldine died; how and with what attendant circumstances of pain and regret, I will not, dare not state. The blow struck to the core of my being. I stood shaken before God. The past, with its one grim remembrance—a remembrance that in the tide of business successes and the engrossing affection which had of late absorbed me, had been well-nigh swamped from sight—rose before me like an accusing spirit. I had sinned, and I had been punished; I had sown, and I had reaped.

"More than that, I was sinning still. My very enjoyment of the position I had so doubtfully acquired, was unworthy of me. My very wealth was a disgrace. Had it not all been built upon another man's means? Could the very house I lived in be said to be my own, while a Japha existed in want? In the eyes of the world, perhaps, yes; in my own eyes, no. I became morbid on the subject. I asked myself what I could do to escape the sense of obligation that overwhelmed me. The few sums with which I had been secretly enabled to provide Colonel Japha during the final days of his ruined and impoverished life, were not sufficient. I desired to wipe out the past by some large and munificent return. Had the colonel been living, I should have gone to him, told him my tale and offered him the half of my fortune; but his death cut off all hopes of my righting myself in that way. Only his daughter remained, the poor, lost, reprobated being, whom he was willing to curse, but whom he could not bear to believe suffering. I determined that the debt due to my own peace of mind should be paid to her. But how? Where was I to find this wanderer? How was I to let her know that a comfortable living awaited her if she would only return to her friends and home? Consulting with a business associate, he advised me to advertise. I did so, but without success. I next resorted to the detectives, but all without avail. Jacqueline Japha was not to be found.

"But I did not relinquish my resolve. Deliberately investing a hundred thousand dollars in Government bonds, I put them aside for her. They were to be no longer mine. I gave them to her and to her heirs as completely and irrevocably, I believed, as if I had laid them in her hand and seen her depart with them. I even inserted them as a legacy to her in my will. It was a clear and definite arrangement between me and my own soul; and after I had made it and given orders to my lawyer in Grotewell to acquaint me if he ever received the least news of Jacqueline Japha, I slept in peace.

"Of the years that followed I have small need to speak. They were the years that preceded your coming, my Paula, and their story is best told by what I was when we met again, and you made me know the sweet things of life by entering into my home. Woman as a thoughtful, tender, elevated being had been so long unknown to me! The beauty of the feminine soul with its faith fixed upon high ideals, was one before which I had ever been ready to bow. All that I had missed in my youth, all that had failed me in my maturing manhood, seemed to flow back upon me like a river. I bathed in the sunshine of your pure spirit and imagined that the evil days were over and peace come at last.

"A rude and bitter shock awoke me. Ona's father, who had followed us to New York, and of whose somewhat checkered career during the past few years, I have purposely forborne to speak, had not been above appealing to us for assistance at such times as his frequently unfortunate investments left him in a state of necessity. These appeals were usually made to Ona, and in a quiet way; but one day he met me on the street— it was during the second winter you spent in my home—and dragging me into a restaurant down town, began a long tale, to the effect that he wanted a few thousands from me to put into a certain investment, which if somewhat shady in its character, was very promising as to its results; and gave as a reason why he applied to me for the money, that he knew I had not been above doing a wrongful act once, in order to compass my ends, and therefore would not be liable to hesitate now.

"It was the thunderbolt of my life. My sin was not then buried. It had been known to this man from the start. With an insight for which I had never given him credit, he had read my countenance in the days of my early temptation, and guessed, if he did not know, where the five thousand dollars came from with which I began my career as speculator. Worse than that, he had led me on to the act by which he now sought to hold me. Having been the secret agent in losing my aunt's money, he knew at the time that I was cherishing empty hopes as regarded a legacy from her, yet he let me dally with my expectations, and ensnare myself with his daughter's fascinations, till driven mad by disappointment and longing, I was ready to resort to any means to gain my purpose. It was a frightful revelation to come to me in days when, if I were not a thoroughly honest man, I had at least acquired a deep and ineradicable dread of dishonor. Answering him I know not how, but in a way that while it repudiated his proposition, unfortunately acknowledged the truth of the suppositions upon which it was founded, I left him and went home, a crushed and disheartened man. Life which had been so long in acquiring cheerful hues, was sunk again in darkness; and for days I could not bear the sight of your innocent face, or the sound of your pure voice, or the tokens of your tender and unsuspecting presence in my home. But soon the very natural thought came to comfort me, that the sin I so deplored was as much dead now, as it was before I learned the fact of this man's knowledge of it. That having repented and put it away, I was as free to accept your gentle offices and the regard of all true men, as ever I had been; and beguiled by this plausible consideration, I turned again to my one visible source of consolation, and in the diversion it offered, let the remembrance of this last bitter experience pass slowly from my mind. The fact that Mr. Delafield left town shortly after his interview with me, and smitten by shame perhaps, forbore to acquaint us with his whereabouts or afflict us with his letters, may have aided me in this strange forgetfulness.

"But other and sharper trials were in store; trials that were to test me as a man, and as it proved, find me lacking just where I thought I was strongest. Paula, that saying of the Bible, 'Let him that thinketh he standeth take heed lest he fall,' might have been written over the door of my house on that day, ten months ago, when we two stood by the hearthstone and talked of the temptations that beset humanity, and the charity we should show to such as succumb to them. Before the day had waned, my own hour had come; and not all the experience of my life, not all the resolves, hopes, fears of my later years, not even the remembrance of your sweet trust and your natural recoil from evil, were sufficient to save me. The blow came so suddenly! the call for action was so peremptory! One moment I stood before the world, rich, powerful, honored, and beloved; the next, I saw myself threatened with a loss that undermined my whole position, and with it the very consideration that made me what I was. But I must explain.

"When I entered the Madison Bank as President, I gave up in deference to the wishes of Mr. Stuyvesant all open speculation in Wall Street. But a wife and home such as I then had, are not to be supported on any petty income; and when shortly after your entrance into my home, the opportunity presented itself of investing in a particularly promising silver mine out West, I could not resist the temptation; regarding the affair as legitimate, and the hazard, if such it were, one that I was amply able to bear. But like most enterprises of the kind, one dollar drew another after it, and I soon found that to make available what I had already invested, I was obliged to add to it more and more of my available funds, until—to make myself as intelligible to you as I can—it had absorbed not only all that had remained to me after my somewhat liberal purchase of the Madison Bank stock, but all I could raise on a pledge of the stock itself. But there was nothing in this to alarm me. I had a man at the mine devoted to my interests; and as the present yield was excellent, and the future of more promise still, I went on my way with no special anxiety. But who can trust a silver mine? At the very point where we expected the greatest result, the vein suddenly gave out, and nothing prevented the stock from falling utterly flat on the market, but the discretion of my agent, who kept the fact a secret, while he quietly went about getting another portion of the mine into working order. He was fast succeeding in this, and affairs were looking daily more promising, when suddenly an intimation received by me in a bit of conversation casually overheard at that reception we attended together, convinced me that the secret was transpiring, and that if great care were not taken, we should be swamped before we could get things into working trim again. Filled with this anxiety, I was about to leave the building, in order to telegraph to my agent, when to my great surprise the card of that very person was brought in to me, together with a request for an immediate interview. You remember it, Paula, and how I went out to see him; but what you did not know then, and what I find some difficulty in relating now, is that his message to me was one of total ruin unless I could manage to give into his hand, for immediate use, the sum of a hundred thousand dollars.

"The facts making this demand necessary were not what you may have been led to expect. They had little or nothing to do with the new operations, which were progressing successfully and with every promise of an immediate return, but arose entirely out of a law-suit then in the hands of a Colorado judge for decision, and which, though it involved well-nigh the whole interest of the mine, had never till this hour given me the least uneasiness, my lawyers having always assured me of my ultimate success. But it seems that notwithstanding all this, the decision was to be rendered in favor of the other party. My agent, who was a man to be trusted in these matters, averred that five days before, he had learned from most authentic sources what the decision was likely to be. That the judge's opinion had been seen—he did not tell me how, he dared not, nor did I presume to question, but I have since learned that not only had the copyist employed by the judge turned traitor, but that my own agent had been anything but scrupulous in the use he had made of a willing and corruptible instrument—and that if I wanted to save myself and the others connected with me from total and irremediable loss, I must compromise with the other parties at once, who not being advised of the true state of affairs, and having but little faith in their own case, had long ago expressed their willingness to accept the sum of a hundred thousand dollars as a final settlement of the controversy. My agent, if none too nice in his ideas of right and wrong, was, as I have intimated, not the man to make a mistake; and when to my question as to how long a time he would give me to look around among my friends and raise the required sum, he replied, 'Ten hours and no more,' I realized my position, and the urgent necessity for immediate action.

"The remainder of the night is a dream to me. There was but one source from which I could hope in the present condition of my affairs, to procure a hundred thousand dollars; and that was from the box where I had stowed away the bonds destined for the use of the Japha heirs. To borrow was impossible, even if I had been in possession of proper securities to give. I was considered as having relinquished speculation and dared not risk the friendship of Mr. Stuyvesant by a public betrayal of my necessity. The Japha bonds or my own fortune must go, and it only remained with me to determine which.

"Paula, nothing but the ingrained principle of a lifetime, the habit of doing the honest thing without thought or hesitation, saves a man at an hour like that. Strong as I believed myself to be in the determination never again to flaw my manhood by the least action unworthy of my position as the guardian of trusts, earnest as I was in my recoil from evil, and sincere as I may have been in my admiration of and desire for the good, I no sooner saw myself tottering between ruin and a compromise with conscience, than I hesitated—hesitated with you under my roof, and with the words we had been speaking still ringing in my ears. Ona's influence, for all the trials of our married life, was still too strong upon me. To think of her as deprived of the splendor which was her life, daunted my very soul. I dared not contemplate a future in which she must stand denuded of everything which made existence dear to her; yet how could I do the evil thing I contemplated, even to save her and preserve my own position! For—and you must understand this—I regarded any appropriation of these funds I had delegated to the use of the Japhas, as a fresh and veritable abuse of trust. They were not mine. I had given them away. Unknown to any one but my own soul and God, I had deeded them to a special purpose, and to risk them as I now proposed doing, was an act that carried me back to the days of my former delinquency, and made the repentance of the last few years the merest mockery. What if I might recover them hereafter and restore them to their place; the chances in favor of their utter loss were also possible, and honesty deals not with chances. I suffered so, I had a momentary temptation towards suicide; but suddenly, in the midst of the struggle, came the thought that perhaps in my estimate of Ona I had committed a gross injustice, that while she loved splendor seemingly more than any woman I had ever known, she might be as far from wishing me to retain her in it at the price of my own self-respect, as the most honest-hearted wife in the world; and struck by the hope, I left my agent at a hotel and hurried home through the early morning to her side. She Was asleep, of course, but I wakened her. It was dark and she had a right to be fretful, but when I whispered in her ear, 'Get up and listen to me, for our fortune is at stake,' she at once rose and having risen, was her clearest, coldest, most implacable self. Paula, I told her my story, my whole story as I have told it to you here. I dropped no thread, I smoothed over no offence. Torturing as it was to my pride, I laid bare my soul before her, and then in a burst of appeal such as I hope never to be obliged to make use of again, asked her as she was a woman and a wife, to save me in this hour of my temptation.

"Paula, she refused. More than that, she expressed the bitterest scorn of my mawkish conscientiousness, as she called it. That I should consider myself as owing anything to the detestable wretch who was the only representative of the Japhas, was bad enough, but that I should go on treasuring the money that would save us, was disgraceful if not worse, and betrayed a weakness of mind for which she had never given me credit.

"'But Ona,' I cried, 'if it is a weakness of mind, it is also an equivalent to my consciousness of right living. Would you have me sacrifice that?'

"'I would have you sacrifice anything necessary to preserve us in our position,' said she; and I stood aghast before an unscrupulousness greater than any I had hitherto been called upon to face.

"'Ona,' repeated I, for her look was cold, 'do you realize what I have been telling you? Most wives would shudder when informed that their husbands had perpetrated a dishonest act in order to win them.'

"A thin strange smile heralded her reply. 'Most wives would,' returned she, 'but most wives are ignorant. Did you suppose I did not know what it cost you to marry me? Papa took care I should miss no knowledge that might be useful to me.'

"'And you married me knowing what I had done!' exclaimed I, with incredulous dismay.

"'I married you, knowing you were too clever, or believing you to be too clever, to run such a risk again.'

"I can say no more concerning that hour. With a horror for this woman such as I had never before experienced for living creature, I rushed out of her presence, loathing the air she breathed, yet resolved to do her bidding. Can you understand a man hating a woman, yet obeying her; despising her, yet yielding? I cannot, *now*, but that day there seemed no alternative. Either I must kill myself or follow her wishes. I chose to do the latter, forgetting that God can kill, and that, too, whom and when He pleases.

"Going down to the bank, I procured the bonds from my box in the safe. I felt like a thief, and the manner in which it was done was unwittingly suggestive of crime, but with that and the position in which I have since found myself placed by this very action, I need not cumber my present narrative. Handing the bonds to my agent with orders to sell them to the best advantage, I took a short walk to quiet my nerves and realize what I had done, and then went home.

"Paula, had God in his righteous anger seen fit to strike me down that day, it would have been no more than my due and aroused in me, perhaps, no more than a natural repentence. But when I saw her for whose sake I had ostensibly committed this fresh abuse of trust, lying cold and dead before me, the sword of the Almighty pierced me to the soul, and I fell prostrate beneath a remorse to which any regret I had hitherto experienced, was as the playing of a child with shadows. Had I by the losing of my right arm been able to recall my action, I would have done it; indeed I made an effort to recover myself; had my agent followed up with an order to return me the bonds I had given him, but it was too late, the compromise had already been effected by telegraph and the money was out of our hands. The deed was done and I had made myself unworthy of your presence and your smile at the very hour when both would have been inestimable to me. You remember those days; remember our farewell. Let me believe you do not blame me now for what must have seemed harsh and unnecessary to you then.

"There is but little more to write, but in that little is compressed the passion, longing, hope and despair of a lifetime. When I told you as I did a few hours ago that my sin was dead and its consequences at an end, I repeat that I fully and truly believed it. The hundred thousand dollars I had sent West, had been used to advantage, and only day before yesterday I was enabled to sell out my share in the mine, for a large sum that leaves me free and unembarrassed, to make the fortune of more than one Japha, should God ever see fit to send them across my pathway. More than that, Mr. Delafield, of whose discretion I had sometimes had my fears, was dead, having perished of a fever some months before in San Francisco; and of all men living, there were none as I believed, who knew anything to the discredit of my name. I was clear, or so I thought, in fortune and in fame; and being so, dreamed of taking to my empty and yearning arms, the loveliest and the purest of mortal women. But God watched over you and prevented an act whose consequences might have been so cruel. In an hour, Paula, in an hour, I had learned that the foul thing was not dead, that a witness had picked up the words I had allowed to fall in my interview with my father-in-law in the restaurant two years before; an unscrupulous witness who had been on my track ever since, and who now in his eagerness for a victim, had by mistake laid his clutch upon our Bertram. Yes, owing to the similarity of our voices and the fact that we both make use of a certain tell-tale word, this patient and upright nephew of mine stands at this moment under the charge of having acknowledged in the hearing of this person, to the committal of an act of dishonesty in the past. A foolish charge you will say, and one easily refuted. Alas, a fresh act of dishonesty lately perpetrated in the bank, complicates matters. A theft has been committed on some of Mr. Stuyvesant's effects, and that, too, under circumstances that involuntarily arouse suspicion against some one of the bank officials; and Bertram, if not sustained in his reputation, must suffer from the doubts which naturally have arisen in Mr. Stuyvesant's breast. The story which this man could tell, must of course shake the faith of any one in the reputation of him against whom it is directed, and the man intends to repeat his story, and that, too, in the very ears of him upon whose favor Bertram depends for his life's happiness and the winning of the woman he adores. I adore you, Paula, but I cannot clasp you to my heart across another sin. If the detectives whom we shall call in to-morrow, cannot exonerate those connected with the bank from the theft lately committed there—and the fact that you have been allowed to read this letter, prove they have not—I must do what I can to relieve Bertram from his painful position, by taking upon myself the onus of that past transgression which of right belongs to my account; and this once done, let the result be for good or ill, any bond between you and me is cut loose forever. I have not learned to love at this late hour, to wrong the precious thing I cherish. Death as it is to me to say good-bye to the one last gleam of heavenly light that has shot across my darkened way, it must be done, dear heart, if only to hold myself worthy of the tender and generous love you have designed to bestow upon me. Bertram, who is all generosity, may guess but does not know, what I am about to do. Go down to him, dear; tell him that at this very moment, perhaps, I am clearing his name before the wretch who has so ruthlessly fastened his fang upon him; that his love and Cicely's shall prosper, as he has been loyal, and she trusting, all these years of effort and probation; that I give him my blessing, and that if we do not meet again, I delegate to him the trust of which I so poorly acquitted myself. But before you go, stop a moment and in this room, which has always symbolized to my eyes the poverty which was my rightful due, kneel and pray for my soul; for if God grants me the wish of my heart, he will strike me with sudden death after I have taken upon myself the disgrace of my past offences. Life without love can be borne, but life without honor never. To come and go amongst my fellow-men with a shadow on the fame they have always believed spotless! Do not ask me to attempt it! Pray for my soul, but pray too, that I may perish in some quick and sudden way before ever your dear eyes rest upon my face again.

"And now, as though this were to be the end, let me take my last farewell of you. I have loved you, Paula, loved you with my heart, my mind and my soul. You have been my angel of inspiration and the source of all my comfort. I kneel before you in gratitude, and I stand above you in blessing. May every pang I suffer this hour, redound to you in some sweet happiness hereafter. I do not quarrel with my fate, I only ask God to spare you from its shadow. And He will. Love will flow back upon your young life, and in regions where our eye now fails to pierce, you will taste every joy which your generous heart once thought to bestow on

"Edward Sylvester."

XL.

HALF-PAST SEVEN.

"I would it were midnight, Hal, and all well."—Henry IV.

The library was dim; Bertram, who had felt the oppressive influence of the great empty room, had turned down the lights, and was now engaged in pacing the floor, with restless and uneven steps, asking himself a hundred questions, and wishing with all the power of his soul, that Mr. Sylvester would return, and by his appearance cut short a suspense that was fast becoming unendurable.

He had just returned from his third visit to the front door, when the curtain between him and the hall was gently raised, and Paula glided in and stood before him. She was dressed for the street, and her face where the light touched it, shone like marble upon which has fallen the glare of a lifted torch.

"Paula!" burst from the young man's lips in surprise.

"Hush!" said she, her voice quavering with an emotion that put to defiance all conventionalities, "I want you to take me to the place where Mr. Sylvester is gone. He is in danger; I know it, I feel it. I dare not leave him any longer alone. I might be able to save him if—if he meditates anything that—" she did not try to say what, but drew nearer to Bertram and repeated her request. "You will take me, won't you?"

He eyed her with amazement, and a shudder seized his own strong frame. "No," cried he, "I cannot take you; you do not know what you ask; but I will go myself if you apprehend anything serious. I remember where it is. I studied the address too closely, to readily forget it."

"You shall not go without me," returned Paula with steady decision. "If the danger is what I fear, no one else can save him. I must go," she added, with passionate importunity as she saw him still looking doubtful. "Darkness and peril are nothing to me in comparison with his safety. He holds my life in his hand," she softly whispered, "and what will not one do for his life!" Then quickly, "If you go without me I shall follow with Aunt Belinda. Nothing shall keep me in the house to-night."

He felt the uselessness of further objection, yet he ventured to say, "The place where he has gone is one of the worst in the city; a spot which men hesitate to enter after dark. You don't know what you ask in begging me to take you there."

"I do, I realize everything."

With a sudden awe of the great love which he thus beheld embodied before him, Bertram bowed his head and moved towards the door. "I may consider it wise to obtain the guidance of a policeman through the quarter into which we are about to venture. Will you object to that?"

"No," was her quick reply, "I object to nothing but delay."

And with a last look about the room, as if some sensation of farewell were stirring in her breast, she laid her hand on Bertram's arm, and together they hurried away into the night.

BOOK V.

WOMAN'S LOVE.

XLI.

THE WORK OF AN HOUR.

Base is the slave that pays."—Henry V.

"Heaven has no rage like love to hatred turned,Nor hell a fury like a woman scorned."—Congreve.

Mr. Sylvester upon leaving the bank, had taken his usual route up town. But after an aimless walk of a few blocks, he suddenly paused, and with a quiet look about him, drew from his pocket the small slip of paper which Bertram had laid on his table the night before, and hurriedly consulted its contents. Instantly an irrepressible exclamation escaped him, and he turned his face to the heavens with the look of one who recognizes the just providence of God. The name which he had just read, was that of the old lover of Jacqueline Japha, Roger Holt, and the address given, was 63 Baxter Street.

Twilight comes with different aspects to the broad avenues of the rich, and the narrow alleys of the poor. In the reeking slums of Baxter Street, poetry would have had to search long for the purple glamour that makes day's dying hour fair in open fields and perfumed chambers. Even the last dazzling gleam of the sun could awaken no sparkle from the bleared windows of the hideous tenement houses that reared their blank and disfigured walls toward the west. The chill of the night blast and the quick dread that follows in the steps of coming darkness, were all that could enter these regions, unless it was the stealthy shades of vice and disease.

Mr. Sylvester standing before the darkest and most threatening of the many dark and threatening houses that cumbered the street, was a sight to draw more than one head from the neighboring windows. Had it been earlier, he would have found himself surrounded by a dozen ragged and importunate children; had it been later, he would have run the risk of being garroted by some skulking assassin; as it was, he stood there unmolested, eying the structure that held within its gloomy recesses the once handsome and captivating lover of Jacqueline Japha. He was not the only man who would have hesitated before entering there. Low and insignificant as the building appeared—and its two stories certainly looked dwarfish enough in comparison with the two lofty tenement houses that pressed it upon either side—there was something in its quiet, almost uninhabited aspect that awakened a vague apprehension of lurking danger. A face at a window would have been a relief; even the sight of a customer in the noisome groggery that occupied the ground floor. From the dwellings about, came the hum of voices and now and then the sound of a shrill laugh or a smothered cry, but from this house came nothing, unless it was the slow ooze of a stream of half-melted snow that found its way from under the broken-down door-way to the gutter beyond.

Stepping bravely forward, Mr. Sylvester entered the open door. A flight of bare and rickety steps met his eye. Ascending them, he found himself in a hall which must have been poorly lighted at any time, but which at this late hour was almost dark. It was not very encouraging, but pressing on, he stopped at a door and was about to knock, when his eyes becoming accustomed to the darkness, he detected standing at the foot of the stairs leading to the story above, the tall and silent figure of a woman. It was no common apparition. Like a sentinel at his post, or a spy on the outskirts of the enemy's camp, she stood drawn up against the wall, her whole wasted form quivering with eagerness or some other secret passion; darkness on her brow and uncertainty on her lip. She was listening, or waiting, or both, and that with an entire absorption that prevented her from heeding the approach of a stranger's step. Struck by so sinister a presence in a place so dark and desolate, Mr. Sylvester unconsciously drew back. As he did so, the woman thrilled and looked up, but not at him. A lame child's hesitating and uneven step was heard crossing the floor above, and it was towards it she turned, and for it she composed her whole form into a strange but evil calmness.

"Ah, he let you come then!" Mr. Sylvester heard her exclaim in a low smothered tone, whose attempted lightness did not hide the malevolent nature of her interest.

"Yes," came back in the clear and confiding tones of childhood. "I told him you loved me and gave me candy-balls, and he let me come."

A laugh quick and soon smothered, disturbed the surrounding gloom. "You told him I loved you! Well, that is good; I do love you; love you as I do my own eyes that I could crush, crush, for ever having lingered on the face of my betrayer!"

The last phrase was muttered, and did not seem to convey any impression to the child. "Hold out your arms and catch me," cried he; "I am going to jump."

She appeared to comply; for he gave a little ringing laugh that was startlingly clear and fresh.

"He asked me what your name was," babbled he, as he nestled in her arms. "He is always asking what your name is; Dad forgets, Dad does; or else it's because he's never seen you."

"And what did you tell him?" she asked, ignoring the last remark with an echo of her sarcastic laugh.

"Mrs. Smith, of course."

She threw back her head and her whole form acquired an aspect that made Mr. Sylvester shudder. "That's good," she cried, "Mrs. Smith by all means." Then with a sudden lowering of her face to his—"Mrs. Smith is good to you, isn't she; lets you sit by her fire when she has any, and gives you peanuts to eat and sometimes spares you a penny!"

"Yes, yes," the boy cried.

"Come then," she said, "let's go home."

She put him down on the floor, and gave him his little crutch. Her manner was not unkind, and yet Mr. Sylvester trembled as he saw the child about to follow her.

"Didn't you ever have any little boys?" the child suddenly asked.

The woman shrank as if a burning steel had been plunged against her breast. Looking down on the frightened child, she hissed out from between her teeth, "Did he tell you to ask me that? Did he dare—" She stopped and pressed her arms against her swelling heart as if she would smother its very beats. "Oh no, of course he didn't tell you; what does he know or care about Mrs. Smith!" Then with a quick gasp and a wild look into the space before her, "My child dead, and her child alive and beloved! What wonder that I hate earth and defy heaven!"

She caught the boy by the hand and drew him quickly away. "You will be good to me," he cried, frightened by her manner yet evidently fascinated too, perhaps on account of the faint sparks of kindness that alternated with gusts of passion he did not understand. "You won't hurt me; you'll let me sit by the fire and get warm?"

"Yes, yes."

"And eat a bit of bread with butter on it?"

"Yes, yes."

"Then I'll go."

She drew him down the hall. "Why do you like to have me come to your house?" he prattled away.

She turned on him with a look which unfortunately Mr. Sylvester could not see. "Because your eyes are so blue and your skin is so white; they make me remember her!"

"And who is *her*?"

She laughed and seemed to hug herself in her rage and bitterness. "Your mother!" she cried, and in speaking it, she came upon Mr. Sylvester.

He at once put out his hand.

"I don't know who you are," said he, "but I do not think you had better take the child out to-night. From what you say, his father is evidently upstairs; if you will give the boy to me, I will take him back and leave him where he belongs."

"You will?" The slow intensity of her tone was indescribable. "Know that I don't bear interference from strangers." And catching up the child, she rushed by him like a flash. "You are probably one of those missionaries who go stealing about unasked into respectable persons' rooms," she called back. "If by any chance you wander into his, tell him his child is in good hands, do you hear, in good hands!" And with a final burst of her hideous laugh, she dashed down the stairs and was gone.

Mr. Sylvester stood shocked and undecided. His fatherly heart urged him to search at once for the parent of this lame boy, and warn him of the possible results of entrusting his child to a woman with so little command over herself. But upon taking out his watch and finding it later by a good half-hour than he expected, he was so struck with the necessity of completing his errand, that he forgot everything else in his anxiety to confront Holt. Knocking at the first door he came to, he waited. A quick snarl and a surprised, "Come in!" announced that he had scared up some sort of a living being, but whether man or woman he found it impossible to tell, even after the door opened and the creature, whoever it was, rose upon him from a pile of rags scattered in one corner.

"I want Mr. Holt; can you tell me where to find him?"

"Upstairs," was the only reply he received, as the creature settled down again upon its heap of tattered clothing.

Fain to be content with this, he went up another flight and opened another door. He was more successful this time; one glance of his eye assured him that the man he was in search of, sat before him. He had never seen Mr. Holt; but the regular if vitiated features of the person upon whom he now intruded, his lank but not ungraceful form, and free if not airy manners, were not so common among the denizens of this unwholesome quarter, that there could be any doubt as to his being the accomplished but degenerate individual whose once attractive air had stolen the heart of Colonel Japha's daughter.

He was sitting in front of a small pine table, and when Mr. Sylvester's eyes first fell upon him, was engaged in watching with a somewhat sinister smile, the final twirl of a solitary nickle which he had set spinning on the board before him. But at the sound of a step at the door, a lightning change passed over his countenance, and rising with a quick anticipatory "Ah!" he turned with hasty action to meet the intruder. A second exclamation and a still more hasty recoil were the result. This was not the face or the form of him whom he had expected.

"Mr. Holt, I believe?" inquired Mr. Sylvester, advancing with his most dignified mien.

The other bowed, but in a doubtful way that for a moment robbed him of his usual air of impudent self-assertion.

"Then I have business with you," continued Mr. Sylvester, laying the man's own card down on the table before him. "My name is Sylvester," he proceeded, with a calmness that surprised himself; "and I am the uncle of the young man upon—whom you are at present presuming to levy blackmail."

The assurance which for a moment had deserted the countenance of the other, returned with a flash. "His uncle!" reëchoed he, with a low anomalous bow; "then it is from you I may expect the not unreasonable sum which I demand as the price of my attentions to your nephew's interest. Very good, I am not particular from what quarter it comes, so that it does come and that before the clock has struck the hour which I have set as the limit of my forbearance."

"Which is seven o'clock, I believe?"

"Which is seven o'clock."

Mr. Sylvester folded his arms and sternly eyed the man before him. "You still adhere to your intention, then, of forwarding to Mr. Stuyvesant at that hour, the sealed communication now in the hands of your lawyer?"

The smile with which the other responded was like the glint of a partly sheathed dagger. "My lawyer has already received his instructions. Nothing but an immediate countermand on my part, will prevent the communication of which you speak, from going to Mr. Stuyvesant at seven o'clock."

The sigh which rose in Mr. Sylvester's breast did not disturb the severe immobility of his lip. "Have you ever considered the possibility," said he, "of the man whom you overheard talking in the restaurant in Dey Street two years ago, not being Mr. Bertram Sylvester of the Madison Bank?"

"No," returned the other, with a short, sharp, and wholly undisturbed laugh, "I do not think I ever have."

"Will you give me credit, then, for speaking with reason, when I declare to you that the man you overheard talking in the manner you profess to describe in your communication, was not Mr. Bertram Sylvester?"

A shrug of the shoulders, highly foreign and suggestive, was the other's answer. "It was Mr. Sylvester or it was the devil," proclaimed he—"with all deference to your reason, my good sir; or why are you here?" he keenly added.

Mr. Sylvester did not reply. With a sarcastic twitch of his lips the man took up the nickle with which he had been amusing himself when the former came in, and set it spinning again upon the table. "It is half-past six," remarked he. "It will take me a good half hour to go to my lawyer."

Mr. Sylvester made a final effort. "If you could be convinced," said he, "that you have got your grasp upon the wrong man, would you still persist in the course upon which you seem determined?"

With a dexterous sleight-of-hand movement, the man picked up the whirling nickle and laid it flat on the table before him. "A fellow whose whole fortune is represented by a coin like that"—tapping the piece significantly—"is not as easily convinced as a man of your means, perhaps. But if I should be brought to own that I had made a mistake in my man, I should still feel myself justified in proceeding against him, since my very accusation of him seems to be enough to arouse such interest on the part of his friends."

"Wretch!" leaped to Mr. Sylvester's lips, but he did not speak it. "His friends," declared he, "have most certainly a great interest in his reputation and his happiness; but they never will pay any thing upon coercion to preserve the one or to insure the other."

"They won't!" And for the first time Roger Holt slightly quavered.

"A man's honor and happiness are much, and he will struggle long before he will consent to part from them. But a citizen of a great town like this, owes something to his fellows, and submitting to blackmail is but a poor precedent to set. You will have to proceed as you will, Mr. Holt; neither my nephew nor myself, have any money to give you."

The glare in the man's eyes was like that of an aroused tiger. "Do you mean to say," cried he, "that you will not give from your abundance, a paltry thousand dollars to save one of your blood from a suspicion that will never leave him, *never leave him* to the end of his miserable days?"

"I mean to say that not one cent will pass from me to you in payment of a silence, which as a gentleman, you ought to feel it incumbent upon you to preserve unasked, if only to prove to your fellow-men that you have not entirely lost all the instincts of the caste to which you once belonged. Not that I look for anything so disinterested from you," he went on. "A man who could enter the home of a respectable gentleman, and under cover of a brotherly regard, lure into degradation and despair, the woman who was at once its ornament and pride, cannot be expected to practice the virtues of ordinary manhood, much less those of a gentleman and a Christian. He is a wretch, who, whatever his breeding or antecedents, is open to nothing but execration and contempt."

With an oath and a quick backward spring, Roger Holt cried out, "Who are you, and by what right do you come here to reproach me with a matter dead and buried, by heaven, a dozen years ago?"

"The right of one who, though a stranger, knows well what you are and what you have done. Colonel Japha himself is dead, but the avenger of his honor yet lives! Roger Holt, *where is Jacqueline Japha?*"

The force with which this was uttered, seemed to confound the man. For a moment he stood silent, his eye upon his guest, then a subtle change took place in his expression; he smiled with a slow devilish meaning, and tossing his head with an airy gesture, lightly remarked:

"You must ask some more constant lover than I. A woman who was charming ten years ago—Bah! what would I be likely to know about her now!"

"Everything, when that woman is Jacqueline Japha," cried Mr. Sylvester, advancing upon him with a look that would have shaken most men, but which only made the eye of this one burn more eagerly. "Though you might easily wish to give her the slip, she is not one to forget you. If she is alive, you know where she is; speak then, and let the worth of one good action make what amends it can for a long list of evil ones."

"You really want to see the woman, then; enough to pay for it, I mean?"

"The reward which has been offered for news of the fate or whereabouts of Jacqueline Japha, still stands good," was Mr. Sylvester's reply.

The excited stare with which the man received this announcement, slowly subsided into his former subtle look.

"Well, well," said he, "we will see." The truth was, that he knew no more than the other where this woman was to be found. "If I happen to come across her in any of my wanderings, I shall know where to apply for means to make her welcome. But that is not what at present concerns us. Your nephew is losing ground with every passing minute. In a half-hour more his future will be decided, unless you bid me order my lawyer to delay the forwarding of that communication to Mr. Stuyvesant. In that case—"

"I believe I have already made it plain to you that I have no intentions of interfering with your action in this matter," quoth Mr. Sylvester, turning slowly toward the door. "If you are determined to send your statement, it must go, only—" And here he turned upon the bitterly disappointed man with an aspect whose nobility the other was but little calculated to appreciate—"only when you do so, be particular to state that the person whose story you thus forward to a director of the Madison Bank, is not Bertram Sylvester, the cashier, but Edward Sylvester, his uncle, and the bank's president."

And the stately head bowed and the tall form was about to withdraw, when Holt with an excited tremble that affected even his words, advanced and seized Mr. Sylvester by the arm.

"His uncle!" cried he, "why that is what you—Great heaven!" he exclaimed, falling back with an expression not unmixed with awe, "you are the man and you have denounced yourself!" Then quickly, "Speak again; let me hear your voice."

And Mr. Sylvester with a sad smile, repeated in a slow and meaning tone, "It is but one little *fuss* more!" then as the other cringed, added a dignified, "Good evening, Mr. Holt," and passed swiftly across the room towards the door.

What was it that stopped him half-way, and made him look back with such a startled glance at the man he had left behind him? A smell of smoke in the air, the faint yet unmistakable odor of burning wood, as though the house were on fire, or—

Ha! the man himself has discerned it, is on his feet, is at the window, has seen what? His cry of mingled terror and dismay does not reveal. Mr. Sylvester hastens to his side.

The sight which met his eyes, did not for the moment seem sufficient to account for the degree of emotion expressed by the other. To be sure, the lofty tenement-house which towered above them from the other side of the narrow yard upon which the window looked, was oozing with smoke, but there were no flames visible, and as yet no special manifestations of alarm on the part of its occupants. But in an instant, even while they stood there, arose the sudden and awful cry of "Fire!" and at the same moment they beheld the roof and casements before them, swarm with pallid faces, as men, women and children rushed to the first outlet that offered escape, only to shrink back in renewed terror from the deadly gulf that yawned beneath them.

It was horrible, all the more that the fire seem to be somewhere in the basement story, possibly at the foot of the stairs, for none of the poor shrieking wretches before them seemed to make any effort to escape downwards, but rather surged up towards the top of the building, waving their arms as they fled, and filling the dusk with cries that drowned the sound of the coming engines.

The scene appeared to madden Holt. "My boy! my boy! my boy!" rose from his lips in an agonized shriek; then as Mr. Sylvester gave a sudden start, cried out with indiscribable anguish, "He is there, my boy, my own little chap! A woman in that house has bewitched him, and when he is not with me, he is always at her side. O God, curses on my head for ever letting him out of my sight! Do you see him, sir? Look for him, I beseech you; he is lame and small; his head would barely reach to the top of the window-sill."

"And that was your boy!" cried Mr. Sylvester. And struck by an appeal which in spite of his abhorrence of the man at his side, woke every instinct of fatherhood within him, he searched with his glance the long row of windows before them. But before his eye had travelled half way across the building, he felt the man at his side quiver with sudden agony, and following the direction of his glance, saw a wan, little countenance looking down upon them from a window almost opposite to where they stood.

"It is my boy!" shrieked the man, and in his madness would have leaped from the casement, if Mr. Sylvester had not prevented him.

"You will not help him so," cried the latter. "See, he is only a few feet above a bridge that appears to communicate with the roof of the next house. If he could be let down—"

But the man had already precipitated himself towards the door of the room in which they were. "Tell him not to jump," he called back. "I am going next door and will reach him in a moment. Tell him to hold on till I come."

Mr. Sylvester at once raised his voice. "Don't jump, little boy Holt. If there is no one there to drop you down, wait for your father. He is going on the bridge and will catch you."

The little fellow seemed to hear, for he immediately held out his arms, but if he spoke, his voice was drowned in the frightful hubbub. Meanwhile the smoke thickened around him, and a dull ominous glare broke out from the midst of the building, against which his weazen little face looked pallid as death.

"His father will be too late," groaned Mr. Sylvester, feeling himself somehow to blame for the child's horrible situation; then observing that the other occupants of the building had all disappeared towards the front, realized that whatever fire-escapes may have been provided, were doubtless in that direction, and raising his voice once more, called out across the yard, "Don't wait any longer, little fellow; follow the rest to the front; you will be burned if you stay there."

But the child did not move, only held out his arms in a way to unman the strongest heart; and presently while Mr. Sylvester was asking himself what could be done, he heard his shrill piping tones rising above the hiss of the flames, and listening, caught the words:

"I cannot get away. She is holding me, Dad. Help your little feller; help me, I'm so afraid of being burnt." And looking closer, Mr. Sylvester discerned the outlines of a woman's head and shoulders above the small white face.

A distinct and positive fear at once seized him. Leaning out, the better to display his own face and figure, he called to that unknown woman to quit her hold and let the child go; but a discordant laugh, rising above the roar of the approaching flames, was his only reply. Sickened with apprehension, he drew back and himself made for the stairs in the wild idea of finding the father. But just then the mad figure of Holt appeared at the door, with frenzy in all his looks.

"I cannot push through the crowd," cried he, "I have fought and struggled and shrieked, but it is all of no use. My boy is burning alive and I cannot reach him." A lurid flame shot at that moment from the building before them, as if in emphasis to his words.

"He is prisoned there by a woman," cried Mr. Sylvester, pointing to the figure whose distorted outlines was every moment becoming more and more visible in the increasing glare. "See, she has him tight in her arms and is pressing him against the window-sill."

The man with a terrible recoil, looked in the direction of his child, saw the little white face with its wild expression of conscious terror, saw the face of her who towered implacably behind it, and shrieked appalled.

"Jacqueline!" he cried, and put his hands up before his face as if his eyes had fallen upon an avenging spirit.

"Is that Jacqueline Japha?" asked Mr. Sylvester, dragging down the other's hands and pointing relentlessly towards the ominous figure in the window before him.

"Yes, or her ghost," cried the other, shuddering under a horror that left him little control of his reason.

"Then your boy is lost," murmured Mr. Sylvester, with a vivid remembrance of the words he had overheard. "She will never save her rival's child, never."

The man looked at him with dazed eyes. "She shall save him," he cried, and stretching far out of the window by which he stood, he pointed to the bridge and called out, "Drop him, Jacqueline, don't let him burn. He can still reach the next house if he runs. Save my darling, save him."

But the woman as if waiting for his voice, only threw back her head, and while a bursting flame flashed up behind her, shrieked mockingly back:

"Oh I have frightened you up at last, have I? You can see me now, can you? You can call on Jacqueline now? The brat can make you speak, can he? Well, well, call away, I love to hear your voice. It is music to me even in the face of death."

"My boy! my boy," was all he could gasp; "save the child, Jacqueline, only save the child!"

But the harsh scornful laugh she returned, spoke little of saving. "He is so dear," she hissed. "I love the offspring of my rival so much! the child that has taken the place of my own darling, dead before ever I had seen its innocent eyes. Oh yes, yes, I will save it, save it as my own was saved. When I saw the puny infant in your arms the day you passed me with *her*, I swore to be its friend, don't you remember! And I am so much of a one that I stick by him to the death, don't you see?" And raising him up in her arms till his whole stunted body was visible, she turned away her brow and seemed to laugh in the face of the flames.

The father writhed below in his agony. "Forgive," he cried, "forgive the past and give me back my child. It's all I have to love; it's all I've ever loved. Be merciful, Jacqueline, be merciful!"

Her face flashed back upon him, still and white. "And what mercy have you ever shown to me! Fool, idiot, don't you see I have lived for this hour! To make you feel for once; to make you suffer for once as I have suffered. You love the boy! Roger Holt, I once loved you."

And heedless of the rolling volume of smoke that now began to pour towards her, heedless even of the long tongues of hungry flame that were stretched out as if feeling for her from the distance behind, she stood immovable, gazing down upon the casement where he knelt, with an indescribable and awful smile upon her lips.

The sight was unbearable. With an instinct of despair both men drew back, when suddenly they saw the woman start, unloose her clasp and drop the child out of her arms upon the bridge. A hissing stream of water had fallen upon the flames, and the shock had taken her by surprise. In a moment the father was himself again.

"Get up, little feller, get up," he cried, "or if you cannot walk, crawl along the bridge to the next house. I see a fireman there; he will lift you in."

But at that moment the flames, till now held under some control, burst from an adjoining window, and caught at the woodwork of the bridge. The father yelled in dismay.

"Hurry, little feller, hurry!" he cried. "Get over towards the next house before it is too late."

But a paralysis seemed to have seized the child; he arose, then stopped, and looking wildly about, shook his head. "I cannot," he cried, "I cannot." And the woman laughed, and with a hug of her empty arms, seemed to throw her taunts into the space before her.

"Are you a demon?" burst from Mr. Sylvester's lips in uncontrollable horror. "Don't you see you can save him if you will? Jump down, then, and carry him across, or your father's curse will follow you to the world beyond."

"Yes, climb down," cried the fireman, "you are lighter than I. Don't waste a minute, a second."

"It is your own child, Jacqueline, your own child!" came from Holt's white lips in final desperation. "I have deceived you; your baby did not die; I wanted to get rid of you and I wanted to save him, so I lied to you. The baby did not die; he lived, and that is he you see lying helpless on the bridge beneath you."

Not the clutch of an advancing flame could have made her shrink more fearfully. "It is false," she cried; "you are lying now; you want me to save *her* child, and dare to say it is mine."

"As God lives!" he swore, lifting his hand and turning his face to the sky.

Her whole attitude seemed to cry, "No, no," to his assertion but slowly as she stood there, the conviction of its truth seemed to strike her, and her hair rose on her forehead and she swayed to and fro, as if the earth were rolling under her feet. Suddenly she gave a yell, and bounded from the window. Catching the child in her arms, she attempted to regain the refuge beyond, but the flames had not dallied at their work while she hesitated. The bridge was on fire and her retreat was cut off. She did not attempt to escape. Stopping in the centre of the rocking mass, she looked down as only a mother in her last agony can do, on the child she held folded in her arms; then as the flames caught at her floating garments, stooped her head and printed one wild and passionate kiss upon his brow. Another instant and they saw her head rise to the accusing heavens, then all was rush and horror, and the swaying structure fell before their eyes, sweeping its living freight into the courtyard beneath their feet.

XLII.

PAULA RELATES A STORY SHE HAS HEARD.

"None are so desolate but something dear,Dearer than self, possesses or possessed."—Byron.

n the centre of a long low room not far from the scene of the late disaster, a solitary lamp was burning. It had been lit in haste and cast but a feeble flame, but its light was sufficient to illuminate the sad and silent group that gathered under its rays.

On a bench by the wall, crouched the bowed and stricken form of Roger Holt, his face buried in his hands, his whole attitude expressive of the utmost grief; at his side stood Mr. Sylvester, his tall figure looming sombrely in the dim light; and on the floor at their feet, lay the dead form of the little lame boy.

But it was not upon their faces, sad and striking as they were, that the eyes of the few men and women scattered in the open door-way, rested most intently. It was upon her, the bruised, bleeding, half-dead mother, who kneeling above the little corpse, gazed down upon it with the immobility of despair, moaning in utter heedlessness of her own condition, "My baby, my baby, my own, own baby!"

The fixedness with which she eyed the child, though the blood was streaming from her forehead and bathing with a still deeper red her burned and blistered arms, made Mr. Sylvester's sympathetic heart beat. Turning to the silent figure of Holt, he touched him on the arm and said with a gesture in her direction:

"You have not deceived the woman? That is really her own child that lies there?"

The man beside him, started, looked up with slowly comprehending eyes, and mechanically bowed his head. "Yes," assented he, and relapsed into his former heavy silence.

Mr. Sylvester touched him again. "If it is hers, how came she not to know it? How could you manage to deceive such a woman as that?"

Holt started again and muttered, "She was sick and insensible. She never saw the baby; I sent it away, and when she came to herself, told her it was dead. We had become tired of each other long before, and only needed the breaking of this bond to separate us. When she saw me again, it was with another woman at my side and an infant in my arms. The child was weakly and looked younger than he was. She thought it her rival's and I did not undeceive her." And the heavy head again fell forward, and nothing disturbed the sombre silence of the room but the low unvarying moan of the wretched mother, "My baby, my baby, my own, own baby!"

Mr. Sylvester moved over to her side. "Jacqueline," said he, "the child is dead and you yourself are very much hurt. Won't you let these good women lay you on a bed, and do what they can to bind up your poor blistered arms?"

But she heard him no more than the wind's blowing. "My baby," she moaned, "my own, own baby!"

He drew back with a troubled air. Grief like this he could understand but knew not how to alleviate. He was just on the point of beckoning forward one of the many women clustered in the door-way, when there came a sound from without that made him start, and in another moment a young man had stepped hastily into the room, followed by a girl, who no sooner saw Mr. Sylvester, than she bounded forward with a sudden cry of joy and relief.

"Bertram! Paula! What does this mean? What are you doing here?"

A burst of sobs from the agitated girl was her sole reply.

"Such a night! such a place!" he exclaimed, throwing his arm about Paula with a look that made her tremble through her tears. "Were you so anxious about me, little one?" he whispered. "Would not your fears let you rest?"

"No, no; and we have had such a dreadful time since we got here. The house where we expected to find you, is on fire, and we thought of nothing else but that you had perished within it. But finally some one told us to come here, and—" She paused horror-stricken; her eyes had just fallen upon the little dead child and the moaning mother.

"That is Jacqueline Japha," whispered Mr. Sylvester. "We have found her, only to close her eyes, I fear."

"Jacqueline Japha!" Paula's hands unclosed from his arm.

"She was in the large tenement house that burned first; that is her child whose loss she is mourning."

"Jacqueline Japha!" again fell with an indescribable tone from Paula's lips. "And who is that?" she asked, turning and indicating the silent figure by the wall.

"That is Roger Holt, the man who should have been her husband."

307 | P a g e

"Oh, I remember him," she cried; "and her, I remember her, and the little child too. But," she suddenly exclaimed, "she told me then that she was not his mother."

"And she did not know that she was; the man had deceived her."

With a quick thrill Paula bounded forward. "Jacqueline Japha," she cried, falling with outstretched hands beside the poor creature; "thank God you are found at last!"

But the woman was as insensible to this cry as she had been to all others. "My baby," she wailed, "my baby, my own, own baby!"

Paula recoiled in dismay, and for a moment stood looking down with fear and doubt upon the fearful being before her. But in another instant a heavenly instinct seized her, and ignoring the mother, she stooped over the child and tenderly kissed it. The woman at once woke from her stupor. "My baby!" she cried, snatching the child up in her arms with a gleam of wild jealousy; "nobody shall touch it but me. I killed it and it is all mine now!" But in a moment she had dropped the child back into its place, and was going on with the same set refrain that had stirred her lips from the first.

Paula was not to be discouraged. Laying her hand on the child's brow, she gently smoothed back his hair, and when she saw the old gleam returning to the woman's countenance, said quietly, "Are you going to carry it to Grotewell to be buried? Margery Hamlin is waiting for you, you know?"

The start which shook the woman's haggard frame, encouraged her to proceed.

"Yes; you know she has been keeping watch, and waiting for you so long! She is quite worn out and disheartened; fifteen years is a long time to hope against hope, Jacqueline."

The stare of the wretched creature deepened into a fierce and maddened glare. "You don't know what you are talking about," cried she, and bent herself again over the child.

Paula went on as if she had not spoken. "Any one that is loved as much as you are, Jacqueline, ought not to give way to despair; even if your child is dead, there is still some one left whom you can make supremely happy."

"Him?" the woman's look seemed to say, as she turned and pointed with frightful sarcasm to the man at their back.

Paula shrank and hastily shook her head. "No, no, not him, but—Let me tell you a story," she whispered eagerly. "In a certain country-town not far from here, there is a great empty house. It is dark, and cold, and musty. No one ever goes there but one old lady, who every night at six, crosses its tangled garden, unlocks its great side door, enters within its deserted precincts, and for an hour remains there, praying for one whose return she has never ceased to hope and provide for. She is kneeling there to-night, at this very hour, Jacqueline, and the love she thus manifests is greater than that of man to woman or woman to man. It is like that of heaven or the Christ."

The woman before her rose to her feet. She did not speak, but she looked like a creature before whose eyes a sudden torch had been waved.

"Fifteen years has she done this," Paula solemnly continues. "She promised, you know; and she never has forgotten her promise."

With a cry the woman put out her hands. "Stop!" she cried, "stop! I don't believe it. No one loves like that; else there is a God and I—" She paused, quivered, gave one wild look about her, and then with a quick cry, something between a moan and a prayer, succumbed to the pain of her injuries, and sank down insensible by the side of her dead child.

With a reverent look Paula bent over her and kissed her seared and bleeding forehead. "For Mrs. Hamlin's sake," she whispered, and quietly smoothed down the tattered clothing about the poor creature's wasted frame.

Mr. Sylvester turned quietly upon the man who had been the cause of all this misery. "I charge myself with the care of that woman," said he, "and with the burial of your child. It shall be placed in decent ground with all proper religious ceremonial."

"What, you will do this!" cried Holt, a flush of real feeling for a moment disturbing the chalk-white pallor of his cheek. "Oh sir, this is Christian charity; and I beg your pardon for all that I may have meditated against you. It was done for the child," he went on wildly; "to get him the bread and butter he often lacked. I didn't care so much for myself. I hated to see him hungry and cold and ailing; I might have worked, but I detest work, and—But no matter about all that; enough that I am done with endeavoring to extort money from you. Whatever may have happened in the past, you are free from my persecutions in the future. Henceforth you and yours can rest in peace."

"That is well," cried a voice over his shoulder, and Bertram with an air of relief stepped hastily forward. "You must be very tired," remarked he, turning to his uncle. "If you will take charge of Paula, I will do what I can to see that this injured woman and the dead child are properly cared for. I am so relieved, sir, at this result," he whispered, with a furtive wring of his uncle's hand, "that I must express my joy in some way."

Mr. Sylvester smiled, but in a manner that reflected but little of the other's satisfaction. "Thank you," said he, "I am tired and will gladly delegate my duties to you. I trust you to do the most you can for both the living and the dead. That woman for all her seeming poverty is the possessor of a large fortune;" he whispered; "let her be treated as such." And with a final word to Holt who had sunk back against the wall in his old attitude of silent despair, Mr. Sylvester took Paula upon his arm, and quietly led her out of this humble but not unkind refuge.

XLIII.

DETERMINATION.

"But alas! to make meA fixed figure for the time of scornTo point his slow unmoving finger at!"—Othello.

"Let me but bear your love, I'll bear your cares."—Henry V.

"Paula!"

They had reached home and were standing in the library.

"Yes," said she, lowering her head before his gaze with a sweet and conscious blush.

"Did you read the letter I left for you in my desk up stairs?"

She put her hand to her bosom and drew forth the closely written sheet. "Every word," she responded, and smilingly returned it to its place.

He started and his chest heaved passionately. "You have read it," he cried, "and yet could follow me into that den of unknown dangers at an hour like this, and with no other guide than Bertram?"

"Yes," she answered.

He drew a deep breath and his brow lost its deepest shadow. "You do not despise me then," he exclaimed "My sin has not utterly blotted me out of your regard?"

The glance with which she replied seemed to fill the whole room with its radiance. "I am only beginning to realize the worth of the man who has hitherto been a mystery to me," she declared. Then as he shook his head, added with a serious air, "The question with all true hearts must ever be, not what a man has been, but what he is. He who for the sake of shielding the innocent from shame and sorrow, would have taken upon himself the onus of a past disgrace, is not unworthy a woman's devotion."

Mr. Sylvester smiled mournfully, and stroked her hand which he had taken in his. "Poor little one," he murmured. "I know not whether to feel proud or sorry for your trust and tender devotion. It would have been a great and unspeakable grief to me to have lost your regard, but it might have been better if I had; it might have been much better for you if I had!"

"What, why do you say that?" she asked, with a startled gleam in her eye. "Do you think I am so eager for ease and enjoyment, that it will be a burden for me to bear the pain of those I love? A past pain, too," she added, "that will grow less and less as the days go by and happiness increases."

He put her back with a quick hand. "Do not make it any harder for me than necessary," he entreated, "Do you not see that however gentle may be your judgment of my deserts, we can never marry, Paula?"

The eyes which were fixed on his, deepened passionately. "No," she whispered, "no; not if your remorse for the past is all that separates us. The man who has conquered himself, has won the right to conquer the heart of a woman. I can say no more—" She timidly held out her hand.

He grasped it with a man's impetuosity and pressed it to his heart, but he did not retain it. "Blessings upon you, dear and noble heart!" he cried. "God will hear my prayers and make you happy—but not with me. Paula," he passionately continued, taking her in his arms and holding her to his breast, "it cannot be. I love you—I will not, dare not say, how much—but love is no excuse for wronging you. My remorse is not all that separates us; possible disgrace lies before me; public exposure at all events; I would indeed be lacking in honor were I to subject you to these."

"But," she stammered, drawing back to look into his face, "I thought that was all over; that the man had promised silence; that you were henceforth to be relieved from his persecutions? I am sure he said so."

"He did, but he forgot that my fate no longer rested upon his forbearance. The letter which records my admission of sin was in his lawyer's hands, Paula, and has already been despatched to Mr. Stuyvesant. Say what we will, rebel against it as we will, Cicely's father knows by this time that the name of Sylvester is not spotless."

The cry which she uttered in her sudden pain and loss made him stoop over her with despairing fondness. "Hush! my darling, hush!" cried he. "The trial is so heavy, I need all my strength to meet it. It breaks my heart to see you grieve. I cannot bear it. I deserve my fate, but you—Oh you—what have you done that you should be overwhelmed in my fall!" Putting her gently away from his breast, he drew himself up and with forced calmness said, "I have yet to inform Mr. Stuyvesant upon which of the Sylvesters' should rest the shadow of his distrust. To-night he believes in Bertram's lack of principle, but to-morrow—"

Her trembling lips echoed the word.

"He shall know that the man who confessed to having done a wrong deed in the past, is myself, Paula."

The head which had fallen on her breast, rose as at the call of a clarion. "And is it at the noblest moment of your life that you would shut me away from your side? No, no. Heaven does not send us a great and mighty love for trivial purposes. The simple country maid whom you have sometimes declared was as the bringer of good news to you, shall not fail you now." Then slowly and with solemn assurance, "If you go to Mr. Stuyvesant's to-morrow, and you will, for that is your duty, you shall not go alone; Paula Fairchild accompanies you."

XLIV.

IN MR. STUYVESANT'S PARLORS.

"Was I deceived, or did a sable cloudTurn forth her silver lining on the night?"— Comus.

"Unworthy?"

"Yes."

Cicely stared at her father with wide-open and incredulous eyes. "I cannot believe it," she murmured; "no, I cannot believe it."

Her father drew up a chair to her side. "My daughter," said he, with unusual tenderness, "I have hesitated to tell you this, fearing to wound you; but my discretion will allow me to keep silence no longer. Bertram Sylvester is not an honest man, and the sooner you make up your mind to forget him, the better."

"Not honest?" You would scarcely have recognized Cicely's voice. Her father's hand trembled as he drew her back to his side.

"It is a hard revelation for me to make to you, after testifying my approval of the young man. I sympathize with you, my child, but none the less I expect you to meet this disappointment bravely. A theft has been committed in our bank—"

"You do not accuse him of theft! Oh father, father!"

"No," he stammered. "I do not accuse him, but facts look very strongly against some one in our trust, and—"

"But that is not sufficient," she cried, rising in spite of his detaining hand till she stood erect before him. "You surely would not allow any mere circumstantial evidence to stand against a character as unblemished as his, even if he were not the man whom your daughter—"

He would not let her continue. "I admit that I should be careful how I breathed suspicion against a man whose record was unimpeached," he assented, "but Bertram Sylvester does not enjoy that position. Indeed, I have just received a communication which goes to show, that he once actually acknowledged to having perpetrated an act of questionable integrity. Now a man as young as he, who—"

"But I cannot believe it," she moaned. "It is impossible, clearly impossible. How could he look me in the face with such a sin on his conscience! He could not, simply could not. Why, father, his brow is as open as the day, his glance clear and unwavering as the sunlight. It is some dreadful mistake. It is not Bertram of whom you are speaking!"

Her father sighed. "Of whom else should it be? Come my child, do you want to read the communication which I received last night? Do you want to be convinced?"

"No, no;" she cried; but quickly contradicted herself with a hurried, "Yes, yes, let me be made acquainted with what there is against him, if only that I may prove to you it is all a mistake."

"There is no mistake," he muttered, handing her a folded paper. "This statement was written two years ago; I witnessed it myself, though I little knew against whose honor it was directed. Read it, Cicely, and then remember that I have lost bonds out of my box at the bank, that could only have been taken by some one connected with the institution."

She took the paper in her hand, and eagerly read it through. Suddenly she started and looked up. "And you say that this was Bertram, this gentleman who allowed another man to accuse him of a past dishonesty?"

"So the person declares who forwarded me this statement; and though he is a poor wretch and evidently not above making mischief, I do not know as we have any special reason to doubt his word."

Cicely's eyes fell and she stood before her father with an air of indecision. "I do not think it was Bertram," she faltered, but said no more.

"I would to God for your sake, it was not!" he exclaimed. "But this communication together with the loss we have sustained at the bank, has shaken my faith, Cicely. Young men are so easily led astray nowadays; especially when playing for high stakes. A man who could leave his profession for the sake of winning a great heiress—"

"Father!"

"I know he has made you think it was for love; but when the woman whom a young man fancies, is rich, love and ambition run too closely together to be easily disentangled. And now, my dear, I have said my say and leave you to act according to the dictates of your judgment, sure that it will be in a direction worthy of your name and breeding." And stooping for a hasty kiss, he gave her a last fond look and quietly left the room.

And Cicely? For a moment she stood as if frozen in her place, then a great tremble seized her, and sinking down upon a sofa, she buried her face from sight, in a chaos of feeling that left her scarcely mistress of herself. But suddenly she started up, her face flushed, her eyes gleaming, her whole delicate form quivering with an emotion more akin to hope than despair.

"I cannot doubt him," she whispered; "it were as easy to doubt my own soul. He is worthy if I am worthy, true if I am true; and I will not try to unlove him!"

But soon the reaction came again, and she was about to give full sway to her grief and shame, when the parlor door opened—she herself was sitting in the extension room—and she saw Mr. Sylvester and Paula come in. She at once rose to her feet; but she did not advance. A thousand hopes and fears held her enchained where she was; besides there was something in the aspect of her friends, which made her feel as though a welcome even from her, would at that moment be an intrusion.

"They have come to see father," she thought "and—"

Ah what, Cicely?

Paula, who was too absorbed in her own feelings to glance into the extension room beyond, approached Mr. Sylvester and laid her hand upon his arm. "Whatever comes," said she, "truth, honor and love remain."

And he bowed his head and seemed to kiss her hand, and Cicely observing the action, grew pale and dropped her eyes, realizing as by a lightning's flash, both the nature of the feeling that prompted this unusual manifestation on his part, and the possible sorrows that lay before her dearest friend, if not before herself, should the secret suspicions she cherished in regard to Mr. Sylvester prove true. When she had summoned up courage to glance again in their direction, Mr. Stuyvesant had entered the parlor and was nervously welcoming his guests.

Mr. Sylvester waited for no preamble. "I have come," said he, in his most even and determined tones, "to speak to you in regard to a communication from a man by the name of Holt, which I was told was to be sent to you last evening. Did you receive such a one?"

Mr. Stuyvesant flushed, grew still more nervous in his manner and uttered a short, "I did," in a tone severer than he perhaps intended.

"It will not be too much for me, then, to conclude, that in your present estimation my nephew stands committed to a past dishonesty?"

"It has been one of my chief sources of regret—one of them I say," repeated Mr. Stuyvesant, "that any loss of esteem on the part of your nephew, must necessarily reflect upon the peace if not the honor of a man I hold in such high regard as yourself. I assure you I feel it quite as a brother might, quite as a brother."

Mr. Sylvester at once rose. "Mr. Stuyvesant," declared he, "my nephew is as honest a man as walks this city's streets. If you will accord me a few minutes private conversation, I think I can convince you so."

"I should be very glad," replied Mr. Stuyvesant, glancing towards the extension-room where he had left his daughter. "I have always liked the young man." Then with a quick look in the other's face, "You are not well, Mr. Sylvester?"

"Thank you, I am not ill; let us say what we have to, at once, if you please." And with just a glance at Paula, he followed the now somewhat agitated director from the room.

Cicely who had started forward at their departure, glanced down the long parlor before her, and hastily faltered back; Paula was praying. But in a few moments her feelings overcame her timidity, and hurrying into her friend's presence, she threw her arms about her neck and pressed her cheek to hers. "Let us pray together," she whispered.

Paula drew back and looked her friend in the face. "You know what all this means?" she asked.

"I guess," was the low reply.

Paula checked a sob and clasped Cicely to her bosom. "He loves me," she faltered, "and he is doing at this moment what he believes will separate us. He is a noble man, Cicely, noble as Bertram, though he once did—" She paused. "It is for him to say what, not I," she softly concluded.

"Then Bertram is noble," Cicely timidly put in.

"Have you ever doubted it?"

"No."

And hiding their blushes on each other's shoulders, the two girls sat breathlessly waiting, while the clock ticked away in the music-room and the moments came and went that determined their fate. Suddenly they both rose. Mr. Stuyvesant and Mr. Sylvester were descending the stairs. Mr. Sylvester came in first. Walking straight up to Paula, he took her in his arms and kissed her on the forehead.

"My betrothed wife!" he whispered.

With a start of incredulous joy, Paula looked up. His glance was clear but strangely solemn and peaceful.

"He has heard all I had to say," added he; "he is a just man, but he is also a merciful one. Like you he declares that not what a man was, but what he is, determines the judgment of true men concerning him." And taking her on his arm, he stood waiting for Mr. Stuyvesant who now came in.

"Where is my daughter?" were that gentleman's words, as he closed the door behind him.

"Here, papa."

He held out his hand, and she sprang towards him. "Cicely," said he, not without some tokens of emotion in his voice, "it is only right that I should inform you that we were all laboring under a mistake, in charging Mr. Bertram Sylvester with the words that were uttered in the Dey Street coffee-house two years ago. Mr. Sylvester has amply convinced me that his nephew neither was, nor could have been present there at that time. It must have been some other man, of similar personality."

"Oh thank you, thank you!" Cicely's look seemed to say to Mr. Sylvester. "And he is quite freed from reproach?" she asked, with a smiling glance into her father's face.

A hesitancy in Mr. Stuyvesant's manner, struck with a chill upon more than one heart in that room.

"Yes," he admitted at last; "the mere fact that a mysterious robbery has been committed upon certain effects in the bank of which he is cashier, is not sufficient to awaken distrust as to his integrity, but—"

At that moment the door-bell rung.

"Your father would say," cried Mr. Sylvester, taking advantage of the momentary break, to come to the relief of his host, "that my nephew is too much of a gentleman to desire to press any claim he may imagine himself as possessing over you, while even the possibility of a shadow rests upon his name."

"The man who stole the bonds will be found," said Cicely.

And as if in echo to her words the parlor door opened, and a messenger from the bank stepped briskly up to Mr. Stuyvesant.

"A note from Mr. Folger," said he, with a quick glance at Mr. Sylvester.

Mr. Stuyvesant took the paper handed him, read it hastily through, and looked up with an air of some bewilderment.

"I can hardly believe it possible," cried he, "but Hopgood has absconded."

"Hopgood absconded?"

"Yes; is not that the talk at the bank?" inquired Mr. Stuyvesant, turning to the messenger.

"Yes sir. He has not been seen since yesterday afternoon when he left before the bank was closed for the night. His wife says she thinks he meant to run away, for before going, he came into the room where she was, kissed her and then kissed the child; besides it seems that he took with him some of his clothes."

"Humph! and I had as much confidence in that man—"

"As I have now," came from Mr. Sylvester as the door closed upon the messenger. "If Hopgood has run away, it was from some generous but mistaken idea of sacrificing himself to the safety of another whom he may possibly believe guilty."

"No," rejoined Mr. Stuyvesant, "for here is a note from him that refutes that supposition. It is addressed to me and runs thus:

"Dear Sir.—I beg your pardon and that of Mr. Sylvester for leaving my duties in this abrupt manner. But I have betrayed my trust and am no longer worthy of confidence. I am a wretched man and find it impossible to face those who have believed in my honesty and discretion. If I can bring the money back, you shall see me again, but if not, be kind to my wife and little one, for the sake of the three years when I served the bank faithfully.

"John Hopgood."

"I don't understand it," cried Mr. Sylvester, "that looks—"

"As if he knew where the money was."

"I begin to hope," breathed Cicely.

Her father turned and surveyed her. "This puts a new aspect on matters," said he.

She glanced up beaming. "Oh, will you, do you say, that you think the shadow of this crime has at last found the spot upon which it can rightfully rest?"

"It would not be common sense in me to deny that it has most certainly shifted its position."

With a radiant look at Cicely, Paula crossed to Mr. Stuyvesant's side, and laying her hand on his sleeve, whispered a word or two in his ear. He immediately glanced out of the window at the carriage standing before the door, then looked back at her and nodded with something like a smile. In another moment he stood at the front door.

"Be prepared," cried Paula to Cicely.

It was well she spoke, for when in an instant later Mr. Stuyvesant re-entered the parlor with Bertram at his side, the rapidly changing cheek of the gentle girl showed that the surprise, even though thus tempered, was almost too much for her self-possession.

Mr. Stuyvesant did not wait for the inevitable embarrassment of the moment to betray itself in words. "Mr. Sylvester," said he, to the young cashier, "we have just received a piece of news from the bank, that throws unexpected light upon the robbery we were discussing yesterday. Hopgood has absconded, and acknowledges here in writing that he had something to do with the theft!"

"Hopgood, the janitor!" The exclamation was directed not to Mr. Stuyvesant but to Mr. Sylvester, towards whom Bertram turned with looks of amazement.

"Yes, it is the greatest surprise I ever received," returned that gentleman.

"And Mr. Sylvester," continued Mr. Stuyvesant, with nervous rapidity and a generous attempt to speak lightly, "there is a little lady here who is so shaken by the news, that nothing short of a word of reassurance on your part will comfort her."

Bertram's eye followed that of Mr. Stuyvesant, and fell upon the blushing cheek of Cicely. With a flushing of his own brow, he stepped hastily forward.

"Miss Stuyvesant!" he cried, and looking down in her face, forgot everything else in his infinite joy and satisfaction.

"Yes," announced the father with abrupt decision, "she is yours; you have fairly earned her."

Bertram bowed his head with irrepressible emotion, and for a moment the silence of perfect peace if not of awe, reigned over the apartment; but suddenly a low, determined "No!" was heard, and Bertram turning towards Mr. Stuyvesant, exclaimed, "You are very good, and the joy of this moment atones for many an hour of grief and impatience; but I have not earned her yet. The fact that Hopgood admits to having had something to do with the robbery, does not sufficiently exonerate the officers of the bank from all connection with the affair, to make it safe or honorable in me to unqualifiedly accept the inestimable boon of your daughter's regard. Till the real culprit is in custody and the mystery entirely cleared away, my impatience must continue to curb itself. I love your daughter too dearly to bring her anything but the purest of reputations. Am I not right, Miss Stuyvesant?"

She cast a glance at her father, and bowed her head. "You are right," she repeated.

And Mr. Stuyvesant, with a visible lightening of his whole aspect, took the young man by the hand, and with as much geniality as his nature would allow, informed him that he was at last convinced that his daughter had made no mistake when she expressed her trust in Bertram Sylvester.

And in other eyes than Cicely's, shone the light of satisfied love and unswerving faith.

XLV.

"THE HOUR OF SIX IS SACRED."

"Mightier farThan strength of nerve or sinew, or the swayOf magic potent over sun and star,Is love, though oft to agony distrest,

And though its favorite seat be feeble woman's breast."—Wordsworth.

It was at the close of a winter afternoon. Paula who had returned to Grotewell for the few weeks preceding her marriage, sat musing in the window of her aunt's quaint little parlor. Her eyes were on the fields before her all rosy with the departing rays of the sun, but her thoughts were far away. They were with him she best loved—with Cicely, waiting in patience for the solution of the mystery of the stolen bonds; with Bertram, eagerly, but as yet vainly, engaged in searching for the vanished janitor; and last but not least, with that poor, wretched specimen of humanity moaning away her life in a New York hospital;—for the sight of the Japha house, in a walk that day, had reawakened her most vivid remembrances of Jacqueline. All that had ever been done and suffered by this forsaken creature, lay on her heart like a weight; and the question which had disturbed her since her return to Grotewell, viz., whether or not she ought to acquaint Mrs. Hamlin with the fact that she had seen and spoken to the object of her love and prayers, pressed upon her mind with an insistence that required an answer. There was so much to be said for and against it. Mrs. Hamlin was not well, and though still able to continue her vigil, showed signs of weakening, day by day. It might be a comfort to her to know that another's eyes had rested on the haggard form for whose approach she daily watched; that another's kiss had touched the scarred and pallid forehead she longed to fold against her breast; that the woman she loved and of whose fate she had no intimation, was living and well cared for, though her shelter was that of a hospital, and her prospects those of the grave.

On the other hand, the awful nature of the circumstances which had brought her to her present condition, were such as to make any generous heart pause before shocking the love and trust of such a woman as Mrs. Hamlin, by a relation of the criminal act by which Jacqueline had slain her child and endangered her own existence. Better let the poor old lady go on hoping against hope till she sinks into her grave, than destroy life and hope at once by a revelation of her darling's reckless depravity.

And yet if the poor creature in the hospital might be moved to repentance by some word from Mrs. Hamlin, would it not be a kindness to the latter to allow her, though even at the risk of her life, to accomplish the end for which she indeed professed to live?

The mind of Paula was as yet undecided, when a child from the village passed the window, and seeing her sitting there, handed her a small package with the simple message that Mrs. Hamlin was very ill. It contained, as she anticipated, the great key to the Japha mansion, and understanding without further words, what was demanded of her, Paula prepared to keep the promise she had long ago made to this devoted woman. For though she knew the uselessness of the vigil proposed to her, she none the less determined to complete it. Easier to sit an hour in that dark old house, than to explain herself to Mrs. Hamlin. Besides, the time was good for prayer, and God knows the wretched object of all this care and anxiety, stood in need of all the petitions that might be raised for her.

Telling her aunts that she had a call to make in the village, she glided hurriedly away, and ere she realized all to which she was committed, found herself standing in the now darkened streets, before the grim door of that dread and mysterious mansion. Never had it looked more forbidding; never had the two gruesome poplars cast a deeper shadow, or rustled with a more woful sound in the chill evening air. The very windows seemed to repel her with their darkened panes, behind which she could easily imagine the spirits of the dead, moving and peering. A chill not unlike that of terror, assailed her limbs, and it was with a really heroic action that she finally opened the gate and glided up the path made by the daily steps of her aged friend. To thrust the big key into the lock required another effort, but that once accomplished, she stilled every tumultuous beating of her heart, by crying under her breath, "She has done this for one whom she has not seen for fifteen years; shall I then hesitate, who know the real necessity of her for whom this hour is made sacred?"

The slow swinging open of the door was like an ushering into the abode of ghosts, but she struck a light at once, and soon had the satisfaction of beholding the dismal room with its weird shadows, resolve into its old and well remembered aspect. The ancient cabinet and stiff hair-cloth sofa, Colonel Japha's chair by the table, together with all the other objects that had attracted her attention in her former visit, confronted her again with the same appearance of standing ready and waiting, which had previously so thrilled her. Only she was alone this time, and terror mingled with her awe. She scarcely dared to glance at the doors that led to other portions of the house. In her present mood it would seem so natural for them to swing open, and let upon her horrified gaze the stately phantom of the proud old colonel or the gentler shade of Jacqueline's mother. The moan of the wind in the chimney was dreadful to her, and the faint rumbling sounds of mice scampering in the walls, made her start as though a voice had spoken.

But presently the noise of a sleigh careering by the house recalled her to herself, and remembering it was but early night-fall, she sat down in a chair by the door, and prepared to keep her vigil with suitable patience and equanimity. Suddenly she recollected the clock on the mantel-piece and how she had seen Mrs. Hamlin wind it, and rising up, she followed her example, sighing unconsciously to find how many of the sixty minutes had yet to tick themselves away, "Can I endure it!" she thought, and shuddered as she pictured to herself the dim old staircase behind those doors, and the empty rooms above, and the little Bible lying thicker than ever with dust, on the yellowed pillows of Jacqueline's bed.

Suddenly she stood still; the noise she had just heard, was not made by the pattering of mice along the rafters, or even the creaking of the withered vines that clung against the walls! It was a human sound, a clicking as of the gate without, a crunching as of feet dragging slowly over the snow. Was Mrs. Hamlin coming after all, or—she could not formulate her fear; a real and palpable danger from the outside world had never crossed her fancy till now. What if some stranger should enter, some tramp, some—a step on the porch without made her hair rise on her forehead; she clasped her hands and stood trembling, when a sudden moan startled her ears, followed by the sound of a heavy fall on the threshold, and throwing aside all hesitation, she flung herself forward, and tearing open the door, saw—oh, angels that rejoice in heaven over one sinner that repenteth, let your voices go up in praise this night, for Jacqueline Japha has returned to the home of her fathers!

She had fainted, and lay quite still on the threshold, but Paula, who was all energy now, soon had her in the centre of the sitting-room, and was applying to her such restoratives as had been provided against this very emergency. She was holding the poor weary head on her knee, when the wan eyes opened, and looking up, grew wild with a disappointment which Paula was quick to appreciate.

"You are looking for Margery," said she. "Margery will come by-and-by; she is not well to-night and I am taking her place, but when she hears you have returned, it will take more than sickness to keep her to her bed. I am Paula, and I love you, too, and welcome you—oh, welcome you so gladly."

The yearning look which had crept into the woman's bleared and faded eyes, deepened and softened strangely.

"You are the one who told me about Margery," said she, "and bade me bring my baby here to be buried. I remember, though I seemed to pay no heed then. Night and day through all my pain, I have remembered, and as soon as I could walk, stole away from the hospital. It has killed me, but I shall at least die in my father's house."

Paula stooped and kissed her. "I am going to get your bed ready," said she. And without any hesitation now, she opened the door that led into those dim inner regions that but a few minutes before had inspired her with such dread.

She went straight to Jacqueline's room. "It must all be according to Mrs. Hamlin's wishes," she cried, and lit the fire on the hearth, and pulled back the curtains yet farther from the bed, and gave the benefit of her womanly touch to the various objects about her, till cheerfulness seemed to reign in a spot once so peopled with hideous memories. Going back to Jacqueline, she helped her to rise, and throwing her arm about her waist, led her into the hall. But here memory, ghastly accusing memory, stepped in, and catching the wretched woman in its grasp, shook her, body and soul, till her shrieks reverberated through that desolate house. But Paula with gentle persistence urged her on, and smiling upon her like an angel of peace and mercy, led her up step after step of that dreadful staircase, till at last she saw her safely in the room of her early girlhood.

The sight of it seemed at first to horrify but afterwards to soothe the forlorn being thus brought face to face with her own past. She moved over to the fire and held out her two cramped hands to the blaze, as if she saw an altar of mercy in its welcoming glow. From these she passed tottering and weak to the embroidery-frame, which she looked at for a moment with something almost like a smile; but she hurried by the mirror, and scarcely glanced at a portrait of herself which hung on the wall over her head. To sink on the bed seemed to be her object, and thither Paula accompanied her. But when she came to where it stood, and saw the clothes turned down and the pillows heaped at the head, and the little Bible lying open for her in the midst, she gave a great and mighty sob, and flinging herself down upon her knees, wept with a breaking up of her whole nature, in which her sins, red though they were as crimson, seemed to feel the touch of the Divine love, and vanish away in the oblivion He prepares for all His penitent ones.

When everything was prepared and Jacqueline was laid quiet in bed, Paula stole out and down the stairs and wended her way to Mrs. Hamlin's cottage. She found her sitting up, but far from well, and very feeble. At the first sight of Paula's face, she started erect and seem to forget her weakness in a moment.

"What is it?" she asked; "you look as though you had been gazing on the faces of angels. Has—has my hope come true at last? Has Jacqueline returned? Oh, has my poor, lost, erring child come back?"

Paula drew near and gently steadied Mrs. Hamlin's swaying form. "Yes," she smiled; and with the calmness of one who has entered the gates of peace, whispered in low and reverent tones: "She lies in the bed that you spread for her, with the Bible held close to her breast."

There are moments when the world about us seems to pause; when the hopes, fears and experiences of all humanity appear to sway away and leave us standing alone in the presence of our own great hope or scarcely comprehended fear. Such a moment was that which saw Paula re-enter Jacqueline's presence with Mrs. Hamlin at her side.

Leaving the latter near the door, she went towards the bed. Why did she recoil and glance back at Mrs. Hamlin with that startled and apprehensive look? The face of Jacqueline was changed—changed as only one presence could change it, though the eyes were clearer than when she left her a few minutes before, and the lips were not without the shadow of a smile.

"She is dying," whispered Paula, coming back to Mrs. Hamlin; "dying, and you have waited so long!"

But the look that met hers from that aged face, was not one of grief; and startled, she knew not why, Paula drew aside, while Mrs. Hamlin crossed the room and quietly knelt down by her darling's side.

"Margery!"

"Jacqueline!"

The two cries rang through the room, then all was quiet again.

"You have come back!" were the next words Paula heard. "How could I ever have doubted that you would!"

"I have been driven back by awful suffering," was the answer; and another silence fell. Suddenly Jacqueline's voice was heard. "Love slew me, and now love has saved me!" exclaimed she. And there came no answer to that cry, and Paula felt the shadow of a great awe settle down upon her, and moving nearer to where the aged woman knelt by her darling's bedside, she looked in her bended face and then in the one upturned on the pillow, and knew that of all the hearts that but an instant before had beat with earth's deepest emotion in that quiet room, one alone throbbed on to thank God and take courage.

And the fire which had been kindled to welcome the prodigal back, burned on; and from the hollow depths of the great room below, came the sound of a clock as it struck the hour, seven!

XLVI.

THE MAN CUMMINS.

Oh day and night, but this is wondrous strange."—Henry V.

"Shut up in measureless content."—Othello.

The lights were yet shining in Mr. Stuyvesant's parlors, though the guests were gone, who but a short time before had assembled there to witness the marriage of Cicely's dear friend, Paula.

At one end of the room stood Mr. Sylvester and Bertram, the former gazing with the eyes of a bridegroom, at the delicate white-clad figure of Paula, just leaving the apartment with Cicely.

"I have but one cause for regret," said Mr. Sylvester as the door closed. "I could have wished that you and Cicely had participated in our joy and received the minister's benediction at the same moment as ourselves."

"Yes," said Bertram with a short sigh. "But it will come in time. It cannot be but that our efforts must finally succeed. I have just had a new idea; that of putting the watchman on the hunt for Hopgood. They are old friends, and he ought to know all the other's haunts and possible hiding-places."

"If Fanning could have helped us, he would have told us long ago. He knows that Hopgood is missing and that we are ready to pay well for any information concerning him."

"But they are old cronies, and possibly Fanning is keeping quiet out of consideration for his friend."

"No; I have had a talk with Fanning, and there was no mistaking his look of surprise when told the other had run away under suspicion of being connected with a robbery on the bank's effects. He knows no more of Hopgood than we do, or his wife does, or the police even. It is a strange mystery, and one to which I fear we shall never obtain the key. But don't let me discourage you; after a suitable time Mr. Stuyvesant will—"

He paused, for that gentleman was approaching him.

"There is a man outside who insists upon seeing me; says he knows there has just been a wedding here, but that the matter he has to communicate is very important, and won't bear putting off. The name on his card is Cummins; I am afraid I shall have to admit him, that is, if you have no objection?"

Mr. Sylvester and Bertram at once drew back with ready acquiescence. They had scarcely taken their stand at the other end of the apartment, when the man came in. He was of robust build, round, precise and business-like. He had taken off his hat, but still wore his overcoat; his face in spite of a profusion of red whiskers and a decided pair of goggles, was earnest and straightforward. He walked at once up to Mr. Stuyvesant.

"Your pardon," said he, in a quick tone. "But I hear you have been somewhat exercised of late over the disappearance of certain bonds from one of the boxes in the Madison Bank. I am a detective, and in the course of my duty have come upon a few facts that may help to explain matters."

Mr. Sylvester and Bertram at once started forward; this was a topic that demanded their attention as well as that of the master of the house.

The man cast them a quick look from behind his goggles, and seeming to recognize them, included them in his next question.

"What do you think of the watchman, Fanning?"

"Think? we don't think," uttered Mr. Stuyvesant sharply. "He has been in the employ of the bank for twelve years, and we know him to be honest."

"Yet he is the man who stole your bonds."

"Impossible!"

"The very man."

Mr. Sylvester stepped up to him. "Who are you, and how do you know this?"

"I have said my name is Cummins, and I know this, because I have wormed myself into the man's confidence and have got the bonds, together with his confession, here in my pocket." And he drew out the long lost bonds, which he handed to their owner, with a bit of paper on which was in-scribed in the handwriting of the watchman, an acknowledgment to the effect that he, alone and unassisted, had perpetrated the robbery which had raised such scandal in the bank and led to the disappearance of Hopgood.

"And the man himself?" cried Bertram, when they had all read this. "Where is he?"

"Oh, I allowed him to escape."

Mr. Sylvester frowned.

"There is something about this I don't understand," said he. "How came you to take such an interest in this matter; and why did you let the man escape after acknowledging his crime?"

With a quick, not undignified action, Cummins stepped back. "Gentlemen," said he, "it is allowable in a detective in the course of his duty, to resort to means for eliciting the truth, that in any other cause and for any other purpose, would be denominated as unmanly, if not mean and contemptible. When I heard of this robbery, as I did the day after its perpetration, my mind flew immediately to the watchman as the possible culprit. I did not know that he had done the deed, and I did not see how he could have possessed the means of doing it, but I had been acquainted with him for some time, and certain expressions which I had overheard him use—expressions that had passed over me lightly at the time, now recurred to my mind with startling distinctness. 'If a man knew the combination of the vault door, how easily he could make himself rich from the contents of those boxes!' was one, I remember; and another, 'I have worked in the bank for twelve years and have not so much money laid up against a rainy day, as would furnish Mr. Sylvester in cigars for a month.' The fact that he had no opportunity to learn the combination, was the only stumbling-block in the way of my conclusions. But that obstacle was soon removed. In a talk with the janitor's wife—a good woman, sirs, but a trifle conceited—I learned that he had once had the very opportunity of which I speak, provided he was smart enough to recognize the fact. The way it came about was this. Hopgood, who always meant to do about the right thing, as I know, was one morning very sick, so sick that when the time came for him to go down and open the vaults for the day, he couldn't stir from his bed, or at least thought he couldn't. Twice had the watchman rung for him, and twice had he tried to get up, only to fall back again on his pillow. At last the call became imperative; the clerks would soon be in, and the books were not even in readiness for them. Calling his wife to him, he asked if she thought she could open the vault door provided she knew the combination. She returned a quite eager, 'yes,' being a naturally vain woman and moreover a little sore over the fact that her husband never entrusted her with any of his secrets. 'Then,' said he, 'listen to those three numbers that I give you; and turn the knob accordingly,' explaining the matter in a way best calculated to enlighten her as to what she had to do. She professed herself as understanding perfectly and went off in quite a nutter of satisfaction to accomplish her task. But though he did not know it at the time, it seems that her heart failed her when she got into the hall, and struck with fear lest she should forget the numbers before she got to the foot of the stairs, she came back, and carefully wrote them down on a piece of paper, armed with which she started for the second time to fulfil her task. The watchman was in the bank when she entered, and to his expressions of surprise, she answered that her husband was ill and that she was going to open the vaults. He offered to help her, but she stared at him with astonishment, and waiting till he had walked to the other end of the bank, proceeded to the vault door, and after carefully consulting the paper in her hand, was about to turn the knob as directed, when Hopgood himself came into the room. He was too anxious, he said, to keep in bed, and though he trembled at every step, came forward and accomplished the task himself. He did not see the paper in his wife's hand, nor notice her when she tore it up and threw the pieces in the waste-basket near-by, but the watchman may have observed her, and as it afterwards proved, did; and thus became acquainted with the combination that unlocked the outer vault doors."

"Humph!" broke in Mr. Sylvester, "if this is true, why didn't Hopgood inform me of the matter when I questioned him so closely?"

"Because he had forgotten the circumstance. He was in a fever at the time, and having eventually unlocked the vault himself, lost sight of the fact that he had previously sent his wife to do it. He went back to his bed after the clerks came in, and did not get up again till night. He may have thought the whole occurrence part of the delirium which more than once assailed him that day."

"I remember his being sick," said Bertram; "it was two or three days before the robbery."

"The very day before," corrected the man; "but let me tell my story in my own way. Having learned from Mrs. Hopgood of this opportunity which had been given to Fanning, I made up my mind to sift the matter. Being as I have said a friend of his, I didn't, want to peach on him unless he was guilty. To blast an honest man's reputation, is, I think, one of the meanest tricks of which a fellow can be guilty: but the truth I had to know, and in order to learn it, a deep and delicate game was necessary. Gentlemen, when the police have strong suspicions against a person whose reputation is above reproach and whose conduct affords no opportunity for impeachment, they set a springe for him. One of their number disguises himself, and making the acquaintance of this person, insinuates himself by slow degrees—often at the cost of months of effort—into his friendship and if possible into his confidence. 'Tis a detestable piece of business, but it is all that will serve in some cases, and has at least the merit of being as dangerous as it is detestable. This plan, I undertook with Fanning. Changing my appearance to suit the necessities of the case, I took board in the small house in Brooklyn where he puts up, and being well acquainted with his tastes, knew how to adapt myself to his liking. He was a busy man, and being obliged by his duties to turn night into day, had not much time to bestow upon me or any one else; but heedful of this, I managed to make the most of the spare moments that saw us together, and ere long we were very good comrades, and further on, very good friends. The day when I first ventured to suggest that honesty was all very well as long as it paid, was a memorable one to me. In that cast of the die I was either to win or lose the game I had undertaken. I won. After a feint or two, to see if I were in earnest, he fell into the net, and though he did not commit himself then, it was not long before he came to me, and deliberately requested my assistance in disposing of some bonds which he was smart enough to acquire, but not daring enough to attempt to sell. Of course the whole story came out, and I was sympathetic enough till I got the bonds into my hands, then—But I leave you to imagine what followed. Enough that I wrung this confession from him, and that in consideration of the doubtful game I had played upon him, let him go where he is by this time beyond the chance of pursuit."

"But your duty to your superior; your oath as a member of the force?"

"My superior is here!" said the man pointing to Mr. Sylvester; "an unconscious one I own, but still my superior; and as for my being a member of the force, that was true five years ago, but not to-day." And brushing off his whiskers with one hand and taking off his goggles with the other, Hopgood, the janitor, stood before them!

It was a radiant figure that met Cicely, when she came down stairs with Paula, and a joyous group that soon surrounded the now blushing and embarrassed janitor, with questions and remarks concerning this great and unexpected development of affairs. But the fervor with which Mr. Stuyvesant clasped Bertram's hand, and the look with which Cicely turned from her young lover to bestow a final kiss upon the departing bride, was worth all the pains and self-denial of the last few weeks—or so the janitor thought, who with a quicker comprehension than usual, had divined the situation and rejoiced in the result. But the most curious thing of all was to observe how, with the taking off of his goggles, Hopgood had relapsed into his old shrinking, easily embarrassed self. The man who but a few minutes before had related in their hearing a clear and succinct narrative, now shrank if a question was put him, and stammered in quite his ancient fashion, when he answered Mr. Sylvester's shake of the hand, by a hurried:

"I am going to see my wife now, sir. She's a good woman, if a little flighty, and will be the last one in the future to beg me to put more confidence in her. Will you tell me where she is, sir?"

Mr. Sylvester informed him; then added, "But look here, Hopgood, answer me one thing before you go. Why is it that with such talents as you possess, you didn't stay in the police force? You are a regular genius in your way, and ought not to drone away your existence as a janitor."

"Ah, sir," replied the other, shaking his head, "a man who is only capable of assuming one disguise, isn't good for much as a professional detective. Goggles and red whiskers will deceive one rogue, but not fifty. My eyes were my bane, sir, and ultimately cost me my place. While I could cover them up I was all right. It not only made a man of me, leaving me free to talk and freer to think, but disguised me so, my best friends couldn't recognize me; but after awhile my goggles were too well known for me to be considered of much further use to the department, and I was obliged to send in my resignation. It is too bad, but I have no versatility, sir. I'm either the clumsy, stammering creature you have always known, or else I am the man Cummins you saw here a few minutes ago."

"In either case an honest fellow," answered Mr. Sylvester, and allowed the janitor to depart.

One more scene, and this in the house which Paula is henceforth to make a home for herself and its once melancholy owner. They have come back from their wedding-journey, and are standing in their old fashion, he at the foot, and she half way up the stairs. Suddenly she turns and descends to his side.

"No, I will not wait," said she. "Here, on this spot we both love so well, and in this the first hour of our return, I will unburden my mind of what I have to say. Edward, is there nothing of all the past that still rests upon you like a shadow? Not one little regret you could wish taken away?"

"No," said he, enfolding her in his arms with a solemn smile. "The great gift which I hold is the fruit of that past, perhaps; I cannot wish it changed."

"But the sense of obligation never fulfilled, would you not be happier if that were removed?"

"Perhaps," he said, "but it cannot be now. I shall have to live without being perfectly happy."

She lifted her face and her smile shone like a star. "Oh God is good," she cried, "you shall not lack being perfectly happy;" and taking a little paper out of her pocket she put it in his hand. "We found that hidden in Jacqueline Japha's breast, when we went to lay her out for burial."

It was only a line; but it made Mr. Sylvester's brow flush and his voice tremble.

"Whatever I own, and I have been told that I am far from penniless, I desire to have given to the dear and disinterested girl that first told me of Margery Hamlin's vigil."

"Paula, Paula, Paula, thou art indeed my good gift! May God make me worthy of your love and of this His last and most unexpected mercy!"

And the look which crossed her face, was that sweet and unearthly radiance which speaks of perfect peace.

[1] A fact.

End of the book.